A NEW INTERNATIONAL ENGAGEMENT FRAMEWORK FOR NORTH KOREA?

Contending Perspectives

A NEW INTERNATIONAL ENGAGEMENT FRAMEWORK FOR NORTH KOREA?

Contending Perspectives

Editors: Ahn Choong-yong, Nicholas Eberstadt, Lee Young-sun

The Korea Economic Institute of America (KEI) is registered under the Foreign Agents Registration Act as an agent of the Korea Institute for International Economic Policy, a public policy research foundation in Seoul established by the government of the Republic of Korea. This material is filed with the Department of Justice, where the required registration statement is available for public inspection. Registration does not indicate U.S. government approval of the contents of this document. KEI is not engaged in the practice of law, does not render legal services, and is not a lobbying organization.

The views expressed in this publication are those of the authors and do not necessarily reflect the views of individual members of KEI's Board of Directors or its Advisory Council.

KEI Editorial Board
Editor in Chief   James M. Lister
Contract Editor   Mary Marik
Proof Editor   Mary Chaves

Library of Congress Cataloging-in-Publication Data
A new international engagement framework for North Korea? : contending perspectives / Ahn Choong-yong, Nicholas Eberstadt, and Lee Young-sun, editors.
    p. cm.
 Includes bibliographical references.
 ISBN 0-9747141-2-7
 1. Korea (North)--Economic policy. 2. Korea (North)--Economic conditions. 3. Korea (North)--Foreign economic relations. I. An, Ch'ung-yæong. II. Eberstadt, Nick, 1955- III. Yi, Yæong-sæon, 1947-
HC470.2.N49 2004
338.91'095193--dc22
                              2004026623

Korea Economic Institute of America
1201 F Street, Northwest
Suite 910
Washington, D.C. 20004
202/464-1982
www.keia.org

Contents

Preface and Acknowledgments

Political developments on the Korean peninsula have taken several turns recently. The historic North Korea–South Korea summit of 15 June 2000 suggested both the possibility and desirability for both Koreas and the neighboring powers to establish a new framework for regional peace to replace the structure inherited from the Cold War. By normalizing diplomatic relations with Western countries, particularly in Europe, North Korea has sought to overcome its image of being a "rogue state." It has attempted to create conditions favorable for the inflow of economic assistance and also, to some degree, for the expansion of trade. In July 2002, North Korea introduced several economic improvement measures, such as a strengthened incentive system, that actually incorporated some market mechanisms. It has been reported that markets have been expanding continuously since July 2002. These prominent movements toward normalizing diplomatic relations with Western countries and increasing international activities as well as internal institutional changes are viewed as policy attempts to overcome North Korea's severe economic distress during the 1990s.

However, North Korea has also moved backwards in recent years. The hastily unveiled special administrative region for the border city of Sinuiju, which promised to launch the DPRK's first experimental market-oriented export zone, proved a fiasco when its designated boss, the mysterious Chinese entrepreneur Yang Bin, was arrested by Chinese authorities just days after Yang's appointment was announced in the summer of 2002. Thereafter the project went into limbo; finally, in the summer of 2004, according to Japanese press reports, DPRK officials notified China that the project had been scrapped. More ominously, in October 2002 during deliberations with visiting U.S. Assistant Secretary of State James A. Kelly, Pyongyang admitted to conducting a major clandestine nuclear weapons development program. Since then, the situation on the Korean peninsula and in East Asia has become substantially more fluid. Work of the Korean Peninsula Energy Development Organization (KEDO) was suspended because of North Korea's violation of the agreement, and Pyongyang pushed its nuclear program forward. Throughout its advances, North Korea openly stated its desire to develop nuclear weapons.

The paradoxical attitudes of the North revived mistrust about its political course. The new revelations have called into question the South's Sunshine Policy of engagement toward the North. Because North Korea may be trying to find a possible strategy for economic security as well as political stability, some observers believe that North Korea may voluntarily transform its system into one that is market based and subsequently adopt an open-door policy. These possible shifts imply that any changes in the country's economic system will be conditional. Thus, "uncertainty" aptly describes the situation in North Korea.

Moreover, dramatic changes in the global and regional environments are heightening the degree of uncertainty and complexity. The United States and the international community have focused on intervening against proliferation of weapons of mass destruction, especially since the 11 September 2001, terrorist attacks in the United States. U.S. interests are linked to preventing the proliferation of nuclear arms, protecting its allies—South Korea and Japan—in East Asia, and preserving the balance of power in the region. Japan's interests are linked to the destabilizing effects of a conflict on the Korean peninsula and its own political and economic relations with South Korea. China, also, has vital interests in maintaining stability on the peninsula and in East Asia so that it may continue to focus on its domestic economy. By and large, Russia shares China's interests. The differing priorities of the major powers involved increase the uncertainty and complexity of the issues surrounding North Korea.

South Korea, the United States, and Japan have agreed to resolve the North Korean nuclear issue within a multilateral formula, convincing North Korea that it must cease its nuclear programs and recognizing that, if it does so, assistance from the international community will follow. The six-party talks were introduced under these circumstances.

An effective international policy on North Korea needs a foreseeable program for international assistance. Research is lacking, however, about how to guide North Korea into the international community under a framework of multilateral cooperation.

Against this background, the Korea Institute for International Economic Policy (KIEP) and the American Enterprise Institute (AEI) agreed to conduct joint research with a view to providing an academic and practicable basis for the concept of North Korea's international engagement. Afterwards, the *Chosun-Ilbo* newspaper joined this project.

This edited volume—the outcome of this joint research—identifies major issues and provides comprehensive analyses, policy implications, and recommendations based on various points of view. The volume comprises the papers from the 12–13 February 2004 conference, "Towards a Peaceful Resolution with North Korea: Crafting a New International Engagement Framework," organized jointly by AEI, KIEP, the Korea Economic Institute (KEI), and *Chosun-Ilbo* and held in Washington, D.C. The project was sponsored by the Ford Foundation and Kookmin Bank.

We would like to thank Dr. Yoon Deok-ryong and Dr. Nicholas Eberstadt for coordinating the conference and preparing this volume for publication. Special thanks go to Dr. Wang Yun-jong for coordinating the conference in its early stages. Among staff at AEI, thanks are extended to Heather Dresser, Assia Dosseva, and Elizabeth Bowen; and at KEI appreciation is due especially to Joseph A. B. Winder, president, and Peter Beck (former director of academic affairs and research) and JooRi Park. We also thank the authors of the papers, the discussants, and other participants who contributed to the success of the conference and this publication.

Ahn Choong-yong
President
Korea Institute for International Economic Policy

Note on Names

In Korea, as in much of Asia, surnames (family names) generally precede given names. Therefore, in this volume, most Asian names begin with the surname and conclude with the given name. For example, for the name Kim Jong-il, Kim is the family name, and Jong-il is the given name. Exceptions to this custom exist; in that case the editors have rendered the name as it is commonly understood or as the individual prefers.

A NEW INTERNATIONAL ENGAGEMENT FRAMEWORK FOR NORTH KOREA?

Contending Perspectives

1

Introduction and Overview

Ahn Choong-yong, Nicholas Eberstadt, and Lee Young-sun

Can the economic system of the Democratic People's Republic of Korea (DPRK, or North Korea) be successfully reformed? That is to say: Is it possible for contemporary North Korea, with its autarkic, hypermilitarized, and ostensibly centrally planned economic structure (institutions and arrangements, one must note, whose post–Cold War performance has been so woeful that the nation suffered peacetime famine in the middle and late 1990s), to move toward and eventually embody an economic regimen akin to the ones that have permitted so much material progress in East Asia's two exemplars of "reform socialism"—China and Vietnam—over the past generation?

Could the rulers of the North Korean state maintain control if the economy under their command evolved from the current variant of "socialism with Korean characteristics" into something with a more peaceable, pragmatic, market-friendly, and internationally open orientation? Can North Korea's highest authorities seriously entertain the notion of inculcating a comprehensive, far-reaching refashioning of what they formally and officially extol as "our own way of socialism" [urisik sahoejuii]? Do they entertain such notions today?

If North Korean authorities did determine to undertake such a transformation, would they be expected to possess the know-how necessary for such a venture? Are there resources—intellectual, institutional, financial—that outside parties could provide that might improve the odds of success for an incipient North Korean economic reform? And, if so, under what conditions — and conditionalities—might those resources most prudently be offered?

This volume attempts to examine these questions in a detailed, rigorous, and systematic manner. The following chapters address the status and outlook for the North Korean political economy; the likelihood of an official DPRK shift toward economic pragmatism, and the practical pitfalls any such move would encounter; the record and lessons of economic liberalization in socialist and post-socialist economies and development assistance initiatives in such locales; the identification and analysis of key sectors of the North Korean economy, whose revitalization might be abetted through outside efforts; the prospects for an international mobilization of private and public capital in the service of North Korean economic reconstruction; and the role that particular external stakeholders might be expected to play in such a venture. Each of the chapters in this book addresses one aspect or another of the North Korea economic reform *problematik;* taken together, they present an in-depth perspective on the issues that would have to be faced if the international community were to resolve to support the economic reform process in North Korea through comprehensive—but also selective—commitments and investments.

As readers will quickly see, the specialists we have assembled—all authorities in their respective fields and areas—do not speak with a single voice about the prospects for North Korean economic reform or the odds that such reform could be bolstered through an external framework for international cooperation. On many critical points, our authors take issue with each other; at more than a few points, the reader will encounter powerfully argued but strikingly discrepant judgments about the questions we pose at the outset of our introduction.

We do not believe this well-informed controversy is a bad thing. Quite the contrary: In our view, it is precisely on such an elevated and varying intellectual terrain that the quest to understand the possibilities and pitfalls of encouraging North Korean economic reform may be more fruitfully pursued.

While it may be the case that none of the basic questions we pose about North Korean economic reform can as yet be said to have a clear and definitive answer, it is also clearly the case that attempting to get the answers to each of these questions right—or close to right—is more than an abstract academic exercise. These days, in fact, the actual, real-world answers to those several questions qualify as high-stakes propositions for a great many interested parties, including the people of the Korean peninsula, the neighboring regions of Northeast Asia, and a number of peoples and places more geographically removed from the locus of such inquires but nevertheless still directly affected by the dramas these inquiries reflect. Indeed, the reformability of the North Korean economic system is now an issue absolutely central to the future security and prosperity of Northeast Asia.

Ever since the end of the Cold War, the DPRK has emerged as the central locus of instability and tension within the Northeast Asian region. Whether it was the threats to turn Seoul into a "sea of fire" in 1994, the indications that the DPRK state might collapse in the mid 1990s, or the off-and-on nuclear crisis that started in the early 1990s and now, in 2004, is very much "on", it is North Korea that is generating the most immediate and acute challenges to the security of this increasingly important economic neighborhood. And all of the solutions to the "North Korean problem" would seem to require a successful economic transition within North Korea itself.

The specter of mass hunger in that unhappy land would be exorcized once and for all through the embrace of sounder economic institutions and implementation of more productive economic policies. With a more economically rational regime, genuine financial self-reliance—as opposed to the false, foreign-aid-focused, "self-reliance" of *juche* in practice—will be possible for North Korea, and the threat of state collapse will be to that degree correspondingly mitigated. No less important, if the North Korean government develops its commercial exports through a more open economic orientation, it would be in a position—unlike its situation today—in which international military extortion would no longer *have to* figure centrally in the state's finances. And, needless to say, economic reform and reform-based development in the North would greatly ease the ultimate burdens that would have to be shouldered by an eventual peaceful and voluntary reunification of the two halves of a too-long-divided Korean peninsula.

We should remind some readers of what others are already well aware: namely, that the notion of promoting and reinforcing from outside those tendencies for economic reform that exist within North Korea itself—addressed and evaluated by every chapter in this volume—is no mere blackboard exercise nowadays. Rather, with whatever measure of success, this objective has been enshrined as a top priority of government in the Republic of Korea under two successive governments, the administration of President Kim Dae-jung (1998–2003) and President Roh Moo-hyun (in office as this is written). Although the name for the policy has undergone changes—Sunshine, Engagement, Peace and Prosperity—the constant mission defining it has been the conviction that Pyongyang can be enticed, through external incentives and commitments, to change gradually but also deliberately into a more economically open and less militarily menacing polity.

In greater or lesser measure, additional governments and international institutions have revealed themselves to be sometime adherents to variations of the same theory. In the United States, for example, the Clinton administration subscribed to a similar viewpoint with its "Perry process" of engagement during 1999–2000, but the George W. Bush administration has adopted a decidedly more skeptical posture toward the potentialities of this theory. Other sometime adherents have included the governments of Japan, China, and Russia (albeit sotto voce in these cases), parts of the European Union, organizations within the United Nations family, and many nongovernmental organizations around the globe. With this background, a "new international engagement framework for North Korea" for promoting and reinforcing economic reform in the DPRK—the concept bruited in the title of our volume—would entail not so much a breaking of new ground as a revitalizing and intensifying of preexisting interests and activities.

Proponents of existing or expanded engagement frameworks for North Korea argue that genuine economic reform is already under way in the DPRK. The evidence they adduce includes the package of new economic measures promulgated by Pyongyang in July 2002, the attempted (but aborted) opening of a special autonomous region around the city of Sinuiju in September 2002, and the ongoing preparations (conjointly with South Korean firms) for a massive Kaesong industrial complex just north of the demilitarized zone, the gradual opening of private markets throughout the country, the advent of heretofore unthinkable private advertising and billboards, and other signs of market-consistent change.[1] Skeptics, of course, interpret differently such evidence of incipient stirrings of economic reform in North Korea and question the practicability of manipulating any reform tendencies from a long distance and through the blunt and limited instruments at the disposal of the international community.

Proponents of continuing and intensifying engagement with Pyongyang believe theirs is the compelling and, ultimately, the overwhelmingly persuasive case. For many of the unconvinced, however, the case for a new international engagement framework for North Korea sounds strangely ahistorical. Despite its ambitious objectives, they counter, there is scant evidence that such engagement has ever before been successful elsewhere.[2]

It is interesting that most of the "engagement optimists" in our volume happen to be Korean; the non-Korean authors tend generally to be decidedly more pessimistic about the difficulties that a new international engagement framework would confront and the probability that these difficulties would be surmounted. We suspect this cleavage is more than purely coincidental.

Nationalistic pride still runs deep on the Korean peninsula; the conviction that Koreans are an extraordinary people, not bound by ordinary rules or constraints of history, can be readily identified on both sides of the demilitarized zone today. Such attitudes may have been reinforced by South Korea's remarkable economic accomplishments over the past two generations, for Korean policy circles tend to be not only acutely aware that the outside world is deeply impressed by the progress they have managed to achieve but also

---

1 For a guardedly optimistic compilation and assessment of these tendencies, consult Ahn Choong-yong, ed., *North Korea Development Report 2003/2004* (Seoul: KIEP, forthcoming).

2 Perhaps the closest recent historical analogy to the international engagement framework currently considered for promoting North Korean reform would be the "Grand Bargain" proposals for Soviet economic reform advanced at the end of the Cold War era. Grand Bargain theorists hoped to entice the policymakers of glasnost into committing to a faster and deeper program of reform through a promise of, inter alia, an additional $15–$20 billion a year in Western foreign aid, although the Soviet Union collapsed before these proposals could be brought into application [cf. Graham T. Allison and Robert D. Blackwill, "America's Stake in the Soviet Future," *Foreign Affairs* 70, no. 3 (Summer 1991); Graham Allison and Grigory Yavlinsky, eds., *Window of Opportunity: The Grand Bargain for Democracy in the Soviet Union* (New York: Pantheon Books, 1991)]. With the USSR's collapse, the move toward an open political system and market economy in the former Soviet Union therefore took place much faster—and with considerably less foreign aid—than the Grand Bargain had originally suggested, making it an ever grander bargain than the one theorists had envisioned.

entirely unforgetting of the fact that foreign voices doubted the viability of the Republic of Korea's path to national affluence at almost every critical step of that long ascent.

Might that same Korean confidence come into positive play through a new international engagement framework for North Korean economic reform, making such a venture workable despite its daunting and manifold challenges? This is another question that as yet cannot be answered. It is our sincere hope, however, that readers will find in our volume some grounding for responding to it—and for dealing more capably with other profound and as yet still obscure aspects of the future of reform and international cooperation for North Korea.

Summaries of Subsequent Chapters

The Political Economy of North Korea

Political Economy of North Korea: Historical Background and Present Situation
by Marcus Noland

The current reforms in North Korea—marketization and the dysfunctional dual-price strategy—may generate unmanageable social changes, including greater social differentiation and inequality. This problem is exacerbated by the regime's emphasis on the military, which in effect diverts wealth away from society. A similar logic applies to foreign aid: aid acts as regime-sustaining walking-around money, facilitating poor governance while supporting patronage. Anecdotal evidence of growing social differentiation in the DPRK, in part caused by the misappropriation of aid for private and military purposes, is consistent with this view. An early collapse of North Korea is unlikely under current conditions. A prerequisite for the successful application of multilateral coercive diplomacy will be convincing the South Korean government and public of the correctness of this strategy. No coercive plan can succeed without South Korean support. To eliminate the North Korean nuclear program through negotiation or to establish the diplomatic precursors to eliminate it through other means requires the reengagement of the six-party talks as a first step.

The Structure of North Korea's Political Economy: Changes and Effects
by Lee Young-sun and Yoon Deok-ryong

This study finds that, since the early 1990s, North Korea's official economy has shrunk because of the collapse of state-owned enterprises, and the private economy has grown as a result of the people's effort to survive amid economic difficulties. Meanwhile, the military economy has maintained its relative fitness despite a small contraction in military spending, demonstrating the military's important role in maintaining domestic stability and external security. Gradually, and often under state-initiated reforms (for example, the reform measures introduced in July 2002), the private sector in North Korea has expanded at the expense of the official economy, thereby transforming the North into a market economy. International engagement toward a peaceful resolution with North Korea should begin with efforts to support growth in the private sector.

North Korea's Survival Game: Understanding the Recent Past, Thinking about the Future
by Nicholas Eberstadt

This paper argues that North Korea was set on a trajectory for an imminent economic collapse in the middle and late 1990s. Such a collapse was averted, however, as the regime experienced an upsurge in imports. This widening of the trade deficit has been financed through a variety of clandestine and illicit channels such as international counterfeiting and drug trafficking. A major source of funding also came in the form of international payments and aid. As South Korea embarked on its Sunshine Policy and other countries began to engage rather than isolate the North, funds were transferred to Pyongyang, which helped the regime pay for its imports and, on the whole, sustain its economy. At the strategic level, the current policy of the DPRK is to finance state survival by exporting insecurity—either through the sale of weapons and weapons technology or through military extortion. Since the regime's survival is contingent and sustained development is unlikely, this strategy is inherently unstable and only defers the question of economic collapse. The current attempt at reform does not address the crux of the problem unless North Korea pursues three policies: economic opening to foreigners, military demobilization, and normalization of relations with South Korea.

Preconditions and Rationale for International Economic Support for North Korea

Managing Collateral Catastrophe: Rationale and Preconditions for International Economic Support for North Korea
by Moon Chung-in

The dynamics of system change in North Korea are by and large a function of internal and external constraints; ideological stance, institutional arrangements, and power structure serve merely as intervening variables in influencing the leadership's choice. In light of this, North Korea can choose among three possible paths. Neither the status quo nor a sudden collapse of the regime is beneficial to all concerned parties, especially South Korea. The most desirable scenario is a gradual transformation through opening and reforms. However, the North cannot achieve a successful transition without obtaining considerable international economic support. To win international support, North Korea must satisfy several preconditions: the alleviation of international security concerns; a more proactive pursuit of ideational, behavioral, and institutional changes in the economic domain; improvement of human rights conditions; and the demonstration of a more credible international behavior.

Strategic Dimensions of Economic Assistance for North Korea
by Paul Bracken

Dealing with North Korea should be viewed as a problem of crisis management. As countries began to engage rather than isolate the DPRK during the 1990s, there was a surprising degree of convergence on the engagement framework, accompanied by the appearance of important thresholds. First, it has been consensual that North Korea should not be allowed to acquire any substantial number of atomic weapons. Second, the various countries involved have assumed various roles in the process. Third, norms, formal procedures, and standards have been institutionalized over time. Two approaches have emerged: the strategic approach that stipulates the clear goal of disarmament in exchange for economic assistance and security guarantees, and the multilateral approach that emphasizes international norms. In a crisis, miscommunication and counterintuitive behavior are common, and development becomes more unpredictable as economic assistance becomes a larger issue and as more countries and groups become involved. Therefore, crisis management cannot be reduced to formal plans drawn up in advance. Instead, a flexible and pragmatic framework that incorporates both the strategic approach and the multilateral approach should be drawn up. Furthermore, sound management assumes the ability to command and control a slow-motion crisis that cascades into a fast-breaking one as well as the ability to distinguish among declaratory, programmed, and actual policies.

Foreign Aid and International Norms: The Case of North Korea
by Carol Lancaster

This paper discusses the underlying norms in the provision of international aid and applies them to the case of North Korea. These norms include the needs, human rights record, and aid effectiveness of the recipient country; the recipient's participation; aid ownership and parity vis-à-vis the donor; and accountability of the donor to its constituency. In turn, aid effectiveness is determined by factors such as the quantity of infrastructure, the level of education and health, the strength of institutions, the degree of governance, the rule of law, the spread of corruption, market freedom, the ability to monitor aid implementation, and, most important, development expenditures compared with military expenditures. North Korea fails by most, if not all, of these indicators. It also barely meets the norms for humanitarian relief and aid in exchange for security cooperation because, in the past, foreign aid was diverted for military purposes and the regime frequently reneged on its international commitments.

Prospects and Preconditions for Market Economic Transformation in North Korea
by Anders Åslund

North Korea is likely to go through a great crisis when its socialist economic system crumbles, and the process of swift economic disruption is already under way. Strong indicators are the decentralization of economic reforms, the empowerment of state-enterprise managers, the emergence of substantial private markets, huge price and wage increases, and massive devaluations. It is not obvious that these indicators will lead to early Korean unification. South Korea could be seriously destabilized by a collapsing North Korean economy, and the North Korean elite would not look favorably upon their own dispossession. Both the North Korean preconditions and the precedents of other postcommunist countries suggest that the country needs to undertake radical market reforms. Three keys are thorough deregulation, radical financial stabilization, and a swift privatization. Foreign assistance will be vital for the success of these reforms. It is essential that foreign assistance is early and is brought in to support market reform rather than to support the rent-seeking interests of the old establishment. The amounts required are likely to be much smaller than usually considered because the absorption capacity of the North Korean economy is likely to be limited.

Possible Forms of International Cooperation and Assistance to North Korea

Unlikely Partners: Humanitarian Aid Agencies and North Korea
by Edward P. Reed

Since 1996, some members of the humanitarian aid community have attempted to respond to the call by the North Korean government for assistance in the face of severe food shortages and related human suffering. Inside North Korea, however, these aid agencies have encountered the unique emergency situation of a garrison state—in total control of its population, information, and distribution systems—confronting a hostile international environment. Delivering emergency aid with accountability under these conditions has been difficult, while assisting affected populations in efforts to regain food security and addressing underlying problems have been almost impossible. The widely held consensus is that fundamental changes in the North Korean system are essential for attaining humanitarian goals, yet systemic change depends on internal and external political factors beyond the control of aid agencies. The creativity of a number of humanitarian agencies has demonstrated that this conundrum actually opens the space for aid agencies to play a critical, if limited, role in saving lives, introducing new ideas, encouraging risk-taking behavior, and building standby capacity for more rapid change when the situation allows.

Designing Public Sector Capital Mobilization Strategies for the DPRK
by Bradley O. Babson

This paper explores issues that will need to be addressed during efforts to mobilize public capital for the DPRK. In general, experience illustrates the tension between political interests of donors and the DPRK leadership on the one hand, and the humanitarian and developmental needs of the DPRK society on the other. Any future efforts to mobilize public capital will need to take into account a number of factors: initial conditions in the DPRK, strategy for reform and institution building, macroeconomic stability, DPRK creditworthiness, multilateral assistance, bilateral interests and political constraints, and aid coordination and management mechanisms. Furthermore, the DPRK needs to address a number of issues while it builds a new fiscal capability: reform of state-owned enterprises, tax system restructuring, domestic debt strategy, role for contractual savings, and the allocative efficiency of public expenditures. Several options are available for international cooperation with the DPRK: arrangements that are led by the two Koreas, the World Bank/IMF, or the six core countries; a KEDO-based framework; a greater role for trust funds; and the creation of a Northeast Asia development bank.

Coping with North Korea's Energy Future: KEDO and Beyond
by Kent E. Calder

Integrating economic and political considerations, this paper outlines elements of a post–Korean Peninsula Energy Development Organization (KEDO) approach to North Korean energy. Given KEDO's original imperfections (the result in significant part of the crisis during which it originated), the irrelevance of its original time frame, and its loss of legitimacy caused by persistent violations of its provisions, the KEDO framework should be rethought and revised. North Korea's energy problems can be resolved through the modernization of its electric power grid and the development of a transnational network of gas-fired power plants that allows both North and South Korean access to Russia's natural gas reserves. Not only can such an approach avoid controversy over nuclear power, it also provides a solution to the fundamental energy need of Northeast Asia, namely, the region's overdependence on imported oil. Nevertheless, the indispensable condition for any form of continued cooperation with North Korea must be a verifiable nonproliferation agreement. If such an agreement is forthcoming, the nuclear dimension of the energy-support program should be scaled down.

Mobilizing Private Capital for North Korea:
Requirements for Attracting Private Investment
by Malcolm Binks and Carl Adams

Pyongyang needs to find some way to diffuse the issue of nuclear materials deployment and make a conscious effort to become a reasonable and opportunistic destination of choice for private foreign capital. To facilitate funds inflow and provide the private sector with sufficient information to improve risk predictability, it must establish a capital infrastructure that complies with a list of 12 financial codes and standards that can be categorized into three broad areas: macroeconomic policy and data transparency, institutional and market infrastructure, and financial regulation and supervision. Certain institutions should be introduced: an economic czar, a ministry of finance, a ministry for economic reconstruction and development, a central bank, and a functioning commercial banking system. Further steps can be undertaken to improve the investment environment; they include investor education and professional country presentations, identification of key industries and projects, regular provision of economic data and information, permission for foreign control of North Korean businesses, creation of mechanisms for foreign currency transfer and settlement of disputes, and the introduction of tax holidays.

Possible Role of South Korea and Other Major Stakeholders

A Proactive Approach to Engaging North Korea: Boldness, Flexibility, and Inclusiveness
by Choo Young-shik and Wang Yun-jong

Despite the significant drawbacks of the Sunshine Policy as a peace plan for the Korean peninsula and the limitations of engagement as a policy strategy for curbing North Korea's nuclear development program, engagement is still the alternative with the fewest number of drawbacks for peaceful resolution of the North Korean crisis. Although engagement remains the preferred strategy, it must undergo a major overhaul. Modified engagement would embody a proactive strategy comprising four major elements: (1) a bold diplomatic initiative to counter North Korea's alarming capability for nuclear weapons, (2) a disciplined means of engagement to counter Pyongyang's bluffing, (3) a comprehensive political, economic, and military engagement policy, and (4) a focus on the regime's long-term self-sustainability and the question of Korean reunification. South Korea should play a key role in the new proactive strategy; to accomplish this, its duties and responsibilities would include, but would not be limited to, persuading other nations that the ultimate goal for North Korea would be regime change through reforms, maintaining solid bilateral relations with the United States, and coordinating international cooperation for resolving the crisis.

Payback Time: Japan–North Korean Economic Relations
by Richard J. Samuels

Strong anti-DPRK public sentiment has been nurtured, and then captured, by the Japan's Liberal Democratic Party for electoral gain. Japan-DPRK economic relations, idled by Japanese government policy, have little sustained business or popular support. The Japanese government insists that normalization cannot proceed without resolution of the abduction issue and cessation of nuclear and missile threats, but the abduction issue is the deal breaker that will block massive infusion of Japanese capital. A multilateral grand bargain on the military threat may be accompanied by token payments from Japan reminiscent of the Korean Peninsula Energy Development Organization or in the form of tied aid earmarked for repayment of long-standing debt. In either event, Japanese firms will follow cautiously with projects for infrastructural development and with investments likely to be tied to those negotiated by South Korean firms.

China's Role in the Course of North Korea's Transition
by Liu Ming

As North Korea's traditional patron, China can take advantage of their close relationship to influence the outcome of the North Korean crisis. This relationship, however, is challenged by several trends. First, there has been a lack of consultation and coordination on important issues. Second, Pyongyang has dubious feelings toward Beijing's influence, given Beijing's collaboration with South Korea and the United States. Third, in China's view, North Korea's erratic foreign policy and unilateralism have failed to adapt to the international situation and have threatened Chinese interests. Fourth, Pyongyang doubts China's credibility as a partner and protector in times of crisis. Last, economic cooperation has been unbalanced and backward. In a plan that involves all major countries, China should act as monitor of North Korea's fulfillment of international agreements on the one hand and as guarantor for North Korean security and U.S. commitment on the other, show understanding toward North Korea's sense of vulnerability and insecurity, push forward inter-Korean reconciliation and soften the stances of Washington and Tokyo, deal with North Korea in a multilateral rather than a bilateral setting, assist North Korea in joining several key international financial organizations, continue with interpersonal exchanges, and advise on North Korea on its economic situation.

Russian–North Korean Relations and the Prospects for Multilateral Conflict Resolution on the Korean Peninsula
by Alexandre Y. Mansourov

This paper provides an overview of the Russia-North Korea rapprochement during the early years of the 2000s. In particular, it attempts to explain the motivations of the two parties throughout this process. For North Korea, the establishment of ties provides several benefits. First, during Kim Jong-il's meetings with Vladimir Putin, Kim outlined a framework for a possible deal between Pyongyang and Washington. Second, the DPRK signified to Chinese leaders that China is not the DPRK's only sponsor (in other words, it tried to play Russia against China). Last, North Korea has learned from the Russian experience of reform and opening, which some Russian analysts believe stimulated Kim's decision to introduce reform policies in July 2002. Russia has several objectives. To ensure a good relationship with a foreseeable unified Korea and a unification process that suits its interests, Russia has striven to influence North Korea and obtain information about developments there, to maintain a proper balance in its relations with Seoul and Pyongyang, to mediate inter-Korean differences, and, finally, to restrain the bargaining position of the United States and thereby reduce the U.S. military presence on the peninsula.

Expected Role of South Korea and Major Stakeholders:
NGO Contributions to and Roles in North Korea's Rehabilitation
by Scott Snyder

This paper outlines the origin and history of activities of nongovernmental organizations (NGOs) in North Korea and their implications for the country's rehabilitation and integration with the outside world. The rise of South Korean NGOs has influenced the development of inter-Korean relations and is likely to play an even more important and complex role in the fields of advocacy and of grassroots exchange and service delivery that are vital to North Korea's rehabilitation. This prospect, however, depends on the continued support from Seoul and the DPRK's admittance of NGO activities. U.S. and European NGOs have been less active than South Korea in the DPRK (a function of their respective governments' policies). European NGOs have been more successful than their U.S. counterparts in establishing a sustained program in the DPRK., in part owing to differences in the requirements that accompany governmental funding of European NGO work in North Korea and the relatively depoliticized European response to DPRK needs.

The Political Economy of North Korea

2

Political Economy of North Korea: Historical Background and Present Situation

Marcus Noland

By standard statistical measures, North Korea (Democratic People's Republic of Korea [DPRK]) is the world's most militarized society,[1] and domestic propaganda incessantly proclaims the virtues of "military-first" politics.[2] If comparable statistical measures were available for politicization, North Korea might rank first on this criterion, too. Internally, all aspects of society are suffused with politics, and externally, politics thoroughly permeates not only the country's diplomatic relationships but also its economic relations.

A famine in the late 1990s resulted in the deaths of perhaps 600,000 to 1 million people out of a pre-famine population of roughly 22 million. Given the regime's extreme preference for guns over butter, the North Korean economy does not produce enough output to sustain the population biologically, and population maintenance is aid dependent. Yet the October 2002 revelation of a nuclear weapons program based on highly enriched uranium (in addition to a plutonium-based program acknowledged a decade earlier), undertaken in contravention of several international agreements, and North Korea's subsequent withdrawal from the Nuclear Non-Proliferation Treaty have put continued international assistance in doubt.

---

1 According to U.S. Department of State figures (DOS 2003), North Korea has traditionally led the world in measures such as military expenditure as a share of national income, or share of the population under arms. During its war with Ethiopia, the percentage of Eritrea's population under arms and military expenditures as a share of gross domestic product (GDP) actually exceeded the comparable figures for North Korea, as did Angola in the midst of its civil war, but, with the cessation of hostilities in the Horn of Africa and the end of the Angolan civil war, in all likelihood North Korea has reasserted its historic primacy on these measures. It is assuredly the case that no other country during peacetime is militarized to the degree North Korea is.

2 According to Koh (2004) the modifier *songun* (military-first) was used 40 times in the 2004 New Year's Day joint editorial of *Rodong Sinmun* (Labor News), *Choson Immigun* (The Korea People's Army), and *Ch'ongryon Chonwi* (Youth Vanguard).

The situation is further complicated by internal economic policy changes initiated in July 2002. These reforms included marketization of the economy, a large increase in the overall price level, the promotion of special economic zones, and a diplomatic opening to Japan intended to secure the provision of billions of dollars in post-colonial claims.

Unlike the diplomatic maneuvering of the past few years, which has had little immediate impact on most North Koreans, the economic reforms have directly affected the masses, altering economic, political, and social relations at the grassroots level. The reforms are contributing to growing social differentiation and inequality, creating what both United Nations (UN) officials and nongovernmental organization (NGO) representatives have described as a new class of urban poor. Those such as senior party officials with access to foreign exchange will be relatively insulated from the effects of inflation. Agricultural workers may benefit from "automatic" pay increases as the price of grain rises, but salaried workers without access to foreign exchange will fall behind. In other words, the process of marketization and inflation will contribute to the exacerbation of existing social differences in North Korea.

The implications for "losers" could be quite severe. According to a World Food Programme (WFP 2003b) survey, most urban households are food insecure, spending 75–85 percent of their incomes on food. In December 2003 Masood Hyder, the UN's humanitarian relief coordinator in North Korea, told the world press that the food problem was concentrated among up to 1 million urban workers, a view echoed by Rick Corsino, head of the WFP's local operation, who claimed that "some people are having to spend all their income on food."[3] According to the UN Food and Agricultural Organization (UNFAO 2003), for the period 1999–2001, 34 percent of North Korea's population was malnourished, though it is unclear on what basis the organization reached such a precise figure, especially in light of the problematic nature of the survey evidence as outlined in Noland (2003). Similarly, in December 2003 the UN's Office for the Coordination of Humanitarian Affairs claimed that the rate of "severe malnourishment" among children was 42 percent, apparently on the basis of the questionable 2002 stunting estimate.

Even if one is skeptical as to the precise figures, there is less room to doubt the rupture of the traditional social compact, necessitating a reinterpretation of the North Korean doctrine of *juche*, or self-reliance, to legitimate the reforms and justify the departure from the country's socialist tradition. The response has been to intensify the military-first campaign, elevating the military above the proletariat in the North Korean political pantheon (Frank 2003a, Noland 2004). The effect has been to overturn the traditional paths to power and status: captains and entrepreneurs have now replaced party

---

3 See Watts (2003) and Cho (2003). Kim (2003, 147–64) and Amnesty International (2004) contain a more general analysis of food insecurity issues.

cadres and bureaucrats as preferred sons-in-law. As the military waxes while the commitment to socialism wanes, North Korea increasingly resembles the totalitarian fascist regimes its propaganda excoriates, albeit a dynastic one. The central issue is whether the current regime can manage this internal change while it confronts the implicit legitimization challenge posed by prosperous, democratic South Korea and diplomatic tensions emanating from its nuclear weapons program.

Background on North Korea

Before the partition of the Korean peninsula at the end of the Second World War, most Korean industries were located in the North; the South was the breadbasket. In 1950, North Korea invaded South Korea. The see-saw character of the war, which saw armies of both sides twice traversing nearly the entire length of the peninsula, destroyed most of the physical capital stock. There was considerable population movement as well, mostly from the North to the South. It is impossible to ascertain with any degree of certainty the capacities of the two countries at the end of the hostilities in 1952.[4]

Under Soviet tutelage, the North set about establishing a thoroughly orthodox centrally planned economy, remarkable only in the degree to which markets were suppressed. In 1955, founding leader Kim Il-sung proclaimed *juche* the national ideology, and under his leadership North Korea developed as the world's most autarkic economy, never joining the Council of Mutual Economic Assistance and going so far as to time its central plans to frustrate linkage with those of fraternally allied socialist states.

Under such relatively autarkic conditions, North Korean industrial development was characterized by excessively diverse, subscale, high-cost production. These inefficiencies were compounded by national security considerations that contributed by a lack of agglomeration in the spatial location of industrial activities and the placement underground of industrial assets and facilities such as the electrical grid.

Following the Korean War, agriculture was collectivized, quantitative planning in production was introduced, state marketing and distribution of grain were established, and private production and trade were prohibited. Collectivization was accompanied by an increase in electrically powered irrigation and the use of industrial inputs such as tractors, chemical fertilizers, and pesticides.

In response to food shortages in 1970–73, the degree of centralization of agricultural planning was intensified. The authorities altered planting patterns, specifically replacing traditional food crops such as tubers, millet, and potatoes with maize. Yields were increased, but they were susceptible to a fall in inputs. A Cultural Revolution–type movement was created, and young

---

4 For general background on the North Korean economy, see Hwang (1993) and Noland (2000).

Communists were dispatched to initiate ideological, cultural, and technical education of farm households. New rural educational institutions were established, and existing rural officials and staff were reassigned and required to enroll in these *juche* curriculum programs. This social engineering eroded knowledge of, respect for, and influence of traditional farming techniques; rural life was thoroughly regimented by the state, and any sort of individual initiative stifled (Lee 2003; Gey 2004, 115–33).

The present crisis has its origins in a multifaceted set of developments in the late 1980s, although the precise causal relationships are unclear. Throughout its history, the country has run recurring balance-of-payments deficits, posing a chronic financing issue. After defaulting on international creditors in the 1970s, North Korea was frozen out of international capital markets and came to rely increasingly on aid from fraternally allied socialist states, remittances from ethnic Koreans in Japan, and illicit activities such as drug trafficking and counterfeiting to generate foreign exchange.

Despite its *juche*-inspired declarations of self-reliance, North Korea has been dependent on outside assistance throughout its entire history, with first the Soviet Union and later China playing the role of chief benefactor or patron. The North Koreans have compensated for this dependence by ferociously denouncing it,[5] portraying aid as tribute paid to the ideologically pure North Korean state (Eberstadt 1999) and trying to play patrons off against each other.[6] Eventually, frustrated by North Korean unwillingness to repay accumulated debts, the Soviets withdrew support and, according to U.S. Central Intelligence Agency (CIA) figures, the net flow of resources turned negative in 1987.[7]

That same year the North Koreans initiated a number of at times conflicting policies in the agricultural sector, including the expansion of state farms, tolerance of private garden plots, expansion of grain-sown areas, transformation of crop composition in favor of high-yield items, maximization of industrial inputs subject to availability, and the intensification of double-cropping and dense planting. Continuous cropping led to soil depletion, and the overuse of chemical fertilizers contributed to acidification of the soil

---

5   For example, in 2000, the day after South Korea began shipping $100 million of assistance to the DPRK and while the UN agencies were urging international donors to commit to new aid to avert catastrophe, *Rodong Sinmun*, the official newspaper of the North Korean government, ran a commentary that read in part, "The imperialists' aid is a tool of aggression . . . a dangerous toxin which brings about poverty, famine, and death, not prosperity."

6   In a somewhat different context, Flake (2003, 39) describes a similar set of attitudes toward a different set of patrons: "DPRK officials were successfully able to come across not as the beggar, but instead as the recipient of entreaties from the outside world. In contrast, the would-be donors, the NGOs, became the supplicants, asking the DPRK for the 'privilege' of helping the North Korean people."

7   There is some controversy as to how seriously to take the CIA's numbers. It is unclear, for example, to what extent the figure takes into consideration the implicit subsidy of the USSR's oil exports to North Korea. The figures developed by Eberstadt et al. (1995, 87–104) show the USSR (Russia) continuing to run a significant trade surplus with North Korea until 1991.

and eventually a reduction in yields. As yields declined, hillsides were denuded to bring more and more marginal land into production. This contributed to soil erosion, river silting, and, ultimately, catastrophic flooding. Isolation from the outside world reduced genetic diversity of the North Korean seed stock, making plants more vulnerable to disease.

These effects were compounded by the tremendous trade shocks that hit the economy starting in 1990 as the Soviet Union disintegrated and the Eastern bloc collapsed. The Soviets had supplied North Korea with most of its coal and refined oil and one-third of its steel. Trade with the Soviet Union accounted for more than half of North Korea's two-way trade. The fall in imports from Russia in 1991 was equivalent to 40 percent of all imports, and by 1993 imports from Russia were only 10 percent of their 1987–90 average (Eberstadt et al. 1995, 87–104). North Korea proved incapable of reorienting its commercial relations in the face of this massive trade shock. The North Korean industrial economy imploded and, deprived of industrial inputs, agricultural output plummeted.

In response, the government initiated a number of retrenchment campaigns, but by the spring of 1995 the situation had become so dire that the North Korean government approached first the Japanese government and then the South Korean government for food assistance, reaching agreements in June. In July it announced to the public that it was receiving external assistance, although it failed to mention the South Korean role. In August 1995, North Korea made a formal request for emergency assistance to the United Nations and immediately began receiving aid from the UN. According to Moody's (2003), food assistance has been running at approximately $500 million annually since 1998.

The provision of this aid has posed a variety of challenges and ethical dilemmas for private and official providers of humanitarian assistance. While it is fair to say that cooperation has improved since assistance was initiated in the mid-1990s, the situation in North Korea remains highly nontransparent. Almost nine years after its arrival, the WFP is still barred from areas accounting for approximately 15 percent of the population, is unable to employ Korean speakers, and is forced to submit to prenotification for site visits. There can be little doubt that North Korea violates minimum standards of nondiscrimination with respect to the distribution of aid. Confronted with this situation, a number of private NGOs have withdrawn from the country.[8]

Catastrophic floods in July and August 1995 added to North Korea's suffering.[9] Although flooding contributed to the food crisis in North Korea, agriculture, like the rest of the economy, has been in secular decline since the

---

8 See Hawk (2003), Noland (2003), and Amnesty International (2004) for discussion.

9 The government announced that 5.4 million people had been displaced, 330,000 hectares of agricultural land had been destroyed, and 1.9 million tons of grain had been lost. The government put the total cost of the flood damage at $15 billion. While the flooding was considerable, the consensus of outside observers was that the government's claims were exaggerated. For example, a UN

beginning of the decade. On the basis of their econometric analysis of North Korean agricultural production, Smith and Huang (forthcoming) conclude that "the dominant triggering factor in the crisis was the sharp loss of supplies of agricultural inputs following the disruption of the trade with the socialist bloc from the late 1980s. . . . The contribution of climatic factors to the agricultural crisis, as stressed by North Korea's policy-makers was at most a secondary cause." This conclusion is reinforced by the computable general equilibrium model–based simulation of Noland et al. (2001), who found that restoration of flood-affected land and capital would have but a minor impact on the availability of food. Taking at face value the WFP's estimates of human needs, even without flooding, North Korea would have entered the mid-1990s with a substantial, apparent food deficit.

Given the secrecy of the North Korean regime, it is unsurprising that the timing and impact of the resulting famine are still not well understood. Contemporaneous estimates of the excess death toll vary enormously, ranging from 220,000 to 3.5 million, but the most recent and sophisticated attempts to measure excess deaths put them in a range of roughly 600,000 to 1 million, or approximately 3 to 5 percent of the pre-crisis population (Goodkind and West 2001, 219–38; Lee 2003).[10] It did not have to be this way. Morocco, a country of similar size and in certain respects with economic characteristics similar to the DPRK's, suffered a similar fall in domestic output in the late 1990s, but a combination of increased exports and increased foreign borrowing allowed it to cover its food deficit through imports. Times were hard, but Morocco did not experience famine—and it recovered.

In parallel with the famine, North Korea became embroiled in a diplomatic confrontation with the United States over its nuclear weapons program. North Korea adroitly used the concerns of the world community to extract resources from the outside world in return for the North's supposed adherence to international norms. Aid was repeatedly provided to North Korea as a quid pro quo for North Korean participation in diplomatic meetings. Between 1995 and 2002 North Korea received more than $1 billion in

---

survey concluded that the flooding displaced 500,000 people, not the 5.4 million the government initially claimed. Nevertheless, the floods played an important public relations role inasmuch as they facilitated the North Korean government's portrayal of the famine as a product of natural disaster (the government unit charged with obtaining international assistance was renamed the Flood Damage Rehabilitation Committee), a guise that a number of foreign relief agencies found advantageous. The floods of 1995 were followed by more, though less severe, floods in July 1996, and renewed appeals for help.

10 North Korean officials have provided a low-end estimate of famine-related deaths of 220,000 people, or roughly 1 percent of the pre-crisis population. Robinson et al. (1999, 291–5) reconstructed mortality rates for a single heavily affected province and concluded that between 1995 and 1997 nearly 12 percent of that province's population had died. The Buddhist Sharing Movement, an NGO, extrapolating to the entire country from an analysis of refugee interviews and observations on the ground, produced estimates of famine-related deaths on the order of 2.8 to 3.5 million. In 2003, the USAID administrator, Andrew S. Natsios, testified that "2.5 million people, or 10 percent of the population" had died in the famine (Natsios 2003). This is almost surely an exaggeration. See Noland (2003) for a further discussion of these and other estimates.

food and energy assistance from the United States, making it in the late 1990s Washington's largest bilateral aid recipient in East Asia.

These trends were reinforced by the election of Kim Dae-jung as president of South Korea and the initiation of his Sunshine Policy. The level of South Korean financial support to the North Korean government is uncertain because, as documented in the 2003 corruption trials, some of the assistance has been made illegally, under the table. However, the ratings agency Moody's puts the budgetary costs to South Korea at $1.7 billion during Kim Dae-jung's presidency. Official aid has continued under the administration of Roh Moo-hyun, reaching $315 million in 2003.

Aid is a pure rent to the incumbent who can dole it out with the sole object of maintaining his incumbency. It acts as regime-sustaining walking-around money, facilitating poor governance while supporting patronage. Anecdotal evidence of growing social differentiation in the DPRK, in part caused by the misappropriation of aid for private purposes, is consistent with this view. As the public distribution system (PDS), the traditional mechanism through which roughly two-thirds of the population obtained food, failed and the famine intensified, food was increasingly allocated through informal markets. In these circumstances control of aid potentially conveys astronomical rents, a situation abetted by the inability of the WFP to monitor continuously the distribution of supplies from port of entry to final recipient.[11]

Beyond the issue of diversion, even in the case of in-kind humanitarian assistance, food obtained on concessional terms has largely crowded out commercial imports, acting as implicit balance of payments support (Noland 2003). There is a large economics literature demonstrating that aid tends to be fungible, simply supporting government consumption according to the preexisting preferences of the recipient governments (Pack and Pack 1990, 188–94; 1993, 258–65). Given the strong propensity of the North Korean government to spend on its military, the implications are obvious.[12]

July 2002 Reforms

In July 2002, the government of North Korea announced changes in economic policy that could be regarded as having four components: microeconomic policy changes, macroeconomic policy changes, special economic

---

11 Snyder (2003, 119) observes: "[T]he amount of food distributed through the PDS is no longer an accurate indicator of imminent distress within the North Korean system, yet it has remained the WFP's primary indicator of distress and the primary vehicle through which the WFP distributes food inside the country. In this respect, the WFP is an ally of the government in its efforts to reestablish control over the means of production." An MSF researcher (Terry 2001) explains: "[B]y channeling [aid] through the regime responsible for the suffering, it has become part of the system of oppression." See Manyin and Jun (2003) for a more extensive discussion of aid diversion issues.

12 Simulations reported in Noland et al. (2001) illustrate how military spending, for example, could be expected to increase with the provision of humanitarian aid. Noland (2004) contains a more general discussion of the political preconditions for effective use of aid.

zones, and aid seeking.[13] These initiatives followed moves begun in 1998 to encourage administrative decentralization (Oh 2003). A September 2003 cabinet reshuffle holds forth the promise of younger, and perhaps more technocratic, leadership. Amid these changes, there has been no mention of the military's privileged position within the economy; indeed, the military-first campaign has intensified.

Microeconomic reforms involve, among other things, an attempt to increase the importance of material incentives. Opinions range widely about what the North Koreans are trying to accomplish.[14] In the industrial sector there is some thought that the government was attempting to adopt a dual-price strategy similar to what the Chinese have implemented in the industrial sphere.[15] In essence, the Chinese instructed their state-owned enterprises to continue to fulfill the plan, but when planned production obligations were fulfilled, the enterprises were free to hire factors and produce products for sale on the open market (Lau et al. 2000, 120–43). In other words, the plan was essentially frozen in time, and marginal growth occurred according to market dictates. Yet the North Korean planning apparatus may have reached such an advanced stage of decline that the conditions under which such an approach might have been viable have passed (Babson and Newcomb 2004).

North Korean enterprises have been instructed that they are responsible for covering their own costs—that is, no more state subsidies. But, at the same time, the state has administratively raised wage levels, and certain favored groups such as military personnel, party officials, scientists, and coal miners receive supernormal increases (Gey 2004, table 2). This alteration of real wages across occupational groups could be interpreted as an attempt to enhance the role of material incentives in labor allocation or, alternatively, as a simple attempt to reward favored constituencies. Likewise, the state continues to maintain an administered price structure, although by fiat the state

---

13 Assessments of both the impact of the policy changes and the political motivations behind their introduction vary. See Lee (2002, 357–64), Chung (2003, 43–53), Frank (2003b), Nam (2003, 18–22), Newcomb (2003, 57–60), Oh (2003, 72–8), and Gey (2004).

14 Oh (2003, 72) disputes this notion, arguing that the aim of the policy changes was "to shift the country's economic control mechanism from one based on material balances in a traditional socialist mandatory planning system to one managed through a monetary mechanism. . . . The situation is quite different from that in China at the beginning of its reform process, where reform-minded leaders boldly argued that economic reform measures were imperatives, not policy options." Newcomb (2003, 59 [emphasis added by Newcomb]) also emphasizes the shift from quantitative planning to a monetized economy and reports a statement by one official that could also be interpreted as suggesting a more limited aim of the policy changes: "this objective (or reform) will only be achieved by removing the last 'vestiges' of the *Soviet system* from the DPRK economy." Frank (2003b) also quotes a similar denunciation of "Soviet-type" practices. These statements could be interpreted as manifestations of a North Korean attempt to justify ideologically a uniquely North Korean "third way" policy package.

15 Gey (2004, 2) strongly disputes this view, at least in regard to the agricultural sector: "[T]he measures taken so far suggest that the North Korean leadership has decided against Chinese-style reform and for the sort of reform deployed repeatedly from the 1960s by the state and party leaders of the formerly socialist countries of central and eastern Europe as they attempted to improve the performance of their planned economies. . . . [T]his will fail in North Korea as well."

prices are being brought in line with prices observed in the markets. The North Koreans have not announced any mechanism for periodically adjusting prices, however; over time, disequilibria—possibly severe—will develop.

In essence, enterprise managers are being told to meet hard budget constraints, but they are being given little scope to manage. Managers have been authorized to make limited purchases of intermediate inputs and to make autonomous investments out of retained earnings. They are also permitted to engage in international trade. Yet it is unclear to what extent managers have been sanctioned to hire, fire, and promote workers, or to what extent remuneration will be determined by the market.

This is problematic (as it has proved to be in other transitional economies): the state has told the enterprises that they must cover costs, yet it continues to administer prices; and, in the absence of formal bankruptcy or any other exit mechanism, there is no prescribed method for enterprises that cannot cover costs to cease operations nor, in the absence of a social safety net, any indication of how workers from closed enterprises would survive.

Anecdotal evidence suggests that North Korean enterprises are exhibiting a variety of responses: some have set up side businesses, either as a legitimate coping mechanism or as a dodge to shed unwanted labor; some have cut wages (despite the official wage increase); and some have closed. It is likely that some enterprises will be kept in operation, supported by implicit subsidies, either through national or local government budgets or through recourse to a reconstituted banking system, which is being restructured. Indeed, the North Koreans have sent officials to China to study the Chinese banking system, which, although it may well have virtues, is also the primary mechanism through which money-losing state-owned firms are kept alive. Officials have also traveled to Vietnam to study the Vietnamese reform experience.

In the agricultural sector, the government has implemented a policy of increasing the procurement prices of grains to increase the volume of food entering the PDS, along with a dramatic increase in PDS prices to consumers, with the retail prices of grains rising 40,000–60,000 percent in the space of six months (Noland 2003, table 4). The increase in the procurement price for grain was in part motivated to counter the supply response of the farmers who, in the face of derisory procurement prices, were diverting acreage from grain to tobacco and using grain to produce liquor for sale.

The maintenance of the PDS as a mechanism for distributing food is presumably an attempt to maintain the social contract that everyone will be guaranteed a minimum survival ration while narrowing the disequilibrium between the market and plan prices. Residents are still issued monthly ration cards; if they do not have sufficient funds to purchase the monthly allotment, it is automatically carried over to the next month. Wealthy households are not allowed to purchase through the PDS quantities in excess of the monthly allotment. The system is organized to prevent arbitrage in ration coupons between rich and poor households.[16]

Some have questioned the extent to which this is a real policy change and how much this is simply a ratification of system-fraying that had already occurred—there is considerable evidence that most food, for example, was already being distributed through markets, not the PDS. But this may indeed be precisely the motivation behind the increases in producer prices—with little supply entering the PDS, people increasingly obtained their food from nonstate sources; and, by bringing more supply into state-controlled channels, the government can try to reduce the extent to which food is allocated purely on the basis of purchasing power. Yet another motivation may be to reduce the fiscal strain imposed by the implicit subsidy provided to urban consumers.

The WFP (2003a) reports that, since the July 2002 price changes, prices for grain in the farmers' markets have risen "significantly" while the PDS prices have remained largely unchanged. Anecdotal accounts suggest that, as a consequence, despite the increase in procurement prices, the policy has not been successful in coaxing back into the PDS domestic supply (as distinct from international aid). Indeed, some anecdotal reports indicate that the PDS is not operating in all areas of the country.

When China began its reforms in 1979, more than 70 percent of the population was in the agricultural sector. (The same held true for Vietnam when it began reforming the following decade.) De-bureaucratization of agriculture under these conditions permits rapid increases in productivity and the release of labor into the nascent non-state-owned manufacturing sector. The key in this situation is that change is likely to produce few losers: farmers' incomes go up as marginal and average value product in the agricultural sector increase; incomes of those leaving the farms rise as they receive higher-wage jobs in the manufacturing sector; and urban workers in the state-owned heavy-industry sector benefit as their real wages rise as a result of lower food prices associated with expanded supply. The efficiency gains in agriculture essentially finance an economy-wide Pareto improvement (that is, no one is made worse off). This dynamic was understood by Chinese policymakers, who used a combination of the dual-price system (allowing the market to surround the plan, to use a Maoist metaphor) and side payments to state-owned enterprises, their associated government ministries, and allied local politicians to suppress political opposition to the reforms. The existence of a large, labor-intensive agricultural sector is one of the few robust explanators of relative success in the transition from central planning to the market (Åslund et al. 1996, 217–313).

---

16 Oh (2003) claims that the rationing coupons have been abolished and that, in theory, wealthy households can buy unlimited supplies through the PDS.

In contrast, North Korea has perhaps half that share employed in agriculture. As a consequence, the absolute magnitude of the supply response is likely to be smaller and the population share directly benefiting from the increase in producer prices for agricultural goods roughly half as big as in China and Vietnam. This means that reform in North Korea is less likely to be Pareto-improving than the cases of China or Vietnam. Instead, reform in North Korea is more likely to create losers and, with them, the possibility of unrest, as discussed in the next section.

One result of these changes has been a noticeable upsurge in small-scale retail activity, with Gey (2004) estimating that 6–8 percent of the workforce is engaged in informal trading activities. Yet there is little if any evidence of a resurgence in industrial activity, and consensus among most outside observers is that, at this writing, marketization has not delivered as hoped. The fall 2003 harvests were fairly large, but it is unclear how much of this is due to favorable weather, provision of fertilizer aid by South Korea, and incentive changes.

At the same time the government announced the marketization initiatives, it also announced tremendous administered increases in wages and prices. To get a grasp on the magnitude of these price changes, consider this: when China raised the price of grains at the start of its reforms in November 1979, the increase was on the order of 25 percent. In comparison, North Korea has raised the prices of corn and rice by more than 40,000 percent. In the absence of huge supply responses, the result will be an enormous jump in the price level and possibly even hyperinflation.[17] Unfortunately, macroeconomic stability at the time that reforms are initiated is the second robust predictor of relative success in transition from the plan to the market (Åslund et al. 1996).[18] High rates of inflation do not portend well for North Korea.

Under these conditions, access to foreign currency may act as insurance against inflation, and, in fact, the black-market value of the North Korean *won* has dropped steadily since the reforms were announced, with one recent report putting it at approximately 1,200 *won* to the dollar in April 2003. In this respect, the authorities' treatment of the external sector has been confused. After announcing the dramatic price increases, the government initially maintained that it would not devalue the currency (though this would have caused a massive real appreciation that would have destroyed whatever

---

17 See Frank (2003b), Noland (2003), and Oh (2003) for recitations of other, non-agricultural, price increases.

18 North Korea looks better on another explanator of success in the transition—the viability of a pre-socialist commercial code. The commercial code of South Korea has its origins in the colonial era Japanese commercial code that in turn was transplanted from Prussia. North Korean scholars and officials at legal workshops have exhibited some familiarity with the concepts of the contemporary South Korean commercial code on the basis of their understanding of their common pre-socialist legal system. Presumably this has helped the two countries over the past several years to conclude the handful of agreements that provide a conventional legal framework for inter-Korean economic relations.

international price competitiveness the North Korean economy has); then it periodically began devaluing the currency as its value in the black market fell.[19] Tariffs on consumer products such as textiles, soap, and shoes have doubled, from 20 percent to 40 percent (Oh 2003), possibly as an attempt to deal with the overvaluation of the real exchange rate and the surge of imports into the country but more likely as an attempt to simply generate revenue in the absence of a functioning tax system.

The government apparently continues to insist that foreign-invested enterprises pay wages in hard currencies (at wage rates that exceed those in China and Vietnam). For a labor-abundant economy this curious policy would seem to be the very definition of a contractionary devaluation, blunting the competitiveness-boosting impact of the devaluation by aborting the adjustment of relative labor costs while raising the domestic resource costs of imported intermediate inputs.

In yet another wheeze to extract resources from the population, in March 2003 the government announced the issuance of "people's life bonds" that, despite their name, seem to more closely resemble lottery tickets than bonds as conventionally understood. These instruments have a 10-year maturity, with principal repaid in annual installments beginning in year five (there does not appear to be any provision for interest payments and no money for such payments has been budgeted). For the first two years of the program, there would be semi-annual drawings (annually thereafter), with winners to receive their principal plus prizes. No information has been provided on the expected odds or prize values other than that the drawings are to be based on an "open and objective" principle. The government's announcement states, without irony, that "the bonds are backed by the full faith and credit of the DPRK government." Committees have been established in every province, city, county, institute, factory, village, and town to promote the scheme—citizens purchasing these "bonds" will be performing a "patriotic deed."[20] Both the characteristics of the instrument and the mass campaign to sell it suggest that politics, not personal finance, will be its main selling point.[21] According to Kim (1998), when the government has resorted to lottery-like

---

19 After about two weeks, in August 2002, the government announced a devaluation of the currency from 2.1 *won* to 150 *won* to the dollar, which approached the contemporaneous black-market rate of around 200 *won* to the dollar. A second devaluation, this time to 900 *won* to the dollar (again approaching the black-market rate) was announced in October 2003.

20 The discussion in Chung (2003) suggests that purchases of the bonds may be compulsory. According to a Korea Trade-Investment Promotion Agency (KOTRA) translation of a 23 May 2003 Itar-Tass account, although purchases are not mandatory, the authorities use purchases as "a barometer of the buyers' loyalty and support for the party and the state."

21 Frank (2003b) argues that the issuance of these instruments is a response to the large expansion in expenditures associated with the increased procurement price for grains, and, indeed, North Korean government expenditures appeared to increase by double digits in 2003. However, the rise in outlays associated with the increase in the procurement price for grain ought to be offset by a similar increase in revenues from the expanded PDS sales. Some have claimed that these instruments could ultimately serve as a basis for privatizing state-owned enterprises.

instruments in the past to deal with monetary overhang problems, they have been unpopular.

The third component of the North Korean economic policy change is the formation of various sorts of special economic zones (SEZs).[22] In September 2002 the North Korean government announced the establishment of a special administrative region (SAR) at Sinuiju. In certain respects the location of the new zone was not surprising; the North Koreans had been talking about doing something in the Sinuiju area since 1998. Yet in other respects the announcement was extraordinary. The North Koreans announced that the zone would exist completely outside North Korea's usual legal structures, that it would have its own flag and issue its own passports, and that land could be leased for 50 years. To top it off, the SAR would be run not by a North Korean but by a Chinese-born entrepreneur with Dutch citizenship named Yang Bin. Yang Bin was promptly arrested by the Chinese authorities.[23]

Ultimately, the planned industrial park at Kaesong, oriented toward South Korea, may have a bigger impact on the economy than either the Rajin-Sonbong or Sinuiju zones. In the long run, South Korean small- and medium-size enterprises (SMEs) will be a natural source of investment and transfer of appropriate technology to the North. However, in the absence of physical or legal infrastructure, they are unlikely to invest. The eventual signing of four economic cooperation agreements between the North and the South on issues such as taxation and foreign exchange transactions could be regarded as providing a legal infrastructure for economic activity by SMEs of negligible political influence.

The industrial park at Kaesong has not yet fulfilled its promise, however. The park has its origins in Hyundai's 1998 deal that set up the Mt. Kumgang tourism venture, and the conglomerate's subsequent dissolution forced the South Korean parastatal KOLAND to take over the project. The North Koreans have inexplicably failed to open the necessary transportation links to South Korea on their side of the demilitarized zone although negotiations with the South on this issue continue.

The fourth component of the economic plan consisted of passing the hat. In September 2002, during the first-ever meeting between the heads of gov-

---

22 The first such zone was established in the Rajin-Sonbong region in the extreme northeast of the country in 1991. It has proved to be a failure for a variety of reasons, including its geographic isolation, poor infrastructure, onerous rules, and interference in enterprise management by party officials. The one major investment has been the establishment of a hotel-casino-bank combination. Given the obvious scope for illicit activity associated with such a horizontally integrated endeavor, the result has been less Hong Kong and more Macau North. See Jung et al. (2003) for an appraisal of the North Korean SEZ policy.

23 Press reports subsequently touted first Park Tae-joon, former South Korean general, head of POSCO, and prime minister, and later Eric Hotung, a Hong Kong philanthropist, as Yang's successor. Now it is reported that Jang Song-thaek, brother-in-law of Kim Jong-il, is running the project. One possible ray of hope in these events was the removal of the ceiling of less than 50 percent foreign ownership in joint ventures.

ernment of Japan and North Korea, Chairman Kim managed to extract from Prime Minister Koizumi a commitment to provide a large financial transfer to North Korea as part of the diplomatic normalization process to settle post-colonial claims, despite the shaky state of Japanese public finances.[24] Each of the leaders then expressed regrets for their countries' respective transgressions and agreed to pursue diplomatic normalization. However, Kim's bald admission that North Korean agents had indeed kidnapped 12 Japanese citizens and that most of the abductees were dead set off a political firestorm in Japan. This revelation, together with the April 2003 admission that North Korea possesses nuclear weapons in contravention of multiple international agreements, has effectively killed the diplomatic rapprochement and with it the prospects of a large capital infusion from Japan, as well as already dim prospects of admission to international financial institutions such as the World Bank and Asian Development Bank.

Implications for Political Stability

Noland (2004) contains an examination of the likelihood of political instability or, more precisely, regime change, based on formal statistical analysis. The models are estimated from three separate cross-national data sets on political developments worldwide since 1960.[25] Several dozen explanatory variables, generally falling into three categories, were considered. The first category consists of political, legal, and cultural variables that tend to change slowly if at all. These would include such things as the origin of the country's legal system; whether it originated that system, adopted it, or had it imposed by a colonial power; and proxies relating to the quality of domestic political institutions. A second group of variables involves demographic and social indicators that tend to change slowly. These include things like the level of urbanization and the degree of ethnic or religious heterogeneity within a country. Economic policy and performance indicators make up the final category. These measures tend to exhibit the greatest temporal variability. As a consequence, the more slowly changing political and social variables tend to determine whether a particular country is generally prone to instability, while the more rapidly changing economic variables tend to impact whether the likelihood of regime change is rising or falling.

These models were estimated and then used to generate the probability of regime change in North Korea. The data for North Korea come primarily

---

24 Japanese officials did not deny formulas reported in the press that would put the total value of a multiyear package in the form of grants, subsidized loans, and trade credits at approximately $10 billion. This magnitude—adjusted for population, inflation, exchange rate changes, and interest foregone—is consistent with the size of Japan's 1965 post-colonial settlement with South Korea. Given the puny size of the North Korean economy, this is a gigantic sum. See Manyin (2003) for further discussion.

25 The underlying sample consisted of 71 countries. In some applications, the sample size was reduced because of missing data on the explanatory variables.

Figure 1: Hazard of Regime Change under Three Scenarios

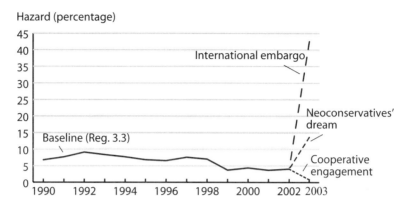

from statistics reported by the Bank of Korea (BOK).[26] The results from one such model are displayed in *Figure 1*. In this particular model, the hazard of political regime change is a function of per capita income, per capita income growth, openness to international trade, inflation, the share of trade taxes in total tax revenue, aid receipts per capita, and whether the country has a tropical climate (a proxy of institutional quality). (Stability is a positive function of income level and growth, trade openness, and aid and is a negative function of inflation, trade taxes, and institutional quality.)

According to this particular model, the probability of regime change peaked at nearly 10 percent in 1992, declined, peaked again in the late 1990s, and has since declined to approximately 4 percent in 2002, the most recent year in the simulation. (Other models reported in Noland [2004] generally yield higher probabilities though a similar time-series pattern.) Statistically speaking, one implication of these models is that those observers who, during the 1990s, predicted North Korea's collapse probably were not making such a bad bet—the cumulative likelihood of regime change in all of these models rises above 50 percent over the course of the decade.

---

26 The quality of the data for North Korea is poor. The BOK estimate of North Korean national income is reportedly constructed by applying South Korean value-added weights to physical esti-mates of North Korean output derived through classified sources and methods; the estimate of na-tional income reputedly was subject to pre-release interagency discussion within the South Korean government. This raises a variety of concerns: that the reliance on physical indicators may augur an overemphasis on the industrial sector (where output is relatively easy to count) relative to the service sector, that pre-release discussions may imply interagency bargaining and a politicization of the estimate, and that the methods through which the figures are derived are not subject to independent verification. The use of South Korean value-added weights is surely inappropriate. It is rumored that a classified mock North Korean input-output table exists, although what role this might play in the BOK's calculations is obviously speculative. For all of these reasons, outside analysts have at times questioned the reliability, if not the veracity, of the BOK figures. See the appendix to Noland (2004) for a more complete description of the data used in this analysis.

Another implication is that economic performance critically influences regime stability and that the North's external relations play a crucial role in this regard. To explore this theme, the models were simulated under three alternative scenarios:

• Under one scenario, which might be labeled "cooperative engagement," diplomatic tensions are eased, and North Korea successfully globalizes in a diplomatically supportive environment. Compared with the status quo, North Korea receives higher levels of aid from South Korea, China, the United States, and other countries. It normalizes diplomatic relations with Japan and begins to receive post-colonial-claims settlement payments. It joins the multilateral development banks and begins receiving aid from them as well. Total aid reaches $3 billion annually. Under the less threatening environment, North Korea liberalizes its economy. The share of trade in national income rises to 71 percent, what it would exhibit if it were as integrated into the world economy as a "normal" country with its characteristics (Noland 2000, table 7.2), and trade taxes are cut to the South Korean level. The rate of economic growth rebounds to its 1999 peak of 6 percent. All other variables stay at their 2002 values.

• In the "neoconservatives' dream" scenario, the global community puts the squeeze on the Kim Jong-il regime. Aid is cut off. Growth falls to its previous low of −6 percent. The inexpertly enacted July 2002 economic policy changes drive inflation up to 300 percent, reputedly its rate over the course of the year since the introduction of the reforms.

• In the "international embargo" scenario, North Korea's relations with the rest of the world deteriorate precipitously, perhaps under suspicion of exportation of nuclear weapons, and all international trade is cut off. Admittedly, this scenario is a stretch for the underlying statistical model, which does not distinguish between food, oil, and video games in the maintenance of a society, and some might object that a total embargo is politically unrealistic as well. It may not be without some utility, however, revealing something about the nature of regime dynamics, at least in a cross-country sample.

For heuristic purposes, the predicted hazard rates associated with each of these alternatives are appended to the graph as "2003," although there is nothing unique in the scenarios to link it to that date, and, indeed, some of the changes envisioned in the cooperative-engagement scenario would probably take more than one year to realize. Nevertheless, the simulations may be revealing in terms of how outside forces might impact regime survival in North Korea.

According to these results, under the cooperative-engagement scenario, the likelihood of regime change falls to less than 1 percent. Kim Jong-il dies in his sleep, and one of his sons dons his grandfather's crown. In the neoconservatives' dream, the likelihood of regime change rises to about a one-in-seven probability, growing thereafter, and in all probability Kim Jong-il is out of power before George W. Bush. (Remember, in the neo-con dream, George W. Bush is in power until 2008.) In the final scenario, international embargo, the likelihood of regime change is greater than 40 percent in the first year, and the Kim Jong-il regime probably collapses within two years. Hufbauer et al. (1990) find that sanctions aimed at destabilization succeed about half the time. When comparing the results obtained in this simulation with the historical track record, it should be kept in mind that the scenario modeled involves a successful complete embargo. An embargo that was less complete by design (i.e., allowing exceptions for certain categories of exchange) or less thoroughly implemented (i.e., there was cheating) would have an attenuated impact on regime stability.

One caveat should be underlined: there may be psycho-political phenomena that are not well captured by these models. In particular, foreign pressure may provide the regime with a rationale for poor performance while, conversely, a lack of foreign pressure (i.e., an absence of enemies) may deprive the regime of an excuse. This is simply to say that the models may overstate the impact of these alternative scenarios on regime stability—the good scenario may not be quite as good and the bad scenario not quite as bad as depicted in Figure 1, regardless of how one defines good and bad outcomes. Given the complexity of the underlying conceptual issues and the poor quality of the data used in the analysis, in statistician-speak these estimates could be thought of as coming with wide confidence intervals attached. Caveat emptor.

Character of Successor Regimes

Suppose that the current regime is unable to manage this transition. Regime change—at least the internally generated variety—would not necessarily imply the disappearance of the North Korean state, though this is surely one possibility. The key issues would be the viability and character of the successor regime. Would any non-Kim Il-sung-ist North Korean regime be viable? Would it be able to legitimate itself, or would this simply be a transitional state toward unification? Is a post-*juche* North Korean state possible?

The current military-first ideological campaign, which at first blush would appear to signal the ascendance of the most reactionary element of the polity, may actually be the mechanism through which a broad-ranging top-down modernization of a society subject to external threat is justified. By elevating the military to the vanguard, the military-first ideology justifies all manner of departures from past practice—including the jettisoning of socialism in practice if not as a teleological ideal—in pursuit of military modernization.

There is historical precedent for this: in the Meiji Restoration as well as the founding of modern Turkey under Mustafa Kemal, revolutionary changes were justified as responses to external threats and legitimated in terms of restoring past historical glory. Yet in this North Korean production, Kim Jong-il would be playing the roles of both the Tokugawa Shogun and the Emperor Meiji. Perhaps this is consistent with Kim's comment to former U.S. secretary of state Madeleine Albright that he was interested in the "Thai model" in which he would reign but not rule (Albright 2003).

In a positive sense, top-down military-centered modernization may be a successful political development strategy. Of course, from a normative perspective, the results of that strategy—a nuclear-armed and possibly proliferating North Korea—may be antithetical to U.S. interests. And there is no guarantee that a military modernizer would be the Park Chung-hee or Augusto Pinochet of North Korea, and not its Alexander Kerensky or Lothar de Maizière. The legitimization challenges for a post-*juche* North Korea could be profound, and there is no certainty of success—even if the regime were supported by a South Korea fearful of the implications of collapse and absorption.

South Korea would be key, because of the resources that it could provide to a new North Korean regime and also because of the challenge that its very existence poses for the legitimization of any successor regime in North Korea. Ironically, one can imagine a situation in which the most radical forces in North Korea would be revolutionary nationalist unifiers who might well be opposed by a South Korean government that—fearing a collapse-and-absorption scenario—might try to prop up the North Korean state.

Implications for South Korea

The collapse-and-absorption outcome would have tremendous economic and political ramifications for the South (and of course be accompanied by an enormous reduction in poverty in the North). Over the course of a decade, the "costs" of unification—the amount of capital investment needed in the North—might be on the order of $600 billion. Although remaining positive, economic growth in the South would slow relative to a no-unification baseline, and, unless compensatory policies were undertaken, the process of economic integration with the North would lead to an increase in income and wealth inequality (Noland 2004).

Even less apocalyptic gradual integration scenarios pose significant challenges for South Korea as well. One can think of these as falling into three categories: real, institutional, and risk. With respect to the first, the real impact of gradual economic integration between North and South Korea in macroeconomic terms would be minor for the South—similar to the impact of NAFTA on the United States or the accession of small, central European countries to the European Union—although the impact might be profound on particular South Korean firms or households. This would hold as long as economic integration was largely limited to goods markets—that is to say that markets for capital and labor would remain segmented.

A second channel of impact on South Korea would be institutional in nature. South Korea has considerable problems with nontransparent and corrupt government-business relations. In the North, there is no real difference between the state and the economy. Large-scale economic integration between the North and the South will be, by its very nature, a highly politicized process and will in all likelihood retard progress in cleaning up business-government relations in the South. Recent corruption scandals involving the Blue House and the Korean Development Bank with respect to Hyundai Asan's activities in the North are emblematic. There are alternatives—encouraging a more transparent and efficient approach to integration through tax policy, for example—but these have not been pursued by Seoul.

Finally, regardless of its economic progress or policy stance, South Korea remains exposed to the vagaries of North Korean behavior. Financially, South Korea is increasingly integrated into the world economy, creating new vulnerabilities. In 1994, during the previous nuclear crisis, foreign participation in South Korean financial markets was limited. Now, however, foreign institutions play a major role in South Korean financial affairs, and foreigners account for nearly 40 percent of the transactions on the Seoul stock exchange. Conversely, restrictions that impeded the ability of South Korean residents to invest abroad and hold non-*won*-denominated assets have been largely eliminated. Last, the use of complex off-balance-sheet transactions and financial derivatives, which did not exist in 1994, has expanded rapidly in recent years.

While it is true that the South Korean stock market actually rose during the 1994 nuclear crisis, the expanded role of foreign participants and the increased complexity of the financial transactions mean that the market today is far less susceptible to political intervention than it was a decade ago.

The popular image of capital flight occurring when foreigners flee for the exits is belied by historical experience the world over—almost invariably it is the better-informed locals who are out the door first. During periods of uncertainty, BOK data reveal that, while foreigners were net buyers in the stock market, South Koreans were net sellers, although to date these incidents appear to have amounted to flights to quality—funds shifted into government-insured bank accounts and not into offshore assets. And while President Roh Moo-hyun has been justly praised for mobilizing young people for political participation, the converse is also true: President Roh's support is relatively weak among older South Koreans, who are the predominant owners of the country's savings and who evince the greatest wariness with respect to North Korea.

Conclusions

North Korea launched economic reforms in July 2002. The results to date have been uneven, and it is by no means preordained that even additional reforms more adroitly implemented will deliver success in the short run. The three robust predictors of success in transitional economies are the degree of macroeconomic stability at the time that reform is initiated, the legacy of a functional pre-socialist commercial legal system, and the size of the agricultural sector (Sachs 1995, 454–85; Åslund et al. 1996). North Korea is already experiencing significant macroeconomic instability, and, in terms of the sectoral composition of output and employment, the North Korean economy resembles Romania and parts of the former Soviet Union more closely than it does the agriculture-led Asian reformers, China and Vietnam.

Moreover, from a broader perspective, the reforms may well be setting in motion social forces that will prove politically destabilizing. From an ideological perspective, the current military-first campaign could be regarded as the opening of a reinterpretation of *juche* that would emphasize modernization over socialism and provide the regime with an ideological rationale for reform. The regime can also draw upon two generations of unparalleled political indoctrination, a complete monopoly on social organization, and a massive apparatus for internal social control that it deploys ruthlessly.

That said, the problem of social control is surely aggravated by the divided nature of the Korean peninsula and the cognitive dissonance created by a prosperous and democratic South Korea. Ironically, this problem is intensifying as the reforms are having the presumably unintended effect of exposing the isolated North Korean populace to an increasing amount of information originating beyond the borders.

Yet even if the North were able to successfully navigate these shoals domestically, it is hard to see the initiative coming to fruition as long as the country remains, in essence, a pariah state, brandishing its nuclear weapons and missiles, subject to diplomatic sanctions. The signs on this front are inauspicious. In January 2004 the world was treated to yet another round of North Korean brinkmanship: the display to visiting Americans of an empty spent-fuel pond at the Yongbyon nuclear site and a substance alleged to be reprocessed plutonium. The North Koreans seem to be content to pressure the United States: as time passes, their nuclear activities proceed, and after a year—after the 2004 U.S. presidential elections—they hope to face a more pliant set of interlocutors.

Nor does it appear that the Bush administration is in any rush to negotiate seriously. Reluctant in an election year to request a congressional appropriation to compensate North Korea for reneging on past promises, the administration instead appears to be content to bide its time, hoping for a North Korean collapse.

Those hopes may well be in vain. North Korea's reforms may ultimately generate unmanageable social changes, but, in the short run, subject to serious caveats about the ambition of the modeling exercise and the quality of the underlying data, the statistical analysis discussed in this paper indicates that today the odds on regime change are not particularly high, perhaps on the order of 5 percent in any given year, down roughly half from its previous peak. Cumulated over a decade, those odds shorten quite appreciably, but neither the Bush administration nor the world community can afford to wait a decade to end the North Korean nuclear program. If the Bush administration seeks regime change in North Korea, it will have to give history a shove. North Korea is unlikely to collapse anytime soon under current conditions.

No coercive plan can succeed without South Korean support—South Korean resources could frustrate any plan to strangle North Korea economically, and lack of South Korean political support for such a scheme would give China and others the diplomatic cover to defect.

Yet today a growing majority of South Koreans, accustomed to living for decades in the shadow of the North's forward-deployed artillery, do not regard the North as a serious threat. Growing prosperity and confidence in the South, in marked contrast to the North's isolation and penury, have transformed fear and loathing into pity and forbearance. Instead, it is the United States, an ocean away, that regards the North and its nuclear weapons program with alarm. As the United States has focused on the nuclear program, its ally, South Korea, has observed the North Koreans' nascent economic reforms, heard their talk of conventional-forces reduction, and perceived that the gap in the two countries' respective assessments of the North Korean threat has patently widened. *Chosun Ilbo* on 12 January 2004 reported on a recent public opinion poll in which more South Koreans identified the United States as the principal threat to peace than those who specified North Korea. The younger the respondent and the higher the level of educational attainment, the wider is this gap. Fifty-eight percent of respondents in their twenties and 52 percent of students and white-collar workers polled singled out the United States as the primary threat to peace. Another survey (Bong 2003) found that more than three-quarters of South Korean students polled actually supported North Korea's development of nuclear weapons.

In these circumstances, a prerequisite for the successful application of a U.S.-led strategy of multilateral coercive diplomacy will be to convince the South Korean government and public of the correctness of the U.S. case. This will be an uphill battle.

The indispensable first step—to either eliminate the North Korean nuclear program through negotiation or to establish the diplomatic precursors to eliminate it through other means—is the reengagement of the six-party talks. There were no breakthroughs at the second round of talks in February 2004 although the participants did agree to a face-saving proposal to establish technical-level working groups. Most commentary pinned the lack of obvious progress on the inflexibility of the United States and/or North Korea. The subsequent political turmoil in South Korea around the impeachment of President Roh further dims the likelihood of progress in the short term.

The historical record of countries forgoing nuclear weapons is subject to multiple interpretations. Three of the four cases in which states gave up nuclear weapons (Ukraine, Belarus, and Kazakhstan) were clearly associated with regime change—in all three cases, newly installed governments seeking to assert democratic credentials and gain international acceptance voluntarily surrendered weapons left over from the Soviet Union, albeit supported with technical and financial assistance from the international community. The fourth example, that of South Africa, is somewhat more complicated. The apartheid-era government of F. W. de Klerk made the decision to surrender its weapons in 1990, before a regime change in the context of a reduced external threat from Soviet proxies in southern Africa after the collapse of the Soviet Union, because of concerns about the use of weapons by a post-apartheid successor regime, and, as in the cases of three former Soviet republics, in a bid to gain international legitimacy and acceptance.

The list of states that have terminated programs before actually fabricating weapons is longer and includes South Korea, among others. Again, the joint decision in 1988 by Argentina and Brazil to halt their programs occurred in the context of newly installed democratic regimes asserting their authority over their militaries by reversing decisions undertaken by preceding military governments.

The most recent case, that of Libya, is interesting in that it appears to deviate from the pattern of terminating nuclear weapons in the context of internal regime change, although it does highlight the role of gaining international acceptance, and it provides some obvious similarities—and differences—compared with the case of North Korea. Like North Korea, the Qadhafi regime has a history of bad relations with the United States, starting with Libya's support for international terrorist groups following the coup d'état that brought Qadhafi to power in 1969 and Libya's placement on the U.S. government list of state sponsors of terrorism in 1979. Relations worsened following a military air engagement in 1981 and the imposition by the United States of economic sanctions the following year. In 1986, in response to evidence of Libyan involvement in a bombing in Germany that killed two U.S. servicemen, the United States launched air strikes in which Qadhafi's home was targeted and an infant adopted daughter killed.[27] Libya retaliated

---

27 Qadhafi's security concerns, though perhaps understandable, verge on the paranoiac: he seldom travels by air outside Libyan airspace and instead wheels around the Maghreb in a massive convoy of 4×4 vehicles, carrying his own food and water and providing his hosts no more than a couple of days' notice of his imminent arrival. I should know: in March 2003, I was expelled on a few hours' notice from my hotel in Bamako, Mali, to make way for the peripatetic Col. Q. and his massive entourage.

by bombing a U.S. airliner over Scotland in 1988. It had earlier bombed a French airliner over Chad.

The Libyan decision to end its nuclear program comes in the context of external events, most notably the U.S.-led destruction of Saddam Hussein's regime in Iraq as well as a broad Libyan attempt to come in from the cold, concluding agreements to resolve issues associated with the airline bombings. Moreover, Libya does not possess nuclear weapons—only a nuclear weapons program—so presumably the value of the program, and the cost of surrendering it, are less to the government compared with actual weapons.

In 2003, when a shipment of uranium enrichment equipment bound for Tripoli was interdicted, Qadhafi's response was contrite, in stark contrast to Pyongyang's bellicose defiance (Sokolski 2004). After making the decision to forgo nuclear weapons, Qadhafi made an appeal to other countries, including North Korea, to follow the Libyan example. The North Korean foreign ministry, as reported by the KCNA on 9 January 2004 (in an article entitled "Spokesman of DPRK FM Dismisses Any Change from DPRK as Ridiculous"), in its inimitable style responded that "[t]his is the folly of imbeciles. . . . To expect any 'change' from the DPRK stand is as foolish as expecting a shower from the clear sky."

Even if one is dubious about the prospects of eliminating the North Korean nuclear program through negotiation with a Kim Jong-il regime—and there are myriad reasons for skepticism—earnest and sincere participation in the talks is essential to place on Pyongyang the onus for the failure to make consensual progress and thereby secure South Korean (as well as Chinese) support for more coercive measures.

In the meantime, while the global community has an ethical obligation to feed hungry North Koreans, it has no obligation to do so in ways that strengthen a totalitarian regime that is itself the source of the problem. Specifically, if the world community is serious about addressing the humanitarian crisis in North Korea, it should be willing to fund a multilateral initiative to create temporary refugee feeding and resettlement camps in China, modeled on the response to the Vietnamese boat-people crisis two decades ago. Governments like those of the United States and the European Union, which censure North Korea on human rights grounds (UN 2003), should be willing to put their money (and their refugee resettlement policies) where their mouths are.[28] China has an understandable wariness of a flood of Korean refugees, and those who criticize China for its treatment of North Korean refugees should be willing to go beyond mere criticism and formulate constructive solutions that would address both the underlying humanitarian disaster in the DPRK and China's understandable domestic political concerns. The North Korean Freedom Act, introduced into the U.S. Senate in

---

28 Regrettably, Japan and South Korea (the latter abstained from the UN human rights vote on North Korea) have the worst refugee resettlement records among OECD member countries.

November 2003 by Senators Sam Brownback (R-KS) and Evan Bayh (D-IN) and in the House by Representatives by Jim Leach (R-IA), Eni Faleomavaega (D-AS), and Chris Smith (R-NJ), would go part way by making it easier for North Koreans to get refugee status and enter the United States, and it puts pressure on the administration to encourage China to live up to its obligations under UN refugee covenants. It would not, however, address the core underlying issue of how to take North Korean refugees off China's hands permanently.

References

Albright, Madeleine. 2003. *Madame Secretary.* New York: Miramax.

Amnesty International. 2004. Starved of Rights: Human Rights and the Food Crisis in the Democratic People's Republic of Korea (North Korea). Report no. ASA 24/003/2004. 17 January. http://web.amnesty.org/library/index/engasa240032004.

Åslund, Anders, Peter Boone, and Simon Johnson. 1996. How To Stabilize: Lessons from Post-Communist Countries. Brookings Papers on Economic Activity 1996:1.

Babson, Bradley O., and William J. Newcomb. 2004. Economic Perspectives on Demise Scenarios for DPRK. Photocopy.

Bong, Young-shik. 2003. Anti-Americanism and the U.S.-Korea Military Alliance. In *Confrontation and Innovation on the Korean Peninsula.* Washington, D.C.: Korea Economic Institute.

Cho, M.A. 2003. Money Replacing Rationing Tickets in N. Korea: Charity Official. Yonhap, 19 December.

Chung, Yun Ho. 2003. The Prospects of Economic Reform in North Korea and the Direction of Its Economic Development. *Vantage Point* 26, no. 5 (May).

Department of State (DOS). 2003. *World Military Expenditures and Arms Transfers.* Washington, D.C.: U.S. Department of State. www.state.gov/t/vc/rls/rpt/wmeat/1999_2000/.

Eberstadt, Nicholas. 1999. *The End of North Korea.* Washington, D.C.: American Enterprise Institute.

Eberstadt, Nicholas, Marc Rubin, and Albina Tretyakova. 1995. The Collapse of Soviet and Russian Trade with North Korea, 1989–1993: Impact and Implications. *Korean Journal of National Unification* 4.

Flake, L. Gordon. 2003. The Experience of U.S. NGOs in North Korea. In *Paved With Good Intentions: The NGO Experience in North Korea,* ed. L. Gordon Flake and Scott Snyder. Westport, Conn.: Praeger.

Frank, Ruediger. 2003a. The End of Socialism and a Wedding Gift for the Groom? The True Meaning of the Military First Policy. 11 December. www.nautilus.org/DPRKBriefingBook//transition/Ruediger_Socialism.html.

———. 2003b. A Socialist Market Economy in North Korea? Systemic Restrictions and a Quantitative Analysis. Working paper, Columbia University, New York, N.Y.

Gey, Peter. 2004. Nordkorea: Reform sowjetischen Typs und Erosion der Staatswirtschaft (North Korea: Soviet-style reform and the erosion of the state economy). *Internationale Politik und Geschellschaft,* no. 1. www.fes.de/ipg/ONLINE1_2004/ARTGEY.HTM.

Goodkind, Daniel, and Lorraine West. 2001. The North Korean Famine and Its Demographic Impact. *Population and Development Review* 27, no. 2.

Hawk, David. 2003. *The Hidden Gulag.* Washington, D.C.: U.S. Committee for Human Rights in North Korea. www.hrnk.org/HiddenGulag.pdf.

Hufbauer, Gary C., Jeffrey J. Schott, and Kimberly Ann Elliott. 1990. *Economic Sanctions Reconsidered,* 2nd ed. Washington, D.C.: Institute for International Economics.

Hwang, Eui-gak. 1993. *The Korean Economies.* Oxford: Clarendon Press.

Jung, Eliot, Kim Young-soo, and Takayuki Kobayashi. 2003. North Korea's Special Economic Zones: Obstacles and Opportunities, in *Confrontation and Innovation on the Korean Peninsula.* Washington, D.C.: Korea Economic Institute.

Kim, Pyung-joo. 1998. Monetary Integration and Stabilization in the Unified Korea. In *Policy Priorities for the Unified Korean Economy,* ed. Il SaKong and Kwang Suk Kim. Seoul: Institute for Global Economics.

Kim, Sungwoo. 2003. North Korea's Unofficial Market Economy and Its Implications. *International Journal of Korean Studies* 7, no. 1.

Koh, Byung-chol. 2004. North Korea in 2003 and 2004: Pyongyang's View. *IFES Forum* (7 January).

Lau, Lawrence J., Yingi Qian, and Gérard Roland. 2000. Reform without Losers: An Interpretation of China's Dual-Track Approach to Transition. *Journal of Political Economy* 108, no. 1.

Lee, Jung-chul. 2002. The Implications of North Korea's Reform program and Its Effects on State Capacity. *Korea and World Affairs* 26, no. 3.

Lee, Suk. 2003. Food Shortages and Economic Institutions in the Democratic People's Republic of Korea. Ph.D. diss., Department of Economics, University of Warwick, Coventry, UK.

Manyin, Mark E. 2003. Japan-North Korea Relations: Selected Issues. Report no. RL32161. Washington, D.C.: Congressional Research Service, Library of Congress. 26 November. www.au.af.mil/au/awc/awcgate/crs/rl32161.pdf

Manyin, Mark E., and Ryun Jun. 2003. U.S. Assistance to North Korea. Report no. RL31785. Washington, D.C.: Congressional Research Service, Library of Congress. 17 March. www.nautilus.org/DPRKBriefingBook/uspolicy/CRSUSAidtoDPRK.pdf.

Moody's. 2003. Uncertainties over North Korean Nuclear Threat Continue to Limit South Korea's Ratings. Special Comment. New York: Moody's Investor Service. December.

Nam, Sung-wook. 2003. Moves Toward Economic Reforms. *Vantage Point* 26, no. 10.

Natsios, Andrew S. 2003. Life inside North Korea. Testimony before the Subcommittee on East Asian and Pacific Affairs, Committee on Foreign Relations, U.S. Senate. 5 June. www.state.gov/p/eap/rls/rm/2003/21269.htm.

Newcomb, William. 2003. Reflections on North Korea's Economic Reform. *Korea's Economy 2003*. Washington, D.C.: Korea Economic Institute.

Noland, Marcus. 2000. *Avoiding the Apocalypse: The Future of the Two Koreas*. Washington, D.C.: Institute for International Economics.

———. 2003. Famine and Reform. Working Paper series WP 03-5. Washington, D.C.: Institute for International Economics.

———. 2004. Korea after Kim Jong-il. Washington, D.C.: Institute for International Economics.

Noland, Marcus, Sherman Robinson, and Tao Wang. 2001. Famine in North Korea: Causes and Cures. *Economic Development and Cultural Change* 49, no. 4.

Oh, Seung-yul. 2003. Changes in the North Korean Economy: New Policies and Limitations. *Korea's Economy 2003*. Washington, D.C.: Korea Economic Institute.

Pack, Howard, and Janet Rothenberg Pack. 1990. Is Foreign Aid Fungible: the Case of Indonesia. *Economic Journal* (March).

———. 1993. Foreign Aid and the Question of Fungibility. *Review of Economics and Statistics.*

Robinson, W. Courtland, Myung Ken Lee, Kenneth Hill, and Gilbert Burnham. 1999. Mortality in North Korean Migrant Households: A Retrospective Study. *Lancet* 354 (July–December).

Sachs, Jeffrey. 1995. Reforms in Eastern Europe and the Former Soviet Union in Light of the East Asian Experience. *Journal of the Japanese and International Economies* 9, no. 4.

Smith, Heather and Yiping Huang. Forthcoming. Trade Disruption, Collectivisation and Food Crisis in North Korea. In *Achieving High Growth: Experience of Transitional Economies in East Asia*, ed. Peter Drysdale, Yiping Huang, and Masahiro Kawai. London: Routledge.

Snyder, Scott. 2003. Lessons of the NGO Experience in North Korea. In *Paved With Good Intentions: The NGO Experience in North Korea,* ed. L. Gordon Flake and Scott Snyder. Westport, Conn.: Praeger.

Sokolski, Henry. 2004. The Qaddafi Precedent. *Weekly Standard* 9, no. 19 (26 January).

Terry, Fiona. 2001. Feeding the Dictator. *The Guardian,* 6 August.

United Nations Economic and Social Council (UNESC). 2003. Situation of Human Rights in the Democratic People's Republic of Korea. Document no. E/CN.4/2003/L.31. 11 April. www.northkoreanrefugees.com/un-ecosoc-resolution.pdf.

United Nations Food and Agricultural Organization (UNFAO). 2003. The State of Food Insecurity in the World 2003. Rome: FAO. www.fao.org/docrep/006/j0083e/j0083e00.htm.

Watts, Jonathon. 2003. How North Korea is Embracing Capitalism. *The Guardian,* 3 December.

World Food Programme (WFP). 2003a. Child Nutrition Survey Shows Improvements in DPRK But UN Agencies Concerned About Holding Onto Gains. Press release. Pyongyang, Geneva: WFP. 21 February.

———. 2003b. Wide-Ranging Reforms Are Introduced. Pyongyang: WFP Country Office. 21 May.

Marcus Noland is a senior fellow at the Institute for International Economics in Washington, D.C. He thanks Paul Karner for research assistance and Nicholas Eberstadt for helpful comments on an earlier draft.

3

The Structure of North Korea's Political Economy: Changes and Effects

Lee Young-sun and Yoon Deok-ryong

Socialist economic systems traditionally have been characterized by a centrally planned economy, in which a planning agency plans and organizes production as well as consumption to reach given objectives. The government carries out the plan while prohibiting unregulated economic activities. However, increasing difficulties in planning and severe shortages have resulted in a marked growth of unplanned economic activities in socialist countries. Activities outside the so-called plan have been termed the "second economy," the "unofficial economy," or the "private economy." This paper will focus on the private economy.

The private economy in socialist countries refers to all production or trade for private gain and is usually run by the market mechanism (Grossman 1977). Private economic activity has increased in every sector and has helped ease economic scarcity in socialist countries during the transition period. Another important contribution of the private economy is that it has allowed entrepreneurial people in transitional economies to make use of their abilities during the period of transition (Lee and Chun 2001, 199–226).

While numerous changes have impacted every sector of North Korea (the Democratic People's Republic of Korea, or DPRK), the military sector has not shown much change. It continues to take priority as far as receiving resources and investment. In fact, government military expenditures have remained stable while the rest of the economy has undergone a severe contraction. Kim Jong-il made the military his primary concern after his official takeover of power, and it takes only one visit to North Korea to recognize that the military is of the greatest importance. The military sector continues to be given priority in resources and investment, and government military expenditures have been stable even though the whole economy has undergone a severe contraction. North Korea's impoverishment since the 1990s has made the military relatively stronger.

The private economy in North Korea has also gained significance in terms of its increasing scale as well as in its role of easing material scarcity. North Korea introduced reform measures to facilitate market mechanisms in 2002; these reforms were regarded by many experts as approval of already existing market mechanisms within the society. Since then, however, North Korea has added to these reform measures by stimulating the private economy further. The increase in market mechanisms through these reforms will expand the unplanned portion of the North Korean economy more rapidly, which may then strengthen the private economy and market mechanisms.

The changes to North Korea's economic structure and economic capacity reflect changes in North Korean society. This paper attempts to show the changes to economic relations and draw implications from the political and economic points of view. This paper first explains changes to North Korea's economic structure and then analyzes the reform measures with regard to a possible economic transition. The final section summarizes the paper briefly and draws conclusions.

Structure of North Korean Economy and Changes Thereto

The North Korean economy is composed of three main economies: the official economy, the military economy, and the private economy.[1] The official economy refers to all economic activities occurring under central planning, and the private economy is defined as all activities outside the planning structure.[2] The military economy implies economic activities for the military sector. These three are only loosely related and do not appear to be closely integrated with each other. The absolute size and weight of each economy within the whole country's economy have changed greatly since the 1990s. The evolving differences have changed the daily lives of citizens and the significance of each economy. To comprehend the changes in the North Korean economy and the economy's influence on the sociopolitical environment, it is necessary to understand the internal dynamics of these three economies and how they interact.

Official economy. The official economy is the main body of North Korea's economy and is the formal economic system comprising state enterprises

---

1   Yoon and Babson (2002, 69–89) discuss the three economies in North Korea but do not include a fourth economy, the "party economy," because it is not extensive. Sometimes, however, the party economy of North Korea's elites is counted as another important economy there. The party economy refers to the economic consumption by the small governing elite, who extract rent from the people's economy and own profitable enterprises such as gold and mining that earn foreign exchange.

2   This definition follows the classifications of first economy and second economy of Dennis O'Hearn (1980). There are numerous discussions of the definitions, each with a slightly different emphasis; see Grossman (1977), Kemény (1982, 349–66), Ericson (1984, 1–24), and Wellisz and Findlay (1986, 646–58).

Table 1: Weight of North Korea's Government Budget in Gross National Income (GNI), 1990–2001

Year	Budget (U.S. dollars, billions)	GNI (U.S. dollars, billions)	Weight (%)
1990	16.6	23.1	72
1991	17.2	22.9	75
1992	18.5	21.1	87
1993	18.7	20.5	91
1994	19.2	21.2	91
1995	n.a.	22.3	—
1996	n.a.	21.4	—
1997	9.1	17.7	52
1998	9.1	12.6	72
1999	9.2	15.8	58
2000	9.6	16.8	57
2001	9.8	15.7	65
2002	n.a.	17.0	—
2003	n.a.	18.4	—

Source: BOK, various years.

and agricultural collectives; it is a centrally planned and controlled monocratic system. The means of production are owned by the state or by cooperatives. Through its rationing system, the state distributes resources for production as well as consumption. In a command economy such as North Korea's, the social preference for production is decided through value judgments made by the ruling body. The North Korean economy is understood to have put great emphasis on social equity and welfare as the other socialist economies have done.

The State Planning Commission is supposed to drive the budget planning process by composing detailed plans; however, in reality, the annual budget is decided after compiling negotiated agreements on production for each enterprise and deriving an allocation of turnover and taxes on profits. Public finance plays an important role in carrying out planned capital accumulation as well as distribution. The budget and the public distribution system (PDS) serve as the core mechanisms of the people's economy for the allocation of resources. Similar to other centrally planned economies, North Korea manages its economy through a governmental budget, and the government uses a large share of the North Korean national income. The government share of total expenditures is normally above 70 percent, and it reached 90 percent in 1993 and 1994 (*Table 1*, above). Even if the government budget uses approximately 60 percent of gross domestic product (GDP), as in recent years, the government still controls most of the national income.

The principal sources of revenue for the budget are turnover taxes,[3] profits from state enterprises, and user fees for working capital. From 1994 to 1998, North Korea's budget declined almost 50 percent, from $19.2 billion to $9.1 billion.[4] Subsequently, the total budget approved by the Supreme People's Assembly has increased slightly and has stabilized at approximately $9.8 billion (Table 1). The collapse of the North Korean industry sector is the prime reason for the decline in total revenues.

In the financial system in North Korea, the central bank plays a major role. The state uses the central bank as another important instrument to realize its plan. The central bank provides funds from the national budget that are needed for business activities of government agencies and state enterprises; these include construction funds, maintenance funds, and operating funds. Loans are extended to meet additional demands for funds. In this system, financing is simply a measure to support the national budget system.

North Korea's central bank carries out the usual functions of any central bank, including issuance of banknotes, monetary control, payments and debt settlement, and the supply and receipt of national funds. It also functions as a commercial bank by offering loans and savings and insurance services. The central bank controls the supply of and demand for money, taking account of money in circulation in cash as well as in non-cash, based on the state's financial plan. North Korea controls resource allocation by controlling money to carry out the state plan. Prices in the people's economy are essentially accounting prices that are set to make supply meet demand. In other words, the monetary policy serves the national plan by controlling the money.

The official economy is run by the state, which plans, invests, produces, and distributes goods and services produced in society. The state manages all the production processes and consumption.

Military economy. North Korea has managed the military economy separately from its other economies (the military economy is called the second economy). The state established the Second Economy Committee in the early 1970s to manage the production of military goods. The Second Economy Committee decides independently on production and distribution and has first priority in allocation of necessary materials and resources. The committee is privileged to manage not only production organizations under the committee, but also the production institutions under the cabinet if necessary. The Second Economy Committee became affiliated with the National Defense Commission in 1993, shortly after its establishment in the constitution in 1992.

---

3   These are taxes on state enterprise production turnover.

4   Data from the Bank of Korea (BOK) are in U.S. dollars in order to make comparable assessments. For a discussion of problems contained in data from the BOK, see Noland (2000).

As the head organization of the defense industry, the Second Economy Committee oversees production activities under the control of the National Defense Commission. The committee manages the planning, production, distribution, and external trade of all military goods in North Korea. It directly controls about 130 munitions factories and about 60 facilities for weapons repair and parts production. In addition, the committee supervises about 100 civilian factories that can be converted to the production of military goods in contingencies such as war.

North Korea's armed forces operate an independent munitions manufacturing system that is a major player in the country's economy. The defense manufacturing industry is divided into two sectors: one producing weapons and technical equipment for combat such as guns, cannons, ammunition, tanks, warships, and aircraft; and the other producing military necessities such as uniforms, shoes, clothing, and food (Suh C. 2002, 28–36). To meet these demands, the military economy runs its own farms, mines, and even banks in addition to its factories.

Manpower in the second economy is estimated at more than 1 million, many of whom are employed in military-owned farms and factories. The North Korean military force includes 1 million troops on active duty and about 4.7 million reservists. The severe contraction of the economy has, however, weakened North Korea's conventional military capabilities, and the country cannot afford significant replacements or upgrades for its conventional military hardware. As a significant part of the labor force, the military economy includes activities or enterprises that meet the needs of the North Korean military establishment; this includes food production, military industries, and businesses that earn foreign exchange.

The military economy does not appear to be closely integrated with the official economy, although the national budget approved by the Supreme People's Assembly does specify allocation for military expenditures. This is probably best understood as "rent" paid by the people's economy to the military, and it supplements the resources mobilized within the military economy itself.

Private economy.   A private economy implies one that exists outside the state plan and that operates according to market mechanisms. In North Korea, as in other socialist countries, informal markets seeking to make private profits have existed for many years. They developed from the farmers' markets, where farmers within cooperative farms can sell agricultural products from their private plots to consumers. The farmers' markets expanded gradually in the 1980s, and, since the sharp economic contraction of the early 1990s, these markets have grown in both number and variety. North Korean defectors report (Chun 1999, 179) that the markets, once open only every 10 days in rural areas, have proliferated and are now open daily. The farmers' markets deal not only with agricultural products but also with industrial goods. The state finally accepted the markets and in March 2003 changed the name from farmers' market (*Nong-min Si-jang*) to market (*Si-jang*).

Several factors have caused the markets to grow rapidly (Chun 1999, 178–80). First, severe food shortages have driven people to the markets because the state has been unable to provide necessary food. Since the collapse of the PDS, the state has been forced to tolerate the markets' growth. Many North Koreans have been able to make a living thanks to the markets. Second, North Koreans have learned necessary market skills from Chinese peddlers (Korean-Chinese constitute the main group of Chinese tradespeople), and cross-border trade has become an important channel for learning and goods transfer. Third, the North Korean government has allowed its citizens to engage in the production of consumer goods. Workers and farmers were organized into auxiliary work units through the "August 3 Consumer Good Production Movement" in 1984 by order of Kim Jong-il. They were to produce consumer goods outside of state planning, using whatever materials were available. The economic crisis of the 1990s forced others to engage in similar activities on an individual basis.

Resources are now flowing into the markets from several sources (Yoon and Babson 2002, 76): agricultural surpluses that exceed state purchases that are produced by cooperatives and households; "leaked goods" from overseas food aid; commodities from cross-border trade with China; items stripped, pirated, and salvaged from state enterprises; commodities diverted from the PDS; goods from small family enterprises; and services offered in the markets.

Numerous reports indicate that the private economy has grown significantly since the early 1990s as households have responded to the food crisis and the failure of the PDS to supply basic human necessities. The PDS had been the mechanism for feeding the urban population, and, since its breakdown in the late 1990s, private markets have been stimulated by demand for basic consumption items. Prices in the markets are generally set in reference to border prices in China. A report by the South Korea Ministry of Unification estimated that 60–70 percent of urban households are now meeting their needs through the markets (Ahn 2002). Although there have been several crackdowns on the operations of informal markets, it seems clear that they will continue to expand. The informal market economy is not officially recognized, but it is accepted as a way of providing normal households with industrial goods as well as agricultural products.

Recent Changes in North Korea's Economic Structure

Drawing on data and estimates from the BOK, we venture a number of comments about structural changes in the DPRK's economy during the period since 1990. A number of these changes appear to be consequential—and, we argue, quite portentous.

First, the weight of government in the economy declined after 1994. The total expenditure of government started with an estimated $16.66 billion and increased to $19.22 billion in 1994. In 1994, the North Korean government absorbed almost 90 percent of the country's GDP, including the PDS, to preserve the socialist economic system. However, natural disasters—flood and drought—caused further deterioration in North Korea's economic situation. Industry was destroyed, and the government has lost its capability to manage the economy according to socialist principles. In addition, the government lost the greater portion of its income sources, causing government expenditures in the early 2000s to decrease to roughly half of what they were in the early 1990s. Although government expenditures increased a little in 2001, they have maintained a relatively constant level ($9.6 billion in 2000 and $9.8 billion in 2001.). Even though overall GDP has decreased dramatically, the decrease was seen mainly in the reduction of government income. The reason behind that loss is that state-owned enterprises became obsolete, and the government lost an important income source. The planning mechanism of the government was no longer able to function, and the PDS collapsed. Consequently North Koreans began to supply themselves with food and necessities from the farmers' markets (Park 2002).

Second, there are indications that the private economy is continuing to expand. At first, the government claimed a great portion of the household income, but by 1994 that income had dropped sharply—perhaps (we might surmise) even as low as one-third of the 1990 level. After the economic breakdown in the mid-1990s, household income rose above the level before the crisis. To make a good enough living to survive, households became active in the farmers' markets; at the same time, production in state-owned enterprises faltered and, in fact, never recovered. The government's ineffectiveness has led to the growing influence of the private economy. Total income might in fact have surpassed the governmental revenues since 2000. Because the private economy follows market mechanisms, the increasing weight of households in the economy reflects the growth of market mechanisms, indicating that more and more money is flowing into the private economy.

Third, government investments have decreased dramatically. The collapse of the official economy has led to this abrupt decrease because the government has no capital for economic rehabilitation. And, even though the private economy has the capacity for investment, there are no channels in place to facilitate it. In socialist countries, the government functions as the only investor; therefore, if the government does not have funds, investment cannot occur. North Korea finds itself in that double bind.

Fourth, the volume of contributions from foreign countries has declined markedly, especially in terms of total trade volume. Both imports and exports dropped because of the breakdown of the international cooperation network as well as internal industrial degradation. The trade deficit, however, remains at a level similar to the earlier level. More than one-third of North Korea's investment is being provided through foreign credit.

These changes confirm that:

- North Korea does not have the capacity for investment needed to escape poverty.
- The North Korean government is losing its influence over the economy.
- North Korea's economy runs in part through market mechanisms; both the private economy and market mechanisms are becoming more important.

All the above findings are interrelated. The government has neither the income nor sufficient capacity for investment. The expansion of household expenditures is a natural consequence of a helpless government: household income has now outstripped government income. Finally the government must find an alternative source of income and reinvigorate its investment scheme.

Changes in the Military Economy and the Military-First Strategy

North Korea appears to allocate about 15 percent of its total budget for defense; however, many experts suspect that the North conceals defense spending within other categories (*Figure 1*). The exorbitant military expenses and the huge volume of military spending have become severe burdens for the North Korean economy.[5] However, North Korea regards military power as the foundation of its internal as well as external security, and the North cannot and will not reduce the military sector as expressed by the government's military-first strategy, even if the power of the military sector hampers economic recovery. The military-first strategy is a literal translation of a Korean term, *songun jongchi*, referring to the politics of giving first priority to the military. The term does not imply a single policy for a particular purpose; rather, it expresses the emphasis on the military throughout society (Suh D. 2002, 148–9).

The military-first strategy has dominated the management style of Kim Jong-il since 1995 even though it was not spelled out until 1998. The military-first strategy was a reaction to the economic crisis that stabilized after the floods of 1995 and 1996 and the drought of 1997 that severely aggravated food shortages. At the least, hundreds of thousands of people were killed by famine during these years.[6] According to Koh Byung-chul (2004):

---

5   Some military experts argue that the North Korean defense industry makes up 30 percent of total national production and that the production volume of defense enterprises surpasses the production volume of civilian industries (Suh C. 2002, 28–30).

6   North Korea reported to the United Nations that the number of deaths resulting from famine was fewer than 300,000, but some workers in nongovernmental organizations estimated the figure to be greater than 2 million (FIDH 2003).

Figure 1: Military Expenditures in North Korea, 1990–2002

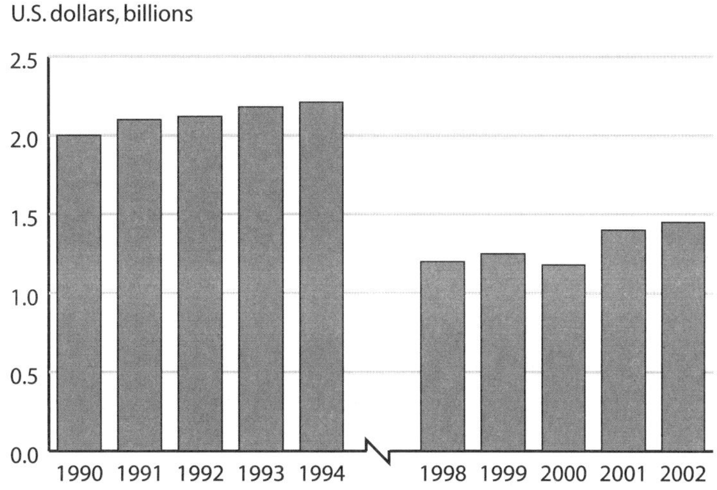

U.S. dollars, billions

Source: BOK, various years.

A great number of people strayed everywhere to seek something to eat at that time. The traditional system of ruling by party faced limits in controlling society in those harsh times. It was inevitable that the military would take over the role of managing political, economic, and social stability. The army had to be strengthened to lead from a position of power both the socialist revolution and construction. That is Kim Jong-il's peculiar style of policy.

The weak economic power of the government threatened to destabilize the state itself. The North Korean government reacted to this situation by strengthening military power within society. The government has given priority to the military to stabilize the power system. The needs of the economy, therefore, were placed behind those of the military. North Korea's JoongAng Broadcasting reported on 18 February 2001 that Kim Jong-il had said: "If I would put the first priority on the economy, more fabric will be made and the quality of life of people may become a little better. However, for awhile yet, I can't endanger our socialist country, forged through blood and fire, for the goal of stuffing our mouths."

Despite its worsening economic conditions, North Korea gives priority to the military sector in distributing food and other available resources. Even if it has become a burden for economic recovery, the military has contributed to the economy by constructing roads, buildings, and dams on a large scale. The military sector guaranteed minimum production even at a time when most people left their places of employment to seek food, and a large number of North Korean soldiers are workers in army uniforms, spending the majority of their service periods at construction sites. The military sector has functioned as a stabilizer for industrial construction as well as for military objectives.

The defense industry has also earned foreign currency. This sector is the most economically competitive sector in North Korea because the country has exported military products continuously and gained international competitiveness. Even though the defense industry is relatively competitive in North Korea, it has too many problems to be relied upon to sustain the economy. But this situation has caused North Korea several problems. First, the defense industry expanded the country's heavy industry too much, causing an imbalance in the industrial structure. The industrial imbalance resulted in agriculture and light industries being underdeveloped relative to heavy industry. Second, the defense industry in North Korea became an important source of foreign exchange. This sector, however, uses much of this foreign exchange to catch up with new developments, and it becomes increasingly difficult for the munitions industries to find new external demand. Third, the defense industry in North Korea is isolated and is usually located close to military bases. This increases production costs and disturbs technology diffusion to other sectors.

Even though the military sector has been given priority in resource allocation, investment in the military sector has decreased significantly because of North Korea's absolute capital shortage. Government expenses for the military sector decreased abruptly in the 1990s, as shown in Figure 1. This implies that the defense industry may begin to fall behind.

Kim Jong-il has chosen the military as a principal tool to overcome a wide range of difficulties both inside and outside the country. The military has helped the state to stabilize economic and social conditions. North Korea is taking advantage of this strategy to strengthen its negotiating position in talks with neighboring countries, especially with the United States and South Korea. It seems clear that the North will stick to its military-first policy as long as Kim Jong-il is convinced of the lack of an external threat and of the necessity of the military to the country's economic recovery. As a result, the military sector will remain a burden in an economic sense and will not contribute significantly to economic improvement.

North Korea's Reform Measures and Their Implications

July 1 Reform Measures

North Korea introduced reform measures at the beginning of July 2002, raising wages and prices to bring the state sector into line with market valuations in the growing private sector. It has scrapped the system of rationing goods, and foreign currency currently can be exchanged for normal North Korean currency rather than coupons to be used in state-designated markets.

Table 2: July 2002 Reform Measures in North Korea and the Direction of Economic Changes

Direction of economic changes	Contents of reform	Policy measures for reform
Changes in economic management	Planned economy → monetary economy	Increase in prices and wages, abolition of rationing system
Reintegration with the international market	Isolation from international market → connection with international market	Readjustment of exchange rate, abolition of exchange coupons
Change in business management	Ethical, social motivation → material, individual motivation	Strengthening the self-supporting accounting system of corporations, material incentives, increase in the autonomous distribution of agricultural products

Price increases were expected to absorb the monetary overhang. Wage increases would provide the people with purchasing power to counter the increases in prices, securing a higher level of living and returning labor into the fold of government control. Scrapping the rationing system acknowledges the breakdown of the state planning and distribution systems. The abolition of rationing would, however, change the command economy into a monetary economy because money, not political power, would determine resource allocation. These changes would constitute the foundation of a market economy.

Moreover, allowing cash to be used for foreign currency exchange will allow foreign customers to approach North Korean markets directly. All these changes seem to be oriented toward monetization, reflecting the intention of the government to introduce market mechanisms.

According to these changes, money and cash will have a greater weight in the economy because the monetization will allow all the economic activities to be translated into monetary terms, thereby contributing to the reallocation of resources and the improvement of economic efficiency in North Korea. Monetization will ease the severe scarcity of consumer goods at first because family enterprises can decide what to produce.

The July 2002 reform measures included increases in prices and wages, a partial abolition of the rationing system, the abolition of exchange coupons, a realistic readjustment of exchange rates, the strengthening of the self-supporting accounting system of corporations, reinforcement of material incentives, and an increase in the autonomous distribution rate of agricultural products. Reform measures are summarized in *Table 2*, above.

This policy reform is expected to eventually increase the efficiency of the North Korean economy, and already there have been some positive outcomes.

However, it is likely that the reform measures will bring about some problems, especially high inflation and pressure on the budget. Budget pressures on the North Korean government will increase because the government will need to pay for government purchases and for higher wages and prices. Government budget revenue will decrease because the government has begun to strengthen the self-supporting accounting system of corporations and increase the portion of the agricultural sector engaged in autonomous distribution. North Korea will face inflationary pressure because economic activities will all be translated into money at an increased level of wages and prices but at the same production capacity. Even if the North experiences a small measure of success from the 1 July reforms, the country cannot fully enjoy the fruits of the reforms if there are no macroeconomic changes to increase government revenue and stabilize inflation pressures.

The North Korean government has also taken steps to control problems stemming from the reform measures. The main problems expected were decreased government revenue and higher inflationary pressure. In May 2003, North Korea began to issue government bonds. These bonds do not bear any interest; instead the government awards a prize to bondholders according to a lottery held every six months until the end of the bonds' validity. This bond issuance was an attempt to absorb private savings, increase government revenue, and reduce the pressures of inflation. The planned issuance period was extended from the end of August 2003 to the end of December 2003, implying that the government had difficulty meeting its fund-raising goals.

In early 2004, Yang Chang-yoon, vice director of North Korea's Ministry of Finance, confirmed that DPRK government revenue could not meet expenses after the economic crisis and that bonds were issued to finance the investment needed for economic recovery and improved living standards through the use of internal resources.[7]

Economic Changes and Sociopolitical Implications

The 1 July 2002 reforms were generally regarded as enforced reform, in other words, the approval of existing reality rather than active reform measures directed toward a specific goal. North Korea has reportedly had success since the reforms, even if there are no available data on actual outcome. *Chosun Shinbo*, the official newspaper of the Chosen Soren,[8] has reported several times on economic and social changes after the reforms. According to *Chosun*

---

7   Yang was quoted in the January 2004 issue of *Monthly Fatherland,* a magazine for North Koreans published in Japan.

8   Chosen Soren are North Koreans who reside in Japan.

9   JoongAng Broadcasting also reported from 24 to 26 December on the economic achievements of 2003. It reported that the production of electricity, coal, consumption goods, and heavy industry increased and transport expanded. The report also stated that this economic achievement was a direct result of the new economic policy.

Table 3: Major Changes in North Korea's Economic Management System in 2003

Changes	Details of changes
Replacement of managers	Managers aged 30 to 40 named in major enterprises
Revaluation and enlargement of the market's role	Farmers' markets expanded into comprehensive consumers' markets Enhanced diversification of consumption goods Price ceilings set on essential index goods such as rice and oil; prices set every 10 days according to supply and demand Markets run under a government enterprise system Market fees and governmental payments imposed on vendors in the market
Enhanced autonomy of factories and enterprises	Government enterprises and cooperative bodies permitted to participate in market activity Factories and enterprises permitted to supply basic goods within a bound of 30 percent For the Pyongyang Tongil market, about 5 percent of returns allotted to factories and enterprises
Introduction of competition	Competition in soap and toothpaste encouraged via price equalization
Introduction of other economic innovations	Massive commercial ad placed in downtown Pyongyang Economic courses with reorganized emphasis on financial and monetary economics; emphasis on price control mechanisms Science and technology recognized as intellectual market goods Contracts between research labs and enterprises obligatory

Source: Material extracted and reorganized from various reports of *Chosun Shinbo* in 2003; cited in KDI (2004, 11).

Shinbo and other sources,[9] North Korea's economy is showing improvement. The volume of production must have increased because the people are working more actively. North Korea's New Year's Common Editorial for 2004 stated that there were increases in production and modernization in light industry, even though no evidence was provided.

North Korea's continuing reform measures imply that economic reform has had some limited success. North Korea went on to complete a range of reform measures in 2003 (*Table 3*), and the New Year's Common Editorial for 2004 expressed the intention of the government to continue with reform.[10] On 22 December 2003, *Chosun Shinbo* reported that a new way of thinking has prevailed in North Korea since the 1 July reforms. North Korean people no longer expect rationing of necessities from the government as they did in the past. The newspaper reported that the trial implementation of "practical socialism" is being established as an irreversible trend. North

---

10 Kim (2004, 12), referring to an article in the newspaper of Kim Il-sung University, analyzed the New Year's Common Editorial 2004, which explains the important tasks necessary to improve economic management.

Korea has expanded the farmers' markets into general consumers' markets and is trying to systemize the markets that appeared spontaneously in the period of economic crisis. The government revises prices for important goods every 10 days according to supply and demand. This seems to be a trial period for the introduction of price mechanisms into the market. Almost all products are traded in the market as long as the trading does not violate any laws. All this implies that reform measures in the North are much more than a just an approval of existing reality.

The private economy has grown rapidly, especially during the crises of the 1990s. The North Korean government has not been able to suppress the expansion of the private economy because the private economy has been combined with many positive effects.[11] North Korean households produce more agricultural products by cultivating private gardens or factory farms. North Koreans in the private economy produce necessities such as clothes and footwear, rice cakes, cookies, liquor, and so on. These activities do not reduce the products of the official economy because the labor or capital used in the private sector does not substitute for labor and capital in the official economy. Workers in the official economy are not fully employed, and they make use of surplus materials or recycled materials. Production in the private sector eases the shortage of goods.

The major question with regard to the reform measures in North Korea has been whether they will lead to a market-based free economy or whether they are simply a piecemeal collection within the framework of a socialist system. Most observers believe that North Korea might be reluctant to transform its system into a market system. This may be true. However, the choice will be made mainly by economic and political conditions. Therefore, it is important to enrich the supporters of transition in the North and improve the economic and political conditions for success. The expansion of the private economy provides good fundamentals for progressive marketization.

The expansion of the private economy has provided the expected positive effects for economic reform in the North (Chun 1999): First, the private economy can pressure the government for change by representing an alternative system. Second, as the private economy becomes larger, fewer people will lose their investments in the private sector. They will support economic reform. Third, the private economy can become a reservoir of entrepreneurship for transition.

The expansion of the private economy may weaken the spirit of socialism by spreading individualism and materialism and by increasing corruption. It can widen the gap between the rich and the poor. Even if there are some negative effects from the perspective of socialism, the state cannot suppress

---

11 At the beginning of the 1990s, the North Korean government tried to ban illegal private farming and unregulated farmers' markets and reduce the frequency of market opening. The government eased these regulations in 1993 (Chun 1999, 187).

the expansion of the private economy because of the private economy's dominant positive economic effects. The private economy in North Korea has grown rapidly, and the total expenditures (or revenues) of households now likely surpass those of the government.

Summary and Conclusion

The North Korean economy can be divided into three categories: the official economy; the military economy; and the private economy. Many changes have taken place in each economy over the years, especially after 1990. The official economy has fallen off because of the collapse of state-owned enterprises, while the private economy has grown because of people's efforts to survive. The military economy maintains itself at a level of relative fitness and still holds a large portion of North Korea's GDP despite a small contraction. The economic crisis has caused the official economy, in part, to transfer its role to the private economy. This will gradually lead the North toward becoming a market economy. The private sector will expand continuously at a much faster pace than before. Although the military economy requires some sacrifice in the economic sense, it has an important function for security as well as for external negotiations. The military economy also plays a role in crisis management in the country's economy. Above all, it cannot be expected that the military-first policy will change before reconciliation with the United States is achieved.

This study shows that the private economy will expand most rapidly while the military economy stagnates and the official economy is contracting. The private economy will pressure the official economy for change, and its expansion will hurt the society's socialist ideology. However, North Korea has continuously introduced diverse institutional changes since the 1 July reforms. The private sector will grow with the additional reform measures. North Korea began its institutional changes in the style of the Soviet Union, allowing only small changes within a tolerable range, but in the Soviet Union these acted as a catalyst to change and the system eventually collapsed. The reform measures in North Korea since the 1 July reforms, however, are similar to the Chinese style of reform, allowing a gradual but significant expansion of the private economy. To make sure that North Korea does not return to its past, more people must continue to show interest in the development of the market system in the North. Investment in various forms will help enlarge the basis for international cooperation as well.

International engagement toward a peaceful resolution with North Korea should begin with efforts to support growth in the private sector. If production in the private sector surpasses production in the official economy, North Korea may become a transition economy without making abrupt changes as China did.

References

Ahn, Doo-soon. 2002. The Possibility of North Korea's Economic Reform and the Policy Measures of South Korea (in Korean). www.pyung.co.kr/gehuk.htm.

Bank of Korea (BOK). Various years. Estimated GDP of North Korea. Seoul: BOK.

Chun, Hong-tack. 1999. The Second Economy in North Korea. *Seoul Journal of Economics* 12, no. 2.

Ericson, Richard E. 1984. The Second Economy and Resource Allocation under Central Planning. *Journal of Comparative Economics* 8, no. 1 (March).

FIDH. 2003. Misery and Terror: Systematic Violations of Economic, Social and Cultural Rights in North Korea. International Federation for Human Rights (FIDH). November. www.fidh.org/article.php3?id_article=859.

Grossman, Gregory. 1977. The "Second Economy" of the USSR. *Problems of Communism* 26 (September/October).

Kemény, István. 1982. The Unregistered Economy in Hungary. *Soviet Studies* 34 (July).

Kim Sang-gi. 2004. Analysis of New Year's Editorial 2004: Economic Sector (in Korean). In *Review of the North Korean Economy*. Seoul: Korea Development Institute. January.

Koh, Byung-chul. 2004. North Korea in 2003 and 2004: Pyongyang's View. Seoul: Kyungnam University, Institute for Far Eastern Studies.

Korea Development Institute (KDI). 2004. *Review of the North Korean Economy* 1.

Lee, Keun, and Chun Hong-tack. 2001. Secrets for Survival and the Role of the Non-State Sector in the North Korean Economy. *Asian Perspective* 25, no. 2.

Noland, Marcus. 2000. *Avoiding the Apocalypse: The Future of the Two Koreas.* Washington, D.C.: Institute for International Economics.

O'Hearn, Dennis. 1980. The Consumer Second Economy: Its Size and Its Effects. *Soviet Studies* 32 (April).

Park, Seok-sam. 2002. Status of Economic Cooperation of North and South Korea and the Future (in Korean). Seoul: Bank of Korea.

Suh, Choo-suk. 2002. Industry of North Korea: Defense Industry (in Korean). *Tongil Kyeongje* 7/8.

Suh, Dae-sook. 2002. Military-First Politics of Kim Jong-il. *Asian Perspective* 26, no. 3: 145–67.

Wellisz, Stanislaw, and Ronald Findlay. 1986. Central Planning and the "Second Economy" in Soviet-Type Systems. *Economic Journal* 96 (September).

Yoon, Deok-ryong and Bradley O. Babson. 2002. Understanding North Korea's Economic Crisis. *Asian Economic Papers* 1, no. 3 (September).

Lee Young-sun is with the Graduate School for International Studies, Yonsei University. Yoon Deok-ryong is with the Korea Institute for International Economic Policy. The authors would like to thank Nicholas Eberstadt, Shin Dong-cheon, and Bradley Babson for their thoughtful and helpful comments and suggestions.

4

North Korea's Survival Game: Understanding the Recent Past, Thinking about the Future

Nicholas Eberstadt

Can the Democratic People's Republic of Korea (DPRK, also known as North Korea) survive—as a distinct regime, an autonomous state, a specific political-economic system, and a sovereign country?

Can it continue to function in the manner it has been performing since the end of 1991—that is, since the collapse of the Soviet empire? Or is it doomed to join the Warsaw Pact's failed Communist experiments in the dustbin of history? Or might it, instead, adapt and evolve—surviving in the sense of maintaining its political authority and power to rule, but transforming its defining functional characteristics and systemic identity?

My own work on the North Korean economy has generally been associated with what others have termed the "collapsist"[1] school of thought, and not unfairly. As far back as June 1990, I published an op-ed essay entitled "The Coming Collapse of North Korea" (Eberstadt 1990); since then, my analyses have requestioned the viability of the DPRK economy and system.[2]

It is therefore perhaps especially fitting that someone such as I, having imagined the odds of the DPRK's post-Soviet survival to be very low, should be charged with explaining just how the North Korean system has managed to survive these past 13 or 14 years—and to speculate about the possibility of sustainable pathways that might permit regime, state, and system to endure that far, or farther, into the future.

The following pages propose to offer something other than an apologia *pro vita sua* (although the reader will have to decide exactly how well that obvious temptation has been resisted). It will proceed through three sections. The first focuses on some of the factors that may have abetted state

---

1 Compare Noland (2004, 12–19).
2 Perhaps, most memorably, including this quote from Eberstadt (1995): "There is no reason at present to expect a reign by Kim Jong Il to be either stable or long."

survival in the DPRK in recent years. The second will discuss the sustainability of North Korea's current economic modus operandi. The final section will examine some of the questions pertaining to a DPRK transition to a more pragmatic variant of a planned socialist economy.

Financing the Survival of the North Korean State

How close to collapse has the DPRK system veered during the past decade? Could the system have disintegrated if events—domestic or international— had unfolded in a slightly different manner? Those speculative questions are unfortunately unanswerable and, for now, are quite untestable. We will probably have to await the eventual opening of the Pyongyang state archives to delve into those issues with any satisfaction—assuming that the DPRK's official files and data offer a sufficiently coherent and faithful record of events to aid such historical inquiries.

Available data do, however, cast light on one aspect of the DPRK's struggle to avoid collapse in the wake of the Soviet bloc's demise. These are the international data on North Korean trade patterns as reported by the DPRK's trade partners—"mirror statistics," as they are called by their users. Mirror statistics cannot tell us how close North Korea may have come to collapse in recent years, but they can help us explain how North Korea has managed to finance state survival.

Although the analysis of the modern North Korean economy has always been hampered by the extraordinary paucity of reliable data that might facilitate independent assessments, it is not exactly a state secret that the DPRK national economy was in the grip of stagnation—or incipient decline—in the 1980s and began to spiral downward once the aid and subsidized trade from the erstwhile Soviet bloc suddenly ceased at the start of the 1990s.

The steep and apparently unbroken decline in North Korean economic performance in the first half of the 1990s led to the outbreak of famine in the DPRK by the mid-1990s—the first and only instance of such mass hunger in an industrialized and literate society during peacetime. North Korea's patent economic dysfunction, and its leadership's seeming unwillingness or incapability to address and correct it, seemed to me to raise the possibility of one very particular kind of systemic collapse: economic collapse. I discussed this prospect in some detail in my 1999 book, *The End of North Korea*.

In discussing economic collapse, of course, I was not venturing guesses about the possibility of some dramatic political event that might bring the North Korean regime to an end—a coup d'état at the top, say, or a revolt from below. (Then, as now, the kinds of information that might permit such a judgment were clearly unavailable to outside observers, especially to those with no access to confidential sources of intelligence.)

Economic collapse, for its part, seemed an exceedingly elastic term, but Eberstadt (1999a) attempted to use it with some conceptual precision. In my analysis, "economic collapse" was not defined as an economic shock, an economic dislocation, a severe depression, or even a famine. "Economic collapse" was offered instead as a term to describe the breakdown of the division of labor in the national economy—the process through which ordinary people in complex productive societies trade their labor for food.[3]

North Korea in the mid- and late 1990s, I argued, was set on a trajectory for economic collapse because its domestic economy was incapable of producing the requisite goods necessary for the maintenance of a division of labor, and the regime seemed utterly unable to finance its purchases from abroad. Although it was impossible to determine from the outside the precise breaking point at which the division of labor would unravel, events were bringing the DPRK system progressively closer to that point.

The situation in early 2004 admittedly looks somewhat different. The ordinary North Korean today, of course, does not exactly live in the lap of luxury. On the other hand, by most accounts the typical North Korean no longer suffers from the desperate privation that characterized the mid- to late 1990s. As best can be told, the North Korean famine—which almost certainly claimed hundreds of thousands of victims and may well have killed a million people between 1995 and 1998[4]—ceased raging five years ago.

Officially, North Korean leadership indicated a new confidence in the DPRK's staying power back in September 1998, at the same Supreme People's Assembly that formally elevated Kim Jong-il to "the highest position of state." That convocation publicly declared that the "arduous march" of the previous several years was completed and announced that the DPRK was now on the road to becoming a "powerful and prosperous state" (*kangsong taeguk*).[5]

Whether or not the North Korean economy has enjoyed actual growth since 1998 (a question that remains a matter of some contention) it is clear that the economic situation has in some meaningful sense stabilized and improved since the grim days of the arduous march. But how was this accomplished? Mirror statistics provide some clues.

We can begin by looking at reconstructions of North Korea's overall trends for merchandise imports (see Eberstadt 2001 and *Figure 1*). In 1990, the reported value of imports was nearly $3 billion (in current U.S. dollars). By 1998, the reported level had dropped below $1.2 billion—a catastrophic fall of more than 60 percent. After 1998, however, North Korea's imports rebounded markedly. By 2001, the reported level exceeded $2 billion and appears to have risen again in 2002. (Comparable data for 2003 are not yet

---

3 This conception of economic collapse was, to my knowledge, first developed and defined by Jack Hirshleifer (1987) of UCLA and RAND.

4 The modeling of Goodkind and West (2001, 219–38) suggests a range of 600,000 to 1,000,000 deaths for the late 1990s.

5 Not too long thereafter, the Bank of Korea (BOK, of the Republic of Korea) declared that North Korea's economy had resumed economic growth; BOK reports, in fact, have suggested positive growth in the DPRK for 1999 and every subsequent year. Whether the BOK analysis can withstand scrutiny is another question. For a skeptical look, see Eberstadt (2001, 1–25).

Figure 1: North Korea's Merchandise Imports, 1989–2002

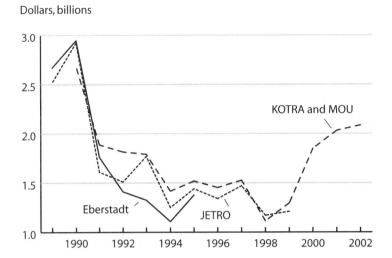

Sources: Eberstadt (2000); JETRO (various years); KOTRA (various years); MOU (various years).

available.) These numbers indicate that North Korea was obtaining nearly 90 percent more in the way of supplies of goods from abroad in 2002 than it had in 1998. In 2002, in fact, the current dollar value of North Korean merchandise imports was at the highest level registered since the collapse of the Soviet Union.

How did North Korea pay for this upsurge in imports? Mirror statistics do not show that it did so through any corresponding jump in reported export revenues (*Figure 2*). Between 1990 and 1998, North Korea's reported merchandise exports collapsed, plummeting from about $2 billion to less than $600 million. By 2002, these had recovered somewhat, to a reported level of just over $900 million. Nevertheless, by any absolute measure, the DPRK's reported export level remained remarkably low in 2002—less than half as high as it had been in 1990 and even lower than it had been in the bitter arduous-march year of 1997.

In a purely arithmetic sense, North Korea succeeded in effecting a substantial increase of merchandise imports despite only modest improvements in its almost negligibly low levels of reported merchandise exports by managing to increase its reported balance of trade deficit appreciably (*Figure 3*). In the arduous march period—the famine years of 1995–98—North Korea's reported surfeit of imports over exports averaged less than $600 million a year. By contrast, in the years 2000–02—the *kangsong taeguk* era—the DPRK's reported trade deficit was more than twice that high, averaging about $1.2 billion annually.

Figure 2: North Korea's Merchandise Exports, 1989–2002

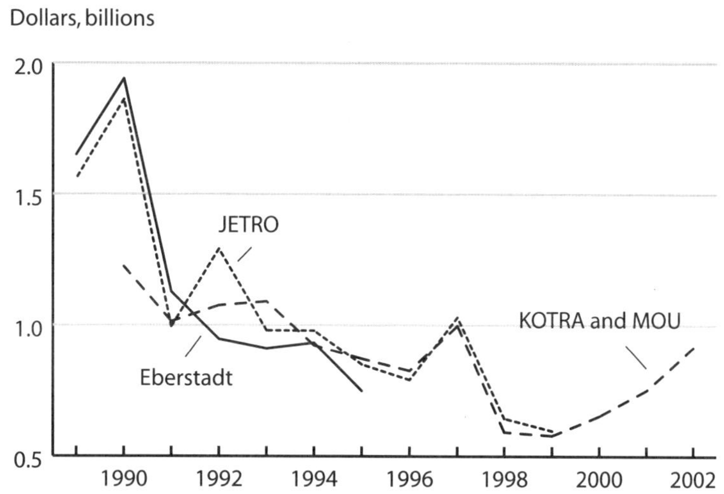

Dollars, billions

Sources: Eberstadt (2000); JETRO (various years); KOTRA (various years); MOU (various years).

But how was this reported trade deficit financed? The answer is not self-evident. After all, North Korea is a state with a commercial creditworthiness rating of approximately zero, having maintained for a generation its posture of defiant de facto default on the Western loans it contracted in the 1970s.

Historically, the DPRK relied on aid from its Communist allies—principally, the Soviet Union and China—to augment its imports. After the collapse of the USSR, China perforce emerged immediately as North Korea's principal foreign patron, and Beijing's largesse extended beyond its officially and episodically announced subventions for Pyongyang. The DPRK's seemingly permanent merchandise trade deficit with China actually constitutes a broader and perhaps more accurate measure of Beijing's true aid levels for Pyongyang (insofar as neither party seems to think the sums accumulated in that imbalance will ever be corrected or repaid).

Implicit Chinese aid, however, cannot account for North Korea's import upsurge of 1998–2002. To the contrary: China's implicit aid to North Korea—its reported balance of trade deficit—fell during these years, dropping from about $0.34 billion to about $0.27 billion. North Korea's non-Chinese balance of trade deficit, by contrast, apparently soared upward (*Figure 4*). Whereas in 1997 the DPRK reportedly managed to obtain only a net of $0.05 billion more merchandise from abroad than its commercial exports would have paid for after factoring out China, by 2002 the corresponding total was more than $0.9 billion.

Indeed, if we remove China from the picture, the line describing North Korea's net imports of supplies from abroad rises steadily upward between

Figure 3: North Korea's Merchandise Trade Deficit, 1989–2002

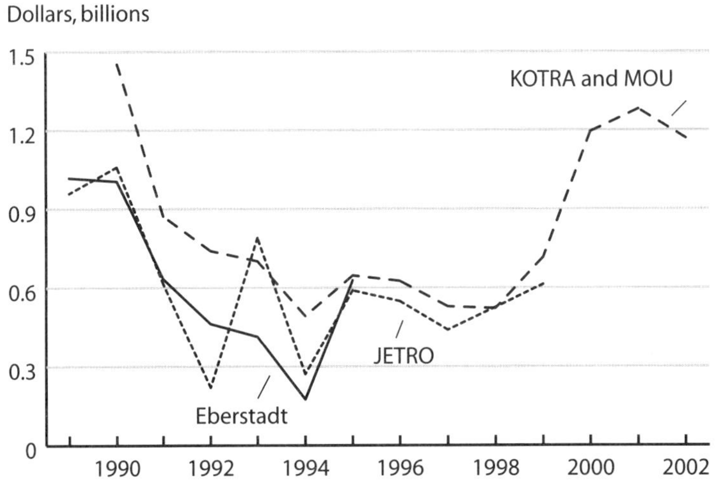

Dollars, billions

Sources: Figure 1 and Figure 2.

1997 and 2002. It is this graphic that captures the economic essence of North Korea's shift from its arduous-march period to its *kangsong taeguk* epoch.

And how was this jump in non-Chinese net imports financed? Unfortunately, we cannot be precise about this because many of the sources of funds involve illicit transactions. North Korea's international counterfeiting, drug trafficking, and weapons and weapons-technology sales all figure here although the sums raised from those activities are a matter of some dispute.

Nor do we yet know exactly how much of the South Korean taxpayers' money was furtively channeled from Seoul to Pyongyang during this period. One set of prosecutorial investigations has convicted former president Kim Dae-jung's national security adviser and several other aides of illegally transferring up to $500 million to Kim Jong-il's Bureau 39 on the eve of the historic June 2000 Pyongyang summit (Ward 2003, 9; Lem 2003, 2). The possibility of other unreported official Seoul-to-Pyongyang payoffs during the 1998–2002 period cannot be ruled out as yet—nor of course can the potential volume of any such attendant funds be determined.

Broadly speaking, however, we can explain the timing and the magnitude of the 1998–2002 upswing in North Korea's non-Chinese net imports in terms of the North Korea policies that were embraced during those years by the United States and its Northeast Asian allies. The year 1998 heralded the inauguration of President Kim Dae-jung in South Korea and the advent of South Korea's Sunshine Policy for détente and reconciliation with the North. In 1999, the United States followed suit with the unveiling of the Perry process (the grand-bargain approach to settling outstanding disputes with the

Figure 4: North Korea's Merchandise Trade Deficit, Excluding Trade with China, 1990–2002

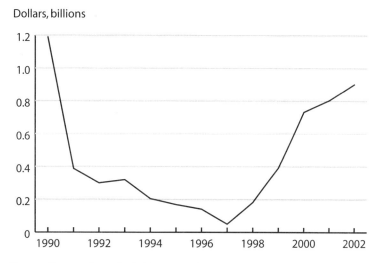

Sources: Figure 1; Figure 2; General Administration of Customs (various years).

DPRK that the *Korea Times* on 7 February 2000 reported was hailed by the ROK foreign minister as "based on our engagement policy toward North Korea"). Both Japan and the European Union (EU) joined in the pursuit of engagement with North Korea during these years as well, although in differing degrees.

In their strict performance specifications—their defining actions, as opposed to their official rationales or stated intentions—Sunshine Policy and engagement policy effectively meant, and continue to mean, organized activity by Western governments to mobilize transfers of public resources to the North Korean state. (If this formulation sounds provocative, reflection on the particulars of those multilateral policies will indicate it is also functionally accurate. They include the Hyundai/ROK National Tourism Office payments for vacations to Mt. Kumgang, the U.S. "inspection fee"[6] of 500,000 tons of food aid granted in 1999 for permission to visit a suspect underground North Korean facility at Kumchang-ri; the continuing food and fertilizer shipments from Seoul and the occasional food transfers from Japan; the secret payment for the historic June 2000 Pyongyang summit; and the new, albeit modest, flows of aid from EU countries in the wake of the flurry of diplomatic normalizations between Pyongyang and EU states in 2000–01.) Thus, it is perhaps not surprising that North Korea's financial fortunes

---

6 This is Pyongyang's description of the transaction.

Table 1: U.S. Assistance to North Korea, 1995-2004

Calendar or fiscal year	Food aid, per fiscal year		KEDO assistance, per calendar year ($ million)	Medical supplies, per fiscal year ($ million)	Total ($ million)
	Metric tons	Commodity value ($ million)			
1995	0	0.0	9.5	0.2	9.7
1996	19,500	8.3	22.0	0.0	30.3
1997	177,000	52.4	25.0	5.0	82.4
1998	200,000	72.9	50.0	0.0	122.9
1999	695,194	222.1	65.1	0.0	287.2
2000	265,000	74.3	64.4	0.0	138.7
2001	350,000	102.8	74.9	0.0	177.6
2002	207,000	82.4	90.5	0.0	172.9
2003	40,170	33.6	2.3	0.0	35.9
2004	60,000	n.a.	0.0	0.0	n.a.
Total	1,953,864	648.8[a]	403.7	5.2	1,057.6[a]

Sources: Figures for food aid and medical supplies from USAID (various years) and USDA (various years); KEDO (various years). Table courtesy of Mark Manyin, Congressional Research Service.
a Through 2003 only.

should have improved so markedly in 1998 and in the years immediately following.

To some readers, it may sound perplexing and counterintuitive to hear the United States—the DPRK's longtime principal opponent and antagonist in the international arena—described as a major contemporary backer of the North Korean state. Yet this is now in fact the case. Figures compiled by Mark Manyin of the Congressional Research Service provide the details (*Table 1*). In the 1996–2002 period, Washington provided Pyongyang with just over $1 billion in food aid, concessional fuel oil, and medical supplies; it is interesting that nearly $350 million of these resources were transferred in 2001 and 2002 under the aegis of the George W. Bush administration.

By the second half of the 1990s, North Korea's reliance on U.S. aid for financing its international purchases and supplies of goods was, in some quantifiable respect, more pronounced than for almost any other state for which Washington funded military, economic, and/or humanitarian assistance programs (*Table 2*). Total U.S. aid allocations to key recipients Israel and Egypt for the five years 1996–2000, for example, amounted to 34 percent and 67 percent of those states' respective export earnings for 2000. U.S. 1996–2000 assistance to North Korea, by contrast, actually exceeded the DPRK's reported year 2000 commercial export revenues. (Incidentally, because most of the U.S. aid resources in Table 1 were not tallied in the inter-

Table 2: U.S. Aid and National Exports, Selected Comparisons

Current Comparison with Selected Countries

Country	Total military and economic aid, 1996-2000 (U.S. dollars)	Exports of goods and services 2000 (U.S. dollars)	Total period aid as percentage of single-year exports (percent)
Pakistan	253,300,000	9,575,000,064	2.65
Ukraine	743,400,000	19,522,000,896	3.81
El Salvador	234,700,000	3,645,691,392	6.44
Nicaragua	206,600,000	962,200,000	21.47
Jordan	1,221,000,000	3,534,132,736	34.55
Israel	14,880,000,000	44,146,860,032	33.71
Egypt	10,595,200,000	15,931,033,600	66.51
Haiti	485,000,000	506,236,864	95.80
DPRK	661,500,000	653,100,000	101.29

Historical Comparison with Taiwan and ROK

Country	Total military and economic aid[1] (U.S. dollars)	Total exports[2] (U.S. dollars)	Total period aid as percentage of single-year exports (percent)
DPRK	1,021,800,000	751,100,000	136.04
Taiwan	2,512,100,000	220,750,000	1,137.98
ROK	4,346,200,000	56,000,000	7,761.07

Sources: Manyin 2004; KOTRA (various years); MOU (various years); USAID (various years); World Bank (2002); and IMF (1962).
1 For the DPRK, figures represent total aid for 1995-2002; for Taiwan and the ROK, figures represent total aid for 1955-1962.
2 For the DPRK, figures represent total exports for 2002; for Taiwan and the ROK, figures represent total exports for 1962.

national commercial ledgers upon which mirror statistics rely,[7] the DPRK's actual level of reliance upon non-Chinese net supplies from abroad was consistently higher for 1998–2002 than Figure 4 suggests.) Ironic though it may seem, when considered in relation to the economy's evident capability to finance its international needs from its own regular commercial exports, Washington's aid lifeline for the DPRK in recent years looks more consequential than any of the bilateral assistance relationships that Washington has arranged for treaty allies or friendly states in any spot on the globe.

---

7 In theory, none of these U.S. assistance resources should be included in mirror statistics, but real-world practice is haphazard. U.S. heavy fuel oil shipped to the DPRK in South Korean vessels, for example, has often been registered as North-South trade in Ministry of Unification inter-Korean trade statistics.

This is not the first time, of course, that U.S. aid has helped a state on the Korean peninsula to survive. After the 1953 Korean armistice, Washington devoted tremendous resources to propping up and strengthening the Syngman Rhee government in Seoul—a regime fascinated with "aid-maximizing stratagems" (Cole and Lyman 1971) and manifestly disinterested in improving its then-miserable export performance. To be sure, judged by the metric of U.S. aid compared with recipient-country exports, the U.S. Cold War project for preserving the ROK was vastly more intensive than Washington's post-Cold War programs sustaining the North Korean state (Table 2). In the late 1950s, on the other hand, U.S. bilateral aid was just about the only game in town for states seeking Western largesse, in marked contrast to today. And if we were able to consider all the aid packages—overt, covert, or semiformal—that were extended to the DPRK by Western governments in the *kangsong taeguk* period, we might well discover that the ratio of such outside assistance to local commercial earnings began to approach the scale of disproportion earlier witnessed in, say, the late-1950s U.S. project to preserve the independence of the Republic of China (Taiwan). (Clearly, that earlier Taiwan effort would have undoubtedly been the more aid intensive by our selected metric; although lower, the aid intensity of the recent DPRK arrangements would perhaps fall within the same approximate order of magnitude.)

We can never know what would have happened if the United States and its allies in Asia and Europe had refrained from underwriting the survival of the North Korean state in the late 1990s and the early years of the present decade. (Such exercises in counterfactual speculation—imaginary history, as they are known to their modern-day devotees[8]—can make for fascinating reading, but they are ultimately inconclusive.) We do not know, furthermore, just how close North Korea came to the critical breaking point of an economic collapse during the arduous-march period between Kim Il-sung's death and Kim Jong-il's formal anointment. What we know—or think we know—can be stated succinctly. The DPRK was failing economically in the mid-1990s, moving closer to the notional point of an economic collapse. In the late 1990s and early years of the current decade, the prospect of economic collapse was diminished materially by an upsurge in provisions of goods from abroad—goods, in turn, that were financed in considerable measure by new flows of Western foreign aid.

Whether or not Western aid flows were the indispensable or instrumental factor in averting a North Korean collapse cannot for now be discussed with the sort of historical knowledge and texture that can be brought to bear in a discussion of the averted collapse of the Ottoman Empire in March 1915. What seems beyond dispute is that the upsurge of Western aid for the DPRK

---

8   A growing number of eminent historians and respected social scientists seem to be engaging in this pastime. See, for example, Polsby (1982), Ferguson (1997), and Cowley (2003).

under Sunshine and engagement policies played a role—possibly a very important role—in reducing the risk of economic collapse and in increasing the odds of survival for the North Korean state.

Current Parameters in Financing State Survival for the DPRK: Ideological and Cultural Infiltration, Military-First Politics

Although North Korea's flirtation with economic collapse did not commence until after the disintegration of the Soviet bloc, the DPRK's relative (and perhaps also its absolute) economic decline has been a long-term process, and by some indicators was already well under way in the Cold War era. The DPRK's trade performance vividly describes this record of long-term economic decline (and, because international trade bears more than incidentally upon the state's risk of economic collapse, it reflects systemic survival prospects as well). From our twenty-first-century vantage point, we may not recall how steep and steady this long decline has been.

There was a time—within living memory—when the DPRK was not known for being an international-trade basket case. In 1970, the level of per capita exports in North Korea and South Korea was roughly comparable ($21 compared with $27—in then-much-more-valuable dollars) (Eberstadt 1995, chap. 1). As late as 1980, in fact, North Korea's export profile, though hardly robust, was also not manifestly disfigured. In 1980, for example, the DPRK's level of reported per capita exports was just slightly higher than Turkey's, and more than five times higher than India's (see *Table 3* on page 87). That same year North Korea's reported imports exceeded reported export revenues, but by a margin that was in keeping with performance of other developing economies, including quite successful ones. The DPRK's 1980 ratio of imports to exports, for example, was just slightly higher than Chile's—but it was a bit lower than either Thailand's or South Korea's (see *Table 4* on page 90).

By 1990 the picture had worsened considerably; see *Table 5* on page 94 and *Table 6* on page 98. Despite a politically determined surge in exports to the USSR under the terms of the 1985–90 Soviet-DPRK economic cooperation accord, per capita exports now ranked in the lowest quartile of the world's economies—in a league with Equatorial Guinea and Kenya—and the ratio of imports to exports had risen so that North Korea was among the quartile of states where this imbalance was greatest. By 1990, North Korea's disproportion between imports and exports placed it in the ranking next to such heavily aid-dependent economies as Jordan and Ghana.

By 2000, as one might suspect, the DPRK was an outlier within the world system (see *Table 7* on page 102 and *Table 8* on page 107). That year, the DPRK's reported per capita export level would have ranked 158 among the 168 countries tracked in the World Bank's world development indicators:

below Chad and at less than half of India's level. (Reported per capita exports from Turkey were now nearly 25 times as high as from the DPRK.) Although the nominal level of per capita exports for the world was nearly 2.5 times higher in 2000 than in 1980,[9] North Korea's nominal reported per capita export level fell by almost two-thirds during those years. At the same time, North Korea's imbalance between reported imports and export earnings (with the former 2.8 times as great as the latter) looked to be among the 10 most extreme recorded that year. A glaring discrepancy between imports and exports does not automatically betoken dependence on aid. In the case of several outliers in Table 8, Lesotho and West Bank/Gaza among them, the discrepancy speaks to the importance of remittances in the local balance of payments. However, North Korea's ratio of reported commercial export revenues to reported imports was even lower in 2000 than in such all-but-permanent wards of the official development assistance community as Haiti and Burkina Faso.

When it comes to trade performance and patterns of international finance, North Korea's downward trajectory and its current straits—its structural descent from Turkey to Haiti in just one generation, at least in terms of the aforementioned particulars—represent in part the misfortune of circumstance. The sudden and unexpected downfall of the Soviet bloc was a disaster for the North Korean economic system: a disaster, indeed, from which the DPRK economy has not yet recovered.

But it would be a mistake to ignore the degree to which North Korea's aberrant and seemingly dysfunctional trade regimen today is actually a result of a conscious purpose, deliberate design, and considered official effort. There exists a deeply embedded regime logic in the DPRK's tangential and precarious relationship with the world economy—and, far from being irrational, it is based on careful and cool-headed calculation of regime survival.

Consider the DPRK's trade performance over the past generation with the 29 countries the International Monetary Fund (IMF) terms the "advanced economies"[10] (or what North Korean terminology would designate as the "capitalist" or "imperialist" countries). Between 1980 and 2000 the total size of the import market for this collectivity grew from about $1.8 trillion to about $6.1 trillion.

The DPRK, we recall, is precluded by Washington's thicket of sanctions and restrictions against U.S.-DPRK commerce from exporting any appreciable volume of goods to the United States, and the United States offers the world's single largest import market. If we exclude the United States from the picture, the remaining advanced-economy market for foreign imports is never-

---

9 Global calculations derived from IMF (2003) and Population Division (2003).

10 This grouping includes 24 of the current 30 Organization for Economic Cooperation and Development (OECD) members (omitting Czech Republic, Hungary, Mexico, Poland, Slovak Republic, and Turkey) and five others (Cyprus, Hong Kong, Israel, Singapore, and Taiwan).

theless vast and (at least in nominal terms) rapidly expanding—growing from about $1.5 billion in 1980 to $4.6 billion in 2000. DPRK exports to this group, however, remained negligible and stagnant during these decades, even after the loss of Soviet bloc markets would seem to have added some urgency to cultivating new sources of commercial export revenue. In 1980 and 1990, North Korea's reported sales to this grouping totaled roughly $430 million and roughly $470 million, respectively. In 2000, the reported aggregate was about $560 million—but that total may have been inflated somewhat by an unusual and perhaps questionable $60 million in North Korean imports recorded that year by Spain. Yet even accepting that year's exceptional Spanish data, the real level of North Korean exports to these "capitalist" countries would have been substantially lower in 2000 than it had been two decades earlier (UN Comtrade 2004).[11]

Pyongyang's remarkably poor long-term performance in the advanced economies' huge markets is no accident. Instead, it is a direct consequence of official DPRK policy and doctrine—most particularly, Pyongyang's concept of ideological and cultural infiltration. Official North Korean pronouncements relentlessly decry the dangers of this phenomenon, which is said to be a technique by which outsiders attempt to undermine the foundations of established Communist states. A recent declamation (FBIS 2003b) will give the flavor of the general argument:

> It is the imperialist's old trick to carry out ideological and cultural infiltration prior to their launching of an aggression openly. Their bourgeois ideology and culture are reactionary toxins to paralyze people's ideological consciousness. Through such infiltration, they try to paralyze the independent consciousness of other nations and make them spineless. At the same time, they work to create illusions about capitalism and promote lifestyles among them based on the law of the jungle, in an attempt to induce the collapse of socialist and progressive nations. The ideological and cultural infiltration is their silent, crafty, and villainous method of aggression, intervention and domination. . . .

> Through "economic exchange" and personnel interchange programs too, the imperialists are pushing their infiltration. . . . Exchange and cooperation activities in the economic and cultural fields have been on the rise since the beginning of the new century. The imperialists are making use of these activities as an important lever to push the infiltration of bourgeois ideology and culture. . . .

---

11 Between 1980 and 2000, the U.S. producer price index—the more appropriate deflator for international tradables—rose by 51 percent. With that deflator, North Korea's inflation-adjusted export volume to this grouping of countries would have declined by about 16 percent between 1980 and 2000. Note that the grouping includes South Korea and that inter-Korean trade is included in the data.

The imperialists' ideological and cultural infiltration, if tolerated, will lead to the collapse and degeneration of society, to disorder and chaos, and even to the loss of the gains of the revolution. The collapse of socialism in the 20th Century—and the revival of capitalism in its place—in some countries gave us the serious lesson that social deterioration begins with ideological degeneration, and confusion on the ideological front throws every other front of society into chaos and, consequently, all the gains of the revolution go down the drain eventually.

DPRK party lecture notes published in South Korea late in 2002 (FBIS 2002) put the point more succinctly:

The capitalist's ideological and cultural infiltration will never cease, and the struggle against it will continue, as long as the imperialists continue to exist in the world. . . .

The great leader, Kim Jong Il, pointed out the following: "Today, the imperialists and reactionaries are tenaciously scheming to blow the wind of bourgeois liberalism into us". . . .

Under these circumstances, if we turn away from reality and we regard it as someone else's problem, what will happen?

People will ideologically degenerate and weaken; cracks will develop in our socialist ideological position; and, in the end, our socialism will helplessly collapse. A case in point is the bitter lesson drawn from the miserable situations of the former Soviet Union and Eastern European countries.

"Economic exchange" with the "capitalist" world, in other words, is explicitly and officially regarded by Pyongyang as a process that unleashes powerful, unpredictable, and subversive forces, forces that ultimately erode the authority of socialist states. Viewed from this perspective, North Korea's record of trade performance vis-à-vis the advanced market economies is not a record of failure (failure to integrate into the world economy) but rather a mark of success (effective containment of a potentially lethal security threat).

Moreover, it is worth recalling that the DPRK's public misgivings about "ideological and cultural infiltration" are of long standing, almost precisely paralleling the state's record over the past generation of minimal export outreach to advanced market economies. Although DPRK pronouncements about ideological and cultural infiltration have attracted some attention abroad since the downfall of Soviet bloc socialism, the slogan itself was not a response to that defining event. To the contrary, North Korean leadership had been highlighting the dangers of that tendency for at least a decade before the final collapse of the Soviet Union. At the sixth congress of the Korean Workers' Party in 1980, for example, Kim Il-sung inveighed against the dangers of cultural infiltration. By 1981 (BBC 1981), he was urging North Korea's "workers and trade union members" to "combat the ideological and cultural infiltration of the imperialists and their subversive moves and sabotage."

It is true that official directives from Pyongyang have from time to time discussed the desirability of significantly increasing the DPRK's volume of international trade. Against such comments, North Korea's extraordinary and continuing weakness in export performance may seem especially curious (insofar as it would be at least in theory so very easy to redress). But Pyongyang's conspicuous neglect of the revenue potential from trade with advanced market economies is not to be explained away as a prolonged fit of absentmindedness. Instead, it speaks to fundamental and abiding calculations in Pyongyang's strategy for state survival.

If staying out of the poisonous embrace of the world economy is viewed as an imperative for state survival by DPRK leadership, a corollary question about state survival inevitably arises: how then to generate sufficient international resources to forestall economic collapse? Pyongyang's answer, to date: through nonmarket transactions. The DPRK has always pursued an aid-seeking international economic strategy, but in the post-Soviet-bloc era the particulars of that approach have perforce mutated. In the *kangsong taeguk* era, North Korea's main tactics for generating international resources are viewed through the prism of the current state campaign for military-first politics (*songun chongchi*).

Like the concept of ideological and cultural infiltration, the theory and recommended practice of military-first politics have received a tremendous amount of airtime in the North Korean media during the past five years. Two recent exegeses may clarify some of the economic implications of this doctrine.

As a long, official analysis in *Nodong Sinmun* on 21 March 2003 instructed, it was a renewed emphasis on military development that enabled North Korea to conclude its arduous march and to step onto the pathway to power and prosperity:

Today, the peoples' struggle for their nations' independent development and prosperity is waged in an environment different from that of the last century.

. . . In building a state in our era, it is essential to beef up the main force of the nation and fortify the revolutionary base, and, in this regard, it is most important to build up powerful military might. In today's world, without powerful military might, no country can . . . achieve development and prosperity.

. . . During . . . "the Arduous March" in our history, great Comrade Kim Jong Il firmly believed that the destiny of the people and the future of the revolution hinged on the barrel of a gun, and that we could break through the difficulties and lead the revolution to victory only by depending on the Army. . . . Through the arduous practice in which the Army was put to the fore and the unheard-of trials were overcome, the revolutionary phi-losophy that the barrel of a gun was precisely the revolution and the barrel of a gun was precisely the victory of socialism was originated. . . .

Our theory on the construction of a powerful state . . . is the embodiment of the profound truth that the base of national strength is military might, and the dignity and might of a country hinges on the barrel of a gun. . . . In a powerful state, the defense industry takes a leading and key position in the economy. . . . Today, by firmly adhering to the principle of putting prime effort into the defense industry and, based on this, by developing the overall economy ceaselessly, our party is brilliantly resolving the issue of consolidating the national strength of a powerful state.

And how exactly does military power conduce to prosperity? The answer (emphasis added) was strongly hinted at in a statement in *Nodong Sinmun* on 3 April 2003:

A country's development and the placement of importance on the mili-tary are linked as one. . . .

Once we lay the foundations for a powerful *self-sustaining national defense industry,* we will be able to rejuvenate all economic fields, to include light industry and agriculture and enhance the quality of the people's lives.

This is a fascinating and revealing formulation. In most of the world to-day, a country's defense outlays are regarded as a weight that must be shoul-dered by the value-adding sectors of the national economy (thus, the phrase "military burden"). In contrast, North Korea's leadership evidently enter-tains the concept of a self-sustaining defense sector—implying that Pyongyang views its military activities as generating resources, not simply absorbing them. In the enunciated view of North Korea's leadership, the DPRK's military sec-tor is the key not only to unlocking the resources necessary to finance its own considerable needs but to financing the recovery of the rest of the na-tional economy as well.

It does not require a great deal of imagination to spell out the operational details of this approach. While it forswears any appreciable export revenues from legitimate commerce with advanced market economies, North Korean today seems to be banking on the possibility of financing state survival by exporting strategic insecurity to the rest of the world. In part, such dividends are derived from exports of merchandise (for example, missile sales and in-ternational transfer of the technology for weapons of mass destruction [WMD]). But these revenues also depend heavily on what might be described as an export of services: in this case, military extortion services (might we better call them "revenue-sensitive threat reduction services"?) that are based on Pyongyang's nuclear development and ballistic missile programs.

The export of strategic insecurity, in its different components, can arguably be said to explain much of the upsurge in North Korea's unexplained surfeit of imports over commercial export revenues since 1998—especially to the extent that Western aid policies in recent years can be described as motivated by appeasement.[12] In an important tactical sense, that approach has enjoyed a success—it has facilitated state survival under imposing constraints. But the territory demarcated by ideological and cultural infiltration on the one side and military-first politics on the other is also, quite clearly, a sort of no-man's-land: an inherently unstable niche in which survival is utterly contingent and sustained development utterly unlikely. North Korea's current strategic policy, in short, may be deferring the question of economic collapse but has not yet answered it.

Avoiding Economic Collapse through Economic Reform Policies?

If the DPRK is currently sustaining its system through aid-seeking stratagems grounded in military menace, as I argue , it would seem to have settled on a particularly meager and highly uncertain mode of state finance. Even today, when this approach is "working," it is not clear that it generates sufficient funding to maintain (much less improve) the nation's aging and badly decayed industrial and transport infrastructure. Moreover, the stratagem may fail for any number of reasons (donor fatigue, DPRK miscalculation, and an external push for regime change in Pyongyang being but three of these).

Under these circumstances, as many foreign observers have argued, a more secure and ultimately satisfactory path for avoiding economic collapse and preserving the sovereignty of the North Korean state might be a pragmatic reorientation of Pyongyang's policy in the name of promoting sustained growth. In some variants of this argument, it is said that China and Vietnam have already demonstrated that it is feasible for a Marxist-Leninist government in an Asian setting simultaneously to execute a shift to an outward-oriented economic regimen, achieve rapid economic growth, and maintain leadership authority and political stability.

Whether reform and outward orientation could be consonant with the preservation of unquestioned power for North Korea's leadership is a question that will not detain us here.[13] Nor will we be diverted by a discussion of

---

12 Even ostensibly humanitarian food aid transfers to North Korea are informed by the reality of military extortion. Think in particular of access to the nuclear facility at Kumchang-ri in exchange for U.S. grain, and, more generally, whether the opaque rules under which food relief is administered in the DPRK would be tolerated by the international donor community in any other setting (Eberstadt 1999b).

13 We may note in passing, however, that both Robert Scalapino (1992) and Ezra Vogel (in discussions from 1994 to 2004) have suggested that North Korea might plausibly evolve from today's hermetic *juche* totalitarian system to a more familiar, Park Chung-hee type of authoritarian state—and the judgment of these two leading U.S. authorities on modern Asia should be respectfully weighed in this consideration.

the potential problems and preconditions of any so-called reform worthy of the name under contemporary North Korean conditions. Instead we will briefly address two practical and subsidiary questions. First, how far have North Korea's much-discussed reforms progressed to date? Second, if the DPRK were truly moving in the direction of reform and self-sustaining growth, how would we tell and what would we see?

North Korea's Economic Reforms to Date

Predictions that the DPRK would soon be embracing economic reform come from a family tree that is, if anything, even more prolific and older than the lineage of predictions about imminent or eventual DPRK collapse. Scholars and analysts have been detecting quiet signs of reform and opening in the North Korean system since at least the 1980s.[14] The intensity of these premonitions typically waxed and waned according to the current temperatures in Pyongyang's relations with Washington and/or Seoul.[15] In July 2002, however, Pyongyang enacted a package of macroeconomic policy changes that marked a notable departure from DPRK practices during the previous generation. Moreover, North Korean leadership now sometimes openly describes these measures as "economic reform"[16]—a term the DPRK had vigorously rejected on the understanding that no reforms were needed for the real existing DPRK system.

The specifics of the July 2002 measures have been described in detail elsewhere (UN 2002, 127–32). Scholars and analysts have in addition offered some initial assessments of their significance and portent.[17]

It may be cheering, of course, to see anything self-described as "reform" emanating from the organs of power in the DPRK. And by comparison with North Korea's economic policy adjustments since, say, the late 1960s, these measures may indeed be described as bold and experimental steps. Yet in a sense this only attests to how impoverished our expectations for DPRK policy have become over the decades. Viewed for what they are—rather than for

---

14 See, for example, Lee (1988), Oh (1990), and Merrill (1991, 139–53); each of these papers was written and initially presented in the 1980s.

15 The announcement of the Pyongyang North-South summit occasioned an especially vigorous pulsation of such premonitions; for example, Marcus Noland (2000, A21): "The secret visit to Beijing last month by Kim Jong Il supports the argument that this is the real deal and that the North Koreans are serious about opening to the outside world." This, of course, was before the outside world learned the true details of the real deal underpinning that historic summit.

16 The president of the Supreme People's Assembly, Kim Yong-nam, in August 2002 said in a conversation with UN (2002, 127) officials: "We are reactivating the whole field of the national economy. . . . We are reforming the economic system on the principle of profitability." The term "reform" has not yet been embraced by the DPRK media, however, who still treat the concept as anathema: "Even though the imperialists are trying to stifle our economy by inducing it to 'reform' and 'opening', our economic management is being improved without deviating even an inch from socialist principles" (FBIS 2003a).

17 For cautiously optimistic analyses, see Noland (2002) and Frank (2003a and 2003b). For a more cautiously skeptical assessment, see Newcomb (2003, 57–60).

what we might hope they will prefigure—the July 2002 package of economic changes can best be described as rather modest in comparison with either economic reforms undertaken in other troubled economies or with the job that needs doing in the DPRK.

In practical terms, the July 2002 package—consumer price increases, wage hikes, currency devaluation, and ration system devolution—accomplished one important function: it remonetized a limited portion of the DPRK domestic economy. By the late 1980s, the DPRK was already a shockingly demonetized operation: back-of-the-envelope calculations for 1987 suggest that the wage bill in that year would have amounted to less than one-fifth of North Korea's official net material product. During the following decade and a half, the role of the national currency in domestic economic activity was progressively diminished. By the turn of the century, North Korea was perhaps the modern world's most completely demonetized economy—excepting only Khmer Rouge Cambodia, where for a time by decree money was abolished altogether.

The reemergence of money in North Korean economic life and, with it, the reemergence of a limited measure of open market activity mark an incontestable and important improvement for the DPRK's tiny consumer sector. It is important also to recognize just what this July 2002 package does not signify. To begin, it does not represent an unambiguous move toward market principles in the DPRK economy. To the contrary: remonetization of the domestic economy would likewise be a sine qua non for the resurrection of the DPRK's badly broken central planning mechanism ("a planned economy without planning" [Kimura 1994]) that has not managed to launch another multiyear national plan since the last one was concluded in 1993.

Limited remonetization of the domestic economy, furthermore, does not signify transformation of the DPRK's badly distorted production structure. To the contrary; the manifestly limited supply response of the DPRK economy to the July 2002 measures is indicated on the one hand by the subsequent steep drop in the black market exchange rate for the DPRK *won*,[18] and on the other by Pyongyang's hurried introduction, barely 10 months after the July 2002 package, of new "people's life bonds"—worthless, utterly illiquid, and involuntarily assigned—in lieu of wages for workers or payments to enterprises (BBC 2003).

To be sure: the limited reintroduction of money in the DPRK domestic economy may elicit some supply response: a Leibenstein-style increase in X-efficiency (Leibenstein 1966, 392–415), for example. But without the possibility of a reallocation of state resources in accordance with new demand conditions—and that possibility currently does not exist in the DPRK—the

---

18 The initial July 2002 exchange rate was set at 153 *won* to the U.S. dollar. By October 2003, as reported on 4 October 2003 by Yonhap (Seoul) in "N. Korea Depreciate [sic] Its Currency. Adopts Floating Rates: Asahi," DPRK government foreign exchange booths in Pyongyang were paying 900 *won* per dollar.

Figure 5: Imports as a Percentage of Exports, 1977–2002, calculated with current U.S. dollars

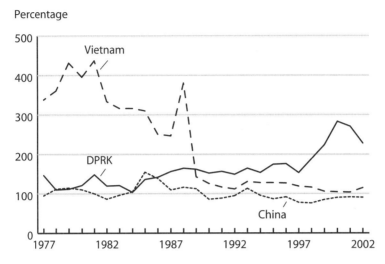

Sources: Eberstadt (2000), KOTRA (various years), MOU (various years), LOC (various years), IMF (2003), World Bank (2003).

supply response must perforce be tepid and superficial. Thus, it should come as no surprise that—heartening signs of newly sprouted "people's markets" notwithstanding—the World Food Program (WFP) has just warned prospective donors that North Korea faces an imminent return to mass hunger barring an influx of new food aid into the relief pipeline (Kim 2004; McDonald 2004).[19] The contrast is not a contradiction but rather a faithful reflection of the scope and limits of the July 2002 reforms.

The July 2002 reforms, in brief, do not in themselves stave off the specter of DPRK economic collapse. Nor do they have any obvious or direct bearing on the prospects for a shift to China-style or Vietnam-style export-led growth. One need only contrast North Korea's patterns of trade performance over the past generation with those of China and Vietnam to appreciate this (*Figure 5* and *Figure 6*). Vietnam began its push for export orientation when its Soviet subsidies abruptly ended, whereas North Korea's export performance markedly worsened and its aid dependence increased after 1991. Although still predominantly agrarian societies, Vietnam and China both manage to export far more merchandise on a per capita basis today than does the ostensibly industrialized DPRK (precisely because of the linkages and supply response mechanisms that the DPRK has assiduously prevented from taking root). At the risk of belaboring the obvious, the DPRK has not even begun to

---

19 The WFP's own institutional interests, to be sure, comport with an alarmist reading of the North Korean food situation, but that does not mean the WFP's latest warnings are wrong.

Figure 6: Per Capita Exports, 1977–2002, calculated with current U.S. dollars

Sources: Eberstadt (2000), KOTRA (various years), MOU (various years), LOC (various years), Census (various years), IMF (various years), World Bank (various years).

tinker with the macro policies or promote the micro institutions that would permit a China- or Vietnam-style export response.[20] Thus, for the time being, economic survival through export orientation is simply not in the cards for North Korea.

What Would Genuine Reform and Opening Look Like?

Instead of sketching out the full contours of a DPRK transition to sustainable export-led growth, it may serve our purposes here to dwell on three essential and inextricably linked features: the outward opening itself, military demobilization, and normalization of relations with the ROK (Eberstadt 2002).

Economic opening.   If Pyongyang were to embark upon a genuine move toward an economic opening, what initial signs would outsiders be able to see? Some of these might include:

• Meaningful departure from old "economic" themes and new dialogue about economic issues in DPRK propaganda and guidance organs;

• Doctrinal reorientation regarding the treatment of profit-generating transactions in official DPRK pronouncements and, especially, profits involving transactions with foreign concerns;

---

20 To date the only appreciable movement in these general areas would seem to be the events that found their denouement in the September-October 2002 Yang Bin fiasco.

- An attempt on the part of the DPRK to settle its long-standing international debt default problems;[21]
- A move toward greater economic transparency, demonstrated by publication of economic and social statistics describing the North Korean domestic situation; and
- Serious attempts to promulgate a legal framework for potential foreign investors that might assist in attracting profit-seeking overseas entrepreneurs to North Korean soil.

Although some observers may see glimmers of the first and second conditions, none of these blinker lights is flashing brightly and consistently in North Korea today.

Military demobilization. Military demobilization would represent a critical aspect of a North Korean program or reform and opening insofar as the following:

- A dismantling of Pyongyang's WMD programs would indicate that North Korean leadership was committed to earning its living from activities other than international military extortion; and
- Reallocation of resources from the hypertrophied military to the civilian sectors would permit much more potentially productive economic activity in the DPRK.

To this date, of course, there is little evidence that North Korea has ever, at any point in its more than five decades of existence, voluntarily abjured any new instrument of military force that might possibly lie within its grasp. (Today, indeed, such a renunciation would seem fundamentally inconsistent with the state's established policies of *kangsong taeguk* and military-first politics.) Moreover, North Korea's commitment to developing WMD was implicitly reaffirmed in the exhortation (FBIS 2001a [emphasis added]), "We should hold fast to the military-first politics and *build up our military strength in every possible way.*"

If North Korea were to head on a different road regarding proliferation, the first clear sign of a change in attitude would be a new stance toward outside verification of North Korean WMD activities. For the time being, however, Pyongyang maintains (BBC 2001) that U.S. calls for verification conceal "a dark ulterior motive to thoroughly investigate our national defense and military bases . . . [a plot to] completely dig out our interior organs [sic]" and (FBIS 2001b) that "the issue [of verification] can never be on the agenda for DPRK-U.S. talks."

---

21 For the past quarter century, the DPRK has been in effective default on roughly $1 billion in European, Japanese, and Australian loans contracted in the early 1970s (Eberstadt 1995, chap. 1).

Normalization of DPRK-ROK relations.   The DPRK cannot execute a successful economic opening unless it demobilizes, and it cannot demobilize unless it comes to terms with the right of the ROK to coexist with it on the Korean peninsula. Consequently, one important and indeed indispensable marker of movement toward reform and opening would be a change in North Korea's official stance concerning the legitimacy of the ROK.

If North Korea were to evidence a new attitude toward the legitimacy of the ROK, the indications of this change would be direct and unmistakable: its highest figures and its official media would simply disclose that they were prepared to accept the existence of the South Korean state, that they recognized the ROK's right to conduct its own foreign policy, and that they respected (while respectfully disagreeing with) Seoul's decision to maintain a military alliance with the United States. Suffice it to say that no such disclosures have been offered to date.

In sum, there is little evidence that North Korea has yet embarked upon a path to reform and opening, with all the transformations in polity that this path would foreshadow. That oft-discussed strategy for economic survival appears to be an option as yet unchosen by the DPRK's own leadership.

How long the DPRK can survive on its current trajectory is anyone's guess—and my personal guesses on this score have admittedly been off the mark, perhaps for reasons indicated above. But if the analysis in this paper is correct, the specter of an economic collapse is a ghost that haunts the DPRK to this very day and one that will not be exorcized unless or until North Korea's leadership agrees to undertake what, in a very different context, they have called "a bold switch-over." Whether Pyongyang accepts such a challenge remains to be seen.

References

Agency for International Development (USAID). Various years. Statistics database. Washington, D.C.: USAID.

British Broadcasting Corporation (BBC). 1981. Kim Il-sung's Speech to Trade Union Congress. BBC Summary of World Broadcasts, no. FE/6896/B/1. Broadcast on 30 November; summary on 3 December.

BBC Worldwide Monitoring (BBC). 2001. North Korea Demands Compensation from USA for Delay to Reactor Project. BBC Monitoring Asia Pacific–Political, 8 July.

North Korea's Survival Game

———. 2003. North Korea reports 'brisk' sale of public bonds. KCNA, 8 May.

Census Bureau (Census). Various years. Statistics database. Washington, D.C.: U.S. Census Bureau.

Cima, Ronald J., ed. 1989. *Vietnam: A Country Study* (Washington, D.C.: Library of Congress, Federal Research Division.

Cole, David C., and Princeton Lyman. 1971. *Korean Development: The Interplay of Politics and Economics.* Cambridge: Harvard University Press.

Cowley, Robert. 2003. *What Ifs? Of American History: Eminent Historians Imagine What Might Have Been.* New York: G. P. Putnam.

Department of Agriculture (USDA). Various years. Statistics database. Washington, D.C.: USDA.

Eberstadt, Nicholas. 1990. The Coming Collapse of North Korea. *Wall Street Journal*, 26 June.

———. 1995. *Korea Approaches Reunification.* Armonk, N.Y.: M. E. Sharpe.

———. 1999a. *The End of North Korea.* Washington, D.C.: AEI Press.

———. 1999b. U.S. Aid Feeds North Korea's Nuclear Designs. *Wall Street Journal*, 23 March.

———. 2000. Economic Recovery in the DPRK: Status and Prospect. *International Journal of Korean Studies* 4, no. 1 (Fall/Winter).

———. 2001. Prospects for Economic Recovery: Perceptions and Evidence. *Joint U.S.-Korean Academic Studies* (Korea Economic Institute, Washington, D.C.).

———. 2002. If North Korea Were Really Reforming, How Could We Tell—And What Would We Be Able To See? *Korea and World Affairs* 26, no. 2 (Spring): 20–46.

Ferguson, Niall, ed. 1997. *Virtual History: Alternatives and Counterfactuals.* London: Picador.

Foreign Broadcast Information Service (FBIS). 2001a. DPRK Daily Full Front-Page Article Discusses National Pride. *Nodong Sinmun*, 1 June. FBIS-EAS-2001-0629, 3 July 2001.

———. 2001b. ROK's Yonhap: N. K. Says U.S. Demands for Verification Ruse to Disarm It. Yonhap News Service, 1 August. FBIS-EAS-2001-0801, 2 August 2001.

———. 2002. Full Text of DPRK Lecture Program in Capitalists' 'Ideological and Cultural Infiltration'. *Chosun Ilbo*, 20 December. Washington, D.C.: FBIS. AFS document no. KPP20021222000016.

———. 2003a. DPRK Cabinet Organ Discusses Improving Economic Management. *Minju Choson*, 6 March. Washington, D.C.: FBIS. AFS document no. KPP 20030313000122.

———. 2003b. DPRK Organ Scores 'Imperialists' for Ideological, Cultural Infiltration Schemes. *Nodong Sinmun*, 20 April. Washington, D.C.: FBIS. AFS document no. KPP20030429000057.

Frank, Ruediger. 2003a. A Socialist Market Economy in North Korea? Systemic Restrictions and a Quantitative Analysis. Columbia University, New York.

————. 2003b. *North Korea: Gigantic Chance and a Systemic Change.* San Francisco: Nautilus Institute at the Center for the Pacific Rim, University of San Francisco. NAPSNET Policy Forum Online PFO 3-31. 9 May. www.nautilus.org/for a/security /0331_Frank.html (accessed 30 January 2004).

General Administration of Customs. Various years. *China's Customs Statistics.* Beijing: General Administration of Customs.

Goodkind, Daniel, and Loraine West. 2001. The North Korean Famine and Its Demographic Impact. *Population and Development Review* 27, no. 2 (June).

Hirshleifer, Jack. 1987. *Economic Behavior in Adversity.* Chicago: University of Chicago Press.

International Monetary Fund (IMF). 1962. *International Financial Statistics.* Washington, D.C.: IMF. http://ifs.apdi.net/imf/about.asp.

————. 2003. *World Economic Outlook database.* Washington, D.C.: IMF.

Japan External Trade Organization (JETRO). Various years. Statistics database. Tokyo: JETRO.

Kim So-young. 2004. WFP Warns of N. K. Food Crisis. *Korea Herald,* 11 February.

Kimura, Mitsuhiko. 1994. A Planned Economy without Planning: Su-ryong's North Korea. Discussion paper no. F-081. Tezukayama University, Faculty of Economics. March.

Korea Trade-Investment Promotion Agency (KOTRA). Various years. Statistics database. Seoul: KOTRA.

Korean Peninsula Energy Development Organization (KEDO). Various years. Statistics database. Seoul: KEDO.

Lee, Hy-sang. 1988. North Korea's Closed Economy: The Hidden Opening. *Asian Survey* 28, no. 12 (December): 1264–79.

Leibenstein, Harvey. 1966. Allocative Efficiency versus X-Efficiency. *American Economic Review* 56, no. 3 (June).

Lem, Samuel. 2003. Seoul Court Convicts 6 over Summit Funds. *International Herald Tribune,* 27 September.

Manyin, Mark. 2004. Unpublished estimates. February.

McDonald, Joe. 2004. WFP Makes Emergency Food Appeal for North Korea, Saying Supplies Nearly Exhausted. Associated Press, 9 February.

Merrill, John. 1991. North Korea's Halting Efforts at Economic Reform. In *North Korea in Transition,* ed. Lee Chong-sik and Yoo Se-hee. Berkeley, Calif.: Institute of East Asian Studies.

Ministry of Unification (MOU). Various years. Statistics database. Seoul: MOU.

Newcomb, William J. 2003. Economic Development in North Korea: Reflections on North Korea's Economic Reform. *Korea's Economy 2003.* Washington, D.C.: Korea Economic Institute.

Noland, Marcus. 2000. The Meaning in the Meeting of the Two Koreas: Out of Isolation. *Washington Post,* 12 June.

———. 2002. West-Bound Train Leaving the Station: Pyongyang on the Reform Track. Washington, D.C.: Institute for International Economics. October. www.iie.com/publications/papers/noland1002.htm.

———. 2004. *Korea After Kim Jong-il.* Washington, D.C.: Institute for International Economics. January.

Oh, Kongdan. 1990. North Korea's Response to the World: Is the Door Ajar? Paper no. P-7616. Santa Monica, Calif.: RAND.

Polsby, Nelson W., ed. 1982. *What If? Explorations in Social-Science Fiction.* Lexington, Mass.: Lewis.

Population Division (United Nations). 2003. World Population Prospects: The 2002 Revision database. New York: United Nations. http://esa.un.org/unpp.

Scalapino, Robert. 1992. *The Last Leninists: The Uncertain Future of Asia's Communist States.* Washington: Center for Strategic and International Studies.

United Nations Commodity Trade Statistics Database (UN Comtrade). 2004. http://unstats.un.org/unsd/comtrade/.

United Nations Office for the Coordination of Humanitarian Affairs (UN). 2002. *Consolidated Inter-Agency Appeal for Democratic People's Republic of Korea 2003.* Geneva: UN Office for the Coordination of Humanitarian Affairs. November. www.reliefweb.int/appeals/2003/files/dprk03.pdf.

Ward, Andrew. 2003. Six Convicted for Korea Payments. *Financial Times,* 27 September.

World Bank. 2002. *World Development Indicators 2002.* Washington, D.C.: World Bank. www.worldbank.org/data/wdi2002/.

———. 2003. *World Development Indicators 2003.* Washington, D.C.: World Bank. www.worldbank.org/data/wdi2003/.

Nicholas Eberstadt holds the Henry Wendt Chair in Political Economy at the American Enterprise Institute in Washington D.C. The author wishes to thank Heather Dresser and Jay Philip Nash for their research assistance with this paper.

Table 3: Per Capita Exports: DPRK Rank in World, 1980

Rank	Country	Exports ($)	Population	Per capita exports ($)
1	United Arab Emirates	23,086,758,915	1,043,000	22,134.96
2	Kuwait	22,438,280,854	1,375,000	16,318.75
3	Luxembourg	4,983,707,216	364,900	13,657.73
4	Saudi Arabia	110,748,188,896	9,372,000	11,816.92
5	Bahrain	3,813,478,376	334,000	11,417.60
6	Libya	23,522,973,568	3,043,000	7,730.19
7	Belgium	70,139,684,426	9,847,000	7,122.95
8	Norway	27,431,630,370	4,091,000	6,705.36
9	Netherlands	90,860,667,073	14,150,000	6,421.25
10	Switzerland	37,344,809,039	6,319,000	5,909.92
11	Iceland	1,176,682,100	228,000	5,160.89
12	Hong Kong, China	25,603,687,962	5,039,000	5,081.10
13	Sweden	37,739,960,268	8,310,000	4,541.51
14	Bahamas, The	939,800,000	210,000	4,475.24
15	Denmark	22,046,713,753	5,123,000	4,303.48
16	Gabon	2,769,522,007	692,000	4,002.20
17	Austria	28,597,132,359	7,553,000	3,786.20
18	Finland	16,872,584,518	4,780,000	3,529.83
19	Oman	3,748,118,124	1,101,000	3,404.29
20	Canada	74,998,056,819	24,593,000	3,049.57
21	Germany	238,163,774,930	78,303,000	3,041.57
22	Puerto Rico	9,402,099,712	3,206,000	2,932.66
23	Trinidad and Tobago	3,145,833,262	1,082,000	2,907.42
24	Malta	1,032,426,445	364,000	2,836.34
25	Ireland	9,639,236,042	3,401,000	2,834.24
26	France	139,022,229,514	53,880,000	2,580.22
27	United Kingdom	145,237,570,626	56,330,000	2,578.33
28	Israel	9,535,564,912	3,878,000	2,458.89
29	Barbados	603,440,519	249,100	2,422.48
30	New Zealand	6,746,600,888	3,113,000	2,167.23
31	Australia	25,737,712,747	14,692,000	1,751.82
32	Suriname	612,885,166	355,000	1,726.44
33	Italy	96,902,633,790	56,434,000	1,717.10
34	Cyprus	974,787,576	611,000	1,595.40
35	Seychelles	100,141,584	64,400	1,554.99
36	Venezuela, RB	19,965,055,658	15,091,000	1,322.98

Rank	Country	Exports ($)	Population	Per capita exports ($)
37	Japan	144,733,545,970	116,782,000	1,239.35
38	United States	279,700,010,000	227,225,000	1,230.94
39	Antigua and Barbuda	74,077,776	61,000	1,214.39
40	Greece	11,526,621,528	9,643,000	1,195.34
41	Malaysia	14,135,948,738	13,763,000	1,027.10
42	South Africa	28,266,759,113	27,576,000	1,025.05
43	Panama	1,933,445,000	1,950,000	991.51
44	Fiji	575,275,520	634,000	907.37
45	Spain	32,740,267,959	37,386,000	875.74
46	Hungary	8,664,422,324	10,707,000	809.23
47	Bulgaria	7,155,711,533	8,862,000	807.46
48	Algeria	14,540,716,612	18,669,170	778.86
49	St. Lucia	89,329,628	115,500	773.42
50	Portugal	7,235,626,562	9,766,000	740.90
51	Belize	107,850,000	146,000	738.70
52	Swaziland	412,961,844	565,000	730.91
53	Jordan	1,579,256,524	2,181,000	724.10
54	St. Kitts and Nevis	32,111,111	44,400	723.22
55	Guyana	490,319,974	761,000	644.31
56	Jamaica	1,368,290,417	2,133,000	641.49
57	Botswana	562,918,168	906,000	621.32
58	Congo, Rep.	1,023,764,785	1,669,000	613.40
59	Chile	6,291,974,407	11,147,000	564.45
60	Costa Rica	1,279,264,964	2,284,000	560.10
61	Mauritius	539,499,795	966,000	558.49
62	Tunisia	3,517,965,181	6,384,000	551.06
63	Korea, Rep.	20,369,193,589	38,124,000	534.29
64	Uruguay	1,523,186,751	2,914,000	522.71
65	Grenada	39,592,592	90,100	439.43
66	Cote d'Ivoire	3,561,287,269	8,194,000	434.62
67	Ecuador	2,951,880,049	7,961,000	370.79
68	Papua New Guinea	1,100,238,663	3,086,000	356.53
69	Solomon Islands	81,585,924	229,000	356.27
70	St. Vincent and the Grenadines	33,137,036	97,800	338.82
71	Vanuatu	37,603,233	115,060	326.81
72	Iran, Islamic Rep.	12,338,107,754	39,124,000	315.36
73	Mexico	20,806,478,261	67,570,000	307.92

Rank	Country	Exports ($)	Population	Per capita exports ($)
74	Zambia	1,607,525,450	5,738,000	280.15
75	Syrian Arab Republic	2,433,274,526	8,704,000	279.56
76	Peru	4,627,898,971	17,324,000	267.14
77	El Salvador	1,220,920,013	4,586,000	266.23
78	Nigeria	18,859,387,259	71,148,000	265.07
79	Honduras	930,000,000	3,567,000	260.72
80	Guatemala	1,748,000,000	6,820,000	256.30
81	Togo	580,217,688	2,519,000	230.34
82	Paraguay	700,999,973	3,114,000	225.11
83	Dominican Republic	1,271,000,064	5,695,000	223.18
84	Zimbabwe	1,560,677,337	7,133,000	218.80
85	Cameroon	1,898,232,186	8,724,000	217.59
86	Colombia	5,414,551,747	28,447,000	190.34
87	Indonesia	26,664,131,299	148,303,000	179.79
88	Nicaragua	519,538,168	2,921,000	177.86
89	Dominica	13,000,000	73,350	177.23
90	Brazil	21,276,141,968	121,616,000	174.95
91	Egypt, Arab Rep.	6,991,666,667	40,875,000	171.05
92	Morocco	3,272,621,044	19,382,000	168.85
93	Mauritania	261,091,421	1,551,000	168.34
94	Thailand	7,801,035,704	46,718,000	166.98
95	Tonga	15,665,473	94,000	166.65
96	Gambia, The	103,028,762	641,000	160.73
97	Philippines	7,661,066,650	48,035,000	159.49
98	Senegal	803,194,592	5,538,000	145.03
99	Argentina	3,895,791,461	28,094,000	138.67
100	Bolivia	682,225,017	5,355,000	127.40
101	Kenya	2,030,403,493	16,632,000	122.08
102	Sao Tome and Principe	10,472,768	89,000	117.67
103	Kiribati	6,551,960	58,100	112.77
104	Niger	616,720,072	5,617,000	109.80
105	Sri Lanka	1,296,327,544	14,603,000	88.77
106	Congo, Dem. Rep.	2,371,496,686	26,908,000	88.13
107	Central African Republic	201,028,393	2,313,000	86.91
108	**DPRK**	**1,414,100,000**	**17,113,626**	**82.63**
109	Turkey	3,660,084,493	44,484,000	82.28
110	Sierra Leone	251,666,984	3,236,000	77.77

Rank	Country	Exports ($)	Population	Per capita exports ($)
111	Lesotho	90,648,365	1,362,000	66.56
112	Benin	222,240,333	3,459,000	64.25
113	Madagascar	539,320,046	8,873,000	60.78
114	Haiti	316,099,994	5,353,000	59.05
115	Malawi	307,474,449	6,183,000	49.73
116	Maldives	7,748,344	158,000	49.04
117	Sudan	805,990,470	19,316,000	41.73
118	Mali	262,685,839	6,590,000	39.86
119	Chad	175,041,754	4,477,000	39.10
120	Bhutan	18,491,906	487,880	37.90
121	Pakistan	2,958,199,994	82,730,330	35.76
122	Ghana	376,348,534	10,740,000	35.04
123	Rwanda	167,923,309	5,163,000	32.52
124	Comoros	10,744,088	335,000	32.07
125	Mozambique	383,020,297	12,095,000	31.67
126	Somalia	200,271,012	6,487,000	30.87
127	Burkina Faso	172,600,568	6,962,000	24.79
128	Burundi	81,022,222	4,130,000	19.62
129	Uganda	242,000,000	12,806,900	18.90
130	Guinea-Bissau	14,039,310	763,000	18.40
131	India	11,249,000,000	687,332,000	16.37
132	Nepal	224,583,339	14,559,000	15.43
133	China	14,327,813,120	981,235,000	14.60
134	Bangladesh	995,270,012	85,438,000	11.65

Sources: World Bank (2003), Census (various years), KOTRA (various years), MOU (various years).

Table 4:   Imports as a Percentage of Exports: DPRK Rank in World, 1980

Rank	Country	Imports ($)	Exports ($)	Imports as percentage of exports (%)
1	Kuwait	9,822,528,552	22,438,280,854	43.78
2	United Arab Emirates	10,215,784,647	23,086,758,915	44.25
3	Libya	11,166,994,610	23,522,973,568	47.47
4	Gabon	1,353,525,793	2,769,522,007	48.87
5	Indonesia	15,766,759,183	26,664,131,299	59.13
6	Oman	2,252,461,204	3,748,118,124	60.10
7	Nigeria	12,324,265,032	18,859,387,259	65.35

Rank	Country	Imports ($)	Exports ($)	Imports as percentage of exports (%)
8	Venezuela, RB	15,142,691,030	19,965,055,658	75.85
9	South Africa	21,837,885,033	28,266,759,113	77.26
10	Trinidad and Tobago	2,430,708,170	3,145,833,262	77.27
11	Norway	23,512,999,569	27,431,630,370	85.71
12	Bulgaria	6,149,883,708	7,155,711,533	85.94
13	Peru	4,011,768,816	4,627,898,971	86.69
14	Algeria	12,846,905,537	14,540,716,612	88.35
15	Bahamas, The	839,600,000	939,800,000	89.34
16	Bolivia	619,875,016	682,225,017	90.86
17	United Kingdom	133,510,736,437	145,237,570,626	91.93
18	Bahrain	3,540,992,306	3,813,478,376	92.85
19	Canada	70,276,949,446	74,998,056,819	93.71
20	Panama	1,842,077,000	1,933,445,000	95.27
21	Malaysia	13,533,271,865	14,135,948,738	95.74
22	Colombia	5,203,045,668	5,414,551,747	96.09
23	Cameroon	1,846,947,983	1,898,232,186	97.30
24	El Salvador	1,188,160,000	1,220,920,013	97.32
25	Congo, Dem. Rep.	2,353,282,237	2,371,496,686	99.23
26	Jamaica	1,367,560,680	1,368,290,417	99.95
27	Congo, Rep.	1,025,658,016	1,023,764,785	100.18
28	Iceland	1,181,205,176	1,176,682,100	100.38
29	Ecuador	2,981,079,941	2,951,880,049	100.99
30	Hong Kong, China	25,872,975,881	25,603,687,962	101.05
31	Barbados	619,897,552	603,440,519	102.73
32	Germany	244,911,978,998	238,163,774,930	102.83
33	Netherlands	93,678,880,027	90,860,667,073	103.10
34	Finland	17,428,091,434	16,872,584,518	103.29
35	China	14,819,450,880	14,327,813,120	103.43
36	Denmark	22,821,562,039	22,046,713,753	103.51
37	New Zealand	7,006,760,042	6,746,600,888	103.86
38	United States	293,799,990,000	279,700,010,000	105.04
39	Sweden	39,801,394,239	37,739,960,268	105.46
40	Hungary	9,142,874,288	8,664,422,324	105.52
41	Luxembourg	5,270,926,204	4,983,707,216	105.76
42	Belgium	74,236,898,364	70,139,684,426	105.84
43	Austria	30,296,804,870	28,597,132,359	105.94
44	Malta	1,094,383,596	1,032,426,445	106.00

Rank	Country	Imports ($)	Exports ($)	Imports as percentage of exports (%)
45	Japan	154,520,933,154	144,733,545,970	106.76
46	Suriname	661,064,438	612,885,166	107.86
47	Ghana	406,950,200	376,348,534	108.13
48	Switzerland	40,930,755,780	37,344,809,039	109.60
49	Zambia	1,763,714,043	1,607,525,450	109.72
50	Fiji	634,761,567	575,275,520	110.34
51	Togo	640,321,806	580,217,688	110.36
52	Puerto Rico	10,477,200,384	9,402,099,712	111.43
53	France	155,661,864,184	139,022,229,514	111.97
54	Guatemala	1,963,299,968	1,748,000,000	112.32
55	Australia	29,069,359,837	25,737,712,747	112.94
56	Tunisia	3,986,911,964	3,517,965,181	113.33
57	Zimbabwe	1,771,437,620	1,560,677,337	113.50
58	Italy	110,003,154,342	96,902,633,790	113.52
59	Guyana	564,839,987	490,319,974	115.20
60	Spain	37,942,881,948	32,740,267,959	115.89
61	Seychelles	116,615,430	100,141,584	116.45
62	Greece	13,560,731,209	11,526,621,528	117.65
63	Cote d'Ivoire	4,189,777,567	3,561,287,269	117.65
64	Chile	7,438,435,984	6,291,974,407	118.22
65	Philippines	9,253,067,162	7,661,066,650	120.78
66	Mexico	25,215,695,652	20,806,478,261	121.19
67	**DPRK**	**1,714,400,000**	**1,414,100,000**	**121.24**
68	Honduras	1,130,499,968	930,000,000	121.56
69	Mauritius	664,753,314	539,499,795	123.22
70	Iran, Islamic Rep.	15,214,810,024	12,338,107,754	123.32
71	Papua New Guinea	1,358,592,035	1,100,238,663	123.48
72	Belize	133,550,000	107,850,000	123.83
73	Korea, Rep.	25,245,953,457	20,369,193,589	123.94
74	Brazil	26,571,483,281	21,276,141,968	124.89
75	Botswana	704,709,213	562,918,168	125.19
76	Thailand	9,825,161,457	7,801,035,704	125.95
77	Vanuatu	47,384,760	37,603,233	126.01
78	Argentina	4,989,979,960	3,895,791,461	128.09
79	Antigua and Barbuda	95,399,998	74,077,776	128.78
80	Ireland	12,575,575,299	9,639,236,042	130.46
81	Uganda	324,000,000	242,000,000	133.88

Rank	Country	Imports ($)	Exports ($)	Imports as percentage of exports (%)
82	Israel	12,923,936,759	9,535,564,912	135.53
83	Swaziland	563,807,476	412,961,844	136.53
84	Uruguay	2,090,439,475	1,523,186,751	137.24
85	Costa Rica	1,778,891,549	1,279,264,964	139.06
86	Cyprus	1,358,356,997	974,787,576	139.35
87	Kenya	2,837,389,828	2,030,403,493	139.75
88	Egypt, Arab Rep.	9,821,666,667	6,991,666,667	140.48
89	St. Lucia	125,699,998	89,329,628	140.71
90	Haiti	445,899,981	316,099,994	141.06
91	Solomon Islands	116,052,061	81,585,924	142.25
92	St. Kitts and Nevis	46,629,629	32,111,111	145.21
93	Portugal	10,763,334,908	7,235,626,562	148.75
94	Gambia, The	153,323,678	103,028,762	148.82
95	Dominican Republic	1,919,000,064	1,271,000,064	150.98
96	Niger	956,555,076	616,720,072	155.10
97	Malawi	480,236,424	307,474,449	156.19
98	India	17,821,000,000	11,249,000,000	158.42
99	Morocco	5,246,862,775	3,272,621,044	160.33
100	Senegal	1,301,502,531	803,194,592	162.04
101	Nepal	364,500,011	224,583,339	162.30
102	Central African Republic	327,434,489	201,028,393	162.88
103	Sierra Leone	420,651,553	251,666,984	167.15
104	Grenada	66,370,369	39,592,592	167.63
105	Sri Lanka	2,204,857,719	1,296,327,544	170.08
106	Chad	298,183,918	175,041,754	170.35
107	Nicaragua	927,803,482	519,538,168	178.58
108	Mauritania	472,621,700	261,091,421	181.02
109	Rwanda	306,872,038	167,923,309	182.75
110	Paraguay	1,314,277,799	700,999,973	187.49
111	St. Vincent and the Grenadines	63,407,406	33,137,036	191.35
112	Pakistan	5,709,197,408	2,958,199,994	193.00
113	Syrian Arab Republic	4,719,467,795	2,433,274,526	193.96
114	Mali	520,165,266	262,685,839	198.02
115	Jordan	3,335,403,206	1,579,256,524	211.20
116	Sudan	1,763,104,152	805,990,470	218.75
117	Madagascar	1,202,017,238	539,320,046	222.88

Rank	Country	Imports ($)	Exports ($)	Imports as percentage of exports (%)
118	Tonga	35,288,259	15,665,473	225.26
119	Turkey	8,456,573,464	3,660,084,493	231.05
120	Benin	524,418,843	222,240,333	235.97
121	Mozambique	964,768,398	383,020,297	251.88
122	Burundi	214,223,333	81,022,222	264.40
123	Somalia	534,102,359	200,271,012	266.69
124	Bhutan	51,138,894	18,491,906	276.55
125	Maldives	24,569,536	7,748,344	317.09
126	Bangladesh	3,239,432,452	995,270,012	325.48
127	Burkina Faso	563,715,097	172,600,568	326.60
128	Guinea-Bissau	46,299,639	14,039,310	329.79
129	Dominica	54,703,703	13,000,000	420.80
130	Kiribati	30,807,885	6,551,960	470.21
131	Lesotho	475,069,333	90,648,365	524.08
132	Comoros	64,152,139	10,744,088	597.09

Sources: World Bank (2003), KOTRA (various years), MOU (various years).

Table 5: Per Capita Exports: DPRK Rank in World, 1990

Rank	Country	Exports ($)	Population	Per capita exports ($)
1	Luxembourg	12,362,136,670	381,900	32,370.09
2	Singapore	67,490,758,621	3,047,000	22,149.90
3	Hong Kong, China	100,410,145,323	5,704,500	17,601.92
4	Belgium	139,596,575,589	9,967,400	14,005.31
5	Switzerland	82,819,232,945	6,712,000	12,338.98
6	United Arab Emirates	22,331,244,892	1,844,000	12,110.22
7	Norway	46,927,176,773	4,241,500	11,063.82
8	Netherlands	158,975,438,651	14,952,000	10,632.39
9	Bahrain	4,887,765,957	503,000	9,717.23
10	Denmark	47,781,564,820	5,140,000	9,296.02
11	Macao, China	3,149,631,083	370,000	8,512.52
12	Iceland	2,143,598,136	254,800	8,412.87
13	Sweden	71,220,806,469	8,559,000	8,321.16
14	Austria	63,966,260,393	7,725,700	8,279.67
15	Ireland	26,950,944,656	3,505,800	7,687.53
16	Finland	31,123,797,001	4,986,000	6,242.24

Rank	Country	Exports ($)	Population	Per capita exports ($)
17	Germany	486,021,890,239	79,433,000	6,118.64
18	Malta	1,971,051,066	360,000	5,475.14
19	Antigua and Barbuda	348,311,111	64,000	5,442.36
20	Canada	149,504,411,733	27,791,000	5,379.60
21	France	258,329,212,002	56,735,000	4,553.26
22	Cyprus	2,880,087,467	681,000	4,229.20
23	United Kingdom	237,735,108,715	57,561,000	4,130.14
24	Israel	18,209,998,320	4,660,000	3,907.72
25	Kuwait	8,281,250,000	2,125,000	3,897.06
26	Italy	217,652,624,643	56,719,000	3,837.38
27	New Zealand	11,785,565,352	3,436,200	3,429.83
28	Oman	5,555,266,580	1,627,000	3,414.42
29	Seychelles	230,302,235	70,000	3,290.03
30	Barbados	839,904,487	258,000	3,255.44
31	Saudi Arabia	48,365,821,095	15,803,000	3,060.55
32	Australia	51,722,133,363	17,065,100	3,030.87
33	Gabon	2,740,354,950	935,000	2,930.86
34	New Caledonia	467,609,332	168,000	2,783.39
35	Libya	11,468,375,887	4,311,000	2,660.26
36	Japan	316,750,515,393	123,537,000	2,564.01
37	Portugal	23,539,775,916	9,896,000	2,378.72
38	United States	557,199,980,000	249,440,000	2,233.80
39	Latvia	5,958,000,133	2,670,700	2,230.88
40	St. Lucia	288,200,000	134,100	2,149.14
41	Spain	83,046,178,502	38,836,000	2,138.38
42	St. Kitts and Nevis	82,385,184	42,030	1,960.15
43	Trinidad and Tobago	2,299,011,765	1,215,000	1,892.19
44	Malaysia	32,816,369,096	18,201,900	1,802.91
45	Korea, Rep.	73,499,499,833	42,869,000	1,714.51
46	Botswana	2,086,912,120	1,276,000	1,635.51
47	Belarus	16,178,861,342	10,189,000	1,587.88
48	Czech Republic	15,768,953,042	10,363,000	1,521.66
49	Greece	15,180,855,017	10,161,000	1,494.03
50	Mauritius	1,529,369,515	1,057,000	1,446.90
51	Belize	257,000,000	189,300	1,357.63
52	Dominica	90,718,517	72,260	1,255.45
53	St. Vincent and the Grenadines	130,462,961	107,050	1,218.71

Rank	Country	Exports ($)	Population	Per capita exports ($)
54	Fiji	878,519,819	736,000	1,193.64
55	Moldova	5,166,666,421	4,362,000	1,184.47
56	Grenada	93,796,295	93,600	1,002.10
57	Hungary	10,294,971,788	10,365,000	993.24
58	Venezuela, RB	19,168,442,360	19,502,000	982.90
59	Jamaica	2,207,161,086	2,390,000	923.50
60	Georgia	4,861,788,618	5,460,100	890.42
61	Namibia	1,220,196,875	1,375,000	887.42
62	Swaziland	660,240,637	770,000	857.46
63	Panama	2,041,586,000	2,398,000	851.37
64	Chile	10,498,261,922	13,099,000	801.46
65	Bulgaria	6,864,383,353	8,718,000	787.38
66	Jordan	2,489,182,055	3,170,000	785.23
67	Slovak Republic	4,110,733,756	5,283,000	778.11
68	South Africa	27,326,969,896	35,200,000	776.33
69	Russian Federation	105,168,547,055	148,292,000	709.20
70	Uruguay	2,185,374,032	3,106,000	703.60
71	Congo, Rep.	1,502,218,435	2,230,000	673.64
72	Tunisia	5,353,409,091	8,154,400	656.51
73	Costa Rica	1,976,163,480	3,049,000	648.13
74	Macedonia, FYR	1,157,243,816	1,903,000	608.12
75	Mexico	48,866,100,761	83,226,000	587.15
76	Algeria	14,545,657,513	25,022,000	581.31
77	Thailand	29,129,804,006	55,595,000	523.96
78	Iran, Islamic Rep.	26,476,358,408	54,400,000	486.70
79	Ukraine	25,245,902,628	51,892,000	486.51
80	Vanuatu	70,912,344	147,300	481.41
81	Argentina	14,643,450,361	32,527,000	450.19
82	Poland	16,895,684,389	38,118,800	443.24
83	Paraguay	1,750,341,449	4,150,000	421.77
84	Angola	3,992,499,897	9,570,000	417.19
85	Armenia	1,443,442,651	3,545,000	407.18
86	Tonga	35,927,637	96,000	374.25
87	Turkey	20,014,163,427	56,154,000	356.42
88	Ecuador	3,499,031,587	10,264,000	340.90
89	Guyana	248,474,060	731,000	339.91
90	Dominican Republic	2,392,771,130	7,061,000	338.87

Rank	Country	Exports ($)	Population	Per capita exports ($)
91	Papua New Guinea	1,308,586,387	3,980,000	328.79
92	Solomon Islands	98,821,575	319,000	309.79
93	Cote d'Ivoire	3,421,251,745	11,800,000	289.94
94	Syrian Arab Republic	3,488,165,260	12,116,000	287.90
95	Morocco	6,829,988,741	24,043,000	284.07
96	Romania	6,406,250,166	23,207,000	276.05
97	Brazil	38,129,059,013	147,957,000	257.70
98	Maldives	52,627,722	213,000	247.08
99	Colombia	8,282,579,458	34,970,000	236.85
100	Mauritania	465,365,250	1,992,000	233.62
101	Honduras	1,108,317,121	4,870,000	227.58
102	Tajikistan	1,206,321,472	5,303,000	227.48
103	Suriname	89,270,302	402,000	222.07
104	Gambia, The	189,845,237	928,000	204.57
105	Philippines	12,198,148,639	61,040,000	199.84
106	Senegal	1,449,717,182	7,327,000	197.86
107	Zimbabwe	2,008,581,937	10,241,000	196.13
108	Cameroon	2,250,713,650	11,614,000	193.79
109	Peru	4,144,927,491	21,569,000	192.17
110	Guatemala	1,608,631,758	8,749,000	183.86
111	El Salvador	892,094,818	5,112,000	174.51
112	Bolivia	1,108,688,320	6,573,000	168.67
113	Egypt, Arab Rep.	8,646,612,831	52,442,000	164.88
114	Indonesia	28,982,530,241	178,232,000	162.61
115	Togo	545,099,635	3,453,000	157.86
116	Kyrgyz Republic	697,564,375	4,423,000	157.71
117	Zambia	1,179,864,265	7,784,000	151.58
118	Guinea	869,736,444	5,755,000	151.13
119	Sri Lanka	2,345,830,231	16,267,000	144.21
120	Lebanon	511,008,107	3,635,000	140.58
121	Bhutan	80,434,166	600,110	134.03
122	Nigeria	12,365,872,842	96,203,000	128.54
123	Cape Verde	43,051,774	341,400	126.10
124	Equatorial Guinea	42,485,125	352,000	120.70
125	**DPRK**	**1,939,000,000**	**20,018,546**	**96.86**
126	Albania	312,500,000	3,277,000	95.36
127	Kenya	2,205,890,747	23,354,000	94.45

Rank	Country	Exports ($)	Population	Per capita exports ($)
128	Comoros	35,635,055	432,000	82.49
129	Haiti	502,200,000	6,473,000	77.58
130	Central African Republic	219,621,201	2,945,000	74.57
131	Congo, Dem. Rep.	2,757,935,431	36,999,000	74.54
132	Sao Tome and Principe	8,336,908	115,000	72.49
133	Nicaragua	251,842,527	3,824,000	65.86
134	Ghana	993,434,057	15,138,000	65.63
135	Lesotho	103,431,308	1,682,000	61.49
136	Yemen, Rep.	689,312,977	11,876,000	58.04
137	Pakistan	6,216,942,715	107,975,060	57.58
138	Benin	263,655,960	4,710,000	55.98
139	China	62,171,591,024	1,135,185,000	54.77
140	Malawi	447,289,731	8,507,000	52.58
141	Mali	415,218,793	8,460,000	49.08
142	Niger	372,432,639	7,707,000	48.32
143	Kiribati	3,309,634	72,340	45.75
144	Madagascar	511,579,180	11,632,000	43.98
145	Chad	234,368,328	5,746,000	40.79
146	Burkina Faso	352,011,283	8,880,000	39.64
147	Marshall Islands	1,700,000	46,200	36.80
148	Sierra Leone	145,827,714	3,999,000	36.47
149	Vietnam	2,332,325,609	66,200,000	35.23
150	India	23,028,000,000	849,515,000	27.11
151	Guinea-Bissau	24,240,000	946,000	25.62
152	Lao PDR	97,939,606	4,132,000	23.70
153	Tanzania	537,502,051	25,470,000	21.10
154	Nepal	381,890,606	18,142,000	21.05
155	Rwanda	145,102,122	6,943,000	20.90
156	Uganda	311,673,602	16,330,000	19.09
157	Bangladesh	1,881,679,563	110,025,000	17.10
158	Burundi	89,130,244	5,456,000	16.34
159	Mozambique	201,346,835	14,151,000	14.23
160	Somalia	89,748,796	7,163,000	12.53
161	Ethiopia	534,884,615	51,180,000	10.45
162	Cambodia	68,528,864	9,145,000	7.49

Sources: World Bank (2003), Census (various years), KOTRA (various years), MOU (various years).

Table 6: Imports as a Percentage of Exports: DPRK Rank in World, 1990

Rank	Country	Imports ($)	Exports ($)	Imports as percentage of exports (%)
1	Argentina	6,546,483,926	14,643,450,361	44.71
2	Venezuela, RB	9,808,102,070	19,168,442,360	51.17
3	Angola	2,147,299,976	3,992,499,897	53.78
4	Oman	3,224,967,490	5,555,266,580	58.05
5	United Arab Emirates	13,780,986,107	22,331,244,892	61.71
6	Trinidad and Tobago	1,448,894,118	2,299,011,765	63.02
7	Nigeria	8,202,785,667	12,365,872,842	66.33
8	Gabon	1,836,820,145	2,740,354,950	67.03
9	Macao, China	2,190,763,357	3,149,631,083	69.56
10	Colombia	5,969,031,672	8,282,579,458	72.07
11	Poland	12,684,210,551	16,895,684,389	75.07
12	South Africa	20,885,728,639	27,326,969,896	76.43
13	Uruguay	1,680,566,177	2,185,374,032	76.90
14	Saudi Arabia	37,834,445,928	48,365,821,095	78.23
15	Libya	8,995,656,320	11,468,375,887	78.44
16	China	50,799,130,824	62,171,591,024	81.71
17	Bahrain	4,001,595,745	4,887,765,957	81.87
18	Ecuador	2,924,891,013	3,499,031,587	83.59
19	Norway	39,356,096,125	46,927,176,773	83.87
20	Brazil	32,371,450,313	38,129,059,013	84.90
21	Congo, Rep.	1,281,844,092	1,502,218,435	85.33
22	Cote d'Ivoire	2,926,981,562	3,421,251,745	85.55
23	Cameroon	1,930,732,109	2,250,713,650	85.78
24	Denmark	41,016,985,847	47,781,564,820	85.84
25	Peru	3,637,681,120	4,144,927,491	87.76
26	Panama	1,796,386,000	2,041,586,000	87.99
27	Germany	430,333,743,238	486,021,890,239	88.54
28	Botswana	1,887,395,861	2,086,912,120	90.44
29	Chile	9,506,460,861	10,498,261,922	90.55
30	Japan	287,928,594,368	316,750,515,393	90.90
31	Hungary	9,431,620,225	10,294,971,788	91.61
32	Netherlands	148,876,183,275	158,975,438,651	93.65
33	Hong Kong, China	94,081,126,006	100,410,145,323	93.70
34	Indonesia	27,157,275,972	28,982,530,241	93.70

Rank	Country	Imports ($)	Exports ($)	Imports as percentage of exports (%)
35	Czech Republic	14,849,886,545	15,768,953,042	94.17
36	Belarus	15,365,853,234	16,178,861,342	94.97
37	Iceland	2,058,188,437	2,143,598,136	96.02
38	Singapore	64,953,655,172	67,490,758,621	96.24
39	Belize	248,100,000	257,000,000	96.54
40	Austria	62,156,580,823	63,966,260,393	97.17
41	Suriname	86,783,149	89,270,302	97.21
42	Luxembourg	12,027,760,483	12,362,136,670	97.30
43	Belgium	135,883,431,979	139,596,575,589	97.34
44	Antigua and Barbuda	340,559,259	348,311,111	97.77
45	Sweden	69,968,357,890	71,220,806,469	98.24
46	Switzerland	81,642,980,856	82,819,232,945	98.58
47	Syrian Arab Republic	3,440,367,093	3,488,165,260	98.63
48	Russian Federation	103,910,115,893	105,168,547,055	98.80
49	Swaziland	653,126,308	660,240,637	98.92
50	Congo, Dem. Rep.	2,729,963,637	2,757,935,431	98.99
51	New Zealand	11,674,600,272	11,785,565,352	99.06
52	Guinea	863,677,673	869,736,444	99.30
53	Zimbabwe	2,002,043,318	2,008,581,937	99.67
54	Canada	149,145,293,651	149,504,411,733	99.76
55	Italy	217,202,682,246	217,652,624,643	99.79
56	Australia	52,259,971,258	51,722,133,363	101.04
57	Zambia	1,203,064,249	1,179,864,265	101.97
58	Latvia	6,122,000,137	5,958,000,133	102.75
59	Fiji	911,607,806	878,519,819	103.77
60	Ukraine	26,229,509,224	25,245,902,628	103.90
61	Korea, Rep.	76,438,756,422	73,499,499,833	104.00
62	France	270,139,456,047	258,329,212,002	104.57
63	Moldova	5,416,666,409	5,166,666,421	104.84
64	Bolivia	1,164,632,090	1,108,688,320	105.05
65	Barbados	884,751,134	839,904,487	105.34
66	Sierra Leone	154,411,646	145,827,714	105.89
67	Mexico	51,767,986,205	48,866,100,761	105.94
68	Algeria	15,472,203,617	14,545,657,513	106.37
69	Seychelles	246,004,235	230,302,235	106.82
70	Finland	33,412,208,899	31,123,797,001	107.35

Rank	Country	Imports ($)	Exports ($)	Imports as percentage of exports (%)
71	Jamaica	2,382,299,679	2,207,161,086	107.94
72	Honduras	1,212,718,817	1,108,317,121	109.42
73	United Kingdom	263,251,055,090	237,735,108,715	110.73
74	Cyprus	3,193,654,425	2,880,087,467	110.89
75	Bulgaria	7,612,328,364	6,864,383,353	110.90
76	Mauritius	1,701,147,705	1,529,369,515	111.23
77	United States	628,600,010,000	557,199,980,000	112.81
78	Haiti	572,400,000	502,200,000	113.98
79	Bhutan	91,916,600	80,434,166	114.28
80	Georgia	5,560,975,610	4,861,788,618	114.38
81	St. Lucia	334,300,000	288,200,000	116.00
82	Malta	2,287,287,707	1,971,051,066	116.04
83	Tunisia	6,219,545,455	5,353,409,091	116.18
84	St. Vincent and the Grenadines	152,266,664	130,462,961	116.71
85	Guatemala	1,900,441,482	1,608,631,758	118.14
86	Paraguay	2,079,153,438	1,750,341,449	118.79
87	Senegal	1,728,127,525	1,449,717,182	119.20
88	Gambia, The	226,861,601	189,845,237	119.50
89	Costa Rica	2,362,835,903	1,976,163,480	119.57
90	Portugal	28,197,186,863	23,539,775,916	119.79
91	Papua New Guinea	1,576,649,215	1,308,586,387	120.48
92	Kenya	2,660,886,776	2,205,890,747	120.63
93	Philippines	14,755,062,729	12,198,148,639	120.96
94	Spain	100,715,749,504	83,046,178,502	121.28
95	Thailand	35,546,453,591	29,129,804,006	122.03
96	Morocco	8,373,834,299	6,829,988,741	122.60
97	Vietnam	2,930,215,427	2,332,325,609	125.63
98	Tajikistan	1,526,559,578	1,206,321,472	126.55
99	Guyana	316,442,091	248,474,060	127.35
100	Dominican Republic	3,090,575,007	2,392,771,130	129.16
101	Namibia	1,584,382,842	1,220,196,875	129.85
102	Sri Lanka	3,053,778,996	2,345,830,231	130.18
103	Turkey	26,464,002,132	20,014,163,427	132.23
104	Armenia	1,910,655,775	1,443,442,651	132.37
105	Mauritania	619,220,700	465,365,250	133.06

Rank	Country	Imports ($)	Exports ($)	Imports as percentage of exports (%)
106	Slovak Republic	5,503,258,837	4,110,733,756	133.88
107	Togo	738,254,023	545,099,635	135.43
108	India	31,485,000,000	23,028,000,000	136.72
109	Yemen, Rep.	969,083,969	689,312,977	140.59
110	Niger	544,691,917	372,432,639	146.25
111	Dominica	133,948,146	90,718,517	147.65
112	Grenada	138,799,998	93,796,295	147.98
113	Jordan	3,727,972,374	2,489,182,055	149.77
114	Pakistan	9,350,911,782	6,216,942,715	150.41
115	**DPRK**	**2,945,405,700**	**1,938,861,818**	**151.91**
116	Ghana	1,521,547,091	993,434,057	153.16
117	Greece	23,434,020,455	15,180,855,017	154.37
118	Solomon Islands	153,748,814	98,821,575	155.58
119	Albania	487,500,000	312,500,000	156.00
120	Romania	10,026,785,816	6,406,250,166	156.52
121	Ethiopia	850,961,538	534,884,615	159.09
122	St. Kitts and Nevis	132,366,664	82,385,184	160.67
123	Egypt, Arab Rep.	14,109,376,402	8,646,612,831	163.18
124	Vanuatu	117,153,596	70,912,344	165.21
125	El Salvador	1,501,185,724	892,094,818	168.28
126	Madagascar	863,630,752	511,579,180	168.82
127	Benin	485,775,428	263,655,960	184.25
128	Nicaragua	467,806,345	251,842,527	185.75
129	Central African Republic	410,926,843	219,621,201	187.11
130	New Caledonia	877,982,022	467,609,332	187.76
131	Tonga	68,866,821	35,927,637	191.68
132	Mali	816,604,472	415,218,793	196.67
133	Nepal	765,387,791	381,890,606	200.42
134	Burkina Faso	708,687,157	352,011,283	201.33
135	Chad	485,190,844	234,368,328	207.02
136	Cambodia	142,458,102	68,528,864	207.88
137	Lao PDR	211,967,256	97,939,606	216.43
138	Equatorial Guinea	91,957,080	42,485,125	216.45
139	Bangladesh	4,108,870,845	1,881,679,563	218.36
140	Rwanda	363,608,848	145,102,122	250.59
141	Comoros	92,878,131	35,635,055	260.64

Rank	Country	Imports ($)	Exports ($)	Imports as percentage of exports (%)
142	Maldives	137,709,373	52,627,722	261.67
143	Uganda	833,722,349	311,673,602	267.50
144	Tanzania	1,595,095,769	537,502,051	296.76
145	Cape Verde	148,025,383	43,051,774	343.83
146	Burundi	314,442,790	89,130,244	352.79
147	Guinea-Bissau	90,350,000	24,240,000	372.73
148	Somalia	346,105,365	89,748,796	385.64
149	Mozambique	888,444,767	201,346,835	441.25
150	Sao Tome and Principe	41,706,779	8,336,908	500.27
151	Lesotho	753,435,684	103,431,308	728.44
152	Marshall Islands	56,000,000	1,700,000	3294.12

Sources: World Bank (2003), KOTRA (various years), MOU (various years).

Table 7: Per Capita Exports: DPRK Rank in World, 2000

Rank	Country	Exports ($)	Population	Per capita exports ($)
1	Luxembourg	29,383,610,297	438,000	67,085.87
2	Singapore	165,812,183,176	4,018,000	41,267.34
3	Hong Kong, China	244,032,761,716	6,665,000	36,614.07
4	Ireland	90,440,955,002	3,794,000	23,837.89
5	Belgium	197,417,360,036	10,252,000	19,256.47
6	Norway	75,393,539,513	4,491,000	16,787.70
7	Netherlands	248,430,008,817	15,919,000	15,605.88
8	Switzerland	110,987,818,287	7,180,000	15,457.91
9	Macao, China	5,819,733,612	438,000	13,287.06
10	Denmark	70,193,357,431	5,340,000	13,144.82
11	Sweden	108,061,847,252	8,869,000	12,184.22
12	Puerto Rico	45,921,200,000	3,815,900	12,034.17
13	Austria	94,610,102,626	8,110,240	11,665.51
14	Kuwait	21,300,733,496	1,984,400	10,734.09
15	Canada	325,049,996,297	30,769,700	10,563.96
16	Iceland	2,947,200,970	280,000	10,525.72
17	Bahrain	6,546,184,739	648,322	10,097.11
18	Finland	51,884,049,305	5,172,000	10,031.72
19	Malta	3,668,190,128	390,000	9,405.62

Rank	Country	Exports ($)	Population	Per capita exports ($)
20	Germany	629,509,287,351	82,210,000	7,657.33
21	Israel	44,146,861,894	6,233,210	7,082.52
22	United Kingdom	401,819,685,180	58,720,000	6,842.98
23	Antigua and Barbuda	448,444,444	68,000	6,594.77
24	France	372,625,407,568	58,893,000	6,327.16
25	Seychelles	458,889,006	81,230	5,649.26
26	Slovenia	10,718,818,509	1,989,000	5,389.05
27	Italy	304,345,757,927	57,690,000	5,275.54
28	Barbados	1,317,058,562	267,000	4,932.80
29	New Zealand	18,656,619,793	3,830,800	4,870.16
30	Malaysia	112,369,211,936	23,270,000	4,828.93
31	Australia	88,780,498,637	19,182,000	4,628.32
32	Korea, Rep.	206,719,689,467	47,008,000	4,397.54
33	Spain	168,203,263,126	40,499,790	4,153.19
34	Japan	512,742,009,270	126,870,000	4,041.48
35	Saudi Arabia	82,368,491,322	20,723,150	3,974.71
36	United States	1,103,100,000,000	282,224,000	3,908.60
37	Trinidad and Tobago	4,841,800,000	1,301,000	3,721.60
38	Estonia	4,819,015,370	1,369,500	3,518.81
39	Czech Republic	35,799,429,904	10,273,300	3,484.71
40	Portugal	33,814,509,108	10,008,000	3,378.75
41	St. Kitts and Nevis	142,333,331	44,000	3,234.85
42	Hungary	28,541,126,231	10,122,000	2,819.71
43	Greece	27,966,531,264	10,560,000	2,648.35
44	Slovak Republic	14,171,825,785	5,401,000	2,623.93
45	St. Lucia	376,435,407	155,300	2,423.92
46	Grenada	235,840,737	99,000	2,382.23
47	Mauritius	2,801,433,106	1,187,000	2,360.10
48	Libya	12,139,647,153	5,290,000	2,294.83
49	Maldives	562,786,724	274,000	2,053.97
50	Dominica	147,240,738	72,000	2,045.01
51	Costa Rica	7,649,024,543	3,810,000	2,007.62
52	Croatia	8,565,394,318	4,380,000	1,955.57
53	Belize	448,250,000	240,000	1,867.71
54	Botswana	3,119,408,836	1,675,000	1,862.33
55	Mexico	180,189,466,559	97,966,000	1,839.31
56	St. Vincent and the Grenadines	178,148,145	115,000	1,549.11

Rank	Country	Exports ($)	Population	Per capita exports ($)
57	Gabon	1,825,332,148	1,230,000	1,484.01
58	Chile	22,468,158,814	15,211,300	1,477.07
59	Lithuania	5,109,125,000	3,506,000	1,457.25
60	Suriname	606,294,896	417,000	1,453.94
61	Venezuela, RB	34,497,624,860	24,170,000	1,427.29
62	Fiji	1,131,571,616	811,900	1,393.73
63	Latvia	3,273,206,271	2,372,000	1,379.94
64	Thailand	80,940,752,405	60,728,000	1,332.84
65	Jamaica	3,422,936,231	2,573,000	1,330.33
66	Uruguay	4,142,365,700	3,337,000	1,241.34
67	Poland	46,245,444,506	38,648,000	1,196.58
68	Panama	3,390,582,000	2,854,000	1,188.01
69	Namibia	1,633,106,146	1,757,000	929.49
70	Guyana	684,547,498	761,000	899.54
71	Tunisia	8,565,842,270	9,563,500	895.68
72	Belarus	8,782,787,255	10,005,000	877.84
73	Bulgaria	7,022,427,995	8,125,000	864.30
74	Congo, Rep.	2,585,746,791	3,018,000	856.77
75	Macedonia, FYR	1,732,960,081	2,026,000	855.36
76	South Africa	36,572,077,414	42,800,990	854.47
77	Swaziland	889,298,475	1,045,000	851.00
78	Argentina	30,936,900,000	37,032,000	835.41
79	French Polynesia	192,401,162	235,000	818.73
80	Russian Federation	115,540,000,000	145,555,000	793.79
81	Algeria	22,715,918,150	30,385,000	747.60
82	Turkey	50,119,000,000	67,420,000	743.38
83	Jordan	3,535,966,192	4,886,810	723.57
84	Kazakhstan	10,760,236,403	15,059,170	714.53
85	Dominican Republic	5,447,142,405	8,373,000	650.56
86	Angola	8,176,127,384	13,134,000	622.52
87	Palau	11,500,000	19,100	602.09
88	El Salvador	3,588,849,229	6,276,000	571.84
89	Romania	12,607,872,935	22,435,000	561.97
90	Philippines	42,076,416,556	76,626,500	549.11
91	Turkmenistan	2,649,500,000	5,285,000	501.32
92	Lebanon	2,140,930,000	4,328,000	494.67
93	Ecuador	5,774,044,126	12,646,000	456.59

Rank	Country	Exports ($)	Population	Per capita exports ($)
94	Samoa	77,149,509	172,000	448.54
95	Syrian Arab Republic	6,845,000,000	16,189,000	422.82
96	Iran, Islamic Rep.	25,243,916,656	63,663,942	396.52
97	Ukraine	19,522,000,384	49,501,000	394.38
98	Colombia	16,571,137,670	42,299,300	391.76
99	Djibouti	246,514,073	632,000	390.05
100	Honduras	2,496,900,000	6,417,000	389.11
101	Brazil	64,160,048,783	170,100,000	377.19
102	Morocco	10,409,377,694	28,705,000	362.63
103	Sri Lanka	6,474,569,483	18,467,000	350.60
104	Guatemala	3,881,472,709	11,385,300	340.92
105	Peru	8,546,053,460	25,939,000	329.47
106	Indonesia	64,474,628,630	206,265,000	312.58
107	Paraguay	1,621,650,049	5,270,000	307.71
108	Cape Verde	130,517,532	434,810	300.17
109	Bosnia and Herzegovina	1,192,000,036	3,977,000	299.72
110	Mongolia	634,796,363	2,398,000	264.72
111	Cote d'Ivoire	4,214,208,377	16,013,000	263.17
112	Azerbaijan	2,118,121,102	8,049,000	263.15
113	Egypt, Arab Rep.	16,174,959,636	63,976,000	252.83
114	Yugoslavia, Fed. Rep.	2,547,084,219	10,637,000	239.46
115	Yemen, Rep.	4,008,397,414	17,507,160	228.96
116	Albania	708,864,277	3,134,000	226.19
117	China	279,561,121,426	1,262,460,000	221.44
118	Vietnam	17,144,000,000	78,522,700	218.33
119	West Bank and Gaza	603,791,679	2,966,000	203.57
120	Cameroon	2,721,361,288	14,876,000	182.94
121	Bhutan	144,200,000	805,000	179.13
122	Bolivia	1,483,613,599	8,328,700	178.13
123	Nigeria	21,499,464,094	126,910,000	169.41
124	Zimbabwe	2,118,004,768	12,627,000	167.74
125	Gambia, The	201,830,095	1,303,000	154.90
126	Moldova	644,430,000	4,278,000	150.64
127	Armenia	446,834,956	3,112,000	143.58
128	Mauritania	377,613,520	2,665,000	141.69
129	Cambodia	1,697,302,624	12,021,230	141.19
130	Senegal	1,338,800,000	9,530,000	140.48

Rank	Country	Exports ($)	Population	Per capita exports ($)
131	Uzbekistan	3,383,400,000	24,746,000	136.73
132	Georgia	703,050,125	5,262,000	133.61
133	Tajikistan	819,000,000	6,193,000	132.25
134	Ghana	2,448,369,037	19,306,000	126.82
135	Kyrgyz Republic	573,184,841	4,915,000	116.62
136	Sao Tome and Principe	16,499,586	148,000	111.48
137	Lesotho	226,049,911	2,035,000	111.08
138	Guinea	734,564,329	7,415,000	99.06
139	Kenya	2,743,864,209	30,092,000	91.18
140	Togo	397,904,436	4,527,000	87.90
141	Madagascar	1,187,439,970	15,523,000	76.50
142	Pakistan	9,930,289,575	138,080,000	71.92
143	Zambia	681,818,182	10,089,000	67.58
144	Haiti	501,946,403	7,959,000	63.07
145	India	63,764,000,000	1,015,923,000	62.76
146	Sudan	1,927,504,667	31,095,000	61.99
147	Mali	628,846,316	10,840,000	58.01
148	Guinea-Bissau	68,442,934	1,199,000	57.08
149	Nepal	1,275,956,679	23,043,000	55.37
150	Comoros	30,679,636	558,000	54.98
151	Benin	333,603,366	6,272,000	53.19
152	Bangladesh	6,611,000,000	131,050,000	50.45
153	Malawi	450,840,100	10,311,000	43.72
154	Tanzania	1,329,795,016	33,696,000	39.46
155	Timor-Leste	25,000,000	737,000	33.92
156	Central African Republic	125,250,709	3,717,000	33.70
157	Chad	233,152,617	7,694,000	30.30
158	**DPRK**	**653,100,000**	**21,647,682**	**30.17**
159	Niger	320,655,075	10,832,000	29.60
160	Uganda	656,000,000	22,210,000	29.54
161	Mozambique	469,194,516	17,691,000	26.52
162	Eritrea	97,489,583	4,097,000	23.80
163	Sierra Leone	110,005,233	5,031,000	21.87
164	Burkina Faso	236,804,405	11,274,000	21.00
165	Rwanda	149,602,258	7,709,000	19.41
166	Congo, Dem. Rep.	963,872,464	50,948,000	18.92
167	Ethiopia	984,250,978	64,298,000	15.31

Rank	Country	Exports ($)	Population	Per capita exports ($)
168	Burundi	62,164,375	6,807,000	9.13

Sources: World Bank (2003), Census (various years), KOTRA (various years), MOU (various years).

Table 8: Imports as a Percentage of Exports: DPRK Rank in World, 2000

Rank	Country	Imports ($)	Exports ($)	Imports as a percentage of exports (%)
1	Libya	5,278,960,692	12,139,647,153	43.49
2	Algeria	11,371,246,346	22,715,918,150	50.06
3	Kuwait	11,370,823,146	21,300,733,496	53.38
4	Iran, Islamic Rep.	13,543,278,076	25,243,916,656	53.65
5	Russian Federation	62,466,000,000	115,540,000,000	54.06
6	Congo, Rep.	1,404,252,928	2,585,746,791	54.31
7	Saudi Arabia	46,987,983,979	82,368,491,322	57.05
8	Venezuela, RB	19,786,888,935	34,497,624,860	57.36
9	Botswana	1,936,345,996	3,119,408,836	62.07
10	Macao, China	3,642,719,197	5,819,733,612	62.59
11	Norway	49,253,100,064	75,393,539,513	65.33
12	Angola	5,724,733,748	8,176,127,384	70.02
13	Ecuador	4,190,657,594	5,774,044,126	72.58
14	Indonesia	48,331,284,154	64,474,628,630	74.96
15	Trinidad and Tobago	3,720,700,000	4,841,800,000	76.85
16	Bahrain	5,056,783,425	6,546,184,739	77.25
17	Finland	40,570,257,444	51,884,049,305	78.19
18	Nigeria	16,884,470,535	21,499,464,094	78.53
19	Syrian Arab Republic	5,391,000,000	6,845,000,000	78.76
20	Yemen, Rep.	3,294,044,411	4,008,397,414	82.18
21	Cote d'Ivoire	3,504,699,647	4,214,208,377	83.16
22	Kazakhstan	9,026,834,588	10,760,236,403	83.89
23	Malaysia	94,349,738,026	112,369,211,936	83.96
24	Ireland	76,915,352,022	90,440,955,002	85.04
25	Denmark	60,795,031,963	70,193,357,431	86.61
26	Japan	444,858,512,233	512,742,009,270	86.76
27	Thailand	70,424,673,375	80,940,752,405	87.01
28	Cameroon	2,376,025,524	2,721,361,288	87.31
29	Uzbekistan	2,961,900,000	3,383,400,000	87.54
30	Turkmenistan	2,336,700,000	2,649,500,000	88.19

Rank	Country	Imports ($)	Exports ($)	Imports as a percentage of exports (%)
31	Canada	288,190,773,747	325,049,996,297	88.66
32	Sweden	95,829,800,993	108,061,847,252	88.68
33	Philippines	37,492,737,483	42,076,416,556	89.11
34	China	250,687,631,994	279,561,121,426	89.67
35	Switzerland	99,548,039,693	110,987,818,287	89.69
36	South Africa	32,842,158,958	36,572,077,414	89.80
37	Singapore	149,173,377,851	165,812,183,176	89.97
38	Fiji	1,034,910,891	1,131,571,616	91.46
39	Zimbabwe	1,956,004,404	2,118,004,768	92.35
40	Netherlands	230,436,041,610	248,430,008,817	92.76
41	Ukraine	18,115,999,552	19,522,000,384	92.80
42	Korea, Rep.	192,619,279,196	206,719,689,467	93.18
43	Congo, Dem. Rep.	905,602,899	963,872,464	93.95
44	Gabon	1,717,521,111	1,825,332,148	94.09
45	Costa Rica	7,283,154,647	7,649,024,543	95.22
46	France	355,593,002,033	372,625,407,568	95.43
47	New Zealand	17,812,969,953	18,656,619,793	95.48
48	Azerbaijan	2,023,533,388	2,118,121,102	95.53
49	Belgium	190,013,653,940	197,417,360,036	96.25
50	Italy	293,859,587,378	304,345,757,927	96.55
51	Chile	21,718,172,820	22,468,158,814	96.66
52	Hong Kong, China	236,267,557,864	244,032,761,716	96.82
53	Sudan	1,870,332,918	1,927,504,667	97.03
54	Colombia	16,300,873,731	16,571,137,670	98.37
55	Germany	622,166,351,422	629,509,287,351	98.83
56	Australia	88,370,602,480	88,780,498,637	99.54
57	Austria	96,414,597,001	94,610,102,626	101.91
58	Mauritius	2,888,333,584	2,801,433,106	103.10
59	Slovak Republic	14,651,895,297	14,171,825,785	103.39
60	Estonia	5,029,191,449	4,819,015,370	104.36
61	Vietnam	17,911,678,193	17,144,000,000	104.48
62	Belarus	9,187,280,919	8,782,787,255	104.61
63	Uruguay	4,337,141,256	4,142,365,700	104.70
64	Czech Republic	37,517,491,578	35,799,429,904	104.80
65	Tajikistan	861,000,000	819,000,000	105.13
66	Seychelles	484,966,222	458,889,006	105.68
67	Argentina	32,738,200,000	30,936,900,000	105.82

Rank	Country	Imports ($)	Exports ($)	Imports as a percentage of exports (%)
68	Slovenia	11,363,086,253	10,718,818,509	106.01
69	United Kingdom	426,397,114,094	401,819,685,180	106.12
70	Mexico	191,497,667,308	180,189,466,559	106.28
71	Hungary	30,415,206,606	28,541,126,231	106.57
72	Spain	180,790,325,419	168,203,263,126	107.48
73	Tunisia	9,256,584,227	8,565,842,270	108.06
74	Bulgaria	7,697,244,590	7,022,427,995	109.61
75	Pakistan	10,912,027,027	9,930,289,575	109.89
76	Barbados	1,456,272,000	1,317,058,562	110.57
77	Malta	4,059,186,472	3,668,190,128	110.66
78	Peru	9,546,638,260	8,546,053,460	111.71
79	Croatia	9,635,041,611	8,565,394,318	112.49
80	Kyrgyz Republic	651,739,255	573,184,841	113.70
81	St. Vincent and the Grenadines	202,592,589	178,148,145	113.72
82	Lithuania	5,832,800,000	5,109,125,000	114.16
83	Antigua and Barbuda	512,962,963	448,444,444	114.39
84	Panama	3,888,600,000	3,390,582,000	114.69
85	Brazil	73,737,994,101	64,160,048,783	114.93
86	Romania	14,767,398,048	12,607,872,935	117.13
87	Suriname	715,546,314	606,294,896	118.02
88	Cambodia	2,005,311,368	1,697,302,624	118.15
89	India	75,656,000,000	63,764,000,000	118.65
90	Morocco	12,458,901,299	10,409,377,694	119.69
91	Iceland	3,544,280,555	2,947,200,970	120.26
92	Central African Republic	154,469,227	125,250,709	123.33
93	Poland	57,138,620,468	46,245,444,506	123.56
94	Madagascar	1,470,853,343	1,187,439,970	123.87
95	Turkey	62,193,000,000	50,119,000,000	124.09
96	Dominica	182,718,515	147,240,738	124.10
97	Swaziland	1,103,622,159	889,298,475	124.10
98	Namibia	2,033,044,012	1,633,106,146	124.49
99	Mongolia	793,927,822	634,796,363	125.07
100	Jamaica	4,328,128,147	3,422,936,231	126.44
101	Sri Lanka	8,234,452,462	6,474,569,483	127.18
102	Macedonia, FYR	2,237,937,022	1,732,960,081	129.14
103	Senegal	1,734,200,000	1,338,800,000	129.53

Rank	Country	Imports ($)	Exports ($)	Imports as a percentage of exports (%)
104	St. Lucia	489,091,259	376,435,407	129.93
105	Gambia, The	262,253,459	201,830,095	129.94
106	Puerto Rico	59,836,200,000	45,921,200,000	130.30
107	Greece	36,862,780,668	27,966,531,264	131.81
108	Honduras	3,312,700,000	2,496,900,000	132.67
109	United States	1,466,900,000,000	1,103,100,000,000	132.98
110	Dominican Republic	7,317,525,140	5,447,142,405	134.34
111	Belize	604,050,000	448,250,000	134.76
112	Mauritania	509,863,010	377,613,520	135.02
113	Portugal	45,922,291,393	33,814,509,108	135.81
114	Bangladesh	9,060,000,000	6,611,000,000	137.04
115	Kenya	3,770,497,558	2,743,864,209	137.42
116	Nepal	1,776,967,509	1,275,956,679	139.27
117	Egypt, Arab Rep.	22,779,979,451	16,174,959,636	140.83
118	Djibouti	347,224,752	246,514,073	140.85
119	Ghana	3,463,756,586	2,448,369,037	141.47
120	Niger	455,490,323	320,655,075	142.05
121	Mali	917,142,335	628,846,316	145.85
122	Zambia	1,017,616,047	681,818,182	149.25
123	Bolivia	2,235,014,010	1,483,613,599	150.65
124	Moldova	971,180,000	644,430,000	150.70
125	Togo	602,545,015	397,904,436	151.43
126	El Salvador	5,575,713,878	3,588,849,229	155.36
127	Yugoslavia, Fed. Rep.	4,003,829,661	2,547,084,219	157.19
128	Tanzania	2,096,692,141	1,329,795,016	157.67
129	Paraguay	2,623,634,441	1,621,650,049	161.79
130	Jordan	5,796,191,890	3,535,966,192	163.92
131	Georgia	1,212,806,558	703,050,125	172.51
132	Guinea-Bissau	125,481,053	68,442,934	183.34
133	Benin	627,397,224	333,603,366	188.07
134	Sierra Leone	212,271,973	110,005,233	192.97
135	Chad	450,855,361	233,152,617	193.37
136	Comoros	60,254,722	30,679,636	196.40
137	Ethiopia	1,960,696,479	984,250,978	199.21
138	Bhutan	291,500,000	144,200,000	202.15
139	St. Kitts and Nevis	295,333,328	142,333,331	207.49
140	Bosnia and Herzegovina	2,542,999,912	1,192,000,036	213.34

Rank	Country	Imports ($)	Exports ($)	Imports as a percentage of exports (%)
141	Albania	1,515,580,821	708,864,277	213.80
142	Uganda	1,413,600,000	656,000,000	215.49
143	Armenia	966,174,535	446,834,956	216.23
144	Sao Tome and Principe	38,382,244	16,499,586	232.63
145	Samoa	193,254,369	77,149,509	250.49
146	Burundi	162,210,166	62,164,375	260.94
147	Haiti	1,321,141,442	501,946,403	263.20
148	Cape Verde	344,211,362	130,517,532	263.73
149	Burkina Faso	657,602,742	236,804,405	277.70
150	**DPRK**	**1,847,800,000**	**653,100,000**	**282.93**
151	Rwanda	441,108,545	149,602,258	294.85
152	Mozambique	1,526,308,504	469,194,516	325.30
153	Lesotho	762,704,061	226,049,911	337.41
154	French Polynesia	952,020,780	192,401,162	494.81
155	West Bank and Gaza	3,085,316,244	603,791,679	510.99
156	Eritrea	498,593,750	97,489,583	511.43
157	Timor-Leste	160,000,000	25,000,000	640.00
158	Palau	127,100,000	11,500,000	1105.22

Sources: World Bank (2003), KOTRA (various years), MOU (various years).

Preconditions and Rationale
for International Economic Support
for North Korea

5

Managing Collateral Catastrophe: Rationale and Preconditions for International Economic Support for North Korea

Moon Chung-in

No country in recent history has been as notoriously branded as North Korea (the Democratic People's Republic of Korea, or DPRK), which has been portrayed as a failed rogue state and a member of an axis of evil playing a dangerous game of proliferating weapons of mass destruction (WMD), violating basic human rights, and starving its own people while pursuing a megalomaniac goal of a strong and prosperous nation (*kangsung daeguk*). North Korea has also even been called an amoral state that not only engages in habitual cheating and blackmail, but also defies international norms and ethics by committing illegal acts such as exporting drugs and counterfeiting currencies. On the basis of this characterization, North Korea does not deserve sympathy or support from the international community, and its early demise through isolation and containment will be a blessing for peninsular, regional, and global peace and stability.

This paper argues that the monolithic and linear interpretations and prescriptions of the North Korean quagmire are misleading and even dangerous. I make this argument not because I believe in an idealistic constructivist view that emphasizes the self-determination of nation-states, the cultural context of national identity, and its intersubjective understanding (Cumings 2004, Bleiker forthcoming), but because a sudden collapse of North Korea and the subsequent negative spillover can bring a collateral catastrophe to South Korea and the Northeast Asian region. Widespread political unrest, an increasing potential for conflict escalation, economic devastation, social instability, and immense human suffering—all of which are likely to be immediate outcomes of a sudden collapse—can jeopardize peace and prosperity on the Korean peninsula and in the Northeast Asian region. Thus, preventing a sudden collapse and avoiding collateral catastrophe seem to be the critical tasks that lie ahead. It is in this context that North Korea deserves international economic support.

To be sure, Pyongyang should be reminded that there is no free lunch. International economic support should be firmly tied to North Korea's corresponding cooperative behavior. Preconditions should include the proactive resolution of security concerns, including the North's nuclear weapons program, extensive structural and institutional realignments for economic opening and reform, political liberalization and improvement of human rights, and accumulation of credible external behavior. This paper aims at addressing these issues within the broad context of systemic changes in North Korea.

System Changes in North Korea and Contending Scenarios[1]

Before we get into a detailed discussion of contending scenarios, it seems essential to define the concept of system change. Although there has been a plethora of scholarly debates on the concept of system change in North Korea, no consensus has yet been reached on its nature. To capture the precise meaning of system change, we need to look into the different levels of change. Changes can take place on the policy, government, regime, and state sovereignty levels (Kim S. 1996; Choi 1996). Depending on the levels of change, we can delineate three basic scenarios on the future of North Korea (Scalapino 1992, 81–9):

- **Status quo** refers to the continuation of existing policy, government, institutions, and the ruling regime. With the status quo, no radical changes can be envisaged with regard to the *suryông* (leader) system, the governing ideology of *juche* (self-reliance), and one-party dominance.

- **System modification** denotes the survival of the current Kim Jong-il regime through incremental adaptation. Thus, modification assumes that the Kim Jong-il regime would endure current hardships through extensive modification of existing policies, institutions, government structure, and ideology.

- **System collapse** is here defined as the radical transformation of policy, institutions, government, and regime.[2] Collapse presupposes primarily the demise of the Kim Jong-il regime, the *suryông* system, and the socialist command economy. Because state sovereignty is presumably retained after the collapse scenario, this scenario also alludes to the possibility of the transfer of power from the Kim Jong-il regime to new

---

1   This section draws partly on Moon and Ryoo (1997) and Moon and Kim (2001).

2   It is assumed here that system collapse does not include the demise of DPRK as a sovereign state. It seems highly unlikely that the North Korean populace will give up sovereignty and go through the process of unification by absorption, as East Germany did. Thus, system collapse should not be automatically equated with the end of North Korea as a sovereign entity.

Figure 1: System Changes in North Korea and Contending Scenarios: An Overview

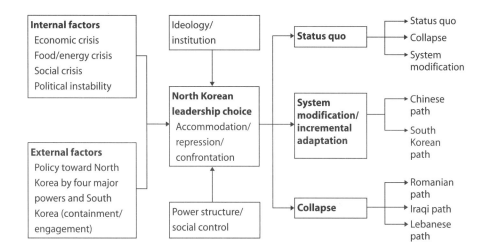

actors such as the military, collective leadership, or populist democratic forces, which may or may not retain elements of the old system.

As *Figure 1* demonstrates, the dynamics of system change in North Korea are by and large a function of leadership choice in the face of internal and external constraints (Moon 2003, 69–131). It is hypothesized that, while the strategic choice of accommodation could prolong system survival at least in the medium term, repression and confrontation could lead to a more immediate collapse or a deformity of the North Korean system. The leadership choice is, in turn, profoundly affected by ideological orientation, power structure, internal institutional arrangements, and the patterns of social control. Rigid adherence to the *juche* ideology and existing institutions, concentration of power in the hands of hard-liners such as the military, and the continuing pursuit of social control through coercion and intimidation could induce the North Korean leadership to choose confrontation and repression as the strategic guide of its governance, which would lead to short-term survival but then to a medium-term to long-term collapse. Meanwhile, ideological and institutional relaxation, decentralization of power, the ascension of soft-liners such as technocrats, and resilience in social control can facilitate the strategic choice of accommodation and system modification.

Ideological stance, institutional arrangements, and power structure serve merely as intervening variables in influencing leadership choice, however. The ultimate trigger variables are objective internal and external situational factors. Although food crises, starvation, economic hardship, and social deviation cannot directly cause system changes, they can serve as crucial variables in invoking leadership responses. In a similar vein, external variables can play an equally important role in affecting leadership choice. No matter how self-reliant North Korea is, its system is closely intertwined with external factors. Although the engagement policy of South Korea and the major regional actors could smooth the strategy of accommodation and incremental adaptation, a shift to policies of denial and containment could cause a reversal of this path by provoking North Korea's corresponding hostile behavior. External factors and impacts on domestic political dynamics in the North should be carefully gauged in forecasting North Korea's political changes.

Against this backdrop, let's examine each scenario by focusing on initial trigger variables; leadership choice; the underlying ideological, institutional, and power structures; and the nature of system changes in the North.

Status Quo and Its Limits

The status quo model asserts that North Korea is likely to continue functioning under the existing political, economic, and social patterns. Changes will be minimal, and the *juche* ideology will continue to serve as the guiding principle of the North Korean polity and economy. Recent gestures of an incremental open-door policy will not be fulfilled but are instead instrumental in alleviating North Korea's short-term economic hardship. As long as Kim Jong-il stays in power, any genuine changes, regardless of whether they are incremental or structural, are quite inconceivable because such changes can undermine the security of the Kim Jong-il regime. The North Korean leadership will not undertake reform measures that put regime survival at risk.

Many observers believe that the status quo will bring about a major system breakdown in the North. But proponents of the status quo criticize this expectation as an oversimplification of the complex North Korean reality. As a matter of fact, since Kim Jong-il's succession in 1994, there have been numerous predictions on the early demise of the Kim Jong-il regime, and outside actors have undertaken hard-line measures to hasten its collapse. These predictions turned out to be wrong (Cumings 2004). Kim's regime has shown its extraordinary reliance and durability by overcoming hard times in the mid-1990s; to date his regime has proved distinctly more capable of surviving than many outside observers had anticipated.

Several factors may account for regime survival even under a status quo policy. First, the *juche* ideology remains intact, serving as the unifying force of the elite and the masses in the North (Bae 2002, 523–603; Lee J. 2000; Lee O. 1996). Second, Kim Jong-il has firmly consolidated his power base, along with his leadership qualities. Since 1972, Kim has had extensive leadership experience. His commanding and charismatic style—revealed internationally during the North Korea–South Korea summit in June 2000—

underscores the fact that his leadership capability should not be underestimated. In addition, he has recently firmly consolidated power in the military and among technocrats. Third, internal cohesion of the ruling elite in the North is unusually high, and friction between hard-liners and soft-liners is more fictional than real. Since elites share a strong sense of common destiny, internal challenges to the Kim Jong-il regime are virtually unthinkable. Fourth, Kim Il-sung's charisma still serves as a valuable asset for regime maintenance. As long as Kim Il-sung is revered and systemic indoctrination in the *suryông* system is sustained, the Kim Jong-il regime is likely to remain intact. The effective working of *yuhun tongch'i* (governance by injunctions of the deceased Kim Il-sung) offers powerful evidence of this interpretation. Finally, North Korea is one of the most regimented societies in the world. Surveillance, intimidation, and social control by the state security apparatus are quite extensive, and punitive measures for any deviation are severe. The geographic compartmentalization of North Korea also makes it difficult for its people to engage in organized or spontaneous mass riots.[3]

External factors suggest a mixed reading of the future of the Kim Jong-il regime under a status quo scenario. None of the regional actors geographically closest to the DPRK favors a DPRK collapse, which could cause major disruptions on the Korean peninsula such as the creation of a unified Korea through absorption or the outbreak of large-scale conflicts.

Since the inauguration in the United States of President George W. Bush, however, the external environment has been changing rapidly. Although South Korea, China, and Russia still favor engagement with North Korea, the United States and Japan have taken a tougher policy stance. Unless North Korea fails to reach a negotiated settlement on the current nuclear standoff, pressures from the outside world will be intensified, taking the form of isolation and containment. Such a hostile external environment will severely undermine North Korea's efforts to maintain its status quo by not only impeding its access to international support but also worsening its domestic food and energy crises.

Ironically, outside pressures from the United States and Japan can contribute to sustaining the Kim regime, at least in the short run, by strengthening the position of the military and enhancing internal cohesion. People's collective memory of the Japanese colonial rule and the destruction wrought on them by the United States during the Korean War will further facilitate Kim Jong-il's staying power.

By taking into account these internal and external factors, the survival of the Kim Jong-il regime might be more than likely. Changes will be minimal, and the gestures of an open door and changes in regime structure will be

---

3 North Korea's policy of encouraging regional autarky (*jiyok charib jui*) seems to have resulted in an increasing closure of its society, because this policy has decreased exchanges of personnel and information among regions (Kim B. 1999, 116).

cosmetic, just to cope with the current economic, food, and energy crises. However, adherence to the status quo cannot assure regime survivability in the medium and long term. If the Kim Jong-il regime cannot effectively muddle through current hardships through incremental adaptation and system modification, it is most likely to encounter the challenges of a sudden collapse. The current economic and ecological crises North Korea is undergoing cannot be solved through cosmetic changes under the continuation of the existing system. These are structural problems, and remedies should be sought at the structural level.

Incremental Adaptation through System Modification

The system modification scenario posits that the continuation of the status quo cannot assure North Korea's long-term survivability. Proponents of system modification argue that in order to manage current difficulties, North Korea needs to modify its system in the direction of opening and reform but that such modification should be incremental so it will not precipitate a major system breakdown (Lee J. 2000, 575–95; Koh B. 1993a; 1993b).

In fact, opening and reform are already under way in the North, albeit at a pace that is slow and in a scope that is limited (Faiola 2003a; 2003b; 2004; Watt 2003; Ward 2004a; 2004b; Zhebin 1995, 230–1; Lee J. 2002; Park Y. 2001; Jeong 2003). The 1998 constitutional amendment that stipulated the introduction of such new concepts as price and profits in the public sector and partial private ownership of farmland exemplifies such efforts.[4] Beneath Pyongyang's repeated rhetoric championing its "own style of socialism," its technocrats are fully aware of the need to carry out opening and reform. More important, the 1 July 2002 administrative reform measures on prices, wages, incentives, and markets have begun to produce erratic but profound and far-reaching changes in the North Korean economy.

Several factors have facilitated the DPRK's willingness to foster moderate reforms through system modification. First is an increasing breakdown of the state-run economy of rations, which has caused enormous supply bottlenecks and a deterioration in people's lives. Second is the example of the dismal failure of the Soviet Union and other East European countries. And, finally, China's stellar performance under market socialism has possibly fostered deliberation on the part of the North Korean leadership about survival through incremental adaptation and system modification (Kim I. 1992, 30–31). In fact, Chairman Kim Jong-il highly praised the Chinese opening and reform during his visit to China in January 2001. Two alternative paths to opening and reform through system modification can be envisaged:

---

4   The full text of the 1998 amendment in Korean is at www.kcna.co.jp/item2/1998/9809/news09/05.htm#11; an abstract in English can be found at www.kcna.co.jp/item/1998/9809/news09/05.htm#24.

- **China's path.** The first alternative is the adoption of the Chinese model in which Kim Jong-il could follow Deng Xiaoping's path of an open-door policy and structural reforms (Chung H. 1999, 124; Yang 2001; McMillan 1997; Park Y. 2001). As China did, Kim can designate selected areas as special economic zones and actively seek foreign investment with preferential treatments. Depending on the success of an open-door policy, Kim can move on to the next step of structural reforms, starting with the agricultural sector and extending to reforms in the price and incentive system, industrial structure, and even patterns of ownership of means of production. Such gradual opening and reform might not instantly lead to political reforms, however; as in the case of China, the current political system would remain intact although there might be some relaxation of political control. In the process of opening and reform, the *juche* economic system would gradually be transformed into market socialism through various institutional and policy reforms, and North Korea could become much more pragmatic and resilient than it had been in managing its national economy as well as in dealing with the outside world.

- **South Korea's path.** The China model represents mainstream thinking on the economic future of North Korea, but there is a possibility of a more radical path. The developmental dictatorship model, which characterized the essence of political and economic governance under Park Chung-hee, may well attract the attention of North Korean leadership.[5] Park Chung-hee was responsible for the transformation of the South Korean economy from poverty and underdevelopment to one of the most dynamic economies in the world in less than two decades through the assertive pursuit of export-led growth and heavy industrialization. In his efforts to overcome North Korea's current economic backwardness and to realize the goal of *kangsung daeguk*, Kim Jong-il might learn something from the developmental dictatorship model. It can expedite the process of economic growth, industrialization, and increased exports without necessarily impairing his regime survival. To emulate the model, however, the North Korean leadership would have to radically reshape its economic template by introducing elements of capitalism, especially private ownership and the use of the market mechanism. Otherwise, the model is not viable because it is predicated on state orchestration of private agents, such as business conglomerates, in fostering growth and industrialization. The transition to a developmental dictatorship would help the North not only to overcome its

---

5 Kim Jong-il has shown a keen interest in learning about South Korea's experience of economic development during the Park Chung-hee period (1961–78); examples include the New Village Movement, the heavy chemical industrialization plan, and an export-led growth strategy (Kim Y. 2003; Mansourov 2003; and press reports in *Weekly Donga* (22 June 2000) and *Hangyerae 21* (6 July 2000).

current economic difficulties but also eventually to become a normal state in the international community.

Both the Chinese model and the developmental dictatorship model can bring about profound effects on economic and political transformation in North Korea. As conservative observers in South Korea and the United States have constantly cautioned, however, the North Korean leadership might not be genuinely interested in economic opening and structural reforms. The current gesture of opening and accommodation might be nothing but a tactical move to manage short-term economic difficulties by attracting foreign economic and humanitarian assistance. With its fear of negative boomerang effects on regime survival, the leadership of North Korea cannot embark on the daring reform measures that were undertaken by Deng and Park. When and if North Korea is able to cope with its current economic hardships, it will return to the old posture of the *juche* economy, delaying or avoiding opening and reform as well as sustaining status quo.

The North Korean leadership's pursuit of Deng's market socialism or Park's developmental dictatorship would definitely contribute to revitalizing its economy, however. Economic recovery resulting from these reforms would sustain the Kim Jong-il regime at least in the medium term, and the DPRK as a sovereign state would be preserved. Improved inter-Korean economic and social exchanges, followed by opening and reform, would produce considerable positive spin-off in the security arena, including tension reduction, confidence building, and arms control. Most important, such developments would be instrumental for forging a direct peace treaty between the two Koreas, ensuring peaceful coexistence on the Korean peninsula.

Inter-Korean economic exchanges and cooperation as well as peace building will be conducive to leveling off the North Korean economy. The North's economic normalization through the selective adoption of market principles and the expansion of the private economy will not only enlarge and activate its civil society, but also precipitate the advent of a new middle class. The expansion of civil society through the rise of a middle class is bound to precipitate political changes in the North. It may not necessarily mean the dismantling of the Kim Jong-il regime, but even if Kim stays in power, the mode of political governance during his reign will depart radically from the old version of totalitarianism, opening a new space for political pluralism.

Three Paths to System Collapse

The blind maintenance of the status quo or the failure to cope with the transitional instability arising from system modification could lead to a sequence of crisis, catastrophe, and implosion, which would bring the North Korean system to an end (Noland 2004; Eberstadt 1999; Pollack and Lee 1998; Downs 1999, chap. 10; Lee D. 1994; Kim G. 1996; Ryu 1997; Kim K.

1996, 22–5). Why crisis and catastrophe? The proponents of this scenario have identified several compelling causal factors.

The most critical factor is economic hardship. Political regimes cannot survive without sustaining economic performance. No matter how ideologically indoctrinated and socially controlled, protracted economic deformity is bound to facilitate the breakdown of a political system by shattering the foundation of its legitimacy and stability. The collapse model identifies North Korea as its classical example. While the structural rigidity of a command economy has skewed the allocation of scarce resources in favor of the defense and heavy industry sectors, the stagnation of the civilian economy, an acute food crisis resulting from continuing natural disasters and poor harvests, and chronic energy shortages have driven the North Korean economy to the brink of total collapse. There are no immediate remedies for the impending collapse. The model predicts that economic catastrophe is inseparably linked to political breakdown.[6]

According to the collapse scenario, Kim's maneuvers to consolidate his political power through various ideological campaigns would not produce satisfactory results. Kim Jong-il could minimize the political backlash of the economic crisis through symbolic and ideological manipulation, social control and intimidation, and projection of the power of leadership. The mass campaign to idolize Kim Jong-il in his father's image reflects this effort, but Kim Jong-il is not Kim Il-sung. The cultivation of new charisma is not easy. Proponents of *yuhun tongch'i* believe that few in the North can challenge Kim Jong-il's leadership position, which he has held since 1973, but his consolidation of power is not complete. Cracks in his leadership, coupled with the pervasive food and energy crises, threaten regime survival by eroding his political legitimacy. Kim's recent championing of the military through the idea of *sunkun jungchi* (military-first politics) cannot rescue his faltering political destiny (Lee D. 1994, 432–3; Koh S. 1995, 73–4; Kim G. 1996, 110).

Supporters of the status quo argue that the social domain also reveals symptoms of crisis and catastrophe. North Korea has traditionally been characterized as a society of purity and discipline. This image of a pristine society has become greatly tarnished. Corruption is known to be pervasive throughout North Korea, where bureaucratic corruption is particularly problematic (Kim S. 1994). In addition, crime, social deviation, demoralization, and even prostitution have become rampant. Defectors from the North have given lively testimonials of growing social decay in North Korea. Economic hardship could produce multiplier effects of social disintegration, resulting in severe social unrest.

According to proponents of the collapse scenario, the Kim Jong-il regime does not seem to have any way out. Reforms, whether systemic or limited,

---

6   In his recent study (Noland 2004, 49), Marcus Noland predicts that, if North Korea is subject to comprehensive economic sanctions, the probability of regime change reaches 50 percent annually.

cannot help the Kim regime avoid an impending collapse (Jung 1994, 249–69; Kim C. 1996, 623–36). Social control and political intimidation can ensure the regime's short-term survival, but in the medium term there is great danger of a sudden implosion in the form of either a military coup d'état or mass riots triggered by food shortages. Limited reforms, through which the Kim regime retains its totalitarian political system while it seeks an early Chinese-style incremental and selective economic opening, cannot secure the medium- to long-term survival of the regime either. Economic opening and increased exposure to the outside world following the reform will instantly trigger political and social instability. At present, collapse theory posits that systemic changes involving such drastic measures as market reforms, economic opening, privatization, and political restructuring are inconceivable because of not only structural contradictions and negative political boomerang effects but also the rather hostile external environment emanating from the current nuclear standoff.

A system collapse in North Korea could take one of three paths: the Romanian, the Iraqi, or the Lebanese:

Romanian path. The Romanian path refers to a collapse of the Kim Jong-il regime and the advent of a new regime, drawing from either the ruling coalition or popular democratic forces, amid severe social, economic, and political unrest (Noland 2000, 324–33). Most critical in this scenario are the initial conditions comprising economic and ecological failures in North Korea. Despite the mandates to cope with these failures through opening and reform, North Korea defies the mandates in fear of a negative political backlash on the stability of its regime and continues its self-reliant strategy, aggravating its economic conditions, seemingly beyond recovery. The acute shortages of food and energy further compound the economic hardship. The failure to satisfy basic human needs and improve living conditions widens and deepens the political and social grievances of the masses, resulting in sporadic riots and an overt defiance of the government. Consequently, domestic hardships increase and the number of economic refugees fleeing across the border into China rises, heightening the fear of neighboring countries.

Facing these internal difficulties, the North Korean leadership continues to repress domestic opposition through coercive measures while it projects a hard-line foreign policy that includes nuclear tests, test launches of long-range missiles, and military provocations meant to defuse domestic instability by invoking contrived external threats. But such moves backfire. Domestic opposition intensifies and unfavorable external environments unfold. North Korea's nuclear ambition and erratic policy behavior force the United States and Japan to intensify their hard-line policies of denial, isolation, and containment by terminating economic and humanitarian assistance, resorting to concerted economic sanctions and blockade, and heightening military preparedness. South Korea also abandons its engagement policy because of increasing domestic and international pressures. Its suspension of economic and social exchanges and cooperation further isolates North Korea. The firm positions of South Korea, Japan, and the United States cause the North to seek alternative sources of assistance such as China and Russia, which do not extend immediate help to North Korea either. Protracted internal political and economic problems prevent Russia from extending immediate relief to the North, and China hesitates to bail out the North not only because of its fatigue over Pyongyang's erratic policy behavior but also because it anticipates mounting pressure from the United States.

In the Romanian model, such internal and external developments narrow the margin of political survival of the North Korean leadership. Enduring social and economic hardship considerably weakens the domestic foundation of governability. The preceptoral power of *juche* as the governing ideology that has buttressed the Kim Jong-il regime would become increasingly questioned, leading to institutional disarray and dismal governance. Internal fragmentation among the leader, the state, the party, and the military becomes all the more pronounced, undercutting Kim's power base. Crisis of governance amid dismal economic performance as well as failure to control and contain social unrest amplifies popular uprising. The North Korean leadership attempts to suppress spiraling social instability through confrontation and intimidation. Such repressive measures could trigger intense debates within the ruling circle, dividing it into soft-liners and hard-liners. While the military and security apparatus might favor the continuation of the Kim regime through further repression and control, soft-liners comprising party cadres and technocrats could advocate a compromise with opposing forces. The elite fragmentation and polarization send signs of weakness of the Kim regime to the public, further fueling domestic crisis. The vicious cycle of repression and resistance without any controlling mechanism ultimately leads to a state of anarchy. As anarchy persists, North Korea becomes totally ungovernable, and high human casualties follow. Under this circumstance, a regime-preserving coup or a genuine revolution could take place, and the North Korean leadership could face the same destiny as Nicolae Ceausescu.

Iraqi path.   The Iraqi path refers to outbreak of a major war and collapse of the North Korean system through occupation, as happened to Iraq at the end of the Saddam Hussein regime. Two possibilities can be envisaged:

- North Korea's preemptive military provocation against the South through a limited war, combined with guerrilla warfare and missile attacks, counterattacks by South Korea and its allied forces, and the eventual occupation of the North by the allied forces; or
- Outbreak of a major war as a result of North Korea's brinkmanship diplomacy, involving WMD, missiles, a surgical strike by the United States and its allied forces on nuclear and missile facilities in the North,

North Korea's counterattack on the South, and allied forces' all-out invasion into the North.

In either case, the end game is likely to be a takeover of the North by South Korea and its allies, resulting in an outcome similar to Iraq.

Under the first possibility, the North Korean leadership might seek a military venture primarily in order to cope with domestic political instability. Internal conditions would deteriorate to the extent that it would cause severe domestic instability and military discontent, threatening the survival of the Kim Jong-il regime. Economic hardship, social disintegration, and political instability could induce the North Korean leadership to deliberate on a military venture as a way of defusing domestic turmoil while consolidating power and control. North Korea's military provocation could instantly trigger massive counterattacks by South Korea and its allies, including the United States and Japan. An all-out counterattack by the allied forces, backed by formidable firepower and abundant logistic support, would eventually destroy the Kim Jong-il regime and place North Korea under the joint occupation of South Korea and the United States. Consequently, the DPRK as an independent government, a socialist system, and a sovereign state would cease to exist, and unification could be achieved through the South's forceful takeover of North Korea.

Another plausible path is conflict escalation emanating from nuclear standoff. North Korea's refusal to undertake a complete, verifiable, and irreversible dismantling of its nuclear programs could derail the six-party talks.[7] And as part of its brinkmanship diplomacy, North Korea might cross critical redlines by exporting nuclear materials to third parties, nuclear testing, and test launching the Taepo-dong 2 missile. The United States and it allies could make concerted efforts to deny and contain the North through comprehensive economic sanctions, naval blockades, and seizure of North Korean vessels carrying nuclear materials and missiles for exports. The United States, as it contemplated in May 1994, could send an ultimatum to the North by signaling a move toward preemptive surgical strikes on suspected nuclear facilities and missile sites. North Korea might then disregard the warning and intensify its hard-line position by crossing redlines such as undertaking nuclear tests, transfer of nuclear materials to third parties, a test launch of the Taepo-dong 2, and premeditated military provocation along its southern border.

Disregarding popular opposition in South Korea and elsewhere, the United States could decide to stage surgical strikes in cooperation with its allies. Upon the surprise attack, the North could mount instant counterattacks on the Seoul metropolitan area and U.S. military assets in the South by launch-

---

7 Participants in the six-party talks are China, Japan, North Korea, Russia, South Korea, and the United States.

ing missiles deployed along the Demilitarized Zone. The North Korean attack could escalate into an all-out counterattack by the allied forces, ultimately defeating North Korean forces. The allied occupation of North Korea would terminate the Kim Jong-il regime as well as the government and sovereignty of the DPRK, paving the way to national unification under South Korean initiatives.

Lebanese path. The Lebanese path implies protracted civil strife, foreign intervention by invitation, and a de facto rule of North Korea under an external trusteeship. Protracted civil war and Syrian intervention in Lebanon exemplify this path, and it is also similar to the Romanian path in its causal sequence. Internal crisis, coupled with a hostile external environment, could force Kim Jong-il to choose the strategy of confrontation and suppression, but he could fail to pacify the domestic turmoil. Failure to control the crisis could trigger internal division and factional struggles within the ruling circle, ultimately resulting in the demise of the Kim Jong-il regime. A power vacuum amid mass riots following the toppling of the Kim regime could bring about a protracted civil war among various social and political forces, resurrecting the image of the Bosnian or Lebanese conflicts. In the middle of this fiasco, the state might still survive if the ruling elite in the North attempts to preserve state sovereignty (to avoid the plight of the East German elite during the process of German unification). But the North Korean elite could well fail to restore order and stability through the establishment of an effective government.

As the domestic situation worsens through protracted civil war and pervasive anarchy, warring factions could invite external intervention in the form of international peacekeeping forces (DIA-ROK 1997, 2). Under these circumstances, China is most likely to intervene. Geographic proximity, historical ties, and the congruity of interests between the Chinese leadership and large segments of the North Korean elite will increase Chinese leverage over North Korea when and if a civil war breaks out in the North. Chinese intervention through the dispatch of its own peacekeeping forces might not come to an end after a short period; it could last longer than expected. As the Syrian intervention in Lebanon illustrates, China could sustain its control over the North even after the North's domestic situation becomes normalized. The North's independence and autonomy would be fundamentally curtailed under a Chinese trusteeship, and China would likely dictate the domestic politics and foreign policy of North Korea.

Costs, Benefits, and Rationale for International Support

The potential paths to system change in North Korea are not likely to be smooth; they vary in different contexts. It is the sequential dynamics of internal and external conditions, leadership choice, and the resulting system changes in North Korea that shape the paths to system change. Which sce-

Table 1: Costs, Benefits, and Rationale for International Support: A Comparison

Scenario	Military dimension	Political dimension	Economic dimension	Social dimension	Humanitarian dimension
Status quo					
	Continuing military tension and conflict potential	Short-term survival/ medium- or long-term collapse	*Juche* economy; chaos and stagnation	Increasing deviation; contradiction	Sustaining human suffering
System modification					
Chinese path	Peaceful management	Reformed political leadership	Incremental opening and reform; leadership-market socialism	Controllable	Improving human condition
South Korean path	Peaceful management	Short- to medium-term dictatorship	Capitalist-radical opening and reform	Controllable	Improving human condition
Collapse					
Romanian path	Civil unrest; heightened tension	Big bang	Chaos and stagnation	High uncontrolled costs	Extensive human suffering
Iraqi path	Conflict escalation	Occupation and transitional chaos	Extensive war damage	Uncontrollable	Extensive human suffering
Lebanese path	Protracted civil war	China's intervention; pro-China regime	Transitional chaos and medium-term recovery	Controllable	Limited suffering

nario is then most desirable and likely? What would be the rationale for international economic support for North Korea?

Desirability and Likelihood

Table 1 shows that system modification seems the most desirable. Though limited in its scope, it not only enhances peaceful coexistence on the Korean peninsula by reducing the potential for conflict escalation, but it also contributes to fostering political reforms in the North. No matter how reformist the Kim Jong-il leadership might be, it will retain either the Chinese form of socialist authoritarianism or the old South Korean version of developmental dictatorship. Nevertheless, political stability can be assured with either model.

The incremental opening and reform (Deng's path) or the radical transformation toward capitalism (Park Chung-hee's path), both of which are integral to the scenario, would significantly level off the North Korean economy. Although transition to opening and reform could entail adverse effects such as transitional social and economic instability, the North Korean leadership would be able to manage these effects through authoritarian political governance and improved material foundation. The most promising aspect would be the improvement of human conditions in North Korea because this scenario is predicated on the effective management of food, energy, and basic necessities.

Although most desirable, the transition to these paths through system modification might not be smooth. The North Korean leadership would have to overcome several formidable hurdles. First to be overcome would be the structural rigidity embodied in the *juche* ideology, the *suryông* system, the socialist planned economy, and bureaucratic inertia. Second, removing such structural rigidities can invite immense domestic political opposition, especially from those hard-liners who fear the negative consequences of opening and reform. Thus, successful transition to the Chinese or South Korean model will be contingent on the North Korean leadership's ability to pacify domestic political opposition. Third, poor physical infrastructure and lack of resources and capital will be other major impediments to opening and reform. Thus, the model's success depends heavily on whether North Korea can acquire international economic support. Finally, international economic support is not likely to arrive unless North Korea alleviates pending security concerns such as its threats of WMD, missiles, and conventional forces. In view of this, the transition will require bold initiatives on the part of the North Korean leadership to overhaul the country's system and remove its nuclear weapons program. The scenario might not be feasible unless the current nuclear standoff is peacefully resolved.

The status quo can be problematic. Because it is predicated on the continuing pursuit of *kangsung daeguk* under the banner of the *juche* ideology and the *suryông* system, North Korea may not give up its nuclear ambition, which would lead to a major escalation of conflict. As long as the North adheres to its old military stance, military tensions may continue to prevail on the Korean peninsula. Immediate adverse political effects may not be visible because North Korea will presumably be under the tight control of the Kim Jong-il regime. But the North Korean economy would continue to deteriorate to the extent that it may not recover. Economic stagnation and chaos, which would be further aggravated by cosmetic economic reform measures, will make the North Korean economy hopeless. Social discontent and deviation would deepen while massive human suffering continues. The more prolonged the duration of status quo, the more intense the internal pressures for system collapse and the higher the costs of fixing the North Korean system after collapse.

Status quo is not likely to last long. The durability of North Korea's regime appears to be approaching the point of diminishing returns. Ideological indoctrination; consolidation of political power; the system of surveillance, control, and intimidation—no matter how sophisticated, firm, and penetrative they are—cannot assure regime survival if the North Korean leadership cannot satisfy the minimal level of basic human needs. The status quo would not work in the medium and long term particularly because cosmetic and stop-and-go opening and reform measures are bound to compound the structural contradictions of the North Korea economy, planting the seeds of economic and social catastrophe. Added to this is the hostile external environment that would arise from North Korea's pursuit of its nuclear ambitions and its unruly behavior. Unless the North Korean leadership makes a drastic shift to opening and reform through major system modification, it is doomed to encounter a big bang, resulting in a collateral catastrophe for South Korea and neighboring countries. Thus, the status quo scenario seems neither desirable nor durable.

The worst case would be system collapse. Of the three likely paths within this scenario, the Iraqi path would be the most devastating because it is predicated on the collapse of North Korea through war and occupation. Given the current structure of military confrontation, conflict escalation and war could well destroy not only North Korea but also all of what South Korea has achieved. It is unthinkable to the South. No matter how limited it might be, war will cause insurmountable human and material damage, as demonstrated by the Korean War. Even if the United States and its allies win the war and liberate the North from the Kim Jong-il regime, there is no guarantee that the North can be pacified easily. As the Iraqi experience shows, managing transitional chaos and unrest can be a daunting challenge. Worse are the negative impacts on the South Korean economy and the astronomical costs of postwar reconstruction. Extensive human suffering, uncontrolled social instability and unrest, and a massive outflow of refugees will make the Iraqi path extremely unattractive.

The Romanian path might be better than the Iraqi one because conflict escalation and war can be avoided, and the economic and social costs will be much lower than the costs of traveling on the Iraqi path. Nevertheless, traumatic regime change and transitional chaos could not only heighten political instability in the North but also severely threaten peace and stability on the Korea peninsula through the negative spillover of an internal power struggle. Ensuing political uncertainty and a lack of clear direction for ideology and governance would continue to deform and stagnate the North Korean economy. If the anarchic situation persists, social instability might become uncontrollable; and, as human suffering worsens, a massive exodus of North Korean refugees into South Korea and neighboring countries can be anticipated. North Korea under this scenario could be better off if it becomes willing to give up its sovereignty and merge with the South—unification by absorption. But this seems implausible not only because of the new political forces in the North that would like to preserve the country's sovereignty, but also because of South Korea's increasing reluctance to accommodate the German unification model in fear of high costs and uncertainty.

Of the three pathways under the scenario of system collapse, the Lebanese path seems the least traumatic and costly. Although protracted civil war might increase military tension on the Korean peninsula, it would not escalate into a major war. Chinese intervention could also reduce economic and social costs in the postcollapse period because it is assumed that China would extend massive assistance to the North to aid in the North's economic recovery and social stability. Political costs would be extremely high, however, because the scenario is based on de facto recognition of Chinese influence over North Korea. Chinese trusteeship of North Korea would be unacceptable to South Korea and some segments of North Korea not only because of historical memory and national pride but also because of the adverse impact on Korean unification. Chinese intervention could perpetuate national division. In addition, China's expanding sphere of influence in the region would also pose a major threat to the United States, Japan, and Russia.

On the basis of the above observations, none of the collapse models seems desirable. Nonetheless, their plausibility cannot be ruled out. If North Korea refuses to reach a negotiated settlement in the current nuclear standoff, as it undertakes dangerous activities such as nuclear testing, proliferation of nuclear materials and missiles, and conventional military provocation, it might be difficult to avoid a major showdown. Blind pursuit of the status quo, amid protracted confrontation with outside powers and subsequent isolation and containment, could also make both the Romanian and Lebanese pathways plausible. In this regard, nothing is unthinkable about the future of North Korea.

Rationale for International Economic Support

After assessing the costs and benefits of the contending scenarios, it becomes evident that opening and reform through system modification is most desirable for all parties concerned. The relevance of international support lies in the desirability of opening and reform and the gradual transformation of North Korea. International support will not only be conducive to North Korea's successful transition to opening and reform but will also be beneficial in other vital areas that affect the international community as a whole.

International support and recognition of North Korea can break a vicious circle of distrust, confrontation, crisis, and uneasy settlements. One of the central causes of the Korean conflict is the lack of recognition and trust. The deep-rooted distrust of and refusal to recognize North Korea as a normal state has compounded already difficult negotiations with North Korea. However, timely and forthcoming international support can serve as a useful vehicle for recognizing North Korea's identity and building trust with the outside world. Although there is always the danger of being cheated by the North, the North's past record shows that positive reinforcements have worked. Engagement and international support will be beneficial not only for the resolution of the current nuclear standoff, but also for inter-Korean military confidence building, arms control, and peacemaking. By reducing military tensions and the potential for conflict, international support will be essential for avoiding collateral catastrophe. Through the improvement of material and social conditions in the North, effective international support will also help alleviate North Korea's aggressive behavior by increasing its dependence on the outside world and depriving the Kim Jong-il regime of its rationale for undertaking provocative actions. Kim would not be able to resort to a scapegoat-driven military adventure designed to pacify domestic political and social instability. Thus, international support, even at the nominal level, would represent more than just material incentives.

The March of Hardship in the mid-1990s, a breakdown in North Korea's ration system, and the success of China have all revealed the structural limits of the *juche* economy. The North Korean leadership is keenly aware of these limitations and has been pushing hard for opening and reform. The 1 July 2002 reform measures involving managerial innovation of state enterprises; a realistic pursuit of price, wage, and foreign exchange rates; and the adoption of incentive systems can be seen as sincere efforts to overcome current economic difficulties. Although these measures have entailed enormous negative consequences such as supply bottlenecks, spiraling inflation, and deepening income inequality, the North Korean leadership has shown a commitment to continuing the process of opening and reform (KIEP 2003).

A little push from the international community can induce profound changes in the North Korean economy. International economic support in terms of expanded trade and foreign direct investment can certainly help sustain and enhance moves toward opening and reform, which would alleviate the North's economic downturn and facilitate its integration with the South Korean and the world economies. Such developments can significantly reduce the economic and social costs for South Korea in a future process of integration and unification.

Systematic international support, particularly in the form of financial support, would also make political changes in North Korea less traumatic and more manageable. A relatively smooth economic operation through opening and reform that is the result of massive external support would most likely entail extensive institutional changes such as new incentive systems, individual property rights, and autonomy and freedom for economic activities. Such changes would require concurrent, albeit limited, political reforms because the monolithic *suryông* system and the existing command and control of the economy and society cannot effectively fulfil the mandates of opening and reform. Moreover, the expansion of civil society through the introduction and diffusion of a market system will facilitate the transition to a reformist political leadership in North Korea.

The opening of North Korea to the outside world, other reforms, and the subsequent introduction of a market system will eventually promote the rise and expansion of civil society. At present, North Korea is devoid of a functioning, normal civil society because voluntary associations are not permitted. In fact, regardless of economic hardship, the Kim Jong-il regime has avoided or delayed the process of opening and reform precisely because of civil society's threats to his regime. Some scholars argue that the exposure of North Korea to the outside world through opening could enhance citizens' awareness of the objective reality of North Korea in a comparative sense, ultimately triggering a shared feeling of cognitive dissonance and even relative deprivation. In particular, newly emerging networks between foreign capital and domestic citizens could easily facilitate the expansion of civil society beyond party and state control. Such developments could cultivate a new foundation for democratic opening in North Korea, making changes from within more plausible.[8]

North Korea is notorious for its miserable living conditions. More than two million North Koreans are known to have suffered from an acute food crisis. In addition, chronic shortages of energy and basic medical supplies have severely deteriorated the living conditions in North Korea. Recognizing the North Korean plight, the international community has offered extensive humanitarian support. Since the nuclear standoff began, however, international support has decreased. Although the United Nations gave $116 million and individual countries and nongovernmental organizations (NGOs) granted $8.16 million and $35.7 million, respectively, to the North in 2003, *Chosun Ilbo* on 21 January 2004 reported that international support decreased by 38 percent, from $257 million in 2002 to $161 million in 2003. If the North Korean nuclear standoff persists, international support, including humanitarian assistance, will continue to decline. But it should be noted that, at present, humanitarian assistance from the outside world is the only way to alleviate the human suffering in North Korea.

International economic support also carries profound implications for Korean unification. South Koreans support neither unification by force nor unification by absorption. Unification by force would be extremely traumatic. Consequently, even if unification were achieved through this path, nation building would require a precarious process of healing fractures. The collective memory of the Korean War is a vivid testimonial to these wounds. A sudden blending of North Korea and South Korea through absorption might also entail painful adjustments. Regional rivalries, institutional differences, and divergent patterns of political socialization and aspirations could lead to another round of animosity and mutual contempt in the post-unifi-

---

8   For detailed discussions of North Korea's civil society, see Suh (1995, 1997, 1998).

cation era. As the German experience testifies, the rise of a second wall dividing the mental geography of a new Korea could hamper the process of genuine integration between the peoples of the two Koreas.[9] Given the high social costs of other modes of unification, unification by consensus appears to be the most desirable for minimizing the trauma of integration, facilitating mutual learning, and fostering national harmony. International economic support, opening and reform, and the eventual transformation of North Korea will be conducive to realizing unification by consensus.

Finally, the extension of international support will ultimately foster a liberal transition on the Korean peninsula. An acceleration of opening and reform by means of international support will contribute to spreading the free market system to North Korea. As commercial liberals argue, the deepening of a market economy and economic interdependence can facilitate the modification of North Korea's external behavior, which would reduce the likelihood of war while it enhances chances for peace (Morse 1976; Keohane 1989, 165–94). The expansion of markets creates vested commercial interests across the border that would oppose an outbreak of war that could destroy wealth; and the spread of a free market system can lead to an enlargement of democracy in the North. No matter how limited they are, openness, transparency, and domestic checks and balances—all of which are associated with democratic changes—would make the conduct of foreign and defense policy more predictable and accountable (Doyle 1997, chap. 8; Russett 1993; Russett and O'Neal 2001, chaps. 2, 3). A market economy and a democratic polity can eventually foster the formation of a community of security through shared norms and values, common domestic institutions, and high levels of interdependence (Deutsch 1959; Adler and Barnett 1998). Thus, international economic support seems indispensable to peace building on the Korean peninsula.

Preconditions for International Economic Support

North Korea deserves support from the international community not simply because of its hardships and human sufferings, but also because of the profound negative effects on peace and prosperity on the Korean peninsula and in the Northeast Asian region that would arise from a traumatic collapse of the North Korean regime. In this sense, international economic support can be seen as a preventive diplomatic move to avoid a major catastrophe. North Korea needs to satisfy several preconditions in order to qualify for international support, however.

---

9 Kucheler (2002) comments on the second wall in a unified Germany.

Resolve Security Concerns

The most urgent precondition is the resolution of the current North Korean nuclear problem. It is believed that North Korea acquired one or two nuclear warheads before it signed the 1994 Agreed Framework. In April 2003 at the Beijing three-party talks, Li Keun, the chief North Korean delegate, indicated to U.S. Assistant Secretary of State for East Asian and Pacific Affairs James A. Kelly that North Korea possessed two nuclear bombs. In addition, North Korea has claimed that it has completed the reprocessing of 8,000 spent fuel rods stored in a water pond. The North is able to reprocess additional spent fuel rods, obtained from the activation of the 5 MW and 50 MW reactors in Yongbyon and a 200 MW reactor in Taechun. Projections of North Korea's plutonium bomb vary according to each analyst, but it is estimated that the reprocessing of 8,000 spent fuel rods will yield about five bombs. The reactivation of the 5 MW reactor is estimated to produce 6–7 kg of plutonium yearly, which can yield about one bomb. The 50 MW reactor is not yet completed, but its completion and activation can produce about 56 kg of plutonium, sufficient to manufacture 11 bombs, per year. The 200 MW reactor is projected to produce 220 kg of plutonium per year, yielding 44 bombs annually (Wolfsthal n.d.; Albright 1994, 78; NTI 2004). More serious is the development of a highly enriched uranium (HEU) program. It is estimated that North Korea will be capable of producing 75 kg of HEU per year, which would be sufficient to manufacture three HEU weapons every year, starting in 2005 (Wolfsthal n.d.; McGoldrick 2003).

Possessing nuclear warheads is one thing; having the capability to deliver them is another. North Korea may have both because the country is known to have a credible delivery capability. It currently possesses various types of missiles: Scud B (range 320 km, payload 1,000 kg), Scud C (range 500 km, payload 770 kg), and Nodong (range 1,350–1,500 km, payload 770–1,200 kg). On 31 August 1998 North Korea alarmed the world by test launching a Taepo-dong 1 missile (range 1,500–2,500 km, payload 1,000–1,500 kg). North Korea is also known to be developing Taepo-dong 2 missiles (range 3,500–6,000 km, payload 700–1,000 kg) but has put a moratorium on test launches. Although the North has been planning to develop an intercontinental ballistic missile, the Taepo-dong 3 (range 15,000 km), it will take more than a decade to complete its development (Nerris et al. 2003, 76–7; Wright 2003). All in all, North Korea is far short of developing a long-range missile to threaten the mainland United States, but it might be able to cause considerable damage in South Korea, Japan, and even Guam.

North Korea is nearing the status of a full-fledged nuclear power. It has already acquired one or two nuclear bombs and is likely to build considerable nuclear arsenals in the short and medium term if left unchecked. Although actual nuclear testing has not been conducted, North Korea has demonstrated its delivery capability.

For peninsular security, the implications of a nuclear North Korea are quite grave. Foremost, a nuclear North Korea is not compatible with the ideal of peace building on the Korean peninsula. Not only would a nuclear North Korea pose formidable nonconventional threats to the South, it would also fundamentally alter the inter-Korean military balance. Equally troublesome are the unintended negative consequences of crisis escalation. If the North Korean nuclear problem cannot be resolved through peaceful means, the use of coercive measures including military options might become unavoidable. Such developments would be bound to cause massive collateral damage to the South. Even a minor surgical strike could escalate into a full-scale war, jeopardizing peace and prosperity on the entire Korean peninsula. Estimates of war casualties reach more than a half million even at the beginning stage of a full scale war (Carter and Perry 1999, chap. 4; Schuman 2003, 38). North Korea's nuclear venture could also easily precipitate a nuclear domino effect, trapping the entire Northeast Asian region in a perpetual security dilemma reminiscent of the late nineteenth century. More important, North Korea could become a threat to global security when and if it begins to export plutonium and other nuclear materials to rogue states and terrorists.

North Korea needs to resolve security concerns arising from its nuclear threats. International economic support will be highly unlikely unless North Korea undertakes a complete, verifiable, and irreversible dismantling of its nuclear weapons program. North Korea should get away from the illusion that nuclear deterrence capability can assure its national security and regime survival. If anything, its obsession with its nuclear ambitions is more likely to accelerate the collapse of its regime through isolation and containment by international society. Moreover, the devastating military and political consequences of conflict escalation cannot be ruled out. The only way out seems to be the path of Libyan leader Mu'ammar Qadhafi.[10]

North Korea needs to resolve other security concerns too. Issues pertaining to missiles, biochemical weapons, and conventional forces are a case in point. The North needs to take a more proactive attitude toward confidence-building measures with South Korea, including the redeployment of offensive forces and the reduction of conventional forces. A concurrent alleviation of security concerns over conventional forces along with nuclear weapons will certainly contribute to cultivating a new international trust in North Korea and facilitating the inflow of international economic support.

---

10 North Korea has repeatedly stated that the Libyan model is unacceptable. However, a relaxation of U.S. demands for complete, verifiable, and irreversible dismantling of the North's nuclear program and an innovative approach such as security assistance through the use of a third-party intermediary (like the British in Libya) might persuade the North to accept the Libyan model.

Expedite Economic Opening and Reform

The fortified *juche* ideology might make the positive transformation of the North Korean economy difficult, but an array of signs including recent economic reform measures points to the fact that North Korea is taking critical steps toward opening and reform. The steady implementation of the 1 July 2002 reform measures seems to be the most vivid testimonial.

Nevertheless, North Korea is still far short of genuine economic changes sufficient to attract international support. First, a realignment of governing ideas seems to be a crucial prerequisite. Neither the *juche* ideology nor the doctrine of *kangsung daeguk* can be compatible with opening and reform. It is ideal when military strength and economic prosperity come together. However, as the experiences of *fukoku gyohei* (rich nation and strong army) in Japan and South Korea demonstrate, military strength can come only after going through capitalist transformation and industrial development. Otherwise, the simultaneous pursuit of the two conflicting goals could derail opening and reform and also undercut a country's national security posture.

Second, there must be profound external behavioral changes. North Korea needs to enhance its international credibility by demonstrating its willingness to comply with international laws and norms. The sanctity of contracts should be assured, and a mechanism for securing financial transactions and arbitration methods of commercial disputes should be put in place. Keeping abreast of international standards on national economic and financial statistics is also required; otherwise, the international community cannot tell what is going on in the North Korean economy. The North should also demonstrate its ability to engage in businesslike conduct at the transaction level, respecting the mutuality of interests in economic and commercial relationships. Proper understanding of concepts and methods of economic, financial, and commercial transactions seems to be essential (Babson 2001, 449–50).

Finally, the North should take much bolder initiatives for the transition from a centrally planned economy to a market mechanism. Such a transition would require major structural and institutional changes, including a more assertive introduction of a market system, a progressive adoption of the private ownership of property, an overhaul of the ration system and state enterprises, and the establishment of new institutions and rules that are friendly to international investment.

Reform Politics; Resolve the Issue of Human Rights

Debate is ongoing about the nature of the political system in North Korea.[11] But it is undeniable that the North Korean political system is monolithic and

---

11 For debates on monolithic vs. pluralistic decision making in North Korea, see Park H. (1998, 225–7), Suh (1998, 199–201), Chung and Lee (1998, 172–3), Merrill (1997, 49–50), Paik (1997, 112).

based on the principle of equating *suryŏng* (leader) with the people, the party, the state, and the military. It is also founded on a totalitarian regime. Although the North Korean regime seeks its legitimacy from such historical legacies as the guerrilla struggle against Japanese colonialism and a major war with the "American imperial power," tight social surveillance, control, and intimidation are what actually sustain the regime. The military has become the most important factor in the North's game of regime survival, and the military has been a major source of opposition to economic opening and reform. It would be extremely difficult for North Korea to undertake meaningful opening and reform without altering its military-centered power structure. More political weight should be given to party and state technocrats. And, in the medium and long run, incremental political opening should be accomplished in the direction of pluralism and decentralization. The North cannot obtain international recognition and support without showing signs of genuine political change.

The gradual improvement of human rights is an urgent issue. North Korea has been classified as the worst violator of human rights in the world. Its murderous criminal codes, lack of procedural justice, complete absence of freedom of association and expression, and large number of political prisoners underscore the stark reality of human rights conditions in North Korea. Because these issues cannot be resolved without a fundamental regime transformation, North Korea will be reluctant to address them officially. Nevertheless, North Korea can deliberate on small steps. For example, North Korea could enhance its human rights record by allowing international organizations or NGOs access to camps for political prisoners. Amendment of its criminal codes could be seen as another meaningful gesture.

Mounting external pressures on the issue of human rights will be unavoidable to the North Korean leadership. But it should be kept in mind that the ultimate resolution of human rights in North Korea cannot be imposed from the outside. It should be resolved from within. To enhance the chances for resolution from within, international support seems to be vital because economic opening and reform, expansion of civil society, and political change are not conceivable without such support.

Demonstrate Normal Behavior

The image of North Korea has been greatly tainted by its track record of unpleasant international behavior. Although the North denounced terrorist activities in the wake of September 11, 2001, memories of the bombing and assassination of South Korean government officials in Burma, the terrorist bombing of a South Korean passenger airplane, and the kidnapping of innocent Japanese citizens still haunt the international community. Equally troublesome is North Korea's alleged extensive engagement in such illicit activities as the smuggling of weapons, drugs, counterfeit currencies, tobacco, and alcohol. Moreover, North Korea's compliance with international norms and laws has been arbitrary and selective, depending on the configuration of its national interests. Its behavior regarding the Nuclear Non-Proliferation Treaty is a case in point. North Korea should take more explicit measures to remove the scarlet letter of terrorism by abandoning its erratic and unruly behavior. This is the only viable way to gain recognition, respect, and trust from international society.

It is highly unrealistic to expect North Korea to satisfy all these preconditions simultaneously. But the North can take step-by-step measures. The most urgent step is the resolution of the current nuclear standoff through the undertaking of a complete, verifiable, and irreversible dismantling of its nuclear program. Depending on progress in the nuclear arena, North Korea would be given a set of incentives and disincentives. Its full cooperation with the dismantling could facilitate its transition to opening and reform by permitting it to have access to international capital, technology, energy, and other forms of support.

Resolution of the nuclear issue should lead to comprehensive measures to ease outside security concerns arising from missiles, biochemical weapons, and conventional forces. The North should engage in direct negotiations with South Korea on the issue of conventional forces along with negotiations about the nuclear issue. Significant progress on inter-Korean military confidence building can produce a positive spillover into nuclear negotiations. North Korea should also take credible steps to restore international trust by settling the issue of the kidnapped Japanese citizens and officially terminating illicit activities such as smuggling drugs and counterfeiting currencies. Finally, regardless of progress on security issues, North Korea should consider taking some visible measures to alleviate its human rights issues.

Policy Options

I have argued that neither the status quo nor a sudden collapse of the North Korean regime is beneficial to all concerned parties, especially to South Korea. The most desirable scenario seems to be a gradual transformation of North Korea through opening and reform. The North cannot make a successful transition to opening and reform without obtaining considerable international economic support. To win international support, North Korea should satisfy several preconditions—alleviate security concerns, including the current nuclear standoff; pursue more proactively ideational, behavioral, and institutional changes in the economic domain; improve human rights; and demonstrate more credible international behavior.

It will not be easy for the North to carry out these preconditions, but it has no other choice. The North Korean leadership should realize the cold reality that its adherence to the status quo in fear of collapse can in fact accelerate the very process of collapse. Only when it ventures into opening and reform through system modification, even while risking regime stability, can it ensure a desired transition and regime survival. Thus, the North Korean leadership should not hesitate to satisfy these preconditions. Paradoxically, although he inherited political power from his father, Chairman Kim Jong-il seems to be the victim of the structural rigidity stemming from the negative legacies of his father's era. All kinds of derogatory rumors notwithstanding, Kim Jong-il seems to be competent, pragmatic, and sensible enough to take new initiatives for opening and reform.

Changes in North Korea can be volatile and unpredictable. But we should be prudent and patient and avoid the trap of wishful thinking. The dialectics of negation embodied in Buddhist teachings deserve close attention. You can change North Korea more easily when you do not speak of change. Changing the North without urging change is perhaps the most effective way of transforming the North. A chorus of outside voices for change will constantly alert and even threaten the North Korean leadership and will backfire with additional unruly behavior from the North. In dealing with North Korea, quiet diplomacy, positive reinforcement, and engagement are much better than coercive diplomacy, negative reinforcement, isolation, and containment.

References

Adler, Emanuel, and Michael Barnett. 1998. *Security Communities.* New York: Cambridge University Press.

Albright, David. 1994. North Korean Plutonium Production. *Science & Global Security* 5.

Babson, Bradley O. 2001. Integrating North Korea with the World Economy. In *Ending the Cold War in Korea: Theoretical and Historical Perspectives,* ed. Moon Chung-in, Odd Arne Westad, and Kahng Gyoo-Hyoung. Seoul: Yonsei University Press.

Bae, Jong-yun. 2002. Korean Unification and Internal Security. In *Constitutional Handbook on Korean Unification,* ed. Jwa Sung-Hee, Moon Chung-in, and Roh Jeong-Ho. Seoul: Korea Economic Research Institute (KERI).

Bleiker, Roland. Forthcoming. *Rethinking Korean Security: Toward a Culture of Reconciliation.* Minneapolis: University of Minnesota Press.

Carter, Ashton, and William Perry. 1999. *Preventive Defense: A New Security Strategy for America.* Washington, D.C.: Brookings Institution Press.

Choi, Wan-kyu. 1996. *Pukhanun Eodiro: Chonhwanki 'Pukhanchok' Jongch'I Hyunsangeui Jaeinsik* [Quo vadis revisited: North Korean political phenomena in the transformative period]. Masan: Kyungnam University Press.

Chung, Chin-wee, and Lee Seok-soo. 1998. Kim Jong Il Regime and the Structure of Crisis: Its Source, Management and Manifestation. In *Understanding Regime Dynamics in North Korea: Contending Perspectives and Comparative Implications,* ed. Moon Chung-in. Seoul: Yonsei University Press.

Chung, Hyun-soo. 1999. Kim Jong Il Chaejeuihan Jungkuksik Gyonhomui Bukhanhwa Ganeunsungaedaehan Yongu [A study of the possibility of North Koreanization of the Chinese experience by Kim Jong-il]. *Bukhanyongu Hakhoibo* [Journal of North Korean Studies Society] 3, no. 1.

Cumings, Bruce. 2004. *North Korea: Another Country.* New York: New Press.

Defense Intelligence Agency (DIA-ROK). 1997. *Jugan kukoikunsajongbo* [Weekly foreign military intelligence]. 31 January.

Deutsch, Karl. 1959. *Political Community and the North Atlantic Area.* Princeton: Princeton University Press.

Downs, Chuck. 1999. *Over the Line: North Korea's Negotiating Strategy.* Washington, D.C.: American Enterprise Institute.

Doyle, Michael W. 1997. *Ways of Peace and Ways of War.* New York: Norton.

Eberstadt, Nicholas. 1999. *The End of North Korea.* Washington, D.C.: American Enterprise Institute.

Faiola, Anthony. 2003a. N. Korea Shifts toward Capitalism. *Washington Post,* 14 September.

———. 2003b. A Crack in the Door in North Korea. *Washington Post,* 24 November.

———. 2004. A Capitalist Sprouts in N. Korea's Dust. *Washington Post,* 23 May 2004.

Jeong, Se-jin. 2003. Ihaenghak jeok Kwanjeom ae seo bon Choikeun Pukhan Kyoungje Pyonhwa Yeonku [A study of recent economic changes in North Korea from a transformative perspective]. *Kukche Jeongchi Nonchong* [International politics review] 43, no. 1.

Jung, Yong-seok. 1994. Kimjongil Ch'eje Pyonhwa Yangsangkwa Tongil Panghyang [Mode of change in Kim Jong-il's regime and direction of reunification]. *T'ongil Munje Yonku* [Studies of the reunification problem] 6, no. 2 (Winter).

Keohane, Robert. 1989. International Liberalism Reconsidered. In *The Economic Limits of Politics,* ed. John Dunn. Cambridge: Cambridge University Press.

Kim, Byong-ro. 1999. *Pukhanui Chiyok Charib Jui* [North Korea's regional autarky system]. Seoul: Korea Institute for National Unification.

Kim, Choong-nam. 1996. The Uncertain Future of North Korea: Soft Landing or Crash Landing? *Korea and World Affairs* 20, no. 4 (Winter).

Kim, Gap-chol. 1996. The Country Still Ruled by the Teachings of the Dead: The Legitimacy of Kim Jong Il. *East Asian Review* 8, no. 3 (Autumn).

Kim, Il-pyong. 1992. The Features of Kim Jong Il Group and Their Possible Choice. *East Asian Review* 4, no. 2 (Summer).

Kim, Kyung-won. 1996. No Way Out: North Korea's Impending Collapse. *Harvard International Review* (Spring).

Kim, Sung-chul. 1994. Bureaucratic Corruption and Its Social Effects in North Korea. *East Asian Review* 6, no. 4 (Winter).

———. 1996. Systemic Change in North Korea and Development of South-North Korean Relationship." In *Proceedings of International Conference on Complex Systems Model of South-North Korean Integration: Systems Perspective,* sponsored by Korean Society for Systems Science Research and International Society for the Systems Sciences, Seoul, 17–18 May.

Kim, Yeon-chul. 2003. Nampukhan Geundaehwa Jeonryak Pikyo [A comparative study of modernization strategy in North and South Korea: Can North Korea adopt the Park Chung-hee model?]. *Yeoksa Munje Yeonku* [Critical studies on modern Korean history] vol. 11.

Koh, Byung-chul. 1993a. The Politics of Succession in North Korea: Consolidation or Disintegration? *Journal of East Asian Affairs* 7 no. 1 (Winter/Spring).

———. 1993b. Prospects for Change in North Korea's Domestic Policy. *Korea Observer* 24, no. 1 (Spring).

Koh, Sung-youn. 1995. Current Crisis Signs and Prospects of Kim Jong Il Regime. *East Asian Review* 7, no. 2 (Summer).

Korea Institute for International Economic Policy (KIEP). 2003. *Bukhan Gyonje Baesuh* [White book on the North Korean economy]. Seoul: KIEP.

Kucheler, Manfred. 2002. Political Culture and Mass Sentiment. In *Constitutional Handbook on Korean Unification,* ed. Jwa Sung-hee, Moon Chung-in, and Roh Jeong-ho. Seoul: Korea Economic Research Institute (KERI).

Lee, Dong-bok. 1994. Kim Jong-il's North Korea: Its Limitations and Prospects. *Korea and World Affairs* 18, no. 3 (Fall).

Lee, Jong-seok. 2000. *Saero Ssun Hyondae Pukhanui Ihae* [A new understanding of contemporary North Korea]. Seoul: Yoksa Pip'yong Sa.

Lee, Jung-chul. 2002. The Implication of North Korea's Reform Program and Its Effect on State Capacity. *Korea and World Affairs* 26, no. 3.

Lee, On-jook. 1996. The Prospects for Changes in North Korean Citizens' Way of Living and Thinking. *East Asian Review* 3 no. 4 (Winter).

Mansourov, Alexandre Y. 2003. A New Life for North Korea's Parliament. *Daily Chosun,* 18 September. www.chosun.com/w21data/ html/news/ 200309/200309170566.html.

McGoldrick, Fred. 2003. The DPRK Enrichment Program: A Freeze and Beyond. Publication no. PFO 03-1A. San Francisco: Nautilus Institute at the Center for the Pacific Rim. January. www.nautilus.org/fora/security/ 0229A_McGoldrick.html.

McMillan, John. 1997. What Can North Korea Learn from China's Market Reform? In *The System Transformation of Transition Economies: Europe, Asia and North Korea,* ed. Lee Doo-won. Seoul: Yonsei University Press.

Merrill, John. 1997. Reading and Misreading North Korea. In *Security Environment in the 21st Century and Korea's Strategic Options,* ed. Yim Yong-soon et al. Seoul: KAIS.

Moon, Chung-in. 2003. Contending Scenarios of Korean Unification and Implications for Constitutional Design. In Vol. 1 of *Handbook of Korean Unification,* ed. Jwa Sung-hee, Moon Chung-in, and Roh Jeong-ho. Seoul: Korea Economic Research Institute.

Moon, Chung-in, and Kim Yong-ho. 2001. The Future Scenarios of North Korea's System. In *The North Korean System in the Post–Cold War Era,* ed. Samuel Kim. New York: Palgrave.

Moon, Chung-in, and Ryoo Kihl-jae. 1997. Crisis Forecasting on North Korea: Contending Models and an Alternative Framework. Paper presented at annual convention of International Studies Association, Toronto, 19–21 March.

Morse, Edward. 1976. *Modernization and the Transformation of International Relations.* New York: Basic Books.

Nerris, Robert S., Hans M. Kristensen, and Joshua Handler. 2003. North Korea's Nuclear Program. *Bulletin of the Atomic Scientists* 59, no. 2 (March/April).

Noland, Marcus. 2000. *Avoiding the Apocalypse: The Future of Two Koreas.* Washington, D.C.: Institute for International Economics.

———. 2004. *Korea after Kim Jong-il.* Washington, D.C.: Institute for International Economics.

Nuclear Threat Initiative (NTI). 2004. North Korea Nuclear Profile. Washington, D.C.: Nuclear Threat Initiative. www.nti.org/db/profiles/dprk/nuc/nuc_overview.html.

Paik, Hak-soon. 1997. North Korea's Unification Policy. In *The Four Powers and Korean Unification Strategies,* ed. Kwak Tae-hwan. Seoul: Kyungnam University Press.

Park, Han S. 1998. Human Needs, Human Rights, and Regime Legitimacy: The North Korean Anomaly. In *Understanding Regime Dynamics in North Korea: Contending Perspectives and Comparative Implications,* ed. Moon Chung-in. Seoul: Yonsei University Press.

Park, Young-Ho. 2001. North Korea in Transition? *Korea and World Affairs* 25, no. 1.

Pollack, Jonathan, and Lee Chung-min. 1998. *Korean Unification: Scenarios and Implications.* Santa Monica, Calif.: Rand.

Russett, Bruce. 1993. *Grasping Democratic Peace: Principles for a Post–Cold War World.* Princeton: Princeton University Press.

Russett, Bruce, and John O'Neal. 2001. *Triangulating Peace.* New York: W. W. Norton.

Ryu, Seok-ryol. 1997. *Pukhan ui Ch'eche Uiki wa Hanbando Tongil* [North Korea's system crisis and Korean unification]. Seoul: Pakyoung Sa.

Scalapino, Robert. 1992. *The Last Leninists: The Uncertain Future of Asia's Communist States.* Washington, D.C.: Center for Strategic and International Studies.

Schuman, Michael. 2003. Peace and War. *Time,* 3 March.

Suh, Jae-jean. 1995. *Tto Hanaui Pukhan Sahoe* [Another North Korean society]. Seoul: Nanam.

———. 1997. Social Change in North Korea and the Stability of Kim Jong-il Regime. *Korea Focus* 5, no. 1.

———. 1998. Class Conflict and Regime Crisis in North Korea. In *Understanding Regime Dynamics in North Korea: Contending Perspectives and Comparative Implications,* ed. Moon Chung-in. Seoul: Yonsei University Press.

Ward, Andrew. 2004a. Hermit Kingdom Peeps Cautiously Out of Its Shell. *Financial Times,* 12 February.

———. 2004b. Shop till You Drop. *Far Eastern Economic Review,* 13 May.

Watt, Jonathan. 2003. How N. Korea Is Embracing Capitalism by Any Other Name. *Guardian,* 3 December.

Wolfsthal, Jon B. n.d. Estimates of North Korea's Unchecked Nuclear Weapons Production Potential. Washington, D.C.: Carnegie Endowment for International Peace. www.ceip.org/files/projects/npp/pdf/JBW/nknuclear weaponproductionpotential.pdf.

Wright, David C. 2003. Assessment of the North Korean Missile Threat. Publication no. PFO 03-20. San Francisco: Nautilus Institute at the Center for the Pacific Rim. March. www.nautilus.org/fora/security/0320A_%20Wright. html.

Yang, Un-chul. 2001. Will Pyongyang Adopt Chinese-Style Reform? *Vantage Point* 24, no. 8.

Zhebin, Alexander. 1995. North Korea after Kim Il Sung: Hard Choices. *Korean Journal of Defense Analysis* 9, no. 1 (Summer).

Moon Chung-in teaches at Yonsei University in Seoul. He is also chairman of the Presidential Committee on Northeast Asian Cooperation. The author wishes to thank Nick Eberstadt and Paul Bracken for their comments.

6

Strategic Dimensions of Economic Assistance for North Korea

Paul Bracken

North Korea's atomic bomb program and the U.S. response to it provide a case study in long-term crisis management. The defining characteristic of a crisis is that it contains turning points, sometimes many of them. In crisis management there are surprises and mistakes. Tight control of policy and especially over the words that go with it are necessary.

Dealing with North Korea's bomb program is a problem in crisis management. It is not a political negotiation or an exercise in economic reform. Although political negotiation and economic reform are part of crisis management, the main reason for outside involvement in North Korea is to forestall its nuclear armaments. Better political relations between the United States and North Korea and major economic reform may happen, but if they happen absent Pyongyang's nuclear disarmament, a major policy failure with implications far beyond Northeast Asia will have taken place.

The main argument of this paper is that crisis management becomes more difficult as it becomes more multilateral. The single-mindedness of the objective—preventing Pyongyang from getting the bomb—is likely to be dissipated. Extraneous issues can be introduced by other parties. The policy of using multiparty talks is likely to become an end in itself instead of a means to an end. Finally, response to North Korean actions becomes more difficult and likely more conservative. A North Korean nuclear test, for example, is a real possibility, but during multilateral talks Washington will likely view this subject as far too complicated to even think through in advance.

U.S. performance in dealing with North Korea over the past 10 years has been quite good. This conclusion will strike some people as astonishing, but much of the criticism of how the United States has managed the North Korean proliferation crisis seems to focus on short-term disagreements between individuals in and out of government and between the United States and other countries. Week-to-week polemics and disputes give too much attention to the immediate but not to the important. This is a bad approach in health care, in buying stocks, and for disarming North Korea.

Policy analysis with a weekly scorecard misses the larger picture. What has happened over the past decade is the discrediting of the North Korean regime, institutionalization of a new coalition bent on stopping its bomb program, a weakening of North Korea's conventional military power, and a contraction of its economy. The disarming of Iraq and Libya and the precedent of using force to replace a regime in Baghdad that violated proliferation standards are major changes in the strategic context of policy toward North Korea. They are having an enormous impact on North Korea's perception of the international environment.

The international economic engagement of North Korea brings new actors and groups (businesses and nongovernmental organizations [NGOs], for example) into the picture much more than in the past. It is a useful development to resolve the North Korean problem as long as it is recognized that the problem remains one of crisis management. One risk is that international economic assistance programs take on an internal momentum of their own that swamps the political objectives for which they were established. This happens in so many different areas that it is virtually a theorem of political science. Policy shapes the politics, rather than politics shaping the policy (Lowi 1964, 677–715). There are clear signs that this dynamic is already in place in the six-party talks dealing with North Korea.[1]

The strategic purpose of international economic assistance—the disarming of North Korea—could be lost sight of because it brings more countries and groups into the picture. A long-term crisis management framework can go a long way toward making sure this does not happen.

Engagement of North Korea and Atomic Weapons

The United States did not engage North Korea until the early 1990s. What typified the U.S.-North Korea relationship before this time was a begrudging relationship forced on Washington to secure the return of the crew of the USS *Pueblo*, a U.S. Navy reconnaissance vessel seized in international waters by North Korea in 1968. The negotiations were vitriolic. Each denounced the other. The United States even disavowed its "apology" to North Korea at the very moment it was signed.

This relationship changed in the early 1990s, when the fact that North Korea might be on track to get atomic weapons began to seep into the consciousness of U.S. leaders. In three years the U.S. policy of isolation was reversed to a policy of engagement. It is surprising how quickly this turnabout came.

---

[1] Participants in the six-party talks are China, Japan, North Korea, South Korea, Russia, and the United States.

There are important reasons that North Korea's nuclear-weapon acquisition sounded the Klaxon in Washington:

- North Korea was a stable regime—but only on the surface. Its behavior toward its people violated every canon of human rights. It was moving toward a hereditary succession of power, and it was easy to imagine atomic weapons playing a role in some inscrutable power game inside North Korea.

- North Korea threatened to undermine the whole fabric of Washington's nonproliferation policies. North Korea's sale of critical technologies throughout the 1990s shows that Washington was quite prescient on this point.

- A North Korea with nuclear weapons had to be seen against the background of a widespread breakdown in the nonproliferation regime established in the late 1960s. In the 1990s, India, Pakistan, China, Iraq, Israel, and Iran advanced their atomic weapons programs—that these countries are not usually grouped together is beside the point. Nuclear programs—including research and development, bombs, and missiles—were spreading fast, and the momentum had to be broken before it became irreversible.

What Game Is Being Played?

What emerged in the 1990s was an engagement framework that can best be called a politics of exchange. With the United States in the lead, the West would give something to the North, and, in exchange, the North would give up its nuclear weapons. Security guarantees, diplomatic recognition, food, and economic assistance have been offered at different times (Cha and Kang 2003). There was not and is not precise agreement on many details. And neither North Korea nor the United States at various times wanted to admit an exchange was going on.

One has to be careful here. This politics-of-exchange framework for disarming North Korea is accepted only grudgingly by some in the United States. An interesting feature of two U.S. administrations—as the Clinton and George W. Bush administrations have proceeded with oil and food transfers and participate in multilateral talks dealing with security assurances for the North—is how far they have gone out of their way to explain to domestic audiences that they are not rewarding North Korea for bad behavior.

But a politics of exchange has developed during two U.S. administrations because the alternatives to it are so unpromising. Pointing out its flaws and inconsistencies is easy. Constructing an alternative is hard. The parties in the framework, both within and between governments, are not united and are often uncomfortable with each other.

Sometimes the politics of exchange is called a grand bargain.[2] Sometimes it is called "oil for nukes." The late 1990s can be viewed as a reconnaissance, an experimentation to discover what exactly North Korea wants. Emergency food and oil shipments certainly looked to be of high priority to Pyongyang then. A problem here is that the North Korean government, which for practical purposes means Kim Jong-il, does not appear to have carefully thought through the politics of exchange. Certainly it is easy to define what Pyongyang wants: status, recognition, aid, and nuclear weapons. But Pyongyang gives every sign of not systematically thinking through the trade-offs and the order of these wishes when it cannot attain them all. It is my strong bet that, when the insider diplomatic history of North Korea's posturing is written, a picture of chaos will emerge. The North Korean side does not understand its own trade space—what it is willing to give up for what it might get in return.

Despite this, a surprising degree of convergence exists about the outlines of the negotiating framework. Salient thresholds quickly appeared, as they usually do. This isn't evident from the week-to-week conflicts and disputes—among policy specialists and government officials or between the United States and other countries. But principles and structure have developed, and they will be hard to overturn.

Number of bombs.   North Korea should not be allowed to acquire any substantial number of atomic bombs. (The wording is carefully chosen here.) Some countries, and some individuals, argue that if North Korea has only one or two "contraption" bombs—those of such a low reliability that they are for all practical purposes unusable—the situation would be not too bad. Nearly all responsible parties, allies, critics, and government officials agree that North Korea should not be allowed to get a substantial number of atomic bombs. The exact number that becomes "substantial" seems to be nowhere defined, reflecting the short-term focus of much of the discussion.

Others argue that even one bomb is completely unacceptable. But this unqualified statement is not clear, at least to me, given the well-known uncertainties about estimating weapons of mass destruction. More important, saying that even one bomb is unacceptable and that we should go to war over it leaves out of the discussion once again an enormous number of additional factors that need to be considered.

Specialization of roles within the politics of exchange framework.   The United States is (usually) the bad cop. China is (often) the good cop. Japan and South Korea are important interlocutors. Other countries are drawn in for special reasons. For example, Russia can sell oil more easily to North Korea because Russia's own economic needs are widely recognized. The role of NGOs is to speak informally with the North, offer trial balloons, and also

---

[2]   O'Hanlon and Mochizuki (2003) provides many variations of possible grand bargains.

persuade some elements of public opinion in the West. NGO observations about famine, health, and social cohesion have been important factors in formulating U.S. government policy.

There is already an internal caucus developing in the six-party talks. The United States tends to consult first with South Korea and Japan before approaching other members. In addition, a silent partner is the European Union. The United States has skillfully set up a "credit line" with the EU that could be tapped to provide assistance to North Korea. This aid could be brought in when needed.

Complete agreement about these roles does not exist, but a structure is taking shape. Ten years ago this structure didn't even exist. Few outsiders were allowed into North Korea. There was a high level of uncertainty about the role of China back then. Now the basic structure of who the actors are and what their roles are is in place.

Increasing institutionalization of the alliance arrayed against the North Korean nuclear program.   The alliance has become institutionalized because norms, formal procedures, and standards have emerged over time. These norms mean that states go beyond the calculation of their own immediate interest. China and Japan, for example, are less likely to offer breakthrough proposals without consultation.

Attempts by North Korea to drive a wedge through this coalition have failed. This is no guarantee that this coalition will hold together in the future, of course, but it is going to be very difficult for North Korea to divide it. China has so many relations with the United States today that, although it is possible that China might radically alter its role with respect to North Korea, such a development does not seem likely. Although it is the norm to list issues like Taiwan and human rights on the U.S.-China agenda, as a business school professor I add another one: China supplies $40 billion per year to the Wal-Mart corporation alone, an amount that is about the size of the entire North Korean gross domestic product. A sharp break with the United States over North Korea would put at risk in China real money and jobs, not just principles.

There are disputes and disagreements within this coalition and within the United States government, but the broader point is that North Korea over the past decade has failed to stop the emergence of an increasingly institutionalized coalition formed to stop her nuclear program. It is difficult to overstate the importance of this development.

This is an outstanding achievement of U.S. foreign policy. The Soviet Union could not stop the creation of the North Atlantic Treaty Organization (NATO) in the late 1940s, and Moscow could never recover from this reversal. The coalition arrayed against North Korea's nuclear program is not nearly as institutionalized as NATO, but it is a great deal more developed than it was ten years ago. Absent a rupture over a policy area that has nothing to do with

North Korea (like Taiwan), the coalition is strengthening. North Korea's erratic statements have helped a great deal here.

Strategic Dimensions of Economic Engagement

There are two approaches to engaging North Korea:

- **Strategic approach.** Washington could take a strategic approach, with the clear goal of disarming the North in exchange for economic assistance, security guarantees, and investments. Here the issues are those of determining the wants of North Korea and applying threats and coercion where needed if the North fails to take the offer.
- **Norm-based approach.** Washington could take a multilateral approach of international economic engagement, which would entail accepting at least partly the international norms that have developed within the multilateral community. This approach means relying on authoritative rules and principles to govern economic assistance toward the North (Lancaster 2004). The issues are issues of conformance with international norms and coordination with allies, possibly with the use of existing or newly created multilateral institutions.

We could debate endlessly which is the better approach, but a crisis management framework points to the conclusion that both are necessary. That is, in a crisis there are so many unpredictable developments and so many cases of miscommunication and counterintuitive behavior by different actors that flexibility and agility are needed during the negotiations. Crisis management cannot be conducted with formal plans drawn up in advance. Such plans are too rigid, and they miss too many developments.

Figure 1 shows a framework for incorporating the strategic dimensions of international economic engagement. Figure 1 combines the strategic approach and the norm-based approach, here restricted to international economic assistance and excluding other kinds of exchange such as security assurances, which could be added to the framework without much difficulty.

Call the first approach "strategic behavior" and the second "norm-based behavior." Each has its own logic, its own rules, and its constraints. It is important to understand, however, that, while the logics of the two are different, they are differences of degree. A program such as food shipments can be interpreted as part strategic and part humanitarian.

Regarding the strategic policies of economic assistance toward North Korea, key points of Figure 1 are that solutions based on pure strategy alone will almost certainly not succeed. For example, if Washington refused to abide by even minimal norms of humanitarian assistance, its refusal would likely weaken the coalition arrayed against North Korea. If the United States declared openly that it was tightening the noose around North Korea to starve

Figure 1: Strategic Dimensions of Economic Engagement

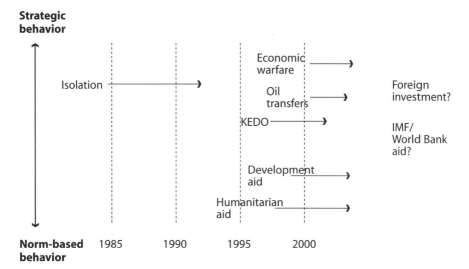

Notes:
Time lines and programs are illustrative.
Programs (KEDO and humanitarian aid, for example) are listed according to their starting years. Suspensions and terminations of programs are indicated by the end of each arrow. New programs that are under discussion but not yet started are shown on the figure without arrows. Because economic warfare is a form of negative economic assistance, that too is listed with an arrow. Economic warfare against North Korea would encompass activities to deny the North needed parts for its weapons program, critical supplies, and money to buy them.

its people into revolt against their governing regime, the resulting worldwide outcry would be justified.

Alternatively, if the United States announced that it was turning over all aspects of economic assistance to either the United Nations, the market, or companies seeking to invest there, every incentive for North Korea to change its behavior would be removed.

The strategic dimension of economic assistance arises from the manipulation of the tensions between the two approaches. This is both the skill and the art. Anyone can pontificate about broad principles, but the mistake is in thinking that getting these right solves the problem. It usually does not. Details matter; and in a crisis that could spill over into war, details matter a lot.

Crises cannot be planned in advance; if there is one conclusion to decades of studies about crisis management, it is that rigid plans almost always lead to trouble. What seemed like an irrefutable fundamental principle six months ago can lead to an unwanted war.

No plan can describe in advance what is going to happen because it is the nature of crises to be fluid, unpredictable, and dangerous. A framework that shows leaders how they can quickly shift up or down toward more strategic or more multilateral approaches, depending on circumstances, offers options that can be adjusted to conditions that can never be known in advance. For example, the termination of food transfers to North Korea is a fairly clear signal that tensions have increased. An increase in economic warfare programs—to disrupt North Korean sales of dangerous technologies or to limit its gains from smuggling, for example—is another signal that could be important to send depending on the circumstances.

Another feature of Figure 1 is that it factors big, complex bargaining proposals into smaller manageable ones. Development aid and humanitarian aid can be separated but at the same time can be understood as part of the larger overall economic engagement. This protects against policies from driving politics too much. For example, the United States has a real tendency to let gestures such as humanitarian aid become self-referential programs, good on their own terms. Despite this tendency, it is the job of U.S. government officials to make sure it does not happen. Officials must look at the larger composite picture.

As more countries consider economic dealings with North Korea, it is essential to not lose sight of the overall objective. Crisis management that preserves the strategic dimensions of economic assistance to North Korea amounts to starting, halting, expanding, contracting, and delaying program elements in a large economic portfolio.

Organizational and Command-and-Control Issues

There are some technical but important issues of how the United States and other countries coordinate their engagement polices with North Korea. The technical issues are sometimes forgotten as different parties argue about whether the United States should follow a unilateral or a multilateral approach.

The need for coordination is increasing as a function of the complexity of the proposals put forward and as a function of the number of countries involved in the negotiations. U.S. governmental structures that have worked over the past few years may be stressed as the number of international actors increases. Serious thought needs to be given to the creation of new structures and to how certain dynamics could develop, dynamics that might overwhelm countries' ability to manage events.

One of the basic doctrines of good crisis management is the requirement for centralized control.[3] The reasons are fairly obvious. In a crisis, the actors are in a heightened state of vigilance, their suspicions are high, and the tendency to shut out new sources of information increases. A mistaken signal can trigger an eruption of violence that is neither desired nor intended.

---

[3]   Among many excellent studies, see Craig and Alexander (1983).

North Korea presents special problems. The premise of economic engagement for strategic purpose developed in this paper, and also contained in many policy proposals, is that the bargaining framework factors a big problem into a sequence of smaller ones. North Korea could follow Libya in 2003 and 2004 in agreeing to a true grand bargain: the abandonment of its atomic weapons program in exchange for recognition as a normal state in the international system. This possibility should not, and cannot, be ruled out. It is not especially likely, however.

As the number of countries working with the United States to formulate policy increases, the difficulty of centralized control increases. Other countries may introduce extraneous issues having little to do with the goal of disarming North Korea. Marcus Noland (2004) has pointed out that the globalization of the South Korean economy has introduced new vulnerabilities arising from South Korea's growing dependence on financial markets. It is conceivable, for example, that an intense crisis like the 1994 showdown of Washington and Pyongyang could have destabilizing impacts on Seoul that would cause a sharp falloff of the South's economy.

The simultaneous coordination of economic, political, and military actions is a great deal harder than pure political-military crisis management. Introducing a third dimension—economics—complicates things, and there is at least some reason to believe that such coordination is not a strength of the United States. Most crises Washington deals with have been short, and financial and economic impacts were therefore negligible. But a crisis that drags on for years could mean that such economic factors become much more important.

A good historical example is the oil embargoes of the 1970s. This crisis continued for years. A number of studies have concluded that the United States did not perform particularly well, and its poor performance was in part due to the demand for coordination of economic, political, and military actions over many years' time. The lateral coordination mechanisms of interagency groups may not be able to manage the complex issues shown on Figure 1, at least over many years.

Another crisis management issue has not received due consideration: the command and control of a slow-motion crisis that cascades to become a fast-breaking one. In my judgment, the transition between the two kinds of crises has barely been considered. Since participating over the past few years in a number of crisis management games focusing on North Korea, I find it striking how artificial and, frankly, implausible was the play of South Korea, China, and Japan. The complexities of economic disruption were usually ignored, and temporizing behavior by allies that is likely in a real crisis was more or less overlooked. Even worse, most of the time the United States as a player quickly transitioned to a narrow military focus that effectively ignored the coalition that had been built to stop North Korea's bomb program.

Another crisis management lesson is the need to separate declaratory, programmed, and actual policy. Failure to clarify the distinctions among these has been a great source of difficulty in the past (Sigal 1988). It remains so. A failure to distinguish among the very different purposes of declaratory, programmed, and actual policy could make us the captives of our own rhetoric. This failure could happen at a time of extreme danger, in a context very different from the one in which the statements were made. In the case of North Korea, U.S. rhetoric that confuses these different policies could deeply alienate or even frighten allies.

The historical tendency in Washington is to view crisis management as largely between two players (Bracken 2003). The United States, working with its allies, should thoroughly examine existing crisis management organizations and command-and-control systems for their performance under a wide range of stressful scenarios. The multiple-player aspects of dealing with North Korea need to be included, and tests of the performance of this system under realistic conditions of peace, crisis, and war should not be postponed (Bracken and Shubik 2001, 47–60). A very good test case would be response to a North Korean atomic test. How would the six-party coalition behave? What economic and military actions would be taken? The questions are difficult, to be sure, but they deserve attention when they are not urgent, as they would be in the event of an actual test.

North Korea's own crisis management system is likely to be terrible. The North's statements about its uranium enrichment program and its threats about defending itself with all necessary means may well have been intended to scare the United States. They may have been designed to buy time so that North Korea could expand its atomic capability. But they did not achieve this effect. In Asia, Pyongyang's words increased the sense that Kim Jong-il was prone to erratic behavior at a time when he ought to have been on his best behavior. No country wants to be tied to a North Korea that plunges the region into war.

Imagining North Korea as a skillful manipulator of international politics, a country that uses the threat of war to extract concessions from the West, is likely to be a dangerous overestimation of the North's behavior if the crisis deepens.

Words matter in a crisis much more than they do in the day-to-day diplomacy of international relations. North Korea's April 2003 statements that it would sell weapons-grade plutonium to whomever it pleased made the North appear reckless and dangerous—even to countries that were seeking a peaceful resolution of the crisis. Words matter a great deal on the Korean peninsula, where the largest concentration of military power in the world pits the United States and South Korea against North Korea. At a time in 2003 when the bulk of U.S. military power was tied down in Southwest Asia, words were even more critical.

Kim Jong-il has led a life that makes Nicolae Ceausescu and Saddam Hussein look sophisticated by comparison. We know now that both these men were near delusional in the years before their falls. It seems entirely likely that the same description could apply to the North Korean leader. At the least, this possibility should be incorporated into our crisis management assessments.

Conclusions

From the end of the Korean War until the early 1990s, Pyongyang was walled off from international relations with the West. Washington followed a policy of strict isolation. But when Pyongyang showed signs of developing atomic bombs, U.S. policy toward North Korea reversed from isolation to political engagement. The United States has done a good job of managing North Korea so far. Now international economic engagement is being considered, which creates a new level of complexity. A number of conclusions can inform this discussion.

First, if the North Korean regime collapses, thus ending its nuclear program, the benefits will far outweigh the costs. A nuclear North Korea is likely to be a very dangerous state. The North's erratic words should be understood as representing a government that is extremely unstable when subjected to stress.

Take the largest estimates of what it will cost to repair the North Korean economy. Double them. This is a cheap price to pay if it rids the world of North Korea's atomic weapons program. At the same time, an abortive economic assistance program that does not accomplish this is likely to exacerbate an already difficult problem.

Clemenceau famously said that revolutions come as a whole. We cannot go back to the French Revolution and select the parts of it we liked and reject the parts we did not like. The same thinking should be applied to North Korea. Although there are preferred ways of ending its arms program, the job is not likely to be one of optimally scheduling transition events so as to minimize the life-cycle cost to outside benefactors. Such schemes can be dangerously misleading because people may start to believe that they can schedule the regime's demise to coincide with economic cycles.

The United States can manage international economic assistance toward North Korea for strategic purpose, but a visible hand is needed—a guiding organization that coordinates programs and words into policy. A control group should be established within the U.S. government to ensure centralized control of North Korea issues. This is badly needed because disputes that already exist will become greater as more countries and more issues are brought into the politics of exchange with North Korea. Washington cannot ensure centralized control of a multilateral coalition, but it must at least insure central control of its own policies. Central control should include the words that are used to declare what these policies mean. The time to learn how to do this is not when a slow-motion crisis accelerates into a fast-breaking one with decisions of war and peace in the balance.

Without central control, market forces alone are not likely to generate capital flows; if they happen to, they will be unconnected to strategic purpose. This is true whether capital comes from the market, South Korea, or international agencies.

Finally, grand bargains need to be decomposed into smaller problem chunks that can be managed better. They can also be negotiated better, which is important because of likely disagreements within the six-party coalition about goals, timing, and who pays the piper.

Too much attention is given to the broad principles needed to kick off multilateral-conference diplomacy, and not nearly enough to managing programs for strategic purpose. Conference diplomacy devoid of hard-edged crisis management systems and organizations may even offer North Korea a way of retaining its nuclear program while receiving outside assistance to pay for it. By cycling around agendas of great complexity, years could pass.

Absent improved organizational capacities in U.S. crisis management of North Korea's nuclear weapons program, the addition of multilateral diplomacy and international economic assistance to the picture risks turning what so far has been a good record into one that not only loses sight of its strategic purpose but also is much more dangerous.

References

Bracken, Paul. 2003. Structure of the Second Nuclear Age. *Orbis* (Summer).

Bracken, Paul, and Martin Shubik. 2001. War Gaming for the Information Age: Theory and Purpose. *Naval War College Review* (Spring).

Cha, Victor D., and David C. Kang. 2003. *Nuclear North Korea, A Debate on Engagement Strategies.* New York: Columbia University Press.

Craig, Gordon A., and Alexander L. George. 1983. *Force and Statecraft, Diplomatic Problems of Our Time.* New York: Oxford University Press.

Lancaster, Carol. 2004. Foreign Aid and International Norms: The Case of North Korea. Chapter 7 of this volume.

Lowi, Theodore J. 1964. American Business, Public Policy Case Studies and Political Theory. *World Politics* 16 (July).

Noland, Marcus. 2004. *Korea after Kim Jong-Il.* Washington, D.C.: Institute for International Economics, 2004.

O'Hanlon, Michael, and Mike Mochizuki. 2003. *Crisis on the Korean Peninsula.* New York: McGraw-Hill.

Sigal, Leon V. 1988. *Fighting to the Finish: The Politics of War Termination in the United States and Japan, 1945.* Ithaca: Cornell University Press.

Paul Bracken is Professor of Management and Political Science, Yale University.

7

Foreign Aid and International Norms: The Case of North Korea

Carol Lancaster

Should the United States or other governments (or international organizations) provide foreign aid to the government of the Democratic People's Republic of Korea (DPRK)? North Korea is an extremely poor country with periodic bouts of severe famine and widespread human suffering. But it is governed by what is arguably the most repressive and secretive government in the world with one of the most mismanaged economies and, despite its poverty, one of the largest expenditures on its military relative to the size of its gross national product of any country on the face of the Earth. What is to be done?

There are no binding international rules of eligibility for receiving foreign aid. The decision to provide or withhold aid rests with the governments and international institutions giving it. But over the half century of aid giving a set of international norms has arisen that has guided who receives aid and who does not. This paper examines those norms, applies them to the case of North Korea, and suggests conditions under which aid should be given or withheld from that peculiar and troubling regime.

Norms for Aid Giving

Let us start at the beginning: What do we mean by norms? What do we mean by foreign aid? And where did foreign aid come from?

Definition: Norms

Norms are principles—widely recognized as legitimate and appropriate—that guide behavior. They may not carry the weight of law or even be written down, but, by being widely accepted, they set standards of behavior against which individuals, groups, states and international bodies can be judged. In the case of foreign aid, there are norms that guide whether an aid-giving agency provides aid as well as how the aid is provided (that is, how much, for what uses, in what forms, and with what terms). We are concerned here with the question of whether, not the many questions of how. What principles, formal or informal, shape whether aid donors provide assistance to particular countries or governments?

Definition: Foreign Aid

Foreign aid is not a policy, as is sometimes thought. It is an instrument for achieving purposes or realizing policies. We use here the definition of foreign aid (also known as official development assistance or ODA) framed by the Development Assistance Committee (DAC) of the Organization for Economic Cooperation and Development (OECD): a transfer of public funds from a government to another government of a developing country, or to an international organization or nongovernmental organization (NGO) for use in such a country, with at least a 25 percent grant element, one purpose of which is to further development and welfare (OECD 2004b).[1] ODA amounted to $58 billion worldwide in 2002. According to DAC data, in that same year, the DPRK received $188 million in foreign aid, $90 million of which was in the form of food aid (OECD 2004a).

Foreign aid is a phenomenon of the second half of the twentieth century, with antecedents in earlier international relief efforts as well as public transfers from colonial powers to their territories in Africa and Asia. But it was the Cold War, beginning in the late 1940s, that led the United States to begin to provide significant and sustained flows of foreign aid to governments under internal or external pressures or threats from communist parties, radical insurgents, the USSR, the People's Republic of China, or their allies. Aid to stabilize and grow economies soon became aid to further their development, used as a means to the end of containing communism.

By the 1960s, most European governments and Japan, now recovered from World War II, established their own aid programs, often with commercial as well as development purposes.[2] Commercial purposes tended to be secondary in most aid-giving countries and were gradually constrained by development goals and international agreements on such things as the amount of tied aid and the use of aid in mixed credit arrangements. Thus, by the end of the twentieth century, foreign aid was provided for three principal reasons:

- To relieve human suffering caused by natural or man-made disasters;

---

1 The DAC would prefer the development and welfare purpose as the main purpose, but aid-giving governments tend to mix their purposes, making this requirement too exacting and difficult to determine. The designation of a developing country is that it had an average per capita income of less than $9,360 in 1998 (a World Bank benchmark).

2 Commercial purposes included securing needed raw materials imports and expanding export markets.

- To support economic and social progress in developing countries (and, with the end of the Cold War, former socialist bloc countries); and
- For national security and international political purposes.[3]

These three goals of aid giving have generated sets of widely shared international norms regarding the conditions under which aid is provided.

Norms: Emergency Relief

Four main norms have come to guide international humanitarian aid:

- The first norm is the humanitarian imperative of saving lives and alleviating suffering where home governments are unable adequately to do so themselves.
- Those providing humanitarian assistance are required to act with impartiality, independence, and neutrality when dealing with the victims of emergencies—that means not taking sides in conflicts and not serving in effect as the agents of external powers that may also have particular interests in emergencies other than providing relief (Sphere Project 2004).[4]
- Those providing relief should treat victims of emergencies with dignity.
- Relief organizations and workers should be accountable to both those they help and those that fund their operations.

In practice, accountability to funders has often meant that governments providing the aid have wanted to ensure it was delivered to its intended beneficiaries. This not usually an issue if an experienced NGO is delivering the aid. It can be a problem if the aid is being provided to governments to distribute and those governments deny donors access to the beneficiaries of the aid.

These principles have not been dispute free. Critics within the relief community suggest that politically blind relief can be abused by manipulative governments or warring factions, hurting the intended recipients in the long run, if not the short run, as well and reinforcing the power and sustainability of abusive regimes. In the case of relief for the refugees in Goma in the wake of the genocide in Rwanda in 1994, Médicins Sans Frontières withdrew from providing relief on the grounds that the relief was controlled by the very *genocidaires* in the camps (remnants of the Hutu militias) who had perpe-

---

3 Other purposes gaining prominence in the 1990s included promoting democracy, managing conflict, and addressing global problems like environmental degradation or the international transmission of disease. For a detailed accounting of the origin and evolution of the purposes of aid, see Lancaster (forthcoming).

4 These principles are found in the code of conduct of the Red Cross and the Red Crescent, which was established in 1994 and is adhered to by numerous NGOs, and in the Humanitarian Charter, drawn from a variety of documents on humanitarian norms and practices and agreed to by a variety of NGOs engaged in relief activities.

trated the genocide in the first place; the relief was permitting them to continue intimidating refugees and purchase arms. Thus, the issue of whether relief, while reducing suffering in the short run, can prolong suffering in the long run is on the international normative agenda.

Norms: Development Aid

International norms guiding the allocation of aid for development are less concrete than those shaping relief assistance and are breached by aid-giving governments far more frequently with much less criticism. Many aid-giving governments have pursued aid giving with mixed motives (often including national security and international political goals) that have obscured the clarity of purpose and the best means for achieving development objectives, which underpin norms. Nevertheless, international norms—involving the characteristics of countries and their governments and make them appropriate recipients for foreign aid—have evolved and have become especially evident since the end of the Cold War. They include economic need, human rights performance, probability of aid effectiveness, aid process, and ability of aid donors to be accountable to their governments for their use of the aid.

Need. It is widely accepted that concessional public transfers for development should be provided to those governments that lack the resources fully to realize their countries' development on their own. Where a country has a pocket of severe poverty but has the resources (through taxes, international borrowing, or foreign investment) to reduce that poverty, the case for development aid is far less compelling. That government has made a choice not to address its domestic problems; it is difficult to argue that the publics in other countries should then do so with their resources.

The benchmark often used to designate needy countries is an average annual per capita income below a certain level. The World Bank designation of countries that are IDA eligible—that is, eligible for soft loans from the International Development Association (IDA)—is the most commonly used norm. The World Bank currently has a cutoff of $875 average per capita gross national income per year (in 2001 prices) for eligibility for IDA loans. The DAC, which is an international club of bilateral aid donors in North America, Europe, and Japan, pushes the norm of neediness further. It undertakes periodic reviews of the aid programs of its member states and makes a point in those reports and in its data generally to highlight the percentage of member states' aid going to the lowest-income countries (with a per capita income of $760 or less in 1998 dollars) in an effort to encourage member states to direct more aid to the poorest.[5]

---

5 The United Nations Development Program (UNDP) has created a Human Development Index comprising a variety of statistical indicators of well-being in addition to per capita income levels, but this index tends to be less used as a common standard of need in the development community; see UNDP (2003).

Human rights. Human rights have long been on the international agenda. They were delineated in 1948 in the United Nations (UN) Universal Declaration of Human Rights and have since been expanded in a number of other international declarations and treaties. For several decades, however, the human rights performance of governments was little debated in international forums because of the sensitivities in particular of newly independent governments about the sanctity of sovereignty and the bipolarity of the Cold War, which made it risky for Western governments to criticize the human rights records of other governments for fear of driving them into the arms of the Socialist bloc (whose regard for human rights was not terribly elevated in any case). Since the 1970s when Jimmy Carter, then the U.S. president, declared that a government's human rights performance was an explicit criterion for the quality of U.S. relations with that country and that the United States would consider that performance in its decisions on aid and on votes in the World Bank on aid loans, human rights has been on the international agenda as a consideration in aid giving. Human rights has been a prominent consideration in the aid programs of a number of other governments as well— the Nordic countries in particular—and has become widely accepted, at least at the rhetorical level.

No common standard is used by aid donors for judging the human rights performances of governments and informing decisions on their aid allocations. The U.S. government often draws on the annual *Country Reports on Human Rights Practices* that, for each country

> . . . cover internationally recognized individual, civil, political and worker rights, as set forth in the Universal Declaration of Human Rights. These rights include freedom from torture or other cruel, inhuman or degrading treatment or punishment; from prolonged detention without charges; from disappearance or clandestine detention; and from other flagrant violations of the right to life, liberty and the security of the person.

> Universal human rights seek to incorporate respect for human dignity into the processes of government and law. All persons have the inalienable right to change their government by peaceful means and to enjoy basic freedoms, such as freedom of expression, association, assembly, movement and religion, without discrimination on the basis of race, religion, national origin or sex. The right to join a free trade union is a necessary condition of a free society and economy. Thus the reports assess key internationally recognized worker rights, including the right of association; the right to organize and bargain collectively; prohibition of forced or compulsory labor; the status of child labor practices and the minimum age for employment of children; and acceptable work conditions (DOS 2003).

Other sources of human rights assessments include the Office of the UN High Commissioner on Human Rights, the United Kingdom (UK) Foreign and Commonwealth Office on Human Rights, Human Rights Watch, Amnesty International, and numerous other public and private organizations worldwide. Although there is no universal standard of human rights to which aid agencies are expected to adhere, there are usually criticisms—from human rights organizations and other governments—of aid-giving countries providing development assistance to governments that are widely recognized as gross violators of human rights.

The U.S. government, for example, was roundly criticized by U.S. human rights groups in the mid-1980s for providing aid to the government of El Salvador in light of the brutality and widespread killings on the part of the military of that country. The government of France has been criticized for providing aid to Togo, where human rights, child trafficking, and political repression have been particular problems over the past decade. In neither of these cases did criticisms prevent the U.S. or French governments from providing aid, but they put governments that have touted their commitment to human rights on the defensive. In another case—the former Zaire—a number of aid-giving governments reduced or halted their aid in the early 1990s after the army there killed a number of students in a demonstration. In this case, the national security or political interests of the aid-giving governments were not perceived to be affected by a cutoff of aid. The realities of aid giving are that, where governments provide the aid for national security reasons or other important political reasons, those reasons usually trump human rights concerns. But that does not mean that human rights standards are not important or influential in aid giving. They clearly are important in today's world.

Aid effectiveness.   Concerns about aid's effectiveness in furthering economic and social development have been around since the beginning of aid giving. Such concerns have taken on a particular prominence since the end of the Cold War (which, in effect, removed a shield against criticism that aid was not furthering development in recipient countries) and since the expansion of quantitative data that has encouraged analysts to take a closer look at aid's impact. Studies—including several from the most influential aid donor, the World Bank—argue that aid has, in fact, been ineffective in a number of situations (Dollar and Burnside 1998).

What are the conditions, apart from the capacity of aid-giving agencies themselves and the quality of their staff's work, that are generally assumed to determine the effectiveness of aid? In the 1960s and 1970s, aid experts would likely have answered that the quantity of infrastructure and the education and health of the population would be critical to the absorptive capacity of a country—that is, the country's ability to use aid effectively. Attitudes are different at present; they reflect the experience of the past several decades on the basis of which it has been recognized that institutions matter. Thus, the general answer today on the conditions of aid effectiveness would include the quality of a country's governance; the degree of openness of its markets (to permit private economic initiative); and the commitment of its government to creating the conditions for economic and social progress, including expanding education and health services (therefore putting less funding into military expenditures). These are the essential conditions President George W. Bush mentioned as qualifications for aid to countries from the new Millennium Challenge Account, but these conditions have been part of the broader development discourse for several years. What do they entail?

Governance is used to refer to several different conditions. One—most often used by the World Bank—refers to capacity of government to perform its functions. This can involve appropriate levels of education and training for staff; adequate amounts of required skills (e.g., auditing); and an efficient, functioning organization of tasks to be accomplished (clarity of responsibilities, delegation, and budgetary planning and controls, for example).

The United States has used the term governance more broadly, often to include democracy, assuming that without the legitimacy and accountability associated with democratic political systems, governments will lack the incentives to ascertain and respond to the public will, to choose and implement workable policies, and to maintain a relatively clean administration with a minimum of corruption. Some in the United States go so far as to assert that, without democracy, development (and, presumably, effective aid) is unlikely to occur.[6] One of the principal and most widely used sources of indicators of the existence and extent of democracy in particular countries is the annual report by Freedom House, called *Freedom in the World*. This report ranks governments according to a number of indicators of political and civil rights.

One aspect of good governance that everyone—both scholars and public officials—appears to support is that essential to effective aid and development are the rule of law and a minimal amount of corruption. Where the rule of law is impaired and corruption rampant, investments (public or private) become extremely risky, and the ability of investments to achieve their objectives and sustain those achievements is diminished. The principal source of indicators of corruption in individual countries is the *Global Corruption Report*, an annual survey produced by Transparency International that ranks countries, on the basis of the perceptions of groups of experts on individual countries.

The degree of **market freedom** is another quality widely considered essential to development and effective aid. Where governments create high barriers to trade; control prices, internal trade and production; levy excessive taxes;

---

6 Research on the relationship between democracy and development, at least in the short run, does not substantiate this view. That has not dampened enthusiasm for it in public discourse, an enthusiasm probably stemming from strongly held and widely shared values that democracy is a good in and of itself—an end as well as a means of policy.

overregulate the economy; and engage in other activities that curb the incentives and opportunities for private entrepreneurs to invest and produce, economies tend to progress more slowly, and opportunities for corruption and mismanagement increase.[7] One source used by the U.S. government for indicators of the degree of free markets is the annual publication by the Heritage Foundation called *Index of Economic Freedom.*

Perhaps the principal indicators of a government's commitment to the development of its country are its **expenditures on health and education** as a portion of its budget and of the country's gross national income. Within these expenditures, development specialists have put special emphasis on funding primary education (it has long been observed that the returns to additional expenditures tend to be high relative to expenditures on secondary and tertiary education) and primary health care. Data on health and educational expenditures are often drawn from World Bank data where data on military expenditures are also available.[8]

Military expenditures as a portion of total government expenditures are sometimes examined by aid-giving governments and consultative groups. Expenditures on weapons of mass destruction have been particularly important to U.S. decisions on aid allocations. The Pressler Amendment, passed by the Congress in 1986, prohibited U.S. aid to Pakistan unless the president could verify that Pakistan did not possess nuclear arms. By 1990, the president could not do so, and U.S. aid to Pakistan was phased out.[9] Other governments have cut their aid when recipient governments exploded nuclear devices; for example, Japan reduced its aid to China in the wake of Chinese nuclear testing in the 1990s. Thus, there may be an emerging norm that governments of developing countries that develop and test such weapons are sanctioned—at least for a time—with reductions in their aid flows.

Aid process.   One of the less-recognized developments of the 1990s was the emergence of what could be called "process conditionality" as part of the norms shaping aid giving. In reaction to the apparent ineffectiveness of aid—especially in sub-Saharan Africa—during the 1980s and early 1990s, practitioners and scholars of aid and development began to look for ways to manage aid to ensure greater effectiveness. Out of this effort came three concepts:

- **Participation.**   Participation means asking people what their preferences are—whether in the form of a national consultation on overall development strategies or in the form of a targeted consultation with the intended beneficiaries of a specific intervention. This is not a new idea;

---

7 This does not mean that there should be no regulation of economic activity. The balance between government regulation and free markets is an area of continuing contention.

8 For a much more detailed examination of the likely indicators used to determine eligibility for the Millennium Challenge Account monies, see Radelet (2002).

9 Aid to Pakistan has since been restored in conjunction with Pakistan's cooperation in the U.S. intervention in Afghanistan and the hunt for members of Al Qaeda.

it has been around since the beginning of development aid and was a prominent element in the community-development focus of aid giving popular in the 1960s. It regained prominence in the late 1980s and 1990s as part of the backlash to structural adjustment programs, which were widely criticized as imposed from the outside, top down, and hurtful to the interests of the poor.

At the core of the current notion of participation is the idea of empowerment—that people should have a measure of control over their lives and not be dictated to or repressed by governments (their own or others) or other powers in society. Deriving from this notion is the belief that, if people are consulted about things intended to affect their lives, their preferences and knowledge can lead to more appropriate interventions, and they will support those interventions in the future—in other words, they will take ownership of the aid interventions, making them more effective and sustainable. Participation in the form of national consultations on development strategies is also regarded by some development practitioners as a means of strengthening democracy in developing countries because it leads the government to consult with its population on these important issues.

- **Ownership.**   Ownership is one of the least satisfactorily defined terms in the aid process category. At its core is the sensible notion that people will take responsibility for things they have had a hand in shaping. However, identifying when ownership exists and when it does not; what sorts of engagement by people create a sense of ownership on their part for particular activities; and what ownership actually leads to in terms of human behavior are also as yet ill defined elements of this concept. Although the term is vague enough to obscure clear thinking, it is virtually a mantra in aid-giving today.

- **Partnership.**   Partnership means a collaboration between aid giver and aid recipient that involves a measure of equality.[10] Again, behind this somewhat vague idea is the assumption that aid recipients will take more seriously aid-funded activities that they have helped to plan and implement; in other words, aid donors should not just arrive in a country and dictate to the government or local communities what will be done for them.

These three ideas—participation, ownership, and partnership—have been given particular prominence by the World Bank in its Comprehensive Development Framework (CDF), a broad concept of what development requires. The three ideas have also become the basis on which the World Bank has

---

10 Partnership can also mean collaboration among different aid-giving organizations, including public aid agencies, NGOs, and private enterprises.

attempted to recast its aid interventions to achieve greater effectiveness and sustainability. The preferred vehicle for ensuring that the World Bank's aid and aid of other aid agencies reflect these principles is the Poverty Reduction Strategy Papers (PRSPs). These are broad national strategies for poverty reduction that are drawn up by recipient governments in consultation with their citizens for maximum participation and ownership and that, after approval by the World Bank Board of Executive Directors will become the framework for World Bank lending and (it is hoped) aid from other governments as well. Having a PRSP is also a requirement for heavily indebted poor countries to gain extraordinary debt relief from the World Bank.

Not all aid agencies have embraced these notions, even at the rhetorical level. Nor have they all made a PRSP a requirement for receiving aid. But these new notions and the reliance on PRSPs are increasingly common among a number of aid-giving agencies. Should it prove possible to demonstrate in a reasonably rigorous manner that these ideas do make aid more effective and sustainable, they could well become full-fledged norms of aid giving.[11]

Accountability.   Few aid-giving agencies are willing to write checks to recipient governments and organizations without some effort to identify the proposed uses of the aid and ascertain whether the funding has, in fact, been used for that purpose. Taxpayers and their representatives in governments in aid-giving countries typically demand such accountings. The more demanding the legislative and public groups are on issues of accountability, the greater the transparency in aid giving and the less opportunity there is for aid-giving and aid-receiving governments and organizations to act corruptly or for the former to turn a blind eye to the latter.

Where public scandals have erupted over the misuse of aid funding—as in Italy during the early 1990s, and periodically in Japan and France—the public can turn against aid and force the government to cut it and to reform. Thus, it has often been the case that governments and organizations receiving the aid must submit to audits, reports, and supervisory visits from aid donors to ensure that the aid is being used as intended. This is a norm in aid giving—more enforced in some aid-giving countries than in others—that is seldom mentioned because it is so widely accepted.

National Security

International norms have minimal influence on the allocation of foreign aid that is based on national security or international political concerns. The decision about whether to use aid in this way is made by aid-giving governments, based on the perceptions and priorities of those in power. This kind of aid has been provided to governments in exchange for agreed actions (for

---

11 In World Bank (2003), the World Bank evaluated the impact of the CDF; it is in the process of evaluating the PRSPs as well.

example, the provision of base rights, the suppression of terrorists), in exchange for general support for the donor government's policies (for example, France vis-à-vis its former colonies in sub-Saharan Africa), or to ensure reliable access to policymakers in recipient countries.

At times, aid for national security purposes is consistent with the norms guiding the allocation of aid for development—that is, provided to governments with good governance, economic policies, and a commitment to their peoples. But it is also the case that governments with poor economic management, poor human rights records, high levels of corruption, and repression have all been the recipients of this type of aid when security or political interests of donor governments have been compelling. The poster child of this type of aid was the former Zaire, which for decades received sizable amounts of aid from the United States, Belgium, and France despite the kleptocratic government of Mobutu Sese Seko.

It appears that aid for national security purposes diminished in the wake of the end of the Cold War, a time when developing countries could exploit their position between the United States and the USSR and assorted allies and surrogates. However, this trend may be reversed with the war on terrorism and an activist policy by the United States to intervene militarily against terrorists and other rogue regimes—actions that often require support from other governments, especially in the region of the intervention. Aid is one instrument for acquiring that support. Aid is also useful as a tool of peacemaking—an incentive for warring parties to negotiate peace. Policies of peacemaking, as in the Middle East and the Balkans, are also likely to make continuing calls on U.S. aid.

Aid for national security or international political purposes, while not much influenced by international norms, is often contested in internal government discussions by officials in development agencies, by development-oriented NGOs, and in books and articles by officials and former aid officials from those governments providing the aid. Much of the long-term tension between the U.S. Agency for International Development and the U.S. Department of State over aid allocations has revolved around this difference of view. Perhaps the country in which such criticisms have been most public and strident is France, where even government officials still in office have published interviews in leading journals (sometimes under noms de plume) and books attacking the misallocation of their government's aid.[12]

If there is a norm in aid giving for national security or international political purposes, it is that those purposes must be regarded by political elites in aid-giving governments as of sufficiently high national priority so as to sus-

---

12 For an interesting example of this criticism, see Michailof (1993). Michailof was a senior official of the Agence Française de Développement at the time this book was published and is again a senior official in that agency. For an attack on U.S. aid for political purposes (in Egypt), see Zimmerman (1993).

tain them in the face of domestic and international criticism. The greater the deviation of the recipient government from the expected norms—especially need, human rights performance, and the qualities leading to greater aid effectiveness—the greater the expected criticism.

Norms and North Korea

How does aid to North Korea stack up against the norms—some weak, some strong—in aid giving at the end of the twentieth century? Let us discuss each set of norms as they apply to North Korea.

Humanitarian Relief

In many ways, this is the most problematic set of norms as applied to the DPRK. We know that much of the population of the DPRK has endured periodic famines (the one in the 1990s is thought to have killed hundreds of thousands at the very least, and perhaps a million or even more), and a large percentage of Korean children are seriously malnourished. In 1998, the UN estimated that 60 percent of Korean children suffered from stunted growth owing to malnutrition (EIU 2004, 13). Since agricultural production—never easy in a country with limited arable land—has diminished because of a lack of inputs and because the DPRK government has opted to spend its diminishing resources on guns rather than butter, the country, according to Noland (2003, 1), "does not produce enough output to sustain the population biologically." What has been necessary since the late 1990s to keep an ongoing humanitarian crisis from turning into a major humanitarian disaster is massive amounts of foreign food aid. It is estimated that one-third of the 22 million North Koreans depend on food aid.

Although food aid has undoubtedly helped avoid widespread starvation in North Korea, providing the food aid does raise practical and ethical concerns. The unwillingness of the Korean government to permit aid donors to monitor the delivery of their aid to ensure it is not diverted to the one-million-strong army leaves doubt about the real beneficiaries of the food. Newspapers have reported that the government of North Korea has denied food to those considered insufficiently committed or loyal, a contravention of the humanitarian commitment to fulfill needs whatever the politics of the needy person or group.

Another difficult ethical problem is that of relieving short-term suffering with food aid while possibly prolonging suffering in the long term by, in effect, strengthening the position of a truly despicable government that is largely responsible for the suffering and starvation of its people and whose existence might be shortened were such aid not available. The ethical choice here, given the unknowns (including the consequences of a collapse of the North Korean regime), is very difficult to make, and most people and organizations have in the past chosen to provide the aid in the short term with the expectation that some of it will reduce suffering.[13]

Development Aid

With regard to the emerging norms that influence the provision of development aid, North Korea at present would never qualify. Although its need cannot be denied (per capita income is believed to be around $750 per year, having declined by half since the early 1990s when the Soviet Union collapsed and its economic subsidies were terminated), it has one of the worst human rights records of any government in the world. For example, recent defectors have alleged that the government has used gas chambers in one of its labor camps to conduct chemical experiments on inmates. Aid for infrastructure and agricultural and industrial inputs might well facilitate greater production and internal trade (earlier investments in these areas have deteriorated dramatically), but North Korea's poor economic management would likely put limits on the sustained impact of these investments.

The DPRK's arbitrary, brutal, and repressive government—a government that in the past has blithely defaulted on its external debts—also limits the opportunities and incentives for individuals to take economic risks or, for that matter, for foreign investors to put their money at risk in the country. The government has invested in the education of its people and has one of the higher average levels of education and life expectancy of governments at its income level, but the government's relatively large expenditures on its large military and on arms production—despite widespread famine in the country—are an indication that the welfare of its population is far from the top of its priority list.

In addition to sizable military expenditures, the DPRK has openly advertised its efforts to develop nuclear weapons and has tested long-range missiles periodically over the past several years. These policies alone might be enough to raise questions about the appropriateness of providing such a government with development aid because such aid might in effect free up more domestic resources for military purposes.

The erratic behavior of the North Korean state—with its extraordinary cults of personality involving its leaders, its kidnaping foreign nationals, and its transfer of nuclear technology to other countries—all set it apart as a rogue state, outside the community of nations and the community of states normally receiving long-term aid for their development.

---

13 In January 2004, it looked like food aid for the DPRK would drop precipitously as food donations through the World Food Program fell. That drop in turn may reflect the growing disillusionment among aid-giving governments with the DPRK and their impatience with Pyongyang's erratic policies regarding weapons of mass destruction. However, the United States and other donors have begun to ship food to North Korea.

Finally, the inability of aid-giving governments to monitor their assistance in Korea would make it difficult for them to be accountable to their own legislatures and publics for the aid they have provided. In the case of development aid, the prospect of people dying if the aid is not provided is not present and does not override normal concerns for accountability.

The only justification for nonemergency aid to North Korea is a compelling national security concern on the part of the aid-giving government, such as was part of the Agreed Framework between the United States and the DPRK when the United States promised energy supplies and two nuclear generating stations in exchange for a promise by the North Koreans to stop production of nuclear weapons and dismantle facilities producing such weapons. This agreement appears to have held for a time, but, after the Koreans decided to commence a new nuclear weapons program, it was then cancelled.

The experience with the DPRK suggests that aid may be useful only in exchange for concrete and immediately delivered benefits and that aid in exchange for long-term commitments does not work. The government in Pyongyang does not regard its international commitments—whether repayment of debts or cessation of the production of nuclear weapons—as something it is obligated to fulfill. One cannot trust or verify because there is no basis for trust and no verification permitted. The only workable basis for exchange appears to be cash on delivery.

References

Department of State (DOS). 2003. Overview and Acknowledgments. In *Country Reports on Human Rights Practices–2002*. Washington, D.C.: Bureau of Democracy, Human Rights, and Labor; U.S. Department of State. 31 March. www.state.gov/g/drl/rls/hrrpt/2002/18133.htm.

Dollar, David, and Craig Burnside. 1998. *Assessing Aid: What Works, What Doesn't and Why*. Washington, D.C.: World Bank.

Economist Intelligence Unit (EIU). 2004. *Country Profile 2004: North Korea*. London: Economist Intelligence Unit.

Lancaster, Carol. Forthcoming. Fifty Years of Foreign Aid. In manuscript.

Michailof, Serge, ed. 1993. *La France et l'Afrique*. Paris: Karthala.

Noland, Marcus. 2003. Famine and Reform in North Korea. Washington, D.C.: Institute for International Economics. www.iie.com/publications/wp/2003/03-5.pdf.

Organization for Economic Cooperation and Development (OECD). 2004a. Aid Statistics. Paris: OECD. www.oecd.org/department/0,2688,en_2649_34447_1_1_1_1_1,00.html.

————. 2004b. Development Cooperation Directorate (DAC), DAC's Glossary. Paris: OECD. www.oecd.org/glossary/0,2586,en_2649_33721_1965693_1_1_1_1,00.html.

Radelet, Steve. 2002. Qualifying for the Millennium Challenge Account. Center for Global Development. December. www.cgdev.org/docs/Choosing_MCA_Countries.pdf.

Sphere Project. 2004. Humanitarian Charter and Minimum Standards in Disaster Response. Geneva: Sphere Project.

United Nations Development Program (UNDP). 2003. Human Development Indicators 2003. New York: United Nations. http://hdr.undp.org/reports/global/2003/indicator/index_indicators.html.

World Bank. 2003. *Toward Country-Led Development: A Multipartner Evaluation of the Comprehensive Development Framework.* Washington, D.C.: World Bank.

Zimmerman, Robert. 1993. *Dollars, Diplomacy and Dependency.* Boulder, Colo.: Lynne Rienner.

Carol Lancaster is a Professor at the School of Foreign Service at Georgetown University, Washington, D.C. She previously served in a number of U.S. government positions, including as Deputy Administrator of USAID from 1993 to 1996.

8

Prospects and Preconditions for Market Economic Transformation in North Korea

Anders Åslund

Since 1989, approximately 30 countries have attempted to move from a socialist system to a market economy in Europe and Asia. The outcomes have been remarkably different. Most have succeeded. In Central Europe and the Baltic countries, normal West European democracies and market economies have been established. In Belarus, Turkmenistan, and Uzbekistan, by contrast, little has happened but the exit of the Communist Party, while dictatorship and socialist economies persist. State ownership and state regulation predominate, and dictatorship remains firm. China and Vietnam have undertaken successful market economic transformation, while their Communist parties remain in power. Other countries fall somewhere in between. Thus, the outcome of postcommunist transformation is by no means given. It varies with initial conditions, the economic policy pursued, and policies of the outside world.[1]

Two true Stalinist states soldier on: Cuba and North Korea. These holdouts cannot be expected to last much longer. This paper offers a discussion of which economic policies might be relevant for North Korea in light of the experiences of the transformation of other postcommunist countries. I do not claim expertise on North Korea, about which my knowledge is rudimentary at best. Yet Communist systems have many features in common, and if one studies many of these economies, one knows what to look for. I have tried to establish relevant North Korean peculiarities and see parallels with countries in the former Soviet bloc that appear reasonable.[2] What lessons can be learned from those countries, and to what extent may they be appli-

---

1 An overall source for this paper is Åslund (2002).
2 I thank Nicholas Eberstadt and Marcus Noland for providing answers to my empirical questions about North Korea.

cable to a future North Korean transformation? Trying to draw the most appropriate parallels, I suggest a scenario for how North Korean Communism may crumble. A key question, of course, is whether the North Korean state will crumble or not. Having drawn up such a scenario, I proceed to prescribe advisable policy actions with regard to economic liberalization, financial stabilization, privatization, and foreign assistance.[3]

North Korean Peculiarities and Relevant Parallels from Other Postcommunist Countries

The postcommunist countries can roughly be divided into four different groups. One consists of China and Vietnam, where market economic reform was initiated by the old Communist establishment. Their outstanding feature was that more than 70 percent of the labor force was employed in agriculture, which made their transition comparatively easy. Quasi property rights could swiftly be introduced in agriculture (Sachs and Woo 1994, 101–45). By contrast, in 1995 no more than 31 percent of the North Korean labor force was employed in agriculture and as much as 37 percent in manufacturing (Eberstadt 2001a, table 5). Because of these structural differences, the Chinese and Vietnamese models appear unattainable. By contrast, Marcus Noland (2004, 60) plausibly argues: "North Korea is probably the world's most distorted economy." These distortions involve all aspects of the economy—its structure, extreme protectionism, prices, and exchange rate.

The Central European and Baltic countries form another group of postcommunist countries. Politically, they had a well-developed public debate before the end of Communism, with strong civil societies. They just needed the signal from Moscow that they were allowed to do their own thing. In Central Europe, economic distortions were comparatively limited. Hungary and Poland had already developed market socialism and had substantial private sectors. No parallel with North Korea is apparent, and their concrete experiences do not appear particularly relevant for that country.

The situation in the former Soviet Union is much more applicable from an economic point of view. Private ownership in the Soviet Union was very limited. Centralized state allocation dominated. Prices and exchange rates were highly distorted. A fiscal crisis was well developed before the collapse of communism. Yet, the former Soviet Union was more reformed and open and had far more markets than North Korea. Post-Soviet cases give us some guidance, but we would expect the situation in North Korea to turn much worse.

---

3 Jeffrey Sachs has published beautiful outlines for what needs to be done after Communism, and they remain true (Sachs 1990, 19–24; 1991, 101–4; Sachs and Lipton 1990, 47–66). A broad relevant literature has developed, notably World Bank (1996), EBRD (1999), Fischer and Gelb (1991, 91–105), Shleifer and Vishny (1998).

With little doubt, the country most similar to North Korea was Albania. Like North Korea, it was a highly national Marxist-Leninist dictatorship, although more orthodox and less original. All power was concentrated in the leader, around whom an incredible personality cult had developed. Even more extreme than contemporary North Korea, Albania had no legal private enterprise. The economy was totally monopolized, essentially with one domestic producer for each product. Foreign trade was completely centralized, and prices were totally distorted. For all practical purposes, no exchange rate existed. Admittedly, Albania is much smaller than North Korea, and it was probably poorer. Yet, no other postcommunist country is likely to tell us as much about the transition in North Korea as Albania.

An additional query concerning North Korea is whether the state itself will collapse and be absorbed by South Korea and, if so, how that will happen. The obvious example is the German unification. However, the parallel is not as self-evident as it may appear. The fundamental difference is that East Germany was continuously subject to Soviet military occupation, which is of course not the case with North Korea. Another East German peculiarity was that the people were very well-informed thanks to West German television, which covered the whole country. Finally, the country experienced a huge and continuous escape of millions of citizens to West Germany, and the refugees were given automatic West German citizenship. Nor is the Vietnamese unification applicable, because it amounted to straightforward military conquest.

A few other examples may be worth contemplating. Moldova was taken from Romania by the Soviet Union during World War II but, although the populations are ethnically united, unification is not a serious issue. Austria is ethnically German and was united with Germany before World War II, but unification with Germany is not suggested by anyone today. Another example is that, after the breakup of the Soviet Union, many thought Belarus would rejoin Russia, as the Belarusian nation is in dispute, but that has not happened so far because the Belarusian elite preferred its independence. Nations are not born but built, and they are vested in their elites. In recent history, it is more common that two nations part company than that two countries of one nation join hands. After a half century of independence, North Korea has developed a strong elite of its own that is unlikely to give up power voluntarily. Considering that few countries are as strange as North Korea, the North Koreans' understanding of their South Korean brethren must be minimal. Why would they then want to merge their state with them?

Nor is it obvious that South Korea would like to absorb North Korea immediately. Economically, the German unification is deterring. The costs to West German taxpayers have been huge—on the order of $150 billion a year. Most of this money has been wasted on social welfare, and East Germans have been caught in a social welfare trap, rendering it unprofitable for them to work, as social benefits have been more ample than wages. Huge public investment in East German infrastructure has proved extremely unprofitable. It is common to blame the currency union, which valued the East German *mark* at an artificially high rate, but a more appropriate target would be the West German trade unions, which insisted on excessive wages in the East for their own benefit. The result was the highest official unemployment in any postcommunist country, rising to 35 percent, as East German labor was priced out of the market. As a consequence, millions of East Germans migrated to the West during the decade after unification. Regardless of policy, the large migration was difficult to avoid after the early unification.

Because of West German insistence on restitution of property to refugees in the West, East Germans did not get much out of the privatization either. Unemployed and deprived, stuck in their social welfare trap, the East Germans grew regretful and voted for left-wing parties and more social welfare, tipping the political balance in unified Germany to the left, so that liberal economic reforms could not be undertaken. Hence, the whole of Germany has been ossified, leading to minimal growth in both the East and the West, at a high cost to society (Pickel and Wiesenthal 1997; Siebert 1992; World Bank 2002). Today Germany is often described as the sick man of Europe, and its sickness is a direct consequence of its unsuccessful unification. Why would anybody like to repeat such a costly failure?

The West German population was four times larger than East Germany's, while South Korea's population is only twice as large as North Korea's. Moreover, West Germany was much richer than South Korea is today. A unification with North Korea could destabilize South Korea both economically and politically, which would harm North Korea as well. Therefore, I shall assume that the North Korean state does not collapse but remains independent during the course of its transformation, which appears to have started already.

A Scenario for North Korean Transformation

The Albanian transformation was instigated by three factors. First, the original despot Enver Hoxha died in 1985. Second, the country was absolutely isolated internationally, and the previously large amount of aid from, first, the Soviet Union and, later, China ceased. Third, the unreformed and autarkic economy ossified and started declining. In addition, the East European revolutions of 1989 had substantial impact on the few thinking members of the elite. As the regime hesitated, it crumbled. Elections were held in the early summer of 1991. While the Communists won, the hard-liners lost out. The ruling elite stayed in power, but it was divided into roughly three groups— hard-liners, reform Communists, and anticommunist opposition. While the small elite fought among themselves, the country ended up in near anarchy by the summer of 1991. The absence of civil society led to a striking lack of compromise and civil peace while the Communist Party stayed strong. Eventually a minor civil war erupted in 1997, but it was swiftly contained.

The situation in North Korea appears reminiscent. Kim Il-sung died in 1994. North Korea is isolated. The difference is that substantial humanitarian assistance of more than $1 billion per year has been given to North Korea for the past few years. As Marcus Noland (2004) argues, this "humanitarian" assistance is likely to prolong the life of the regime. In a country where power and knowledge have been so extremely concentrated, as in North Korea, the old elite is likely to feed all future political groups. As in Albania, an uncompromising anti-Communist Party is likely to emerge, which is more anticommunist than democratic, while a strong, recalcitrant Communist Party is likely to persist. The weaker that civil society was before the end of communism, the less probability of democracy or sophisticated policy in any sphere (Åslund 2002).

The North Korean economic system appears to be unraveling. The economic reforms of July 2002 are largely first-generation Soviet-type reforms, focusing on better incentives within the old system rather than systemic changes. After an enterprise has fulfilled its planned production obligations, it is allowed to trade with its surplus on the open market with retained earnings. Another element has been administratively increased wages and prices. Agricultural procurement prices, especially, have been boosted to make it more attractive to sell grain to the state. Parallel private trade in foodstuffs is permitted (Noland 2004, 46–9; Oh 2003). In short, these reforms can be described as tinkering with the old Soviet-type system, allowing more power to state enterprise managers, more material incentives, and more marginal markets. To a student of Soviet reforms, this sounds like the not-very-successful Kosygin reforms in the 1960s (Kornai 1992, chap. 15, 360–79).

It is interesting that North Korea has immediately moved ahead to what can be described as second-generation reforms, involving elements of market socialism. For food, in particular, the private market appears to have become dominant. Attempts have been made to adjust prices and wages to markets. State enterprises have been given foreign trade rights, further enhancing the rights of their managers. Two huge devaluations were undertaken in August 2002 and October 2003, respectively, in attempts to catch up with the black market exchange rate (Noland 2004, 49–50). This does not sound like the orderly Hungarian economic reforms or even the Polish reforms; it sounds rather worse, as during the Soviet economic crisis around 1990, when Mikhail Gorbachev's regime entered its death throes (Åslund 1991).

Several elements are noteworthy. No concept or blueprint for economic reform appears to exist. Wild price increases of up to 60,000 percent suggest not only massive distortions but also an absence of macroeconomic thinking, which was characteristic of the Soviet Union. Few knew the budget balance or money emission. They were not allowed to study Western economics, so how could they understand the implications of a large budget deficit or the issuance of money? Dollarization is apparently already advanced. Under these circumstances, hyperinflation is likely to be around the corner, and economic collapse usually follows (Åslund 1995).

Again, the Albanian example is illustrative. In the summer of 1991, Albanian output plummeted and probably halved during the third quarter (Åslund and Sjöberg 1992, 135–50). A confluence of factors contributed. The key was that the state could no longer demand that enterprise managers attain plan targets. The stick was gone, and the production of many goods was disrupted. Another reason was that state regulation remained in place, so goods that were no longer produced in sufficient quantities in the country could not be imported. Any regulation could cause enormous damage in this setup. Meanwhile, the combination of collapsing production, declining tax collection, and rising wage demands boosted the budget deficit and led to a financial crisis. The outcome was one of the greatest declines of output recorded in any country in peacetime. Although North Korea has already gone through a decline in output of as much as 25 percent from 1989 to 1999 (Noland 2004), it could face an even worse collapse now, which should also lead to a political unraveling because few societies go through hyperinflation without major political disruption.

Something else also seems to be going on in North Korea. Toward the end of the Soviet Union's existence, state enterprise managers indulged in massive rent seeking, transferring the profits from their enterprises to their private trading companies and accounts. The North Korean system, with large differences between black market prices and state prices as well as between the official exchange rate and the black market rate, appears ideal for the rent seeking so characteristic of the end of the Soviet system (Åslund 1995; Hellman 1998, 203–34).

But there is a way out. Albania recovered fast, and for the next eight years it maintained an average gross domestic product (GDP) growth of 8 percent a year, although it suffered a setback of 7 percent in 1997 because of civil disorder (EBRD 2003). Overall, Albania has been the most dynamic transition country. Essentially, three cures helped:

- It undertook quite a radical liberalization and financial stabilization, allowing economic revival and a growth of 10 percent as early as 1993.

- Albania carried out a radical land reform in the summer of 1991 in spite of anarchy. The government simply declared that every collective farmer was entitled to a certain area of land, but it was up to the peasants themselves to take it. The peasants did so instantly, and, after having set on the land for a brief moment, they started producing briskly (Åslund and Sjöberg 1992). This land reform can be compared with the Chinese agricultural reform that brought about a similar change. This was perhaps the most important cure of the three.

- Huge foreign assistance was also instrumental. At the time, tiny Albania was by far the poorest country in Europe. It no longer is, and the European Union flooded the country with aid to avoid emigration and instability. Initially, foreign assistance reached as much as 40 percent of GDP. It has financed both large budget deficits and large current account deficits. In relation to GDP, no other transition country has received as large a volume of foreign assistance as Albania (though some developing countries have received even more to little benefit (World Bank 2003, 338–40).

Postcommunist economic reform strategies have been well elaborated. First of all, a political breakthrough must occur, which is a very domestic and idiosyncratic matter. But, as the Polish reformer Leszek Balcerowicz (1994, 75–89) has emphasized, there is a window of opportunity or moment of extraordinary politics when people focus on the long-term interest of the nation as a whole. This is the key to the politics of reform. For instance, Poland, Estonia, and Albania succeeded in undertaking sufficient reforms during that short period of time, while most notably Belarus, Turkmenistan, and Uzbekistan failed to do so.

Several elements should preferably be part of a successful reform process. A political leader needs to acquire political legitimacy, best of all through a democratic vote. Political leaders need to elaborate a reform program, which a newly elected parliament preferably should adopt. A comprehensive but small reform program then should be swiftly implemented. It should contain the pillars of the new system; it is vital not to get bogged down in too many details, which only cause delays and rarely matter at the first stage. The keys in the early transition are far-reaching deregulation of prices, trade, and enterprise combined with a rigorous macroeconomic stabilization program and international assistance consisting of both advice and financing. As soon as possible, privatization should be initiated, especially small-scale privatization (Åslund 2002). Inevitably, a transition is messy, and the North Korean transition has the potential of being very messy. Yet, North Korea has several great advantages. First, as a latecomer, it can benefit from the lessons learned from other postcommunist countries. Second, the existence of a successful peer country, that is, South Korea, will greatly facilitate its transition. Third, plenty of international financing is available for North Korea's transition.

Yet, a system as rigid as North Korea's is likely to experience a horrendous economic crisis, and, regardless of how small its output is at present, the economy will probably plummet (Winiecki 1991, 669–76). Extreme financial destabilization is probable, and rent seeking will no doubt be extraordinary. The best cure comprises liberalization, financial stabilization, and privatization, but it will be severely contested and difficult. This concurs with the general lessons from postcommunist transformation that the more democracy, radical liberalization, stabilization, and privatization, the greater the economic growth (Berg et al. 1999; De Melo et al. 1997, 17–72; Havrylyshyn 2001, 53–87).

Early and Profound Liberalization

An outstanding feature of North Korea's current economic situation is shortages. People who have always lived in a socialist economy characterized by shortages cannot imagine they will go away. A market economy can overcome this very fast, but only if it is sufficiently free. Therefore, a radical deregulation of prices and markets brings an immediate political benefit, while a gradual liberalization agitates people.

Also strong economic reasons favor far-reaching and early liberalization. If enterprises cannot acquire inputs, they will produce less, and output can start plummeting, as happened at the end of the Soviet Union and Albania. Furthermore, if workers cannot find anything to buy for their money but have to spend hours queuing or searching for goods, they have little incentive to work more and will naturally work less. A free market, by nature, will provide a better allocation of goods and services, while a semi-liberalized market may cause new distortions (Boycko 1991, 35–45).

Finally, arguments of social justice cry out for far-reaching liberalization. All socialist economies are characterized by their privileged access to goods and services for the elite. In the transition, one of the greatest problems has been rent seeking, as some businesspeople with special access bought goods at low prices fixed by the state while selling these goods on free markets at prices that could be up to 100 times higher (Hellman 1998; Åslund 2002). This rent seeking has generated so-called oligarchs, attracting the greatest political reaction in postcommunist countries. Both shortages and rent seeking can be brought to an end with a swift deregulation.

The required response is the liberalization of virtually all prices of goods and services. Otherwise no supply effect might be apparent. In Poland, which undertook a truly radical liberalization, people just went out into the street and started selling their surplus stocks immediately after price liberalization. In Russia, by contrast, it took quite some time before many goods appeared in the market because the liberalization was not full-fledged. For North Korea, nearly complete price liberalization would be vital. Price increases for a few goods often arouse public reactions and riots, while comprehensive price liberalization is calmly accepted, as it is rightly perceived as a change of the whole economic system and not as an act of redistribution.

Some exceptions are usually made. A few food staples, such as bread and milk, are often left aside, which might accommodate a fearful public. Rents, heating, electricity, and gas for households as well as public transportation are similarly almost always subject to some price regulation in response to political demands. The greatest danger to reform is the continued regulation of wholesale prices of commodities such as energy, metals, and agricultural goods. In the former Soviet Union, such domestic prices were often fixed at artificially low levels to allow a few monopolistic traders to sell these commodities abroad at a level several times higher and pocket the profit, mostly offshore, which contributed to capital flight.

The liberalization of imports is one of the most popular actions in a postcommunist transformation because all kinds of hitherto unknown goods suddenly become available on the domestic market. Because the exchange rate has usually plummeted already, domestic products are incredibly inexpensive, so no competition between imports and viable domestic produce arises. Many countries, ranging from Poland and Estonia to Russia, abolished all import tariffs and quotas at the same time as they liberalized prices. Where this did not happen, for instance, in Ukraine, the dearth of goods continued and a few rent seekers profiteered by privileged foreign trade rights. North Korea should go for full liberalization of imports at the same time as it liberalizes most prices.

The deregulation of exports was, contrary to expectations, very difficult to accomplish in the post-Soviet countries. Because of the prevalent shortages there, a popular misperception was that "the country would become empty" if exports were freed, reflecting the assumption that everybody would prefer to sell everything elsewhere for real money. Behind this popular view was a more sinister objective concealed. Profiteers who bought commodities at home at low state prices needed restrictions on exports to benefit fully from their booty, and domestic price controls for commodities would make little sense if they could be freely traded.

At present, the difference between the black and official exchange rates is huge in North Korea. There is hardly an easier way of making piles of money than arbitraging between an artificial official exchange rate and a free rate. This is a source of rent seeking that must be closed as soon as possible. Huge devaluations as in August 2002, from 2.1 *won* per dollar to 150 *won* per dollar, cannot solve this problem (Noland 2004, 50). After each devaluation to another fixed rate, a new black exchange rate will evolve if the free market exchange rate is plummeting. The exchange rate needs to be unified; as long as the market rate is sinking, the only way of doing so is to let the exchange rate float. The single exchange rate should apply to all transactions regardless of who undertakes them and for what purpose.

A common belief under communism is that people have lost their entrepreneurial spirit. Russians even thought they had degenerated genetically. With the first opening of the market, however, this myth faltered. Yet, many bureaucratic impediments remain. They may not appear significant just after a democratic revolution, when the old bureaucracy is shell-shocked, but sooner than anybody can imagine, they will return with a vengeance. Therefore, it is vital to undertake a full-fledged liberalization of enterprise early on; necessary regulations can be introduced later. The best example was set by Poland, which adopted a simple ruling that anybody could sell anything anywhere at any price at any time. Instantly, thousands of people went out into the streets and started trading. North Korea should follow Poland's example, which led to the early revival of the Polish economy and a swift surge of millions of new small enterprises.

Rigorous but Difficult Financial Stabilization

When communism collapses, inflation is likely to explode for many reasons. A large monetary overhang of unsatisfied demand is in place.[4] The flow of wages presumably exceeds the flow of consumer goods, and imbalances are probably even worse in the enterprise sphere. At the time of revolution, wages and public expenditures typically go out of control. In a Communist state, the Ministry of Finance and the central bank are weak, subordinate institutions, while the state planning committee and industrial ministries are superior. Money is not only passive but is subdivided into enterprise account money and cash. Multiple technical payment problems will lead to arrears and demand for enterprise subsidies and monetary emissions (Sachs and Lipton 1993, 127–62). Naturally, price liberalization will unleash all these inflationary forces.

With retail price increases of 40,000 to 60,000 percent for such key goods as grain already being undertaken (Noland 2004, 48), North Korea is probably already in the throes of hyperinflation. The erratic and huge increases in both prices and wages suggest that large budget deficits and monetary emissions are in place, but this information appears not to be publicly available. That hyperinflation is probably inevitable in North Korea is a strong argument for South Korea not to undertake an instant unification with the North, because then also South Korea could be dragged down by a horrendous macroeconomic destabilization. A nightmare for the South would be that the North could issue credits in its currency and would of course do so without any comprehension whatsoever. If the North needs to maintain its own currency, it will also need to keep its own central bank and Ministry of Finance.

A fundamental lesson from the Soviet transformation is that hardly anybody in the former Soviet Union knew anything about macroeconomics, the teaching of which was banned under communism (Åslund 1995). Fortunately, Russia had a few economists who had managed to study macroeconomics on their own, but presumably nobody in North Korea knows anything at all about macroeconomics. A fair guess is that hardly anybody knows the size of the budget deficit or monetary emission as a share of GDP and that nobody knows that these two phenomena cause inflation. It is even possible that no measure of monetary emission exists.

A number of actions are initially necessary. Nowhere are outside economic advisers as necessary as on macroeconomic stabilization. Whoever wants to

---

4   A helpful overall presentation is Wyplosz (1999).

learn about these matters must be given a swift course in the fundamentals about the nature and causes of inflation. The International Monetary Fund (IMF) is the obvious lead agency on macroeconomic stabilization. North Korea should be admitted as a member of the IMF, the World Bank, and the Asian Development Bank (ADB) as early as possible, and its macroeconomic stabilization should be based on an early standby agreement with the IMF. Although great and swift efforts must be made to establish the real statistical picture, policymakers will have to work for a long time with the most rudimentary data at hand, forcing them to act on principle rather than calculation.

The initial tasks are technical: unify cash and enterprise money and facilitate payments, for instance, by allowing cash payments throughout the economy. The functioning of payments must take precedence over any state control function. Fiscal and monetary powers must be concentrated in the Ministry of Finance and the central bank, which will be priority targets for technical assistance.

As the old system is withering, public expenditures are likely to explode for many reasons. First of all, knowledge of the negative effects of budget deficits is likely to be missing. Various groups may be pandering to the population with wage increases and higher social expenditures. After the transition has started, state enterprises typically come to the fore, and that process seems to be well under way in North Korea. They demand the indexation of their working capital, subsidized credits, and direct subsidies. Given the absence of civil society, the apparent pressure from workers and the population at large will soon be transformed to a pressure from the economic elite, that is, the state enterprise managers (Hellman 1998).

The key task in the early transition is therefore to control public expenditures. Any overall cut of public expenditures should be avoided. Instead, a few major categories of costs of a systemic nature should be cut. Four key items to cut are price subsidies, foreign trade subsidies, enterprise subsidies, and military expenditures. Price subsidies disappear with price liberalization, and foreign trade subsidies with the liberalization of foreign trade. To cut enterprise subsidies is much more difficult, and, as late as 1998, combined direct and indirect enterprise subsidies in Russia amounted to 16 percent of GDP. Throughout the former Soviet Union, it turned out to be surprisingly easy to cut military expenditures, while a major mistake was not to eliminate the secret police. The political economy of the cuts should be to openly target certain elites while leaving most social expenditures, notably health care and education, in place.

The aim should be to keep public expenditures down so that taxes can be kept low. Given the extraordinary power of the elite, which is bound to continue after the end of Communist rule, high public expenditures will inevitably be focused on the elite rather than directed to the poor and suffering. The former Soviet Union has increasingly moved to few, low, and flat taxes with broad tax bases. A certain enterprise tax is sensible, but it could stop at 30 percent. Payroll taxes tend to rise excessively in socialist countries, so they should not be higher than 15 percent. Some sales taxes and excise taxes make sense, as does the flat income tax of 13 percent in Russia. Small entrepreneurs, whether peasants or craftspeople, should be subject only to a fixed lump-sum tax, which requires no accounts and cannot be changed with income in any given period. This has driven Ukraine's economic recovery (Åslund 2002). In any case, North Korea should opt for low taxes and public expenditures. A reasonable revenue for a country at North Korea's level of economic development would probably be 15 percent of GDP, which requires few and small taxes (Tanzi and Tsibouris 2000). Initially, a budget deficit might arise, and the international community should be prepared to finance at least 10 percent of GDP in the early stages of North Korea's transition.

The key task of financial stabilization is to introduce a demand barrier and impose hard budget constraints on all enterprises. Then, surplus stocks that people and enterprises have hoarded will enter the market. Financial stabilization will also bring inflation under control—that is, get it under 40 percent a year. Inflation is not likely to become very low for many years. One reason is that it takes time to get the right relative prices, and prices more easily adjust under moderate inflation. Another is that the exchange rate is bound to plummet because of hyperinflation, and much of the real revaluation under the recovery is likely to come in the form of inflation rather than nominal revaluation.

One of the great disputes at the beginning of each transition is what exchange rate policy to choose and, possibly, what exchange rate to pick. As long as the exchange rate has not been unified and no financial stabilization undertaken, a reasonable exchange rate is nothing but guesswork. Currency reserves are likely to run out, and then exchange rates typically end up in free falls; in Albania and Mongolia, inexperienced and uncontrolled central bankers gambled away each country's whole currency reserve. High inflation and uncontrolled money emission may then drive the exchange rate extremely low even in a relatively rich country such as Russia, where the free market exchange rate fell so low that an average monthly wage amounted to merely $6 in December 1991.

In North Korea, an even more devastating devaluation is likely. In an extreme financial destabilization, a pegged or fixed exchange rate can provide a badly needed nominal anchor, which worked well in some countries, notably Poland. The problem is that a temporary peg is often maintained for too long. A currency board, which provides a more long-term fixation of the exchange rate, is usually considered valid only for small and very open economies and certainly not for commodity producers, exposed to extreme fluctuations on world markets (Williamson 1995). While the choice of exchange rate regime is a subject of dispute, there is no doubt that substantial currency reserves are vital for the success of financial stabilization. Their early intro-

duction can prevent an excessive devaluation and, thus, an excessive inflation. Such reserves can and should be provided by the international community, notably the IMF.

Professional economists tend to be preoccupied with bank systems and
financial markets, but those institutions do not matter much in the early
transition, when the main need is to impose hard budget constraints to force
enterprises to start working normally. While it is true that economic growth
and financial depth are correlated, financial markets need time to develop.
Premature attempts at boosting them tend to lead to financial crises rather
than any tangible benefit.

Privatization: Critical for Systemic Change

Privatization is always difficult because it involves a large number of concrete properties to which multiple people and groups lay claims. Many principles collide. For the North Korean case, a certain prioritization can be made.[5]

First, an early and broad privatization is vital to create a critical mass of
private enterprises to make the market economic transformation irreversible. Among former Communist countries, Belarus, Turkmenistan, and
Uzbekistan have failed to do so. Second, to make the privatization socially
and politically acceptable, privatization should focus on the broad groups
with the strongest claim to property—employees, tenants, and the population at large. For the same reasons, priority should be given to North Korean
nationals. Third, restitution would be a bad idea, especially as many South
Koreans have claim to property in the North. East Germany has illustrated
the hazards. Restitution overwhelmed the courts for years, leading to many
properties remaining idle; and because the East Germans were excluded from
that privatization they became very regretful and many voted for the Communist Party in spite of huge subsidies from West Germany. Fourth, state
revenues are of little or no relevance; it is far more important to cross the
hurdle to a capitalist system swiftly. Tax revenues after the economy has got
going will swiftly exceed the possible privatization dues from run-down
Communist enterprises. Fifth, new property rights should be clearly defined,
definite, and transferable with minimal liens. In short, the main task is to
spread as much state property as possible to as many North Koreans as possible while minimizing political acrimony. Sixth, foreign direct investment
should not be an early aim. Foreign investors will not understand much of
North Korea in the initial transition, and they are not well suited to invest or
run enterprises there. The nascent legal system will be a mess for years. This
means that the simplest and most decentralized methods of privatization
are the best. They should focus on ordinary North Koreans in order to em-

---

5   A useful summary of the experiences is Havrylyshyn and McGettigan (2000, 257–86).

power them and facilitate the transition to capitalism. Objects that appear to be difficult to privatize, such as infrastructure, can be left for later.[6]

The easiest task is to give small enterprises to the their employees for a token payment. Small-scale privatization usually occurs early. It takes some time to arrange, but then it goes fast because everybody wants to get a piece of the action. Two conditions are important. First, it has to be done by the local authorities because their administrative capacity is required. Often local authorities are convinced to sell when they are facing a shortage of funding. Second, property rights must be individualized. Managers often try to keep the property collective for their own benefit. Small-scale privatization is usually popular and arouses little political controversy.

In parallel, agricultural land should be given to those who till it. Land reform usually happens early in countries where agriculture is important regardless of what happens to other reforms. Presumably, North Korea should take its cue from China and undertake a swift distribution of all land to the peasants. A maximal area for each peasant needs to be set, and transferable property titles are preferable although that feature may wait for some time because transferable titles cause controversy: people fear outside purchases of huge areas of land. In Russia and Ukraine, estates with hundreds of thousands of hectares of land have already been formed. In North Korea, by contrast, overpopulation in the countryside will probably lead to fragmentation of farms into very small family farms, which promotes intensive cultivation of the land.

Housing should simply be given away to the tenants. Nobody else can lay reasonable claim to housing. People feel more secure if they own their apartments and houses, and they receive a bit of capital that they can mortgage in due time.

From the very outset, a large sector of small enterprises should arise if total freedom of small entrepreneurs is permitted. Individual entrepreneurs, primarily in trade and crafts, can swiftly employ more than 10 percent of the labor force, providing the poor with incomes, labor, and supplies all at once. North Korea has an extremely small service sector, employing about 30 percent of the labor force (Eberstadt 2001a, table 5), and it could easily absorb an additional one-fifth of the labor force. This employment would naturally occur in small enterprises in retail trade and crafts, as has occurred in many postcommunist countries. Critical for such success is deregulation.

The privatization of large and medium-size enterprises is always technically difficult and politically controversial. No doubt, as transition starts, North Korean state enterprise managers soon will lay claim to the enterprises they manage for the state. They will be strong enough to block any privatization if they do not get their cut. Thus, we have to accept that they

---

6 Compare with Boycko et al. (1995).

will claim their share. They can be balanced partly by their employees, who should also get their share—preferably twice as much as their managers. Finally, a mass privatization through vouchers to the population at large is beneficial. At least the population gets something, privatization becomes definite, and a free float of outside stocks is created. Thanks to spread and transferable stocks, outside owners can in due time purchase the privatized enterprises. The critical condition to fulfill is empowerment of the locals (Boycko et al. 1995).

Certain major enterprises or assets—the telecommunications company, public utilities, mines, and metallurgical companies—can probably be sold to foreign strategic investors and could be sold through international tenders. However, it would be dangerous to harbor any illusions about early foreign direct investment in a country that is as unknown and different as North Korea. It will take time before private foreign direct investment takes off. Privatization is also a way of empowering North Koreans, so a broad South Korean purchase of North Korean enterprises—as West Germans bought East German enterprises—is neither economically nor politically nor socially desirable.

During early transition, a strange hysteria tends to prevail about the shape of enterprises. Everybody thinks that all enterprises will collapse and that everybody will be unemployed, but in reality virtually all companies are making huge profits because of high inflation. The point is that enterprises have more time for their restructuring than people tend to believe. Therefore, there is no reason to be afraid of bankruptcy, which is wrongly perceived as the destruction of physical assets. Instead, bankruptcy is an effective means of accomplishing a clean financial break. Old claims are sorted out; enterprises are forced to pay, which is a major problem in transition; and good physical assets can be put up for auction to new owners without any mysterious concealed liens. In fact, bankruptcy—understood only by chance to be a helpful technique—turned out to be one of the most efficient means of privatization in Poland.

Technically, privatization is the most complex task of transition, requiring a large amount of technical assistance to organize the privatization administration, to design privatization legislation and techniques, and to assess enterprise values. These tasks have typically been carried out by the U.S. Agency for International Development (USAID) and the World Bank, which have great competence in privatization.

Vital Foreign Assistance

Naturally, foreign assistance can play a great role in North Korea's transition to a market economy.[7] However, not all aid is useful, and some is even harmful, benefiting rent seekers and impeding reform.

Right now, North Korea needs and receives humanitarian food assistance. Obviously this will have to continue to avoid starvation, but the huge size of the assistance appears to help maintain the moribund regime. As soon as North Korea is liberalized, foreign donors might pay attention so that foreign food assistance does not amount to dumping, driving domestic peasants out of business. The best way of avoiding that calamity is to sell food aid on the market to the benefit of the state budget.

Presumably, no North Koreans have the relevant knowledge or experience to handle the postcommunist transition. International technical assistance—that is, consulting—is badly needed in this area. First, a few outstanding economists are required in order to aid the leading North Korean economic policymakers with the overall economic reform agenda. The same economists would naturally take care of advice on financial stabilization directed at the Ministry of Finance and the central bank. It is practical to create one central office of economic research for the government and the central bank, which should gather together the leading economic advisors. Because all relevant statistics are uniquely absent in North Korea (Eberstadt 2001b), international donors need to focus on quickly establishing some kind of statistical system. (Initially, policymakers should take care not to bother about what the statistics say because they will be so bad that they will disinform more than they inform. In the absence of plausible data, policymakers have to act on principle more than on anything else.) Privatization in all its forms requires large and expensive technical assistance for a long time. For financial stabilization, the IMF is the key international agency, and the World Bank complements the IMF with a broader structural agenda. USAID has had much experience with post-Soviet transformation and could serve as the leading bilateral agency. The Japanese and South Korean aid agencies should also come in with technical assistance. Technical assistance is cheap because the North Korean reform government will be able to absorb the inputs of only a limited number of consultants.

The funding of financial stabilization will be the big cost in the early transition. These costs fall into three groups:

- **International reserves.** The international reserves of the central bank are likely to be minimal. To stop the free fall of the exchange rate, the international community needs to replenish international reserves from the outset of a financial stabilization policy. Preferably, such reserves should be kept at a safe place abroad during the chaos of the early transition. Financial stabilization must be based on a standby program with the IMF, and that agency can provide the necessary loans for the replenishment of international reserves.

---

7 This section draws primarily on Sachs (1994, 501–23) and Åslund (2002).

- **Foreign debt servicing.**   North Korea has been in default on its foreign debt since the 1970s. It needs to renegotiate its outstanding debts in the Paris Club for government debt, and most likely the country will have to ask for some debt relief as the penalties on the defaulted debt will be huge. An agreement with the Paris Club also presupposes a functioning IMF program.

- **Budget financing.**   North Korea is likely to have a large budget deficit at the outset, and international financing will be the only possible source to cover it. Essentially, five donors—IMF, World Bank, ADB, Japan, and South Korea (the United States does not offer such support)—appear plausible.

An idea that is as common as it is flawed is that international assistance should focus on the private sector. The simple fact is that governments are not very good at enterprise investment, and abroad they are even worse at it. Similarly, attempts at large infrastructure investment projects in early transitions have generally been unsuccessful in the former Soviet Union. The key task during initial transition is to impose hard budget constraints, which is the opposite of providing soft government funding. Similarly, the World Bank and the European Bank for Reconstruction and Development have tried to boost bank lending in the early transition in most postcommunist countries. The unfortunate result has been that virtually all banks supported by these two financial organizations have gone bankrupt. Nascent commercial banks should be encouraged to be cautious and learn their new trade rather than indulge in excessive risk taking. The World Bank and the ADB are well placed to assist with infrastructure investments, to which South Korea and Japan presumably want to contribute as well.

Nor is it realistic that foreign agencies do much to finance the social sector. The international financing of social benefits is usually politically unacceptable in the donor community. Yet, education should be seen as investment in human capital. Especially in the case of North Korea, it is vital that a substantial group of young people receive relevant education in economics, other social sciences, law, and business administration. A large number of students should be financed for both undergraduate and graduate education abroad in economics, business administration, law, politics, and other social sciences because a critical mass of young North Koreans thinking competently about these subjects is crucial for the early success of transformation. Foreigners, even South Koreans, cannot fulfill that role because they know so little about how North Korean society really works.

The amount of assistance that may come into question appears to be exaggerated. The absorption capacity of North Korea is likely to be quite limited. North Korea's GDP per capita is probably very small in current dollars. Nicholas Eberstadt (2001b, table 6) notes that North Korea claimed that its GNP per capita was as low as $239 in 1995 in a submission to the United

Nations. In 1992, the Russian GDP in current dollars was as little as $80 billion. North Korea has only one-seventh of Russia's population, it is clearly a less developed country, and it appears to be suffering worse macroeconomic havoc. Therefore, a common figure of about $20 billion in GDP is likely to be reduced to a fraction of not more than $10 billion. This also suggests limitations in North Korean absorption capacity. For a longer period, international assistance of a maximum of 20 percent of GDP appears possible for North Korea to absorb (World Bank 2003, 338–40). Assuming a steadily revalued currency, this could mean an absorption capacity of something like $20 billion to $40 billion over a decade.

One of the biggest early financing needs is macroeconomic stabilization, notably to replenish international reserves. The World Bank (2003, 203) records that North Korean exports have plummeted by two-thirds in a decade, from $1,857 million in 1990 to $661 million in 2001.[8] The standard requirement for international reserves is three months of imports. If imports were about $800 million, this would only amount to $200 million, which is a trifle in terms of international financing.

At present, North Korea already receives about $1 billion a year in international assistance. That might amount to as much as 10 percent of GDP a year—a very high level. This would mean that the Kim Jong-il regime is entirely maintained by foreign assistance, which could also explain why the steadily falling GDP was turned around in 1999 (Noland 2004, 22). If so, the current assistance is very difficult to defend.

Conclusions

North Korea is likely to go through a horrendous crisis when its socialist economic system crumbles. The less outside support the country is given, the earlier that crisis is likely to come. In any case, the process of swift economic disruption is probably already under way. Strong indicators are decentralizing economic reforms, empowerment of state enterprise managers, emergence of substantial private markets, and huge price and wage increases as well as massive devaluations. All this suggests a swift economic collapse, with hyperinflation reminiscent of the economic collapse of the Soviet Union or Albania. It is not obvious that this will lead to instant Korean unification. South Korea could be seriously destabilized by a collapsing North Korean economy, and the North Korean elite would hardly like to be dispossessed. The example of the German unification is a potent deterrent.

Both the North Korean preconditions and the precedents of other postcommunist countries suggest that the country needs to undertake as radical a market reform as it can, but success will not come easily. Three keys—thorough deregulation, radical financial stabilization, and a swift

---

8 See Noland (2000, 89) for a discussion.

privatization—are politically possible, however. Foreign assistance will be vital for the success of these reforms; it is essential that foreign assistance come early and be brought in to support market reform rather than the rent-seeking interests of the old establishment. The amounts required are likely to be much smaller than usually discussed because the absorption capacity of the North Korean economy is likely to be very limited.

References

Åslund, Anders. 1991. *Gorbachev's Struggle for Economic Reform*, 2nd ed. Ithaca: Cornell University Press.

———. 1995. *How Russia Became a Market Economy*. Washington, D.C.: Brookings Institution.

———. 2002. *Building Capitalism: The Transformation of the Former Soviet Bloc*. New York: Cambridge University Press.

Åslund, Anders, and Örjan Sjöberg. 1992. Privatization and Transition to a Market Economy in Albania. *Communist Economies and Economic Transformation* 4, no. 1.

Balcerowicz, Leszek. 1994. Understanding Postcommunist Transitions. *Journal of Democracy* 5, no. 4 (October).

Berg, Andrew, Eduardo Borensztein, Ratna Sahay, and Jeronim Zettelmeyer. 1999. The Evolution of Output in Transition Economies: Explaining the Differences. International Monetary Fund working paper no. 73. Washington, D.C.: IMF.

Boycko, Maxim. 1991. Price Decontrol: The Microeconomic Case for the "Big Bang" Approach. *Oxford Review of Economic Policy* 7, no. 4.

Boycko, Maxim, Andrei Shleifer, and Robert W. Vishny. 1995. *Privatizing Russia*. Cambridge: MIT Press.

De Melo, Martha, Cevdet Denizer, and Alan Gelb. 1997. From Plan to Market: Patterns of Transition. In *Macroeconomic Stabilization in Transition Economies*, ed. Mario I. Blejer and Marko Skreb. New York: Cambridge University Press.

Eberstadt, Nicholas. 2001a. Socio-Economic Development in Divided Korea: A Tale of Two "Strategies." Working Paper Series, vol. 11, no. 5. Cambridge: Harvard Center for Population and Development Studies.

———. 2001b. "Our Own Style of Statistics": Availability and Reliability of Official Quantitative Data for the Democratic People's Republic of Korea. *Korean Journal of International Studies*. www.hri.co.kr/file_pds/pub02/200001/EUR200001_09.PDF.

European Bank for Reconstruction and Development (EBRD). 1999. *Transition Report 1999*. London: EBRD.

———. 2003. *Transition Report 2003*. London: EBRD.

Fischer, Stanley, and Alan Gelb. 1991. The Process of Socialist Economic Transformation. *Journal of Economic Perspectives* 5, no. 4.

Havrylyshyn, Oleh. 2001. Recovery and Growth in Transition: A Decade of Evidence. IMF Staff Papers, 48, Special Issue. Washington, D.C.: IMF.

Havrylyshyn, Oleh, and Donal McGettigan. 2000. Privatization in Transition Countries. *Post-Soviet Affairs* 16, no. 3.

Hellman, Joel S. 1998. Winners Take All: The Politics of Partial Reform in Postcommunist Transitions. *World Politics* 50.

Kornai, Janos. 1992. *The Socialist System: The Political Economy of Communism.* Princeton: Princeton University Press.

Noland, Marcus. 2000. *Avoiding the Apocalypse: The Future of the Two Koreas.* Washington, D.C.: Institute for International Economics.

———. 2004. *Korea after Kim Jong-il.* Washington, D.C.: Institute for International Economics.

Oh, Seung-yul. 2003. Changes in the North Korean Economy: New Policies and Limitations. In *Korea's Economy 2003.* Washington, D.C.: Korea Economic Institute.

Pickel, Anders, and Helmut Wiesenthal. 1997. *The Grand Experiment.* Boulder, Colo.: Westview.

Sachs, Jeffrey D. 1990. What Is to Be Done? *Economist,* 13 January.

———. 1991. Helping Russia: Goodwill Is Not Enough. *Economist,* 21 December.

———. 1994. Life in the Economic Emergency Room. In *The Political Economy of Policy Reform,* ed. John Williamson. Washington, D.C.: Institute for International Economics.

Sachs, Jeffrey D., and David A. Lipton. 1990. Poland's Economic Reform. *Foreign Affairs* 63, no. 3.

———. 1993. Remaining Steps to a Market-Based Monetary System. In *Changing the Economic System in Russia,* ed. Anders Åslund and Richard Layard. New York: St. Martin's Press.

Sachs, Jeffrey D., and Wing Thye Woo. 1994. Reform in China and Russia. *Economic Policy* 18.

Shleifer, Andrei, and Robert W. Vishny. 1998. *The Grabbing Hand: Government Pathologies and Their Cures.* Cambridge: Harvard University Press.

Siebert, Horst. 1992. *Das Wagnis der Einheit* [The daring of unity]. Stuttgart: Deutsche Verlags-Anstalt.

Tanzi, Vito, and George Tsibouris. 2000. Fiscal Reform over Ten Years of Transition. Working paper no. 113. Washington, D.C.: IMF.

Williamson, John. 1995. *What Role for Currency Boards?* Washington D.C.: Institute for International Economics.

Winiecki, Jan. 1991. The Inevitability of a Fall in Output in the Early Stages of Transition to the Market: Theoretical Underpinnings. *Soviet Studies* 43, no. 4.

World Bank. 1996. *World Development Report 1996: From Plan to Market.* Oxford: Oxford University Press.

———. 2002. *Transition: The First Ten Years.* Washington, D.C.: World Bank.

———. 2003. *World Development Indicators 2003.* Oxford: Oxford University Press.

Wyplosz, Charles. 1999. Ten Years of Transformation: Macroeconomic Lessons. Paper presented at the World Bank's annual Bank Conference on Development Economics, Washington, D.C., 28–30 April.

Anders Åslund is the Director of the Russian and Eurasian Program at the Carnegie Endowment for International Peace in Washington, D.C. He thanks conference participants, especially Nicholas Eberstadt and Magnus Blomström, for their comments. Rashed Chowdhury provided research assistance.

Possible Forms of International Cooperation and Assistance to North Korea

9

Unlikely Partners: Humanitarian Aid Agencies and North Korea

Edward P. Reed

One of the most unsettling aspects of humanitarian work in North Korea (or the Democratic People's Republic of Korea, DPRK) is the disconnect between the country's proud official face and its desperate reality. A scene I witnessed along a dusty road in North Hwanghae province in 1997, when I directed an NGO aid program, was emblematic of this apparent state of denial. Our team was returning to Pyongyang after visiting a hospital where severely malnourished children were being rehydrated with drips fed from discarded beer bottles. An elderly woman, clearly exhausted, was collapsed at the roadside under a large brown bundle. Above her one of the ubiquitous arches across the road proclaimed in large letters: The Victory of Socialism Is in Sight!

North Korea first appealed for international humanitarian assistance in 1995 after devastating floods pushed its already faltering economy over the brink. Since then a number of multilateral, bilateral, and nongovernmental aid organizations (NGOs) have responded to its call. Providing humanitarian assistance to North Korea has posed unique challenges to aid providers, however. Underlying the problem is the fact that the very act of requesting aid contradicts the bedrock ideology of *juche* on which the North Korean state is built. *Juche*, or self-reliance, proclaims that North Korea can build a socialist paradise for its people, relying primarily on its own resources and ingenuity under the "genius leadership" of Kim Il-sung and Kim Jong-il.[1] Acknowledging problems and mistakes is the starting point for seeking solu-

---

1 A number of writers have attempted to interpret *juche* to non-Korean audiences; see, for example, Park (2002), Oh and Hassig (2000), and Cumings (1997). As recently as the official new year's editorial for 2004 (the year of Juche 93 in the DPRK), the centrality of the *juche* concept was reemphasized: "It is necessary to intensify the education in the *juche* idea, strengthen the driving force of the revolution in every way and consolidate the politico-ideological position of socialism as solid as a rock this year. . . ."

tions, but this goes against the national ethos and pricks the personal pride that has been deeply instilled in all DPRK citizens. Indeed, doing so may even border on treason.

In addition to this fundamental contradiction confronting aid agencies, other elements in North Korea differentiate crises there from other humanitarian crises of recent years:

- Although almost all other crises of this magnitude have unfolded in the context of conflict or failed states, the rigid North Korean state is very much intact, compelling all aid providers to negotiate with the government on the terms under which aid will be provided.

- In other crises, aid organizations have usually planned and directly implemented aid distribution to those in need and have also worked with local nongovernmental counterparts. In the DPRK local distribution of aid has been handled, for the most part, by and through government channels, and there is no civil society with which international NGOs can collaborate.

- Although open conflict is absent, North Korea considers its very survival threatened by hostile states, and it is in a constant state of war mobilization. Ironically, it feels most threatened by some of those very states from which it has solicited and received the most aid. Aid agencies must work in this politicized context—in the states where those agencies are based, and in North Korea where the agencies seek to deliver aid—in which an atmosphere of mistrust pervades on both sides.

- Although reliable sources have reported starvation and death on a massive scale, even at its peak this was a famine largely invisible to outsiders. There has been little visible population movement and no gathering in camps by refugees or displaced persons (though thousands have gone into hiding across the border in China), and agencies have had limited direct contact with the affected population inside the country.

- The most basic data on the crisis and its human dimensions have been difficult if not impossible to obtain or verify with any degree of reliability. Government officials insist that agencies accept the government's assessment that the country is facing a major crisis and not insist on details. When we pressed to visit affected households, one official remarked to me, "We have lowered our pants; do you want us to strip naked?"

- Media coverage that has provoked public response to other crises continues to be banned in North Korea. Images of starving children have been rationed to the outside world, and the government insists on carefully controlling all publicity.

- Human rights abuses are not unique to the DPRK; however, the extreme nature of the alleged abuses (for example, torture and execution for political crimes, a system of camps holding political offenders and their families under extreme conditions, and distribution of food and other necessities according to political loyalty[2]) and the fact that aid agencies must work in close collaboration with the government confront aid agencies with a serious moral dilemma.

Other humanitarian crisis spots that reflected to some degree similar challenges include Iraq between the 1991 Gulf War and the 2003 invasion; Cambodia under the Vietnam-backed government (after 1979); and Ethiopia during the 1983–85 famine. In each of these cases, aid agencies were compelled to negotiate the terms of assistance with a generally repressive state apparatus that controlled access to the affected population and the distribution of aid. Ethiopia was a major learning experience for many agencies; some claimed only after the fact to have realized the extent to which their aid was being manipulated for political purposes. Cambodia forced agencies to decide between assisting the majority population inside the country (under the strict control of the government) or helping refugees on the Thai border (infiltrated by the Khmer Rouge). Assisting Iraqis devastated by a decade-long embargo exposed agencies to the charge that they were prolonging suffering by strengthening the regime of Saddam Hussein. What may be unique about North Korea is that all of these issues simultaneously confront aid agencies, and in spades. Furthermore, the existence of a thriving rival Korean state on the peninsula and the formal state of war that persists between North Korea and the United States (under the United Nations flag) greatly complicate the security environment.

This uniquely difficult environment has challenged aid agencies on two levels: first, the widely held humanitarian principles that govern provision of aid by NGOs and other agencies are severely tested in the North Korean context; and, second, the ability to plan and implement effective humanitarian and developmental aid projects is critically limited.[3] Humanitarian assistance for North Korea is not only justifiable, however, but it can be provided with integrity. There are many other places in the world where human suffering deserves an international response and where access is not hindered by the government. Nevertheless, the determined focus on North Korea by United Nations (UN) and NGO agencies should remain a high priority. The impact of aid agencies in North Korea goes beyond the relief of human suffering. As

---

2 Human rights concerns in relation to North Korea range from total control of information, to restrictions on movement, to harsh punishment of border crossers, to cruelties more extreme than those mentioned in the text (Hawk 2003; Amnesty International 2003; OHCHR 2003).

3 I have benefited greatly from Flake and Snyder (2004), a comprehensive study of the experience of U.S., European, and South Korean NGOs operating in North Korea. Articles that attempt an overview of NGO experience in North Korea include Lautze (1997), Bennett (1999), Smith (2002), Weingartner (2003), and Lee J. (2003, 77–93).

a community, the agencies contribute to building an environment and a model for constructive international engagement at a time of serious tensions and dangers. Careful use of this opening for engagement can help forestall a much greater humanitarian and political disaster in a highly charged part of the world.

Human Impact of Economic Collapse

Following the Stalinist economic model, and in spite of supporting a massive military establishment, North Korea was able to feed its growing population and provide for a modest standard of living in the years following the Korean War. Housing, education, medical care, and employment were guaranteed for all citizens at different levels of quality depending on job assignment and political status. However, most observers agree that, by the mid-1980s, the North Korean economy had begun to decline because of systemic constraints. In agriculture, the push for self-sufficiency had exhausted the fragile ecosystems. By the late 1980s, food shortages began to appear. In the early 1990s, North Korea was hit by shocks that sent the economy over the edge. The end of special subsidized trade arrangements with the Soviet Union and China crippled the economy. Oil imports fell to one-fourth of needed supply, leading to widespread closing of industries, including those producing fertilizers, chemicals, and other inputs for agriculture. Floods and drought in 1995–97 were the final straws on the camel's back, but they also provided a politically acceptable rationale for requesting international assistance.

Thus, what has confronted aid agencies is not an underdeveloped economy or third-world society but rather a collapsed industrialized economy that had once met many humanitarian goals, albeit dependent on external subsidies and following a model that could not be sustained. Many of the key factors of a modern economy—most important are the critical human resources and, secondarily, some social institutions—are still scattered around and could be rehabilitated.

Aid agencies have also been confronted with a complex humanitarian crisis. Food shortages caused by falling production and lack of imports have resulted in hunger, malnutrition, and increased mortality throughout the country. Observations by aid workers and interviews with refugees have led to the widely circulated figure of about one million deaths between 1995 and 2000 directly attributable to the food shortage.[4] The victims were disproportionately infants, the elderly, young mothers, and those living in urban areas of the Northeast. Although shortages were felt throughout the population, it is clear that some segments were less affected: the ruling elite,

---

4 Noland (2000, 191–4) summarizes the widely varying estimates of famine-related deaths; they range from 220,000 (by a DPRK official) to 3.5 million (by a South Korean NGO). Goodkind and West (2001) use models and the 1998 nutritional survey to reduce uncertainty, and they estimate between 600,000 and one million deaths can be attributed to famine between 1995 and 2000.

citizens of Pyongyang where the most politically loyal reside, and the military. Massive food aid, stabilization of food production (though at much lower levels than before), and various coping mechanisms led to a precarious and minimum level of food security since 2001 (Natsios 2001, Noland 2003).

North Korea is primarily an urbanized society; about three-fourths of the population live in cities where they are dependent on rations or markets of some kind to obtain food. Unlike the Great Leap famine in China, the farming population in North Korea was less affected than the large urban populations in outlying parts of the country. While rations for cooperative farms were reduced, the government wisely refrained from squeezing the farms to the extent of further depressing production. Also, farm families had access to more coping mechanisms than did urban dwellers, including expansion of private farming, hoarding production, and harvesting wild plants in the mountains.

Most of the population of North Korea today can be considered traumatized survivors of this catastrophe and, no doubt, fearful that the worst is not over. One county official told me, in 1998, that those who could quickly adjust and cope survived, while those who could not, died. The manager of a collective farm wept as she told me of women coming to her begging for a little extra ration for their children that she could not give. It is no exaggeration to say that a large segment of an entire cohort of North Korean children has been permanently damaged physically and mentally by malnutrition.[5]

A nutritional survey (UNICEF 1998), conducted with the cooperation of UNICEF and the World Food Programme (WFP), revealed that 15.6 percent of children under seven years old suffered from acute malnutrition (wasting), and 65.4 percent from chronic malnutrition (stunting). These figures seemed consistent with what aid workers were observing at the time outside of Pyongyang. A second survey (CBS 2002) conducted in the fall of 2002 (after several years of sensitive negotiations), indicated a fairly dramatic improvement in most categories. Wasting fell to 8.1 percent, and stunting to 39.2 percent. Although these survey data must be used with caution, they appear to support the conclusion that food is getting to targeted children. Nevertheless, continued high levels of child as well as maternal malnutrition and geographic discrepancies (for example, wasting was found in 12 percent of children in South Hamgyong province but in only 3.7 percent of Pyongyang children) indicate not only that conditions remain extremely bad, but also

---

5   The collection edited by Lim and Chang (2003) compares the nutritional status of North Korean children with that of children in developing countries and assesses the probable impact of widespread malnutrition on human and social development in North Korea. The chapter by M. Elizabeth Hoffman (Lim and Chang 2003, 117) concludes: "Children lacking the essential assistance for physical, cognitive, emotional, and psychological maturation leaves North Korea with at least one generation of children who will enter adulthood fully underdeveloped."

that supplies are being rationed to benefit certain parts of the country over others.[6]

The health system, once a source of pride for North Korea, was itself a victim of the crisis. Local pharmaceutical plants closed and imports of medicines slowed to a trickle. Hospitals had no medicines, supplies, equipment, or electricity and so could not adequately treat those most in need of care. At one hospital outside of Pyongyang, the highly trained doctors and technicians confessed their feelings of helplessness and frustration, and welcomed all outside support. Lack of supplies for water treatment facilities has created a sanitation crisis, while lack of fuel for heating has further undermined the health of vulnerable populations.

A severe shortage of electricity hobbles every sector of this urbanized and industrialized society: food production, industry, transportation, urban homes and workplaces as well as medical facilities. The largely electrified rail system has been reduced to a crawl.

Assessments by outside observers of the prices, wages, and foreign exchange adjustments introduced by the North Korean government in August 2002 have varied widely from dismissive to optimistic. However, the impact on ordinary North Koreans seems fairly clear. The availability of food and other commodities in newly established local markets has increased. However, inflation has also set in, and a large segment of the population without access to cash income may be falling into even more difficult circumstances. The WFP has identified this group of unemployed and underemployed urban families as a new category in need of emergency assistance (UNOCHA 2003a).

One impact that is profound in its implications is that North Korea, for all its trumpeting of self-reliance, has become fundamentally dependent on the charity of the international community for the survival of a large portion of its population. How this fact affects ordinary North Koreans who are aware of it and officials who serve the regime is hard to estimate. While no doubt a source of shame, it also reveals the fragility of the *juche* system that is at the core of the regime's ideological grounding.

---

6 These dramatic improvements between the 1998 and 2002 nutritional surveys have not gone unchallenged. In particular, an extremely small percentage of low birth weight (LBW) children, even by international standards, has been cited by some as an indication of conflicting and therefore unreliable data. This problem and the general issue of reliability have been thoroughly assessed by Shrimpton and Kachondham (2004, 12), and they conclude: "The verification processes carried out by the authors and international observers support the veracity of the survey results, ruling out the likelihood of false data or manipulation of data." The LBW issue is complicated by the fact that birth weight is based on mother's recall, but the reported weights strongly correlate with measurements of later malnutrition of the same children. International technicians trained North Korean field teams and observed all measurements and interviews in the context of a tightly drawn survey design.

Humanitarian Response

After negotiating quietly with Japan and South Korea for emergency food shipments, the North Korean government issued a general call for international food aid in the fall of 1995. The WFP issued its first appeal for food contributions and opened a small office in Pyongyang in 1996. International NGOs also mobilized to respond but were encouraged by the North Korean government to ship commodities (especially food) rather than set up in-country programs. North Korea established the Flood Damage Rehabilitation Committee (FDRC) within the Ministry of Foreign Affairs to handle relations with all non-Korean aid agencies.[7]

Almost all agencies focused initially on emergency food aid. As the scope of the emergency and the problems associated with delivering food aid to North Korea became clearer, however, delivery of food aid was left primarily to the WFP while most agencies attempted to focus on assisting specific locales through smaller-scale interventions. Other sectors began to receive attention as specialized UN agencies expanded their operations in the country. UNDP and FAO focused on agricultural rehabilitation; and WHO and UNICEF concentrated on health, especially of children. A number of European NGOs were able to establish modest resident programs as part of diplomatic negotiations between the European Union (EU) and the North Korean government. U.S. NGOs were forced to manage as best they could through one- and two-week visits to the country two or three times a year, coinciding with the arrival of commodities. NGOs in South Korea also emerged to advocate for helping North Korea; however, the South Korean government required that the substantial aid they collected be channeled through the Korean Red Cross and delivered through the International Federation of the Red Cross (IFRC). Under President Kim Dae-jung's Sunshine Policy, beginning in 1998, this policy was relaxed to allow South Korean NGO representatives to visit the North, but under fairly close restrictions.[8]

All aid agencies were quickly confronted with a number of sobering realities. Although North Korean officials urged immediate and maximum food aid to stave off disaster, the only clear evidence offered of severe hunger or starvation were brief and carefully orchestrated visits to selected baby homes

---

7 The FDRC has been the hosting unit for all UN and bilateral agencies and for most NGOs. In early years, direct contact with line ministries was rare, which further complicated assessments, planning, and coordination. Recently there seems to be some relaxation of this restriction and more direct cooperation, especially in agriculture and health. A few NGOs have had different hosting units. American Friends Service Committee continues to work with the Committee for Solidarity with the World's People, a relationship established more than a decade before the crisis. World Vision for some time worked with the Asia-Pacific Peace Committee (APPC). The APPC and its "family" of Workers' Party units have also hosted all contacts with South Korean NGOs and companies. Organizations representing ethnic Koreans from outside the peninsula are usually hosted by the Committee for Support of Overseas Compatriots and related units.

8 Flake and Snyder (2004) provide additional detailed descriptions of the activities of the various NGOs.

or hospital wards crowded with malnourished children. There were few in-dicators—common in emergencies elsewhere—of widespread famine such as large population movements, large numbers of obviously weakened adults, bodies of those who had succumbed. This led to a debate among agencies and governments about the extent and severity of the problem, a debate that lasted at least a year and deeply politicized the international response (Becker 1998). In addition, aid workers used to assessing the cause of an emergency in order to design an appropriate response quickly learned that, in spite of clear evidence to the contrary, the only causes that North Korea admitted or discussed were flooding and other natural disasters. It also quickly became clear that North Korean counterparts were under a mandate to obtain the maximum amount of commodity aid with the minimum amount of intru-sion by foreign aid workers. The aid agencies had entered the world of *juche* and quickly had to adjust their modus operandi or withdraw.[9]

Dilemmas for Humanitarian Aid in North Korea

North Korea's plea for assistance came at a time when international aid agen-cies were debating what was frequently referred to as "the crisis of humani-tarian aid." In the wake of the Rwanda genocide and its aftermath and then the militarized humanitarian interventions in the Balkans, aid agencies were reevaluating their role and their operational guidelines. Complex humani-tarian disasters, characterized by massive human suffering and vulnerability as well as armed conflict, challenged the ability to effectively actualize the simple motive of saving lives. In retrospect it became clear that well-inten-tioned aid could do great harm as well as great good. Humanitarian inter-vention in the context of conflict could actually exacerbate the conflict and prolong suffering. A narrow focus on saving lives without attention to the root causes of a crisis could result in dependency that postponed solutions. Strictly separating assistance from attention to human rights abuses could be the equivalent of not seeing the forest for the trees (Rieff 2002; Anderson 1999).

In light of the sobering experience of the 1990s, new emphasis was placed on delivering aid with integrity while avoiding doing further harm. Agencies were urged to go beyond providing relief by working with local communi-ties to rebuild food security and reduce future vulnerabilities. Most aid agen-cies approached North Korea with a heightened sensitivity to complying with these principles, while major donors and the media were looking over their shoulders (Minear 2002; Terry 2002; Humanitarian Studies Unit 2001).

---

9   This paper addresses the operating environment that faces multilateral, bilateral, and nongovern-mental agencies operating in North Korea; however, the primary concern is with the experience and potential contribution of NGOs. The special circumstances under which South Korean NGOs oper-ate make them a particular case, and their experience will be addressed only to the extent the issues are relevant to them. The experience of efforts by South Korean NGOs to deliver aid to North Korea is described in English in Chung (2004) and Kwon and Kim (2003).

Should We Help North Korea?

The most fundamental question for aid agencies considering helping the people in North Korea is whether aid actually prolongs their suffering by prolonging the life of a repressive and ineffective regime. As I worked in North Korea, I framed the question: "When the day comes when they can speak freely, will the farmers, workers, and prisoners of North Korea thank me or condemn me for having collaborated with the state to deliver aid?" Until that day we must make our decision by balancing the positive impacts of aid on individuals as well as on the North Korean system against any negative impacts aid might have.

There can be little doubt that the policies of the North Korean regime have contributed directly and indirectly to the humanitarian crisis in the country. The absolute control over citizens' lives, the distribution of benefits according to political loyalty, and the ultimate threat of banishment of whole families to prison camps for political offenses all point to human rights abuses of the most egregious nature. Many of those who have successfully fled the regime, including the former Workers' Party secretary, Hwang Jang-yop, refer to the North as one large prison camp and suggest that the sooner the regime falls, the sooner relief will come to the people.[10] Others point to the massive misallocation of resources by the regime. Scarce funds and resources are poured into military programs and Kim cult monuments while hospitals lack heat, basic equipment, and medicines. Another argument is that only fundamental changes in economic structure and policies will bring an end to the crisis, and observers find little evidence that the Kim Jong-il regime is willing or able to implement such reforms. So, should aid agencies simply hold back and let nature take its course?

One reply to this position is that in the case of authoritarian regimes nature seldom takes the course that outsiders expect. Sue Lautze (1997), who has studied many famine situations, has noted: "History teaches us that famine may threaten the survival of the people of a communist nation but it will not threaten the dominant political regime." It is impossible to say what the internal political impact would have been if North Korea had not received almost a million tons of food aid per year since 1996. However, the degree of social and political control in North Korea is so total and the level of indoctrination so complete that it is easy to imagine that the Kim Jong-il regime would have survived even under harsher conditions than have prevailed. Furthermore, the most likely result of a breakdown of order would be mass population movements toward the Chinese border and perhaps on the high seas. As other cases have shown, the human costs of such movements

---

10 Hwang made a number of statements during his visit to the United States in November 2003. See, for example, his interview, "Hwang Jang-Yop Calls for Regime Change," with Rebecca Ward on the Voice of America on 4 November 2003.

are staggering, not to mention the potential for dangerous political destabilization in the region.

The primary rationale for intervention provided by aid agencies is the humanitarian imperative: all persons in life-threatening need should be provided assistance no matter what the political environment; in the simple terms attributed to former U.S. president Ronald Reagan, "A hungry child knows no politics." This is a comforting but not entirely satisfying answer. One of the major lessons of recent history is that, under some circumstances, aid intervention can actually make people worse off. Sooner or later most aid agencies have had to add the argument that, rather than bolstering the North Korean regime and its policies, aid has in fact contributed to a gradual process of opening and policy change. What is the evidence of such impact?

Backhanded evidence is provided by the North Korean regime itself. In the now infamous "yellow wind" editorial of January 1998 and in several official statements since, regime spokespersons have starkly warned the North Korean people that international aid is part and parcel of the imperialist plot to undermine the regime through reform and that aid comes mixed with capitalist poison (Weingartner and Weingartner 1999). Meanwhile, other official statements have periodically been issued thanking the United Nations and other agencies for their assistance and urging its continuation. The most obvious explanation for these conflicting statements is that aid and aid workers have introduced a new element into North Korea that, purposely or not, threatens the reigning orthodoxy. Continued acceptance of aid agencies in the country points up the desperate need for assistance that so far has outweighed these concerns in the minds of North Korean decision makers.

Aid workers who were familiar with North Korea before or in the early stages of the crisis speak of the changes they have observed in the openness of North Korean counterparts, assessment of problems, and access to affected areas (Morton 2002; Zellweger 2002). With approximately 100 U.N. and other agency workers resident in the country and many others making frequent and extended visits over the past eight years, many North Koreans have been exposed to information and ways of thinking that fundamentally challenge the official line of the regime. Pyongyang-based North Korean officials, when accompanying aid workers to the field, have learned the extent of the suffering and the depth of the problems in their own country. North Korean program managers have gained a clearer idea of the nature of their problems and seem to value the interaction with foreign aid workers who have opened new space for analyzing and addressing the problems. For example, a senior agricultural official once told me that after an overseas study tour he realized that centrally mandated government policies on fertilizer application had destroyed North Korean soils, and that it would take 20 years to rebuild them. And, because officials and managers are under incredible pressure to show results, many have welcomed assistance no matter what the source.[11]

The information flow is two-way. Aid workers have provided first-hand, ground-level information on conditions throughout North Korea. This has proved to be a reliable basis for assessing humanitarian conditions and has given a human face to the crisis. Indirectly, this information has also assisted analysts seeking to understand social and economic dynamics inside the country. A more accurate and balanced assessment of North Korean society can only be helpful in seeking a peaceful solution to the political issues that separate North Korea from the international community.

Though the debate continues, the predominant view in the international aid community is that, even though operating conditions are problematic, the nature of the regime itself should not be an obstacle to providing humanitarian assistance.[12] Even Hwang Jang-yop has expressed support for food aid as long as there is certainty that it goes to those who need it. The issue then becomes whether the conditions under which agencies operate in North Korea allow for delivery of aid to those in need and enable underlying causes of the problems to be addressed. Hazel Smith (2002, 14), who has evaluated several aid programs in North Korea, has written: "The humanitarian dilemma for the agencies has been, given the acceptance by all agencies of the widespread need for humanitarian aid but given also the constraints placed upon humanitarian operations, on what terms should the agencies continue with humanitarian assistance to the people of the DPRK."

Do Agencies Know Where Their Aid Is Going?

Basic principles governing delivery of humanitarian aid are impartiality and accountability. Aid should go to those in greatest need on the basis of objective and systematic assessment. Aid delivery should be transparent, enabling agencies to confirm that it is distributed to the target group and to assess its impact. These processes require that aid agencies have direct and ongoing contact with the affected populations, are able to collect data on the status of the populations, and are able to monitor directly the distribution of aid. From the beginning these have been sticking points for the North Korean government. Given the state's absolute control over its population, its distribution of social benefits according to political loyalty, and its official mili-

---

11 After a particularly difficult and tense period of interaction with higher officials over issues related to project monitoring, a ministry official took me aside and said: "I know that it is very difficult to work with my government, but please do not give up. We need your help." There are also more subtle impacts of outside contact. A driver once told me that he had been taught that Americans were cruel and evil people who had committed unspeakable atrocities against Koreans during the Korean War, but that he found me to be a good person and wondered about other Americans.

12 There are those who dissent. Sophie Delaunay, the regional coordinator for North Korea for Médecins Sans Frontières testified that "MSF would like to reiterate that access by the population to the aid it needs can only be improved if there are independent needs assessments, independent distribution mechanisms, and independent monitoring by operating agencies (Delaunay 2002)." Fiona Terry (2001), a researcher for MSF, put it more bluntly: "The purpose of humanitarian aid is to save lives. By channeling it through the regime responsible for the suffering, it has become part of the system of oppression."

tary-first policy, most donors have pressured aid agencies for stronger-than-usual assurances that aid is not being diverted.[13]

No one claims that conditions in North Korea fully meet these international standards. (It is unlikely that they are fully met in any crisis intervention.) Although things have improved somewhat since the early years, and the experience of agencies differs, in general North Korea continues to restrict aid agency operations in various ways. Collection of data on affected populations as a basis for operational planning is severely limited. Real-time observation of local aid distribution or delivery is rare. Random checking of delivery points, institutions, or households is seldom allowed. Unmonitored interaction with the affected population is prohibited as well. In late 2003 the executive director of the WFP, after a visit to Pyongyang, urged more openness on North Korea's part in order to satisfy demands of major food donors (Harmsen 2003). "It's important that North Korea be as transparent, accountable and accessible as is humanly possible," he was quoted as saying. "We simply want a list [of hospitals, orphanages, and schools] of where the food is going. For two years now they have not been able to give us that list."

Given the practical and moral dilemmas and the sheer frustration associated with operating in North Korea, it would not be surprising if some, if not all, aid agencies had considered withdrawing at one time or another. Several have actually terminated their programs, citing these and other constraints on their operations. Four European NGOs, Médecins du Monde (MDM), Médecins Sans Frontières (MSF), Action Contre la Faim (ACF), and Cap Anamur, were implementing direct emergency health delivery programs following models they used in other crisis situations. These programs required ongoing presence in medical or child care institutions, direct contact with patients, and intensive training of medical personnel. This approach clearly challenged North Korea's policy of minimizing interaction between foreign aid workers and the general population, and the authorities moved to limit their access or redirect their programs. As they withdrew, some of the agencies also asserted that assistance was not being delivered according to need but perhaps based on political calculations.[14] Oxfam UK discontinued its water treatment project in 1999 following a dispute over the collection of water quality data. CARE withdrew from a U.S. private voluntary organization (PVO) consortium in 1998 (Flake and Snyder 2004, 31), saying that

---

13 The Bush administration has increased pressure on WFP to show improvement in the monitoring of food delivery as a condition for further U.S. contributions (Natsios 2003).

14 See Schloms (2004, 54–7). MSF was most vocal in its criticism of the operating conditions in North Korea. According to MSF's 30 September 1998 statement ("MSF Calls on Donors to Review Their Aid Policy towards DPRK," www.msf.org/countries/page.cfm?articleid=712831EF-EC70-11D4-B2010060084A6370), "MSF is convinced there are serious medical and humanitarian needs in DPRK which need to be addressed, but adheres to the international humanitarian principles of impartiality and of freedom to assess needs, to assist the most vulnerable, and to assess the effectiveness of that assistance."

conditions did not allow implementation of "sustainable rehabilitation and development programs."

Nevertheless, most agencies (UN, bilateral, and NGOs) that initiated programs have continued to work in North Korea. All have engaged in an endless process of negotiation, reevaluation, and adjustment. They have also been buffeted by political and military developments that have affected both North Korean openness and donor generosity. They grapple with the humanitarian dilemmas but cite a number of factors that convince them to stay:

- Many agencies have adjusted their programs to fit the operational conditions. For example, they limit operations to selected locations or institutions that can be visited repeatedly, they supply materials that are targeted for specific projects and can be more easily identified during field visits, and they select entry projects that do not require direct or frequent contact with the general population.

- Some agencies have found more flexibility when they have focused their initial interventions in areas identified as high priorities by the government (e.g., potato cultivation, alternative energy, or information technology [IT]). When an established high-priority project requires wider access to areas and populations, access has usually been provided.

- Agencies have learned how to communicate specific requirements or conditions and, if necessary, cancel or delay delivery of specific shipments or activities (short of canceling the whole program) if these are not met. PMU Interlife, a Swedish NGO, closed an agricultural assistance program when staff access was restricted but has since negotiated a new program in another part of the country (United Nations 2003, 161). Most agencies have had the experience of delaying a subsequent delivery of supplies until monitors can verify on-site the distribution of an earlier delivery.

- A mutual learning experience has occurred when agencies have persisted. North Korean counterparts who, no doubt, were instructed to resist all intrusions as a form of spying have observed that some basic data are essential for good planning and continued donor response. Some agency workers have realized that, given the continuing political and military pressures on the country, it is not unreasonable for North Koreans to be cautious about release of certain information or access to sensitive areas. In particular, agencies have lowered their profiles in the media and become more sensitive regarding information used in fundraising campaigns.

- Above all, agencies point to the importance, over time, of building trust with counterparts based in Pyongyang and with project partners at the local level. It is not uncommon for counterparts to begin to share, at least partially, the perspective of the aid workers and to take the risk of pleading the agency's position in relation to monitoring. It is even more common for local partners (farm managers, hospital administrators, and provincial officials) to exhibit ownership of a project and jealously guard supplies provided by the agencies.[15]

• An additional positive factor is the unusually close cooperation among almost all agencies operating in North Korea. NGOs have recognized and relied on the UN agencies to advocate with the North Korean authorities on behalf of the entire aid community and to coordinate and track aid efforts in the various sectors. NGOs have sought to maximize interagency collaboration and support, including using opportunities to monitor each other's projects during field visits. The entire aid community has issued periodic consensus statements that objectively assess the operating conditions and commit themselves to striving to hold as closely as possible to basic humanitarian principles.

According to aid agencies, these factors have led to gradual improvement in transparency and in the ability to monitor aid projects. WFP points to the opening of five field offices outside of Pyongyang, the presence of about 45 full-time food delivery monitors, and the significant increase in the number of monitoring visits to institutions and homes, among other things. Some resident NGOs now have staff based in the localities where they work. Others report more frequent visits to project sites. Training of local workers and technical staff is being integrated into many projects, allowing closer interaction with affected populations. Another indication of a more positive aid delivery environment is that a number of NGOs have newly initiated residential programs in North Korea over the past two years. This includes Save the Children-UK, AFMAL-FBF (Italy), and Premiere Urgence (France). AFMAL-FBF and Premiere Urgence have initiated programs in the health sector that include rehabilitation of hospitals and training of medical personnel.

None of this means that the operating environment in North Korea yet allows NGOs and other agencies to meet all international standards for delivery of humanitarian assistance. The entire aid community continues to call for further improvements, especially in access to the affected populations. However, it would be fair to say that those eleven residential NGOs, four bilateral agencies, and seven UN agencies operating in North Korea today feel that, with attention to trust building, careful planning, appropriate project choice, clear definition of expectations, and standing on principle when necessary, humanitarian assistance projects can be implemented with sufficient transparency and accountability. In other words, aid agencies are

---

15 After successful overland delivery of a large food shipment by one NGO, a senior official of the remote province informed me that, in order to prevent diversion by officials along the route, he had sent local staff to the border to ride on each rail car until it reached its destination. Such action does not answer all monitoring questions but does reveal a lot about how the system actually works and the role of local officials.

able to claim that they do know whom their programs are helping, they can see the general impact of their work, and they can collect sufficient information to meet accountability expectations of their donors.

What Aid Is Needed? What Is Possible?

In the early days of the crisis, the attention of aid agencies was focused on saving lives. This meant getting as much food as possible into the country. This is the response that the DPRK authorities sought, and this is what governments were willing to provide. There is no doubt that these efforts saved lives, but it quickly became clear that emergency aid was no solution. As more information became available, it was clear this was no short-term emergency to tide over with supplemental food aid. Also, it was not simply a food or agriculture problem. Hunger and starvation were the indicators of a thoroughly broken system, from top to bottom. This assessment was starkly stated (UNOCHA 2002, 7):

> The current humanitarian approach alone cannot lead to sustainable development given the complexity of the country's underlying problems. Unless humanitarian assistance is accompanied by development leading to economic recovery/growth, there will be no end to the emergency.

Full-scale development requires addressing systemic problems that have brought the economy to its knees, including reconstruction of infrastructure, investment in whole new industries, putting agriculture on a sustainable basis, creating institutions necessary to promote and facilitate international trade and investment, and also creating market signals where none existed before. In other words, development requires systemwide reform.

The logic of emergency food aid was to buy time for these underlying problems to be addressed. In fact, the largest single food aid program in modern history is now entering its ninth year, and yet only marginal progress has been made toward rehabilitation and even less toward development. The obstacle to shifting to developmental efforts is a monumental chicken-or-egg problem. Donor countries have refused to provide the massive levels of developmental aid needed without evidence of the systemic changes necessary for such aid to be used effectively. The North Korean authorities, meanwhile, have resisted all but marginal changes because they view these prescriptions as the recipe for destabilization and even regime change. Add to this the increased levels of distrust between North Korea and potential donors created by the renewed nuclear dispute, and the result has been near gridlock. So, with a reform program that would address the systemic problems underlying the human suffering not yet in sight, how can aid agencies justify continuing their relatively small-scale, incremental programs?

My response is that aid agencies must do everything they can to encourage and demonstrate, even on a small scale, what development-oriented programs look like. This can begin with rehabilitation, but every opportunity should be sought to build in activities that prepare for sustainable development, at least at the institutional or sectoral level. Rehabilitation aims to repair or improve elements of the system that can still contribute to meeting human needs and reduce the need for external aid. This could include, for example, providing spare parts for farm machinery, repairing irrigation systems, restarting local food processing, or reequipping hospitals. Development-oriented projects build new local productive and human capacity and introduce new attitudes. Examples would be local production of program inputs, spreading improved agricultural practices through intercooperative workshops, training technicians in new research methodologies, and introducing results-oriented planning tools.

The continuing political standoff actually enhances the importance of NGOs and other aid agencies. Until the large-scale internationally funded development projects can begin, NGOs have shown that they are in a position to pursue rehabilitation and development-oriented projects. The small scale and localization of NGO projects make them appear less threatening than larger projects. Working on a long-term basis in selected locations allows them to build better working relationships. Also, some donors (the EU, for example) are willing to fund small-scale NGO projects in advance of systemic change.

Lessons from Operational Experience

Although all aid agencies face a similarly difficult operational environment in North Korea, some have operated with more success than others. The Appendix provides a summary of the experience of seven resident and nonresident agencies that have had some success in implementing projects with development-oriented impact while minimizing problems with transparency and accountability. Their experience has implications for both the approach to programming and for operating style.

Programming

The community-based, participatory approach to development that NGOs seek to implement elsewhere is not yet possible in North Korea. Nevertheless, years of patient persistence and of trial and error on the part of a number of NGOs have generated important programming lessons. The following recommendations flow from the examples described in the Appendix, but are also based on consultations with aid workers currently in the field as well as my own personal experience. They suggest an approach to NGO programming in North Korea that is most likely to advance the transition from relief and welfare to locally sustainable development.

Focus on development-oriented projects. NGOs and bilateral assistance agencies should continue to focus their efforts primarily on rehabilitation and development programs. The essential point is to model a process based on problem assessment, local participation, impact evaluation, and rapid follow-through on success. Projects should be planned in such a way as to maximize the need for involvement at multiple levels and across administrative lines. Such an approach plays to the strengths and flexibility of NGOs and helps break down barriers to communication and learning across North Korean political and administrative units.

Link with national priorities. NGOs can increase their chances for success by selecting project interventions that can be linked in some way to official North Korean priorities. Rehabilitation and adjustment of agriculture is clearly the top priority for policymakers and receives direct attention from Kim Jong-il himself. World Vision, for example, has responded to the official call for a "potato revolution" through technical and training programs that addressed some of the early problems in a way that ensures greater impact and accomplishes technology and skill transfer. Similarly, the American Friends Service Committee (AFSC) and others have aligned with the "seed revolution." Campus für Christus built on the national call for goat raising that threatened to result in further ecological damage by demonstrating less damaging foraging systems; it then went on to introduce new products (cheese and yogurt) and even start a new export industry (goat hides). More recently, rehabilitation of irrigation has received official attention, and a number of NGOs are working in this area.

Respond to priorities outside of agriculture. NGOs cannot solve the energy crisis in North Korea, but officials have welcomed small-scale innovations on the local level. The Adventist Development and Rehabilitation Agency (ADRA) is assisting with enhancing and expanding the use of biogas, and the Nautilus Institute is introducing wind power technologies. Challenging the image of a closed society, Kim Jong-il has made IT a high priority as a means of modernization leapfrogging. Although not all of North Korea's problems will be solved by waiting for official campaigns, it is hard enough to work in North Korea when swimming with the current, let alone when swimming upstream. Also, many agencies have found it possible to branch into new activity areas once their credibility in the priority area has been demonstrated.

Include capacity building. Training and other forms of capacity building should be a major element of every project. North Korean farmers, technicians, and managers are educated and have demonstrated openness to new ideas and new approaches. The IFRC's efforts to upgrade the knowledge, skills, and educational materials of the North Korean Red Cross is an outstanding example of a long-term capacity-building program at the national level (IFRC 2003). The UNICEF/WFP nutritional surveys incorporated new data-processing technology and skills training on a large scale. Triangle Generation Humanitaire and Concern Worldwide organized a two-day training for managers of 15 tree nurseries; Concern is also organizing a Farmer Field School for training in appropriate use of bio-pesticides; the Swiss Agency for Development and Cooperation (SDC) has set up a training center for farm mechanics in one county. AFSC and Campus für Christus have arranged long-term overseas training programs for North Korean technicians and farm managers.

Bring new technology.   North Korea needs both low-end (appropriate) technologies and high-end (state-of-the-art) technologies in order to deal with a collapsed industrialized economy and infrastructure. Side by side, we see effective projects to introduce integrated pest management, green manures, village water systems, and biogas energy on the one hand and hydroponic seed potato production, IT projects, and the latest technology for detecting and treating tuberculosis on the other. Multiple technologies and processes will create a marketplace of ideas and possible solutions that will help break the rigidity of many years of top-down dictation of cookie-cutter solutions.

Build an information base.   NGOs should try to incorporate collection, analysis, and useful data into their projects. Shifting the basis of project choice and assessment away from political considerations to a scientific basis is key to a development approach. At the national level, the two nutritional surveys, no matter their limitations, have no doubt provided the North Korean government with a clearer picture than ever before of the status of their children's health. Earlier, the UNDP worked with the North Korean Ministry of Agriculture to produce the Agricultural Rehabilitation and Environmental Protection (AREP) plan for rehabilitating the agricultural sector. The process included collection of the best estimates for agricultural sector indicators currently available. At the NGO project level, several agencies have reported careful data collection and analysis by farmers for field trials, and even testing of water quality for sanitation projects (once denied to Oxfam) is now accepted. Linking data collection and analysis to introduction of new IT concepts and technology can encourage acceptance because IT is one of the leadership's highest priorities.

Promote sustainability.   Sustainability requires administrative support, ongoing skill transfer, availability of inputs, maintenance, replication, and ultimately a sense of local ownership and responsibility. It is clear that sustainability is a particular challenge in North Korea. Following directives from above, officials have sometimes pushed for a particular initiative only to drop it when the political winds shifted. Emphasizing capacity building and expanding to as many locations and levels as possible may help prevent dependence on a few skilled persons. Many projects require inputs that are not produced in the country and cannot be imported because of lack of foreign exchange, an obstacle for which there will be no thorough solution until the overarching problem of integrating North Korea into the world economy is solved. However, the project approach itself can limit dependence (for example, green manure over chemical fertilizers, gravity-flow irrigation over pumps). Agencies can also include in project design the rehabilitation or construction of local manufacturing or processing facilities (including food processing, farm machine shops, intravenous-fluid production, irrigation pipe manufacturing). Creating as many backward (through local procurement) and forward (product marketing) linkages to the core project is a way to increase the likelihood that the initiative will be sustained. Finally, the North Korean tendency to build a showcase project should be resisted, and emphasis should be consistently placed on the replicability of innovations over a wide area.

Respond to new opportunities.   Limited market forces have come into play in North Korea, creating new opportunities for some Koreans and perhaps opening new areas for external assistance. As farmers become partially oriented to markets, micro-credit projects could support expansion of production of farm animals and crops on private plots or in small groups. Farmer training could include management skills that the emerging individual farmers need to make a profit. The price and wage reforms have created a new and growing urban unemployed sector that does not have cash to purchase food and other essentials. Innovative programs aimed at creating small-scale handicraft or other export-oriented industries may be welcome by the government. As in other crises, women have borne the brunt of the economic collapse in North Korea. Livelihood projects targeting women, such as the project recently initiated by the Swiss development agency, SDC, may be another way of responding to the new situation that is emerging.

Operating Style

Aid agencies still operate under objectionable restrictions on transparency and accountability. However, some agencies appear to fare better than others in this regard. The question is what approach to working in North Korea is most likely to enhance accountability and encourage a receptive response on the part of North Korean counterparts.

Build trust.   In spite of the polite hospitality most aid agencies encounter, the DPRK considers all international agencies and individuals with which it works as potential security threats until proven otherwise. Sincerity on the part of the organization and its representatives is the key concept for Koreans. An agency demonstrates sincerity by following through on commitments, by appointing sensitive and well-trained staff to the program, by steadily increasing the size of its commitment, and by avoiding negative publicity about the country. Personal sincerity on the part of agency representatives is demonstrated by showing respect for the North Korean system and its leaders, by recognizing the accomplishments of the society under very difficult circumstances, by being flexible in project implementation when possible, and by inquiring respectfully about customs and way of life in the North Korea. None of this is different from ways of building trust in other cultures; in North Korea, however, it is extremely important and it may take more time. Everyone may see things that they don't like about North Korea, but, as long as the commitment has been made to engage the government through humanitarian assistance, it is counterproductive to voice criticism openly.

Appoint good staff.   Careful selection and preparation of staff to reside in or regularly visit North Korea is critical to success. Staff should have the personal qualities suited to living in and working in a closed, monitored, and stressful society with few distractions. Preparation should include orientations with others who have worked in North Korea as well as basic information on the modern history of the Korean peninsula. Maintaining the same organizational representatives over an extended period allows for building personal trust on the part of the Korean counterparts (and the Korean security services) and acquiring needed knowledge and insight on the part of the foreign representative. It is advisable to separate the roles of official agency representative/negotiator (who may be resident or nonresident) and project technical staff who bring specific skills to the program and work directly with counterparts. This will provide an important buffer between the day-to-day working staff and the political pressures inherent in the system.

Cultivate counterpart relations.   The most important personal relationships are those with the political and technical counterparts with whom agency representatives work on a day-to-day basis. Sometimes this relationship can be strained by difficult negotiations, unexpected changes in plans, and denial of reasonable requests. One must always keep in mind that North Korean counterparts are under extreme pressures that we can hardly imagine. They have been entrusted to have intimate dealings with foreigners with whom the general population is prohibited contact. Theirs is a very risky position because serious missteps could bring disaster to them and their families. They are working under strict constraints and they deliver decisions rather than make them. Expressing sympathy for their situation, even when they deliver bad news, can help control frustration. Patience and an even temper are rewarded.

Design transparent projects.   Negotiate projects that by their nature make accountability easier. Focus on a limited number of cooperative farms, institutions, or sites over an extended period of time. This will enable the development of working relationships with local officials and managers and allow impact to be observed. Provide material assistance in the form of equipment and supplies specific to the assessed needs of the project sites. Deliver material inputs in allotments allowing confirmation of delivery, installation, and use of one set before the next is ordered. Require cooperative evaluation in project phases, making it clear that continuation depends on favorable results.

Collaborate with other agencies. In a country where information is controlled, monitoring is constrained, and isolation is policy, it is essential that aid agencies cooperate and collaborate as much as possible. This does not happen easily because the authorities are not comfortable with agencies comparing notes and working together, although this seems to be changing somewhat. The Inter-Agency Forum and other structures already exist for UN-bilateral-NGO cooperation, and these should be continually strengthened. The UN Office for Coordination of Humanitarian Affairs (OCHA) should continually collect and share data on aid agency projects by county, by institution, by cooperative farm, and other jurisdiction in order to create a current matrix of agency activity by location and by project sector. Agencies should continue to explore opportunities for collaboration in the field in order to make their limited resources go further. No agency should initiate work in North Korea without fully consulting with agencies already engaged there.

Persist. Compared with operations in most other countries, the early period of building trust and demonstrating credibility takes much longer in North Korea. It is frequently a bumpy road, subject to misunderstanding and changes in the international environment. It usually takes several years for an agency to arrive at the point where effective, development-oriented projects can be introduced. Senior decision makers in aid agencies must recognize these realities and be ready to make long-term initial commitments. It is no accident that those agencies with the longest history of engagement with North Korea (IFRC, Campus, Concern, Caritas, AFSC, Eugene Bell Foundation) have the best working relationships with the authorities and some of the most innovative programs.

Conclusion

The human suffering in North Korea today is the result of a failed system operating in a hostile international environment. Humanitarian aid organizations cannot solve this problem. Only sustained, multifaceted, systemic change based on political decisions in Pyongyang can set North Korea on the path to building an economy that can meet the basic needs of its people. Change in the international political environment, especially reduction of tensions with the United States and acceleration in South Korean–North Korean rapprochement, are needed to encourage and facilitate this process.

So, what is the role of aid agencies in this constricted and wholly politicized context?

First, resident and visiting aid workers, even though they have limited direct interaction with ordinary Koreans, serve the critical role of witnessing and accompaniment. Imagine the tragedy of famine and the struggle for survival of the last nine years going on behind the old *juche* curtain, unseen by the world. Instead, at least to some extent, we know what North Koreans have suffered and endured. And many North Koreans know that we know. This has created an emergent solidarity that encourages Korean risk taking for the sake of helping their own people. The system may be cruel, but from my own experience I can say that there are North Korean humanitarians who are deeply encouraged by the presence of international aid workers.

Second, by engaging North Korea in cooperative aid programs, aid agencies explicitly or implicitly communicate that the best hope for the North Korean people is evolution of their system. While they must work within the parameters set by the regime, aid agencies do not necessarily strengthen the status quo. Through interaction with North Koreans at national, local, and institutional levels, they create new space and opportunities for many Koreans to consider an alternative future for their society. Most aid workers live and project a very different image of the outside world than that in the official propaganda. This is a world that North Koreans can sense they may be able to live in. In fact, it is my impression that many North Koreans are already dwelling in two worlds: the old, regimented world of "single-minded unity" and the new world of scrambling to sustain themselves by their own wits with openness to anything that might help. That this new world could be termed "authentic *juche*" makes this mental trick bearable.

Third, aid workers have pressed their North Korean counterparts, especially at the local level, to take practical approaches to problem solving on the basis of objective data. This direction happens to coincide with a subtle change in official policy. In the old days, Kim Il-sung (or those speaking for him) decided which crops to plant and how much fertilizer to apply, and everyone waited for his solution to every problem (often through "on-the-spot guidance"). Now local units are told that they are on their own and must solve their problems however they can. But years of waiting for orders and direction have suppressed the North Koreans' native creativity, and many are reticent, if not fearful, to suggest novel solutions. Aid agencies have supported local solutions, usually in dialogue with local administrators: "Instead of waiting for more fertilizer, let's try crop rotation and green manure. Instead of cutting trees from the hillsides, let's cultivate woodlots. Instead of waiting for fuel for old pumps, let's dig gravity flow irrigation systems." Official campaigns are still launched from above, but now many of these innovations originate from initial small-scale collaboration between aid agencies and local units.

Fourth, the work of aid agencies is creating stand-by development capacity.[16] Development-oriented projects, such as those described above, have introduced new ideas, new approaches, new skills, and new knowledge of how the world works. This process along with parallel engagement with outside commercial companies have made North Korea ready to move ahead much more quickly than current official policy allows. Other transitional experiences indicate that policy and its constraints lag behind change on the ground. This is illustrated by the catch-up policy to recognize open markets long after they appeared and to adjust prices closer to black-market realities. If and when a fundamental shift in official policy is rolled out, change in North Korea will undoubtedly surge ahead, building to a significant extent on the experience of many years of working with aid agencies.

Finally, North Korea's isolation from the outside world has contributed to the dangerous political and military confrontation that continues to threaten the region. Through the work of humanitarian aid agencies over the past 10 years more, North Koreans have had more contact with outsiders and their ideas than through any other channel. For all their flaws and mistakes, aid agencies represent some of the best impulses and values of the world community, and the interaction between them and Koreans at many levels can only have improved the environment for resolving the political issues. In this sense every aid program in North Korea is ipso facto a peace-building program. Though the scale of human suffering may be greater in other parts of the world, perhaps it is only in North Korea where a relatively small humanitarian effort can potentially have such a crucial impact on the overall situation.

For aid agencies to fulfill these roles, they must be committed to working in an unusual and difficult environment. They must continue to negotiate and renegotiate the terms of engagement and accept that they will be buffeted by political ups and downs. And they must be prepared to shift gears if the situation changes. Nevertheless, whatever the political future of North Korea might be, the knowledge and skills that the aid agencies impart will be useful in building a better future. Self-reliance is an honored concept in development work. One way of looking at the role of aid agencies is that they are joining with North Koreans to reinterpret *juche* so that it can be the basis for authentic self-reliant, but also participatory and liberating, human development.

---

16 In the UN 2004 Consolidated Appeal for the DPRK (UNOCHA 2003a, sec. 2.4) a similar point is made (emphasis added): "Although aid agencies have been able to achieve significant results with well targeted assistance. . ., the limited sustainable improvements in the humanitarian situation has demonstrated the need for sustained efforts by all parties to create an *enabling environment for development.*"

Appendix
Humanitarian Aid Projects in North Korea:
Selected Examples

Adventist Development and Relief Agency–Switzerland (ADRA)

ADRA–Switzerland is the Swiss national branch of ADRA, a faith-based international organization. ADRA began operating on a small scale in North Korea in 1999, initially providing food aid and winter clothing. The program has expanded to include local production of enriched bread for schools, rehabilitation of hospitals including staff training, and alternative energy. Of particular interest is the project, in collaboration with the North Korean Thermal Institute (housed at the State University of Science), to promote alternative and efficient use of energy. This, of course, is a high-priority issue for the government, which has pushed for local power generation using small-scale hydroelectric generators. ADRA has focused on introducing improved biogas fermenters to produce gas as an energy source for operating farm machinery and trucks, warming homes, and cooking. In 2003, ADRA completed a test model of a family-size digester that makes use of local and imported technology. To enable year-round gas production, the digester is housed in an insulated greenhouse that can also be used to grow vegetables during the winter. After assessment of this trial, ADRA and the Institute plan widespread dissemination of the technology around the country (Wellinger 2003).

American Friends Service Committee (AFSC)

AFSC, the international service agency of American Quakers, began a program in 1998 to support agricultural rehabilitation that has focused on improving soil fertility, upgrading irrigation systems, and reducing post-harvest losses. The project is implemented on several cooperative farms, and a research component is pursued in collaboration with the Academy of Agricultural Sciences (KAAS). The scarcity of chemical fertilizers has created a strong incentive in North Korea to find alternative methods for rebuilding soil fertility. AFSC has sought to introduce selection and wide dissemination of green manures plus crop rotation farming systems. Local and national scientists have run selection trials with a variety of leguminous crops that can be planted in paddy and rain-fed fields in late fall, and then plowed under in the spring before planting the main crop. Two of these green manures have been identified as hardy and compatible, and the scientists claim that if used in an integrated cropping system could provide at least half of the nitrogen needed for rice and corn production. KAAS is now ready to promote this system throughout the country.

AFSC has also facilitated a link-up between KAAS rice breeders and rice scientists in Vietnam. In fall 2003, three North Korean rice breeders traveled to Vietnam where they lived for six months in order to grow a range of rice varieties (996 different experimental lines) to speed up varietal selection processes. Using the winter season could cut in half the time needed to identify improved varieties. The Rice Institute of the Vietnam Agriculture Science Institute hosted the North Koreans and arranged field trips to national and regional agricultural research centers. (Ireson 2003, and personal correspondence)

Campus für Christus (CfC)

Campus für Christus, a non-denominational Christian organization based in Switzerland, began a project in 1997 to support the national call for raising goats. The project began on a small scale in one county of South Hamgyong province, focusing initially on improved fodder and animal care. Over the years the project has expanded to include introduction of modern breeding practices (including importing of frozen semen to improve herds), improved milk processing and preservation, cheese and yogurt making, and more recently tanning to produce high-quality hides for export. The tanning and hides export component has been developed in cooperation with the Ministry of Light Industry with support from the Swiss Agency for Development and Cooperation (SDC). Working closely with the Ministry of Agriculture, Campus has expanded the project to nine sites including North Hwanghae province and the Pyongyang area. The project directly affects an estimated 20,000 people but reaches many others through training held at the nine project centers. Some 67 North Koreans have traveled to Switzerland, where they lived with farm families and learned modern herding methods. According to Campus, the project "concentrates on state-of-the-art technologies and methods which can be operated in the mid-term without dependence or support from abroad and which can be reproduced" (United Nations 2003a, 161).

Eugene Bell Foundation (EBF)

The Eugene Bell Foundation, a nonresident NGO based in the United States and South Korea and working only in North Korea, has selected and focused on one serious health problem: the reemergence and spread of tuberculosis. Starting with donations of essential anti-TB drugs to a few TB clinics, EBF has now developed a full program at multiple sites throughout the country, including hospital and sanitarium rehabilitation, provision of fully equipped mobile diagnostic clinics, introduction of the DOTS treatment, and training of medical staff at all levels in the TB control sector. EBF estimates that its assistance now reaches one-third of all TB patients in the country, or 130,000 persons in 50 hospitals and clinics. Though the program will continue to rely on donated supplies, EBF has succeeded in introducing new treatments and inculcating new attitudes among medical staff and patients. EBF enjoys good access and is able to document its work carefully. This special relationship is due largely to the fact that, beginning with his first trip to the country in 1979, EBF's founder, Dr. Stephen Linton, has been able to develop a high level of trust with senior North Korean officials. Dr. Linton's fluency in the language belies the claim that North Korea will not work with foreign Korean speakers.

International Federation of Red Cross and Red Crescent Societies (IFRC)

The IFRC's primary goal in North Korea has been to strengthen the national Red Cross Society's capacity to respond to human needs caused by the systemic crisis as well as sudden onset disasters. IFRC maintains a small team in the country as advisers and technical assistants but works primarily through the national Red Cross. Projects include provision of essential drugs and supplies to approximately 1,762 hospitals and clinics, improvement of water and sanitation systems, disaster management, and organizational development for the national Society. The IFRC has probably done more than any other agency to demonstrate the possibility and potential impact of human capacity building in the health sector. The IFRC has integrated capacity building in all aspects of health delivery and care, especially in disaster preparedness and management. For example, in 2003 alone, the IFRC supported multiple workshops for health personnel from national to village level in the following areas: malaria prevention, safe delivery practices (for midwives), rational drug use, SARS response, HIV/AIDS, hospital infection control, community-based first aid, water sanitation and health, and disaster management. The IFRC (and ICRC) has helped link the North Korean Red Cross into the world movement by supporting many study visits and training in other countries, including China and Mongolia as well as the headquarters in Geneva. It is generally conceded that North Korea once had an impressive health infrastructure and a large supply of doctors and other professionals that provided cradle-to-grave health care. The IFRC's approach is to build on this foundation while introducing modern technology and management practices (IFRC 2000, IFRC 2003).

Swiss Agency for Development and Cooperation (SDC)

SDC's broad program of assistance to North Korea illustrates the potential for bilateral aid from a country that enjoys normal diplomatic relations with North Korea. SDC's program explicitly supports the transition from aid to development assistance and internal economic reform. Its approach includes support for improved food security, strengthening the efficiency and autonomy of economic units, and building capacity to use aid effectively. There are several projects: a multi-pronged agricultural development project working with KAAS and 20 cooperative farms; a project (financed by UNIFEM) to build management and marketing skills among unemployed women in

Pyongyang and support them to take advantage of the emerging market economy; an IT seeding project that links Swiss companies with units in North Korea; and a program supporting small-scale projects of European NGOs focusing on sloping-land management, integrated pest management, mechanical training, and support to the Campus für Christus goat project. In addition to technical training for participants in the projects outlined above, for its Korean counterparts and Korean technical staff in all aid agencies, SDC has recently begun implementing training modules on project cycle management and on the transition from humanitarian aid to development cooperation (UNOCHA 2003b).

World Vision (WV)

World Vision International and World Vision (South) Korea have worked together in North Korea since 1996 in a range of project areas including agricultural rehabilitation, medical assistance, and food delivery and processing. One project has focused on the national priority to increase rapidly the production of potatoes as a supplementary food source. Potatoes can be grown in less fertile soils and can be harvested in late spring, allowing a second crop to be planted. The fact that Kim Jong-il himself has called for a "potato revolution" has ensured that World Vision has received an unusual level of cooperation and access. The critical limiting factor in potato production is seed quality. World Vision, in close collaboration with KAAS scientists, decided to focus on the problem of producing, protecting, and distributing high-yielding, virus-free seed potatoes. In a major technology-transfer initiative, World Vision introduced an integrated program that includes large-scale hydroponic greenhouses in Pyongyang that supply virus-free minitubers to four regional seed production centers corresponding to the four major agro-geographical areas of the country. The model introduced in the North was developed in South Korea by the government's Rural Development Administration. South Korean scientists regularly visit the North to work with, and provide training for, North Korean scientists at the national and regional levels. Several North Korean scientists have received training in Australia. Initially all the materials and chemicals needed for hydroponic farming were imported, but gradually local materials are being substituted wherever possible. It will take several more years to realize the full potential of this project, but major yield improvements have already been realized in local experiments (Lee Y. 2003).

References

Amnesty International. 2003. North Korea: Human Rights Concerns. Media Briefing, ASA 24/002/2003, 11 April. http://web.amnesty.org/library/Index/ENGASA240022003?open&of=ENG-PRK.

Anderson, Mary B. 1999. *Do No Harm: How Aid Can Support Peace—Or War.* Boulder, Colo.: Lynne Rienner.

Becker, Jasper. 1998. Postscript: North Korea, 1998. In *Hungry Ghosts: Mao's Secret Famine.* New York: Henry Holt.

Bennett, Jon. 1999. North Korea: The Politics of Food Aid. Relief and Rehabilitation Network paper no. 28. London: Overseas Development Institute.

Central Bureau of Statistics (CBS). 2002. Report on the DPRK Nutrition Assessment. Pyongyang: CBS. October. www.humanitarianinfo.org/DPRK/infocentre/library/Library_Documents/Report_on_the_DPRK_Nutrition_Assessment_October_2002.pdf.

Chung, Oknim. 2004. The Role of South Korea's NGOs: The Political Context. In *Paved with Good Intentions: The NGO Experience in North Korea*, ed. L. Gordon Flake and Scott A. Snyder. Westport, Conn.: Praeger.

Cumings, Bruce. 1997. *Korea's Place in the Sun: A Modern History.* New York: W. W. Norton.

Delaunay, Sophie. 2002. The Humanitarian Situation and Refugees: Testimony presented to the U.S. House of Representatives Committee on International Relations, Subcommittee on East Asia and the Pacific. 2 May. http://wwwc.house.gov/international_relations/107/dela0502.htm.

Flake, L. Gordon, and Scott A. Snyder, eds. 2004. *Paved With Good Intentions: The NGO Experience in North Korea.* Westport, Conn.: Praeger.

Goodkind, Daniel, and Lorraine West. 2001. The North Korean Famine and Its Demographic Impact. *Population and Development Review* 27, no. 2.

Harmsen, Peter. 2003. World Food Program Says North Korea Needs to Be More Open with Donors. AFP news release, 20 December.

Hawk, David. 2003. *The Hidden Gulag: Exposing North Korea's Prison Camps.* Washington, D.C.: U.S. Committee for Human Rights in North Korea. www.hrnk.org/HiddenGulag.pdf.

Humanitarian Studies Unit, ed. 2001. *Reflections on Humanitarian Action: Principles, Ethics and Contradictions.* Sterling, Va.: Pluto Press. Originally published as *Los desafíos de la acción humanitaria.*

International Federation of Red Cross and Red Crescent Societies (IFRC). 2000. North Korea's Public Health Pays the Price of Isolation. In *World Disasters Report 2000: Focus on Health*, chapter 4. Geneva: IFRC, 2000. www.ifrc.org/publicat/wdr2000/wdrch4.asp.

———. 2003. Democratic People's Republic of Korea, June–November 2003. Program update no. 2. 16 December. www.ifrc.org/cgi/pdf_appeals.pl?annual03/0167030302.pdf.

Ireson, Randall. 2003. Agricultural Assistance in North Korea: From Fertilizer to Farming Systems. Paper delivered at Ecumenical Consultation on the Korean Crisis, National Council of Churches-USA, Washington, D.C., 16–18 June.

Kwon, Tae-jin, and Kim Yong-hoon. 2003. Inter-Korean Agricultural Cooperation: Current State and Prospects. Paper prepared for the Korean Rural Economics Institute, Seoul.

Lautze, Sue. 1997. The Famine in North Korea: Humanitarian Responses in Communist Nations. Medford, Mass.: Feinstein International Famine Center, Tufts University. http://famine.tufts.edu/pdf/nkorea.pdf.

Lee, Jong-woon. 2003. Outlook for International Agency Assistance for North Korea. *Korea Focus* 11, no. 5 (September–October).

Lee, Yong-beom. 2003. Current Technology in North Korean Agricultural Production. Presented at the conference, "North Korea in Crisis: Food Production, Economics, and Security," North Dakota State University, 26 September.

Lim, Gill-Chin, and Namsoo Chang, eds. 2003. *Food Problems in North Korea: Current Situation and Possible Solutions.* Seoul: ORUEM Publishing House.

Minear, Larry. 2002. *The Humanitarian Enterprise: Dilemmas and Discoveries.* Bloomfield, Conn.: Kumarian Press.

Morton, David. 2002. David Morton Sees Increased Mutual Understanding. Interview by CanKor. Canada/DPR Korea E-Clipping Service. 30 September. www.cankor.ligi.ubc.ca/issues/100.htm#INTERVIEW.

Natsios, Andrew S. 2001. *The Great North Korean Famine: Famine, Politics and Foreign Policy.* Washington, D.C.: United States Institute of Peace.

———. 2003. Life inside North Korea. Testimony before the U. S. Senate Committee on Foreign Relations, Subcommittee on East Asian and Pacific Affairs. 5 June. www.state.gov/p/eap/rls/rm/2003/21269.htm.

Noland, Marcus. 2000. *Avoiding the Apocalypse: The Future of the Two Koreas.* Washington, D.C.: Institute for International Economics.

———. 2003. Famine and Reform. Working Paper series WP 03-5. Washington, D.C.: Institute for International Economics.

Office of the United Nations High Commissioner for Human Rights (OHCHR). 2003. Question of the Violation of Human Rights and Fundamental Freedoms in Any Part of the World. Document no. E/CN.4/2003/L.31. Agenda item no. 9, 59th Session, UN Commission on Human Rights, Economic and Social Council. 15 April.

Oh, Kongdan, and Ralph C. Hassig. 2002. *North Korea through the Looking Glass*. Washington, D.C.: Brookings Institution Press.

Park, Han S. 2002. *North Korea: The Politics of Unconventional Wisdom*. Boulder, Colo.: Lynne Rienner.

Rieff, David. 2002. *A Bed for the Night: Humanitarianism in Crisis*. New York: Simon and Schuster.

Schloms, Michael. 2004. The European NGO Experience in North Korea. In *Paved with Good Intentions: The NGO Experience in North Korea*, ed. L. Gordon Flake and Scott A. Snyder. Westport, Conn.: Praeger.

Shrimpton, Roger, and Yongyout Kachondham. 2004. Food and Nutrition in the Democratic People's Republic of Korea: Children's Nutritional Status. Study prepared for UNICEF Pyongyang.

Smith, Hazel. July 2002. Overcoming Humanitarian Dilemmas in the DPRK (North Korea). Special Report no. 90. Washington, D.C.: U.S. Institute of Peace. www.usip.org/pubs/specialreports/sr90.html.

Terry, Fiona. 2001. Feeding the Dictator. *The Guardian*, 6 August.

———. 2002. *Condemned to Repeat: The Paradox of Humanitarian Action*. Ithaca: Cornell University Press.

UNICEF. 1998. Report on The Multiple Indicator Cluster Survey in the Democratic People's Republic of Korea, 1998. Pyongyang: UNICEF. www.humanitarianinfo.org/DPRK/infocentre/library/Library_Documents/DPRK_MICS_1998.pdf.

UN Office for the Coordination of Humanitarian Affairs (UNOCHA). 2002. *Democratic People's Republic of Korea 2003: Consolidated Appeals Process*. New York, Geneva: United Nations. November. www.reliefweb.int/appeals/2003/files/dprk03.pdf.

———. 2003a. *Democratic People's Republic of Korea 2004: Consolidated Appeals Process*. New York, Geneva: United Nations. November. http://ochadms.unog.ch/quickplace/cap/main.nsf/h_Index/CAP_2004_DPRK/$FILE/CAP_2004_DPRK_SCREEN.PDF?OpenElement.

———. 2003b. DPR Korea OCHA Situation Bulletin, December 2003. Pyongyang: OCHA (United Nations). 21 January. wwww.reliefweb.int/w/rwb.nsf/d2fc8ae9db883867852567cb0083a028/66c1dfe11bc46248c1256e220034bbb1?OpenDocument.

Weingartner, Erich. 2003. NGO Contributions to the Transition from Humanitarian to Development Assistance in DPRK. In *North Korea in the World Economy*, ed. E. Kwan Choi, Yesook Merrill, and E. Han Kim. New York: Routledge.

Weingartner, Erich, and Marilyn Weingartner. 1999. Humanitarian Aid to North Korea: Peace-Building by Example. Paper presented at the seventh annual Canadian Consortium on Asia Pacific Security (CANCAPS) conference, Dalhousie University, Halifax, Nova Scotia, 5 December.

Wellinger, Arthur. 2003. Rural Energy Production: Biogas Plant, A Sustainable Source of Energy for Cooperative Farms. Report for ADRA-DPRK, Pyongyang, 12 December.

Zellweger, Kathi. 2002. Aid for North Korea: Seven Years of Challenges and Change. Paper prepared for Caritas-Hong Kong, Hong Kong, 5 April.

At the time of writing this chapter, Edward P. Reed was Associate Director of the Center for East Asian Studies, University of Wisconsin–Madison. He is currently Korea Representative for the Asia Foundation, based in Seoul. As manager of North Korea emergency response programs of the American Friends Service Committee (1994–97) and World Vision International (1997–2000), he traveled frequently to North Korea to negotiate and monitor relief and rehabilitation programs. His most recent visit was in 2000. The analysis and opinions expressed in this paper do not reflect the policies of the nongovernmental organizations for which he worked.

10

Designing Public Sector Capital Mobilization Strategies for the DPRK

Bradley O. Babson

Estimates of the financial requirements for reconstruction and future growth of the economy of the Democratic People's Republic of Korea (DPRK, or North Korea) vary greatly, as do estimates for meeting the educational, health, and social security needs of its people. Private investment will be critical in this process, but efforts to stimulate private capital, both domestic and foreign, will need to go hand in hand with mobilizing public investment to remove infrastructure bottlenecks and provide essential social services. An early priority will be to launch investigations in order to take stock of the DPRK's needs and improve the basis for estimating financial resource requirements for the short and medium term. There is broad consensus that the needs will be huge.

Major challenges facing the DPRK leadership and international community in any new international engagement framework will include how to mobilize both domestic and foreign public savings to meet capital investment and recurrent expenditure requirements, how to link public resource mobilization with a comprehensive economic reform strategy and viable macroeconomic framework, how to achieve synergy from public and private investment, how to develop absorptive capacity of the DPRK to use funds efficiently and with transparent accountability to minimize what will be great temptations for corruption, and how best to support a new political economy in the DPRK so that it will share the benefits of growth widely among the population and attend to the needs of vulnerable groups.

Aid Lessons from the DPRK's Past

The international community's experience with mobilizing public, international resources for the DPRK during the 1990s highlights a critical tension between political interests of donors and the DPRK leadership on the one hand, and the humanitarian and economic development needs of the DPRK society on the other. The tendency to politicize provision of foreign aid is very high, which reduces the impact of aid on the lives of the DPRK population and distorts incentives for reforms by the authorities.

Subsidized Socialism

It is worth remembering that the DPRK built a socialist economic system in which all domestic resources were public, and subsidies from the Soviet Union and China were major sources of international assistance for many years. The DPRK's long-standing misallocation of resources and aid from Communist states contributed greatly to the breakdown of the North Korean economy in the 1990s and the humanitarian crisis that ensued. While espousing the *juche* philosophy of self-reliance, the DPRK actually built a system that institutionalized economic dependence on foreign public financial assistance, even though this was largely disguised in the form of "friendship prices" and countertrade practices that provided large subsidies, especially for energy. This dependence, plus the distorting effects of prices that did not reflect economic cost, led to energy-intensive investments in industry, transport, and agriculture that were inefficient and ultimately unsustainable. The DPRK's military-first policies and favoritism of the elite amplified these failures, which were not challenged by the suppliers of the DPRK's economic aid during this period.

The experience with aid from Communist states underscores the simple fact that the economic policy context is critical for foreign aid to be effective in promoting economic development, and that aid provided primarily for political purposes—in this case to ensure regime survival—does not necessarily lead to economic viability and can foster aid dependence that acts as an inhibitor of needed economic reform.

Korean Peninsula Energy Development Organization

The international response to both the DPRK's nuclear brinkmanship of the early 1990s and the food crisis of the mid-1990s essentially resulted in mobilization of new forms of international public financial assistance for the DPRK. The establishment of the Korean Peninsula Energy Development Organization (KEDO) under the Agreed Framework, negotiated in 1994 between the United States and the DPRK, created a mechanism through which public resources from KEDO members (primarily the United States, Japan, the Republic of Korea [ROK, or South Korea] and the European Union [EU]) were managed to provide both 500,000 metric tons of heavy fuel oil annually to the DPRK and construction of two light-water reactor (LWR) nuclear power plants.

Although this agreement broke down following disclosure in October 2002 of a secret uranium enrichment program, with suspension of oil shipments in December 2002 and suspension of the LWR project in November 2003, the resources provided by KEDO to the DPRK between 1995 and 2003 did accomplish some positive results. On the political side, the KEDO program did contain the DPRK's plutonium nuclear program and allowed for direct contacts and negotiations between KEDO member states and the DPRK during a period of extreme difficulties for the DPRK, involving both leadership change following the death of Kim Il-sung and the economic and food crises. These stabilizing factors were important for maintaining peace and fostering an environment in which the DPRK could build trust with new foreign partners in cooperative activities. On the economic side, the fuel oil helped offset the trade shock that accompanied the collapse of the Soviet Union in 1992, and the LWR project provided a means to develop practical working modalities for foreigners with the DPRK authorities.

The LWR project itself, however, was never seen by either side as a genuinely economic undertaking for overcoming the DPRK's shortages of electric power. Many issues were left unattended as the project developed, including such elementary questions as how to finance transmission lines to connect the plants to the national electricity grid and how to stabilize the grid itself to absorb power from the LWRs. With the suspension and likely cancellation of the LWR project now a reality, there is a growing realization (especially in the ROK) that significant resources have been deployed without formation of any tangible economic asset.

A lesson emphasized by the KEDO experience is that when public resources are mobilized primarily to achieve political goals—in this case the containment of the DPRK's nuclear program—but are provided as economic assistance that does not meet a test of economic or commercial rationality, the political achievement may be unsustainable and the resources essentially wasted. Although the demise of the KEDO LWR project may have been triggered by the discovery of the secret uranium enrichment program, KEDO was destined in any case to face a crisis at the point when its fundamental lack of economic justification and provision of needed complementary investments could no longer be ignored.

A second lesson is that KEDO did demonstrate the value of multilateralism, both in mobilizing significant public resources from donors with very different interests and in coordinating policies relating to management of these resources and operational relations with the DPRK authorities. For this reason, it may well be desirable to consider a future role for a KEDO-like entity in mobilizing resources for the DPRK under a new international engagement framework if it is provided with a new mandate and is better able to integrate its economic and political functions.

Humanitarian Aid

The international response to the DPRK famine of the mid-1990s also holds valuable lessons for the future. The mobilization of significant humanitarian assistance was accomplished in an orderly way under the leadership of the United Nations (UN). The annual UN appeal is based on detailed crop production and food availability assessments by the World Food Program (WFP) and Food and Agriculture Organization (FAO), with health and educational humanitarian needs defined by the World Health Organization (WHO) and the United Nations Children's Fund (UNICEF). These objectively defined appeals have been supported by donors through contributions to UN-managed delivery programs, bilateral transfers, and support for NGOs active in the DPRK. The willingness of donors, particularly the United States, the ROK, Japan, and the EU, to provide humanitarian assistance while challenging the DPRK on its weapons programs contributed importantly to a growing perception that it is possible to engage the DPRK on multiple fronts concurrently, and that delinking humanitarian assistance from other issues could create an atmosphere conducive to addressing other concerns of the international community.

The fact that the DPRK was willing to ask for international assistance and set up administrative mechanisms to cooperate with foreign partners has contributed to the beginning of a more businesslike way of interacting. While there have been concerns about monitoring delivery of food aid to intended beneficiaries, access to different areas of the country, and restrictions imposed by the government on foreigners working in the DPRK, there have also been improvements over the years, owing in part to mutual trust building and in part to learning from experiences.

There are important limitations, however, on the humanitarian resource mobilization experience of recent years. First is aid fatigue. After seven years of appeals for food aid, the willingness of the international community to continue to meet the food deficit in the DPRK is dwindling. This reflects both frustration that the more fundamental obstacles to improving food security in the DPRK have not been overcome as well as the emergence of new claimants—in Africa, Afghanistan, and Iraq—on resources for humanitarian assistance that compete with the DPRK. A second limitation is the unwillingness of most donors to shift from humanitarian assistance to development assistance, pending resolution of major political security issues. A third limitation is the recent willingness of some donor governments to link humanitarian assistance to other political objectives. Since the reemergence of a nuclear crisis in late 2002, neither the United States nor Japan has made significant efforts to respond to the shortfall in the UN appeal for 2003 and expected for 2004, although official policy is still to maintain a separation of humanitarian aid from other issues.

The overall lesson from the humanitarian experience of recent years is that mobilization of significant public resources for the DPRK depends critically on political will, and this will cannot be assumed to be stable, even for basic humanitarian needs.

Korean Reconciliation

Political will to mobilize resources for the DPRK has been significantly affected by the appeal of inter-Korean reconciliation. The Sunshine Policy adopted by President Kim Dae-jung in the ROK led to significant use of public funds to finance inter-Korean projects, including subsidies to private companies such as Hyundai Assan for its Mount Kumgang tourism project. The ROK Ministry of Unification reported that the Inter-Korean Economic Cooperation Fund, which it administered, grew from 40 billion *won* in 1998 to 1,037 billion *won* in 2002. The Yonhap News Service reported on 10 December 2003 that during the first 11 months of 2003, following the revelation of the DPRK's highly enriched uranium (HEU) nuclear program in late 2002, the ROK provided $125 million in direct economic and humanitarian aid to the DPRK while it continued efforts to resolve the DPRK's nuclear program peacefully through dialogue.

Revelation of under-the-table payments to secure agreement for the June 2000 summit meeting between Kim Jong-il and Kim Dae-jung underscores the risk, however, that public funds can be used in nontransparent ways that ultimately undermine the objectives of reconciliation and distort incentives for the DPRK to adopt businesslike practices in its dealing with foreigners. The lesson is that corruption is an issue that can infect the donor as well as the recipient; and the risk of corruption's playing a major role in use of public resources mobilized for the DPRK is high. Strong efforts will be needed to introduce transparency and safeguards in the mechanisms for decision making about both the granting of funds and the use of funds.

Recent Chinese Aid

The experience of Chinese economic support for the DPRK in the 1990s also contains important lessons. Since the collapse of the Soviet Union, China has been the DPRK's biggest trading partner and largest supplier of concessional assistance, through both subsidized trade and direct transfers. Chinese agricultural and energy assistance have been vital to the DPRK's ability to avoid internal instability that could threaten survival of the regime. China has chosen not to channel resources through the UN appeal mechanism; it has relied on bilateral channels instead. This permits China to use its assistance to pursue its own political goals independently. It is widely believed, for example, that Chinese food aid is channeled to the military, which allows the WFP food aid to be targeted at the general population without risk that the military-first policy or regime stability would be undermined by foreign aid policies of other countries.

Cash versus In-Kind Payments

It is noteworthy that most publicly provided humanitarian aid to the DPRK, inter-Korean economic assistance (for example cross-border road and rail links), subsidized trade with China and the former Soviet Union, and KEDO provision of oil and LWR construction have not been in cash but as in-kind payments. Cash payments have been made openly by the private sector but not openly by the public sector, except in the case of protocols negotiated by KEDO under the LWR project for wage payments for North Korean labor, for example.[1] This preference for in-kind payments over cash illustrates the lack of trust by external providers of publicly funded assistance; they suspect that the DPRK authorities would not use the funds for purposes intended, but would divert them to either the military or the elite for their consumption. Any future effort to address the DPRK's large-scale infrastructure investment needs must involve very different modalities for channeling funds for contracts for civil works, equipment, and technical services. Protocols for procurement of goods and services will need to be negotiated, and the use of funds will need to be supervised during future program of development assistance. These will be major issues for both multilateral and bilateral donors. The KEDO experience will be a valuable starting point in these discussions.

Transition to Market Economy

The failures of the DPRK economic system combined with the limitations of foreign assistance in this environment are the backdrop for the emergence of the informal market economy in the DPRK today. Ordinary people in the DPRK are seeking new means to meet basic needs, and they have responded to incentives to fend for themselves and not depend on the state. Economic reforms introduced by the government since mid-2002 have accepted that market mechanisms are now playing an important role in the DPRK economy and social system and that market incentives are needed to increase both agricultural and industrial production. Lack of resources to finance needed infrastructure and intermediate inputs has constrained a supply response to those reforms. Thus, mobilization of public resources, both domestically and internationally, is critically needed to reinforce the reform process and stimulate economic recovery.

The dilemma for the international community is how to facilitate mobilization of resources for the DPRK without undermining the positive features of the emerging market economy. Just when incentives are beginning to stimu-

---

1   Secret cash payments by the Kim Dae-jung government, recently revealed, are considered a scandal.

late entrepreneurship and whet the appetite for freedom in the DPRK population, the risk exists that foreign aid will be used to suit the political needs of donors and the DPRK authorities and to undercut the transformative processes now under way in the DPRK. The challenge is to design policies and mechanisms that put publicly mobilized resources to best use for accelerating economic system change and putting the country on a path to prosperity for its citizens.

Designing a Public Capital Mobilization Strategy

Any future efforts to mobilize public capital under a new international engagement framework will need to take into account the initial conditions of the DPRK economic situation, proposed strategy for economic reform and institution building, requirements of macroeconomic stability, the DPRK's creditworthiness, requirements for multilateral assistance (including membership in international financial institutions [IFIs]), bilateral interests and political constraints, and aid coordination and management mechanisms. These factors will influence how much public capital will need to be mobilized; the purposes to which it will be applied; the balance of contributions from domestic, multilateral, and bilateral sources; modalities that will be used; and the conditionalities that will accompany commitments of funds.

Initial Conditions

The first questions to be asked by potential suppliers of public capital are what the funds will be used for and how much will be needed in specific time frames. Although general agreement exists that the DPRK public infrastructure in power and transport requires a large investment, there is neither a known inventory of the current state of these assets nor an available assessment of the balance that should be struck between rehabilitation and new investment. Nor are there comprehensive assessments of the condition of urban infrastructure, especially water supply, sanitation, and housing. Because of investigations by UN agencies and the ROK, more is known about the conditions of agriculture, but a comprehensive assessment of irrigation rehabilitation and flood control investment requirements is needed. Similarly, it is generally known that educational and health services in the DPRK require both capital investment and large-scale financing for recurrent costs, particularly for supplies and salaries.

Early priorities in a new international engagement framework will be a detailed needs assessment and preparation of a public investment program in collaboration with the DPRK authorities. How such an assessment will be conducted and who will take the lead should be questions addressed up front. It will set a precedent for future aid mobilization modalities and aid coordination mechanisms no matter which option is chosen for conducting the assessment:

- An inter-Korean team could carry out the assessment, which would then be presented to the international community;

- The DPRK could ask international agencies to conduct the assessment; this could be a collaborative exercise similar to the assessment that was conducted by the World Bank and United Nations Development Program (UNDP) for a donors meeting on Iraq in October 2003, or the assessment could be led by one of these agencies;[2] or

- A core group of countries could commission an assessment; this could provide the political context for the new engagement framework and link the assessment to political conditions associated with earlier agreements on security issues. Such an assessment could be carried out either by a team representing the core group composition or by an inter-Korean team or international organization team working under terms of reference supplied by the core group and reporting to it.

Another initial question will be the absorptive capacity of the DPRK government for funds provided to a public investment program. How would resources actually flow? Although experiences of UN agencies, nongovernmental organizations (NGOs), inter-Korean projects, and KEDO will be useful, the DPRK's actual mechanisms for controlling the flow of funds and managing public works will have to be carefully evaluated. Thus, an institutional assessment will be needed to complement the needs assessment for public investment. This institutional assessment will determine the types of conditions and monitoring requirements that donors will attach to any future funding. Concern about possible diversion of resources to military use and corruption can be expected to be major issues for the international community, and a practical framework for dealing with these concerns will need to be worked out with the DPRK authorities. Multilateral development banks and the UNDP should be given lead responsibility to avoid different standards being demanded by different suppliers of funds.

External technical and financial assistance will have to meet the standards of efficiency and accountability that the international community will require. Use of public capital ultimately requires accountability to the public, in both the DPRK and the countries that supply the DPRK with foreign aid. Attention to this issue by international civil society watchdog groups should be expected.

Strategy for Economic Reform and Institution Building

Money alone will not be the answer to the DPRK's economic troubles. It will be necessary to design a public capital mobilization plan that fits a com-

---

2 Because the DPRK is not a member of any of the IFIs but does host an in-country mission of UNDP, it would be logical for UNDP to play a coordinating role during planning discussions with the DPRK authorities to provide in-country logistical assistance for such an assessment exercise.

monly accepted economic reform strategy and institution-building requirements in a realistic way. The DPRK initially will rely on foreign capital to
kick-start its economy recovery, but from the very beginning it is important
that efforts be made to put in place policies and capacities to mobilize public resources domestically to support the economic reform and development
program. Technical assistance and training funded by foreign aid will be
essential for building the capacity to mobilize public capital domestically.

To begin, a workable consensus between DPRK authorities and foreign
partners on the economic reform strategy and development agenda must be
established. This will require analysis of options available to the DPRK on
the basis of its own conditions and history and an assessment of the lessons
of experience of other countries undertaking the transition from socialist to
market-based economic systems. What should be expected is a debate between advocates of the big-bang reform policy and advocates of paced reform. The implications of these different approaches for both political and
financial dimensions of the management of change and the role of different
foreign partners would vary greatly.

Institutional limitations in the DPRK are likely to be a major factor affecting the ultimate choice. Thus, it will be critically important that the political
context for the economic reform strategy be firmly established before significant public capital is mobilized. The opportunity costs of capital are significant in the DPRK context, and the risks of wasting resources and undermining domestic and foreign political support for the economic strategy should
be minimized through decision making that creates a broad consensus of
the best way to proceed and a willingness to provide the level of financial
support to make the strategy successful.

Engaging the DPRK in policy dialogue must occur from the very start; that
dialogue will have a large effect on the ways public capital will be mobilized
and the atmosphere of cooperation between the DPRK and foreign partners.
Mobilization efforts will be enhanced by building a culture of openness and
dialogue, with the DPRK willing to listen to the advice of foreigners but
ultimately making its own decisions in ways that promote self-confidence
and the political will to follow through on implementation. To achieve this
openness and frank exchange of views, the DPRK will need to be willing to
be much more transparent in sharing information and cooperative about
investigations than it has been in the past.

Macroeconomic Framework

Currently the DPRK economy is not guided by a macroeconomic policy; nor
does it have the institutions and tools in place to exercise macroeconomic
management. Price reforms introduced in 2002 have resulted in inflationary
pressures that the DPRK is ill equipped to constrain. Early in a new engagement framework, it will be necessary to assist the DPRK in developing new

capacities in this area through training and technical assistance. In parallel with work assessing public investment needs and determining the best economic reform and development strategy discussed above, it will be important to work with the DPRK to construct a macroeconomic policy and financing plan that is compatible with these exercises.

The feasibility of any framework will depend critically on the ability to mobilize the resources needed to fulfill the financing plan. Thus, the public capital mobilization process will need to be carefully coordinated with the policy-planning process. This will require a close working relationship between the DPRK authorities and advisers who are in close touch with major potential doors to the program. In many countries, the International Monetary Fund (IMF) and World Bank are called on to perform this coordinating role, but the DPRK does not yet have relations with these institutions. The ROK has the macroeconomic expertise to provide the DPRK with such advice, and, to the extent that the two Koreas are seeking to deepen integration of their two economies, it will be important for the ROK to be closely involved in the macroeconomic policy dialogue with the DPRK because this will also have a direct bearing on macroeconomic policy and management in the ROK itself. Thus, an issue that will need to be addressed is how to balance and coordinate the roles of the IFIs and the ROK in macroeconomic surveillance, policy advice, and technical assistance to the DPRK.

Creditworthiness

Another issue that will need to be addressed is how to factor DPRK creditworthiness into public capital mobilization for the DPRK. The World Bank assesses country creditworthiness on the basis of a number of factors, including gross domestic product (GDP) per capita and public debt–servicing capacity. While the detailed information needed to establish creditworthiness for the DPRK has not yet been made available, the DPRK's low level of economic production and external trade deficits can be expected to constrain its ability to borrow on anything but highly concessional terms.

The DPRK does not have a good reputation as a borrower, and this perception will need to be overcome for public as well as private lenders to the DPRK government in the future. Domestic borrowing is a new phenomenon in the DPRK, but the public bond program introduced in 2003 demonstrated a fundamental lack of appreciation for the role of bonds in public finance, with elements of gambling in the design of the program. Similarly, the ROK Ministry of Unification and the Bank of Korea report that the DPRK has a substantial outstanding external debt, estimated to be as large as $12.5 billion, on which it is paying neither interest nor principal. Of this, a large portion is debt to Russia.

Implications of this situation are that the DPRK is going to have to rely primarily on building a new tax system as the primary means of mobilizing resources domestically. It will also need to restructure its existing foreign debt, and build credibility as a borrower by creating new debt reporting and management capacities. As part of the overall strategy for public resource mobilization, the international community will also likely seek conditions for future financial assistance to the DPRK for economic reconstruction that will lead to improvements in creditworthiness over time. To the extent that DPRK will require grants and concessional loans from donors, it will be expected to comply with standards that have been established globally for access to development assistance. These were reconfirmed in 2002 at the International Conference on Financing for Development in Monterrey, Mexico.

One issue that may arise if the ROK and the DPRK pursue a gradual economic integration policy is that the ROK may be asked to guarantee loans made by other parties to the DPRK government. This would help overcome creditworthiness constraints in mobilizing resources for the DPRK, but it would also place a contingent liability on the ROK. Providing such guarantees would be one way for the ROK to avoid the shock of premature German-style integration while it accepts a burden that is larger than would normally be expected of a donor to another country.

Membership in the International Financial Institutions

The DPRK is not a member of any of the IFIs, although it has had informal contacts on several occasions. Mobilization of public capital for the DPRK will be greatly facilitated by IFI membership, which would allow the DPRK to gain access to financial resources mobilized through well-established multilateral mechanisms, to obtain access to knowledge resources and technical assistance from these agencies, and also to leverage bilateral assistance through assurances that would be provided by the multilateral relationships. To obtain membership, the DPRK will need to apply and to meet technical and legal conditions for membership, and existing member governments will need to vote in favor of the DPRK becoming a member. Thus, both technical and political requirements for membership will need to be satisfied. It is possible, however, for the DPRK to obtain services from the IFIs before formal membership if existing members adopt a resolution calling for such assistance in their own interest.

Regional Economic Cooperation

Another factor that will influence the mobilization of public capital for the DPRK is the evolving agenda of regional economic cooperation in Northeast Asia. The DPRK is a member of the Consultative Commission for the Tumen River Development Area and Northeast Asia (Tumen Commission) and has participated in the Tumen River Area Development Program (TRADP) sponsored by the UNDP. This program has languished in recent years, but a new engagement framework with renewed interest by China, Russia, and Mongolia in expanding cross-border trade and access to the DPRK port of Rajin might well reinvigorate the TRADP framework. Because the Tumen Commission is the only formal intergovernmental body that currently exists to guide regional economic cooperation in this area, it is likely to be used to mobilize support for cooperative projects among local governments.

Regional energy and transport links are also topics of much discussion in Northeast Asia, as a new engagement framework with the DPRK could also be expected to lead to deepening discussions about how to finance a rail link from the ROK through the DPRK to Russia and China and how to trade power supplies and proceed with gas pipeline projects that include the DPRK. While such projects will most likely require private funding, public capital mobilization will also be required; and any regional projects will need to be linked to the public investment program discussed earlier for the DPRK. Any such projects will also require multicountry political and legal agreements in addition to financing. For this agenda to go forward it will be necessary to develop modalities to address all the issues among the concerned states.

Core Group and Second Circle

The six-party-talks framework[3] that has emerged as the mechanism for political engagement with the DPRK might well evolve to become an ongoing security dialogue forum. To the extent that a new engagement framework will link such ongoing political and security arrangements with economic assistance, mobilization of foreign aid to support economic reform and development in the DPRK may well be conditioned by the decisions of this core group. KEDO also represents a core group that has been centrally involved in engagement with the DPRK since 1995.

The configuration of these two groups differs. If public capital mobilization in the future is going to be conducted within a framework of policies set by a core group, a question that will need to be addressed is adjustments to the memberships of these two groups. The six-party talks presently exclude the EU, although the EU is an active member and contributor to KEDO. Because a future program to mobilize public capital for the DPRK is likely to be broadly supported by European countries, the issue of EU participation in a core group can be expected to be an important one from their point of view. Similarly, if KEDO is going to play a role in the future under a new mandate, reconfiguring the membership is also an issue that would arise. Neither Russia nor China is a present member, but both should participate in any future core group coordination effort that KEDO might be asked to undertake.

---

3 Participants in the six-party talks are China, Japan, North Korea, Russia, South Korea, and the United States.

Apart from questions about whether a core group will guide economic cooperation policies and resource mobilization efforts with the DPRK, it will be necessary to consider how best to involve a second circle of countries that do not have a seat at the table for security negotiations but will be important sources of future public capital mobilization and support for economic reforms and institution building in the DPRK. Two Pacific Rim countries already active are Australia and Canada, and others such as Vietnam can provide valuable advice to the DPRK, both on the basis of their own experiences during transition to a market economy and in working with multilateral institutions and bilateral donors in aid mobilization and management. Individual European countries—including Switzerland, Sweden, Italy, Germany, and the United Kingdom—also will want to be involved bilaterally, not only through EU and IFI channels. Finding ways to give second-circle countries a voice in the new engagement framework will be important to the overall effort to help the DPRK integrate with the international community and gain broad financial support for economic transition and development.

Inter-Korean Economic Cooperation

Encouraging inter-Korean reconciliation is a strong motivator for the international community to provide public capital to the DPRK. Thus, it is likely that donor countries will be more forthcoming with resources if the two Koreas are pursuing a policy of deepening inter-Korean economic cooperation in parallel with improving social and political relations within a broadly supported security framework.

Because unification is understood to be a long-term process requiring reduction in the large gap in the two economies and gradual harmonization of infrastructure, financial systems, legal systems, product markets, and labor markets, the inter-Korean economic agenda can be expected to evolve and will need to be calibrated to progress in economic reforms and capabilities in the DPRK. For this reason, mechanisms will be needed to ensure proper coordination between the financing of the DPRK's economic development program and the inter-Korean program. The ROK will probably be expected contribute a large share of the public capital needed for the DPRK to fulfill its side of the inter-Korean economic cooperation program, but it will face limitations consistent with its own macroeconomic stability and economic growth needs. Thus, the international community will need to support the two Koreas in their process and supplement ROK resources with resources mobilized from other donors and will need to contribute knowledge and expertise from global experience that will bring value added to what the two Koreas can do by themselves.

Normalization of Relations with Japan

When Japan normalized relations with the ROK in 1965, it provided a financial package of $800 million (Manyin 2003, appendix). This included a grant of $300 million to be disbursed over a 10-year period, a concessional loan of $200 million to be disbursed over a 10-year period and repaid over 20 years with interest of 3.5 percent, and $300 million in private credits over 10 years from Japanese banks and financial institutions. When Japan normalizes relations with the DPRK, it is widely expected that the DPRK will receive a financial package similar in composition to that received by the ROK, but it will be significantly larger in value in order to take into account the intervening time period. Estimates are in the range of $5–10 billion. Even at the low end, Japan can be expected to be a major supplier of public capital to the DPRK. Thus, the mobilization of public capital for the DPRK will be heavily influenced by Japanese policy with regard to the timing of normalization of relations, the size and composition of the financing package, modalities for transferring resources to the DPRK, and conditionalities that may be applied by the Japanese government.

The Japanese voice will carry significant weight with both the DPRK and other donors, whose own policies toward provision of capital to the DPRK will need to be coordinated with Japanese priorities. Because of concerns about the risk of diversion of funds to the DPRK military, Japan will not want to commit large sums in advance of a more general political agreement with the DPRK on both the multilateral security issues and bilateral issues of concern. Japan will also not want to be the only major player in provision of public capital, and, after normalization of relations, most likely will want close cooperation with the IFIs to multilateralize the risks of extending large-scale capital support to the DPRK.

China's Future Role

After playing a critical facilitator role during the six-party talks, China will be expected to continue to be proactive and collaborative in a new engagement framework. Thus, China's economic assistance policy to the DPRK in the future will need to be more transparent and more coordinated with the policies of other donors than in the past. This would be a significant departure from China's past economic relationship with the DPRK, and would also be widely interpreted as a natural evolution of China's emergence as a regional power following on its success in expanding regional economic cooperation with Central Asia and the Association of Southeast Asian Nations (ASEAN). It should be expected that China's willingness to develop more open and coordinated economic assistance relations with the DPRK will also be reflected in future activism in Northeast Asia regional economic cooperation.

China's future role will also have an impact on economic assistance policies of other countries. If China expands participation in multilateral cooperation both through active collaboration with IFI activities in the DPRK and in regional economic cooperation mechanisms such as TRADP and KEDO, there will be incentives for other donors to support these initiatives and provide complementary funding.

Human Rights and Environmental Protection

A new engagement framework with the DPRK will be shaped not only by political agreements on security and needs for economic reform and reconstruction, but also by human rights and environmental concerns. The policies of the DPRK authorities in these areas will affect the mobilization of capital from donor countries, especially those democracies where public funds for foreign aid are authorized through national legislatures. It can be expected that the United States and Europe will link their assistance programs to progress on human rights issues. Both the World Bank and the Asian Development Bank (ADB) have detailed guidelines for ensuring both social and environmental safeguards in projects that they finance, and the DPRK would be expected to abide by these standards the same as any other borrower from these institutions. Most bilateral development assistance also requires conditionalities to ensure mitigation of adverse social and environmental impacts. Mobilizing public capital for the DPRK will be much easier if the authorities engage in dialogue with foreign partners on these issues and develop policies and action plans that can be supported by the donors.

Strategies for Mobilizing Domestic Public Capital

The DPRK will require a large infusion of foreign capital to stimulate policy reforms and economic growth. It will also need a strategy to foster significant growth in domestic public savings in the medium term, which will be required for public investments that sustain growth as well as maintain macroeconomic stability and meet expanding requirements for social expenditures, operations, and maintenance of economic infrastructure. Along with other socialist economies undergoing the transition to market mechanisms, the DPRK does not have in place the financial and legal institutions that will be needed to achieve this goal. Thus, a high priority initially will be to design an institutional development plan and fiscal policy that is synchronized with the overall economic reform strategy.

A big-bang approach would be somewhat different from a gradual approach. With a big bang, the priority for fiscal policy would be to secure macroeconmic stability and supply public goods that the private sector cannot provide. More gradually, fiscal reform would be a major driver of growth during transition, and the government could both use fiscal stimulus and intervene to give new economic actors incentives to generate growth (Lee 2003).

In both cases, it will eventually be necessary to address a number of fundamental issues in building new fiscal capability in the DPRK. These include reform of state-owned enterprises (SOEs) and incentives for profitability and growth, restructuring of the tax system, strategy for domestic debt, the role of contractual savings, and improvements in allocative efficiency of public expenditures. These issues are complex problems, and building the necessary institutional underpinnings to make significant progress will take time. Foreign aid, both in knowledge services and financial resources, should be calibrated to support the DPRK's process of building these domestic capabilities so that the need for external public savings can diminish over a reasonable time period. The experience of Vietnam under its *doi moi* program would be a useful reference for the DPRK and future donors in addressing this agenda.

Reform of State-Owned Enterprises

Historically the state budget in the DPRK has been financed principally by turnover tax and profits-remittance tax on SOEs and agricultural cooperatives. The industrial sector also accounts for 70–80 percent of state revenue (excluding military). Thus, the sharp contraction of the DPRK economy in the 1990s is reflected in the drop in central government revenues from 37.1 billion *won* in 1991 to 20.3 billion *won* in 1996 (Koh 1999). This drop largely reflects the decline of revenue from SOEs resulting from a breakdown of production. SOE performance was affected by a number of factors, including depletion of capital stock, outdated technologies, failures of central planning, great distortions in prices, lack of access to finance and intermediate inputs, the trade shock induced by the collapse of the Soviet Union, interference of the Workers' Party in enterprise management, rigidity of the labor market, and absence of entrepreneurship. The revitalization of SOEs thus will be essential for any future domestic effort to mobilize public resources.

Beginning with amendments to its constitution in 1998, the DPRK has begun to accept the idea of profit motive to encourage increased industrial production. In the economic reforms introduced in 2002, the country took a number of initiatives to promote enterprise reform, including permitting firms to obtain inputs from market-determined suppliers, reducing the influence of Workers' Party representatives on management decisions at the firm level, placing a hard budget constraint on SOEs, and allowing more flexibility in labor management. The emergence of the informal market economy is also a factor. In a new engagement framework, a major priority will be to support growth of the market economy in a way that promotes leveling the playing field with SOEs, at the same time improving the ability of SOEs to be autonomous and competitive business enterprises (Park 1995). Tax revenues must be increased through buoyancy based on growth and profitability of the enterprise sector.

Restructuring the Tax System

Another major future priority will be to restructure the tax system of the DPRK in order to capture transactions in the market economy as well as the state sector and to create incentives for enterprise investment and entrepreneurship. Turnover and profits-remittance taxes should be replaced by income taxes for enterprises and individuals and a value-added tax on imports and domestic transactions (Park 1995). The design and implementation of tax reform will need to parallel reform of the financial sector and development of a commercial banking system. The legal and administrative framework to support policy shifts will also need to be put in place, and that will take time. Thus, a phased approach will be needed and technical assistance provided to the DPRK to support the transformation of the public finance system. Resistance to tax reforms can be expected at both the enterprise level and the individual level, so tax administration and anticorruption measures will need to be addressed as part of the agenda.

A related issue is the restructuring of the roles of central and local government in mobilization of public revenues. Already some limited and uneven steps have been taken to give local governments more authority to collect fees and local taxes, and some observers advocate rapid decentralization of the fiscal system following the Chinese experience to promote the private economy (Lee 2003). However, over-rapid fiscal decentralization comes with risk because of the needs for capacity building at the local level, an accountability framework, and good coordination of local fiscal management with macroeconomic stabilization.[4]

Domestic Public Debt

In May 2003, the DPRK introduced a bond scheme intended to mobilize private savings for government use. This scheme was designed as a lottery, after which only a few bondholders would eventually receive interest on their investment. Not surprisingly, few takers have been reported. Eventually, however, domestic debt must play a role in public finance in the DPRK, as a way to mobilize resources for public investment and as a tool of macroeconomic management. While this will require, first, growth in enterprise and private savings as well as legalization of property rights for various classes of assets, a new engagement framework should include assistance in developing public debt policies and management capacity consistent with international standards. The DPRK does not have a good reputation as a public borrower, so investor confidence will need to be developed in the domestic population as well as among foreign investors and donors who supply official development assistance (ODA) loans.

---

4   For a good discussion of these issues, see Dabla-Norris and Wade (2002).

Contractual Savings

Similarly, the DPRK will need to develop new mechanisms to finance health care and social security as they undergo transition. The existing social security system, for example, has become essentially irrelevant to households participating in the informal market economy, where prices far exceed social welfare payments. A new engagement framework should include a review of contractual savings schemes adopted by other socialist countries in transition and assistance to the DPRK in developing new policies and programs to meet these essential human needs.

Allocative Efficiency

How well the DPRK performs in reforming public expenditures will also have an impact on mobilization of resources from domestic as well as foreign sources. If public investment is diverted to unproductive expenditures or wasted through mismanagement and corruption, it will not have the buoyant impact on economic growth and state revenues that will be needed. Reduction in military expenditures and redeployment of military assets and personnel to productive activities will require major attention and assistance in a new engagement framework. Price liberalization is also needed to foster more efficient allocation of resources throughout the economy, but the DPRK will need support in managing price reforms in ways that will induce supply responses and contain inflationary pressures. Economic efficiency should also be given primary consideration in public investment planning, especially for infrastructure and in the selection and prioritization of projects for both domestic and foreign funding. The DPRK will need training and technical assistance as well as political discipline in order to make good public investment decisions.

Modalities for Mobilizing Foreign Public Capital

Several basic options are available for arranging international cooperation with the DPRK aimed at mobilizing ODA. They differ in two major respects. One is leadership—in other words, who convenes and chairs the meetings of donors. The other is the extent to which political considerations in addition to economic considerations are explicitly addressed in the mandates and processes of these decision-making mechanisms. The choices that are made in establishing institutional arrangements for mobilizing ODA for the DPRK will have lasting impact not only on the DPRK but also on the conduct of relations among the countries of Northeast Asia and relations between Northeast Asia and the United States and Europe.

These choices should be made with a full understanding of their implications. This section of the paper examines three approaches: Korea-led approaches, World Bank/IMF–led approaches, and core country group–led approaches. The strengths and limitations of each approach are discussed, along with some variations. This is followed by examination of issues relating to future options for KEDO, the potential role for trust funds, and the proposal for a Northeast Asia development bank.

Two Koreas in the Lead

If eventual reunification of the two Koreas is the ultimate goal of both countries and is supported by the international community, a joint sponsorship framework is one option to consider. In this case, the agenda and process for coordinating the mobilization of ODA resources for the DPRK would be guided by the two Koreas together and would reinforce the objectives of reducing the gap between the two economies, deepening inter-Korean economic cooperation, and gradually integrating the two economic systems. This approach has the advantage of keeping the reunification goal at center stage and providing a political incentive for the international community to mobilize resources and provide support for the reunification process for an extended period. The IFIs, the EU, and bilateral development assistance agencies could be commissioned through this framework to work with both Koreas on the program; they could provide advice and technical assistance to both countries and financial support to the DPRK to meet its public investment program requirements. In policy dialogue with the international donors, the two Koreas could describe what each was doing individually, as well as together, to advance the overall economic agenda on the Korean peninsula. Each could also explain where assistance from the international community would be most helpful.

An institutional framework has already been set in place for an inter-Korean economic dialogue and the management of cooperation activities that operate in parallel with frameworks on social-cultural and security matters. It would be relatively easy to build on this existing inter-Korean economic cooperation framework, both to convene meetings with the international donor community and to monitor and supervise implementation of reforms and projects in the DPRK. Capacities that have already been built up in the ROK—in the Ministry of Unification, Ministry of Economy and Finance, Bank of Korea, Korea Institute for International Economic Policy, and Korea Development Institute—could be mobilized rapidly to support the international engagement framework while ROK institutions work with counterpart organs in the DPRK to help the North Korean institutions build their capacity to engage effectively.

One disadvantage of the Korean-led approach is that it could place major powers and other donors in an awkward position of supporting a joint Korean economic agenda that they may find objectionable for one reason or another. If the two Koreas together proceed with an agenda that is inimical to the interests of one or more major donors or that is perceived to be tilted politically, non-Korean donors would have less leverage to influence a change of course than would be the case in the other approaches discussed below. This potential for preemption could be mitigated if processes were put in place for consultations with donors on major issues on an ongoing basis in both Seoul and Pyongyang. Building a culture of openness and cooperation would be essential for long-term success.

Traditional Consultative Group

The typical model used for other countries around the world is a consultative group chaired by the World Bank in close collaboration with the IMF and UNDP. In the early stages of the ROK's economic development, a consultative group was active there. Although consultative group meetings have normally been held in Paris, either annually or on an occasional basis, in recent years it has been common for these meetings to be held in other centers, such as Tokyo, or in the country concerned. Setting up a consultative group for the DPRK along traditional lines would mean that the DPRK would have to become a member of the IFIs at an early stage and work closely with the IFIs in economic and financial reporting and in preparation of reports used as the basis for the consultative group discussions. Because of the inter-Korean economic agenda and long-term unification goals, any IFI-led consultative group framework would need to be designed to work closely with ROK authorities and institutions to ensure that policy dialogue and financing plans are coordinated with the inter-Korean processes.

The advantages of the traditional consultative group are that it has well-established processes known to the donor community and is an efficient mechanism for coordinating policy dialogue and mobilizing formal commitments to finance a well-reasoned macroeconomic framework for economic development. It also would enable the DPRK to learn rapidly the ways of the international financial system and develop intimate working relations with IFI staff responsible for managing the relationship and consultative group preparations. Because both the IMF and World Bank played central roles in the management of the ROK financial crisis of the late 1990s, and because the IMF maintains a surveillance capability and routinely conducts Article IV consultations with the ROK, the IFIs also would be well positioned to play the lead coordinating role for discussions of the interaction of DPRK economic transition and development with the ROK macroeconomic policy and management.

A disadvantage of the traditional model is that the IFIs are forbidden by their articles of agreement to take political considerations into account in the conduct of their work. For the DPRK, it may be difficult to separate political dialogue from discussions of economic policy and mobilization of resources. Issues such as progress in implementation of security agreements, handling of human rights issues, and domestic political dynamics of change in both Koreas are likely to be discussed as part of the context for extending

ODA. For example, representatives of donor countries participating in consultative group meetings usually come from ministries of finance and development assistance organizations, but political discussions are usually led by representatives of foreign ministries. A variation of the consultative group format that might overcome this liability would be to have the meetings cochaired by the UN and World Bank, which would legitimize the integration of political and economic dialogue at the same meetings.

Core Country Group

If the six-party framework for negotiating security agreements for the DPRK is successful, it might naturally be expanded, with some modifications, to address economic assistance issues as well. The pressure to link economic assistance with progress on political agreements is likely to be strong if a step-by-step, road-map approach is adopted by this group. In this approach, it would be necessary for the core group to either have a rotating chair or elect one country to serve as chair for the economic cooperation meetings. Because donors to the DPRK will include the IFIs, the EU, and second-circle countries such as Australia and Canada, participation in the economic meetings would need to be expanded beyond the six-country framework. Conduct of these meetings would be driven by assessments of progress on political agreements and consideration of the implications of economic assistance. In this framework, the issues of concern to all the core countries would be given high priority, and the mobilization of broader international support for the DPRK would be considered in this context. A variant might make use of KEDO as the forum for economic discussions if KEDO were to be given a new and wider mandate and its membership expanded to include China and Russia (see the next subsection).

The advantage of the core country group's taking the lead on the ODA mobilization discussions is that the linkage to the political framework for international engagement with the DPRK would be clear and explicit. The main disadvantage of this approach is that the DPRK's economic reform process and development would be shaped by the strong political interests of members of the core group and dominance of regional perspectives and, thus, delay the DPRK's full integration in the global community and normal workings of the international financial system. Also, inter-Korean reconciliation would be given a second-row seat to the other interests of the large powers, reinforcing a sense of dependency of both Koreas, with potentially negative effects on public opinion in these countries. Some adjustments in the working modalities of the core group would also be needed to fit the requirements of economic policy dialogue and coordination between foreign policy and economic agency participation.

Future Options for KEDO

A successor to KEDO could be given a role in the mobilization of public capital in a new engagement framework in two ways. Both would require changes in the existing KEDO mandate and membership.

- Use KEDO as the primary mechanism to provide energy assistance to the DPRK, keeping broadly with its present mandate but expanding it to cover conventional (not nuclear) energy supply, rehabilitation of the transmission system, and demand-management activities. The package of such assistance would need to be shaped by an energy-sector study that KEDO would undertake. This could be done in partnership with the World Bank and the Asian Development Bank in order to take advantage of their expertise in studies of this kind. The package of assistance to the energy sector would need to be linked to the overall economic development strategy adopted for the DPRK and the resource mobilization coordinated with the more general ODA mobilization efforts managed through one of the frameworks discussed above.

  KEDO would be one important actor in the development assistance to be provided to the DPRK and would need to participate in the general aid coordination processes and have close cooperation with the IFIs, to both ensure consistency in policy dialogue and enlist IFI resources in support of the energy sector program. In addition, KEDO could be the primary mechanism for reaching agreements among the countries of Northeast Asia on cross-border energy trade that involves the DPRK, including potential power trade and gas trade. To undertake this role, both Russia and China would need to become KEDO members, and its activities would become closely linked to the broader discussions of regional energy security. Relatively minor adjustments in the staffing and management of KEDO would be needed for it to be able to undertake this limited expansion in its role.

- The other option would be to give KEDO's successor a much broader mandate to become the "Korea Economic Development Organization" and serve as the primary modality for coordinating all discussions of economic strategy and development assistance for the DPRK. This would operate under the guidance of the KEDO members, who would need to be expanded to include China and Russia, and would thus represent an expanded core country group that would also include the EU. KEDO would become the instrument for linking the political and economic frameworks for engagement, where it would be determined that the political framework would need to tightly guide economic discussions and commitments, not only for the core countries but also for the international community.

The main disadvantage of this approach is that KEDO was never conceived as an economic organization despite its mandate to provide heavy fuel oil and construct two LWRs. As a political organization, KEDO has been managed and staffed primarily by foreign affairs personnel, not by energy experts and economists. For KEDO to assume a broader economic mandate, major adjustments would be needed in its staffing and management as well as in its operating procedures. Another disadvantage is that the inter-Korean economic relationship would be overshadowed by the KEDO organization, potentially causing some inconsistency in the policies adopted by KEDO for economic engagement with the DPRK and the dynamics of inter-Korean cooperation.

Possible Role for Trust Funds

The DPRK requires large-scale public infrastructure investment that will need to be funded by ODA in the short and medium term. Funding for typical projects comes mainly from the multilateral development banks and bilateral development assistance agencies such as the Japan Bank for International Cooperation. Infrastructure funding is usually provided as loans, not grants, even if the loans are at concessional terms for qualifying countries. Large-scale infrastructure projects require much advance preparation:

- A public investment program that is consistent with both an economic development strategy that is widely supported and a prudent macroeconomic management framework;
- Feasibility and engineering studies to ensure that both technical designs and costing are prepared properly;
- Environmental and social studies and mitigation plans, including plans and funding for resettlement of households affected by infrastructure projects; and
- International competitive bidding for contracts, required especially by the IFIs; this requires considerable preparation, especially for a country that has not participated in the international system of procurement before.

For these reasons, even though the DPRK's needs for infrastructure investment are high, there will be a period of several years required to undertake the prerequisite studies and preparations to absorb large amounts of ODA. During this time, high priority will have to be given to funding the studies, technical assistance, and training that the DPRK will need to prepare and implement a large program of international assistance.

The idea of a grant trust fund to launch this process has considerable merit. To reduce complications of multiple donor demands on DPRK administrative capacity, it would be efficient to establish a multilaterally funded facility that is administered by a single agency or a limited number of agencies to take a lead role in organizing a program to use such funds and to supervise their implementation. One option would be to give the UNDP the lead role because it already has a trust fund for the DPRK in place and could ask the IFIs to assist in the execution of specific activities. Another option would be to set up the trust fund in one or more of the IFIs, as has been done for a number of other situations, including East Timor and Bosnia-Herzegovina. If the existing shareholders so desire, such a trust fund could be created quickly, even before the DPRK undergoes the process of obtaining membership in the IFIs. The advantage of establishing IFI-managed trust funds is that it would impel the development of the operational working relations between the IFIs and the DPRK that will be needed for IFIs to play the role they will be expected to play in any of the aid coordination and management scenarios discussed above.

Consideration of the Proposal for a Northeast Asia Development Bank

The idea of establishing a new regional development bank to finance the infrastructure investment envisaged for expanding economic integration in Northeast Asia has been under active discussion in the region for a number of years. If such a new financing institution were to be created, the institution would be expected to be one source of funding for DPRK reconstruction and integration in the regional economy. The case for such an initiative rests on at least two assumptions: (1) that such an institution could mobilize incremental funds to supplement funds that would be mobilized through the World Bank and Asian Development Bank, and (2) that a different governance system would mean the application of standards and conditionalities different from those required by the existing IFIs.[5] In particular, the argument is made that a Northeast Asia development bank (NEADB) would provide political-risk coverage for countries such as the DPRK.

Like the World Bank and the Asian Development Bank, an NEADB could use a public capital structure to intermediate in the private-capital markets in order to provide financing that the private sector would not undertake on its own. The first-tier, founding-member countries would be China, the DPRK, Japan, Mongolia, the ROK, and Russia; they would be expected to subscribe 40 percent of the bank's capital. Another 20 percent would be subscribed by second-tier Asian countries, and the remaining 40 percent would be subscribed by the United States, Europe, and others. Implicit in the NEADB concept is that this organization would respond to the political will of its first-tier members, which would dominate decision making and also staffing. The institution would become an important instrument for regional

---

5   For a detailed discussion of the case for establishing a Northeast Asia development bank, see Katz (2003).

cooperation among governments that, compared with other regions of the world, do not have a good track record of working collaboratively as a group.

Although these objectives are laudable, there are political, financial, and administrative reasons for skepticism about whether and how quickly an effective institution could be established. The first political question is whether the United States and Europe would choose to participate and support the idea that a third development bank could contribute sufficient value added to the capabilities of the World Bank and Asian Development Bank to be worth the additional costs and administrative overhead a new institution would imply. Alternatives would be to encourage the existing organizations to strengthen their capacity to support Northeast Asia regional development and DPRK economic reconstruction through internal organizational adjustments, including staffing. The question of Russia's membership in the Asian Development Bank would also need to be addressed, but this would be simpler than creating a new organization in order to include Russian participation. A second political question is how an NEADB would relate to the emerging core country group framework that is evolving from the six-party talks. In principle, an NEADB could be designed as an economic instrument of this political framework, but in this case the United States would need to be included as a first-tier member, which is not what the promoters of the NEADB concept had in mind.

Financially, there are significant questions about how capital subscriptions and voting power would be distributed in an NEADB, and there are also questions about who the borrowers would be (other than the DPRK and possibly Mongolia). It is difficult to believe that China and Russia would choose to borrow from an NEADB, if they are major shareholders, when they have their own large domestic capacity to finance infrastructure investments and access to international capital markets as sovereign borrowers.

From an administrative perspective, the question is how quickly a new NEADB could establish the operational policies and procedure, and staffing and management, to function effectively. For all these reasons, the establishment of an NEADB can be expected to be controversial and, in any case, protracted. Efforts to mobilize capital for the DPRK should not be distracted by the larger complications of the debate on creating a new financial institution for the region.

Conclusions

A new engagement framework for the DPRK will need to face up to important realities when it comes to mobilizing public financial resources. One reality is that the linkage of political and economic considerations needs to be handled very carefully in order to avoid problems similar to those with past assistance to the DPRK and to ensure that future assistance is effective in meeting expectations of both the DPRK authorities and the international community. A second reality is that there are many complex and difficult challenges to be met in transforming the DPRK economy, setting it on a sustainable growth path, and integrating it with the ROK economy, the regional economy, and the international financial system. Open and constructive policy dialogue between the DPRK and the donor community will be essential so that there is common understanding of what will be required to achieve results, especially in conditionalities that will be placed by donors on access to resources and in the supervision of the implementation of donor-financed activities. A third reality is that building new institutional capacities and laying the groundwork of technical preparation for large infrastructure investments will take some time and require good coordination among those providing support to the DPRK. To be successful, mobilizing resources for a new engagement framework for the DPRK will require goodwill and commitment to sustained cooperation between the DPRK and its foreign partners for some time to come.

References

Dabla-Norris, Era, and Paul Wade. 2002. The Challenge of Fiscal Decentralization in Transition Countries; working paper WP/02/103. Washington, D.C.: International Monetary Fund.

Katz, Stanley S. 2003. Financing the Infrastructure Investment. In *A Vision for Economic Cooperation in East Asia: China, Japan, and Korea*, ed. Cho Lee-Jay, Kim Yoon-hyung, and Lee Chung H. Seoul: Korea Development Institute; Honolulu: University of Hawaii Press.

Koh, Il-dong. 1999. North Korean Budgetary Structure and Analysis of Recent Budgetary Situation. Working paper. Seoul: Korea Development Institute.

Lee, Il-young et al. 2003. Current Progress and Future Direction of Fiscal Policy in North Korea (in Korean). Seoul: Korea Institute of Public Finance (KIPF).

Manyin, Mark E. 2003. Japan-North Korean Relations: Selected Issues. Washington, D.C.: Congressional Research Service. 26 November. http://fpc.state.gov/documents/organization/27531.pdf.

Park, Chong-Kee. 1995. Fiscal System. In *Economic Systems in South and North Korea: The Agenda for Economic Integration*, ed. Cho Lee-jay and Kim Yoon-hyung, chap. 4. Seoul: Korea Development Institute.

Bradley O. Babson is a consultant on Asian affairs with a concentration on Korea and Northeast Asia economic cooperation. He is a retired World Bank offical who received his MPA degree from the Woodrow Wilson School of International and Public Affairs at Princeton University in 1974.

11

Coping with North Korea's Energy Future: KEDO and Beyond

Kent E. Calder

The subject of the energy future of North Korea (the Democratic People's Republic of Korea or DPRK) has many dimensions, conceptualized in a broad variety of ways. For engineers, the energy future can be a problem in boiler efficiency and reactor safety. For energy economists, the future is an issue of trade-offs among fuel sources such as coal, natural gas, and nuclear power.

For economists with structural perspectives, energy is a constraint on economic growth in North Korea. For specialists in regional integration, energy is a catalyst for bringing Northeast Asia together. And for many security analysts and policymakers, energy is a lever for simultaneously blocking dangerous nuclear proliferation and subverting unwanted geopolitical change.

The central economic and security elements of the North Korean energy equation are inseparable in policy terms. Nuclear proliferation in North Korea, a security problem of global importance, deserves its central place in the minds of policymakers. Yet for analytical purposes it is important to disentangle economic and security aspects of the energy problem without denying their legitimate policy interdependence. North Korean politics, after all, could change radically over the coming years, altering the security equation profoundly. Yet the DPRK's resource endowments, which must inevitably shape economic calculations, will remain constant.

Amid the myriad uncertainties of the North Korean energy equation, one strong likelihood is that the Korean Peninsula Energy Development Organization (KEDO), as presently constituted, has little future. Much of the U.S. Congress, not to mention the Bush administration, has been consistently skeptical of KEDO, and economic assistance to North Korea has never had much constituency in the United States in any case (Sigal 1998). The program has, to be sure, survived a remarkable number of crises, including the

North Korean submarine incursion into South Korean waters in the fall of 1996 and the North Korean Taepo-dong missile launch of August 1998 (Snyder 2000). Yet KEDO will find it much harder to survive the major, direct violation of the Agreed Framework involved in North Korea's covert highly enriched uranium (HEU) program, especially given the December 2002 suspension of the heavy fuel oil supply program, the extended suspension of reactor construction activities after November 2003, the lack of U.S. congressional budgetary authorization for future operations, and the continuing heavy skepticism in the Bush administration regarding a seemingly dysfunctional institution inherited from the past.

During KEDO's more than seven years of operation, from its establishment in March 1995 until the HEU program revelations in late 2002, that tri-national organization did, to be sure, quietly foster useful interpersonal networks between North Korea and the broader world while it scored important technical accomplishments in consolidating U.S.-Japan-Korea triangular relations. There are also substantial sunk costs that—rhetoric aside—it is rational to recoup. The United States has expended more than $700 million on heavy-fuel-oil supplies to North Korea and on the administrative costs of running KEDO. South Korea (also, Republic of Korea, or ROK) and Japan have together already invested well over $1 billion in construction of a now partly built light-water reactor (LWR) in Kumho, North Korea (KEDO 2001; KEDO 2002; Brooke 2004).

Future international efforts to cope with North Korea's energy problems can reasonably build, either figuratively or even literally, on these foundations. Yet the duplicity in the covert North Korean HEU program, coupled with the economic irrationality of much of the 1994 Agreed Framework that established KEDO, and domestic political controversies regarding the organization in virtually all of the participating nations make it likely that KEDO will need to be scrapped and reconfigured. Thus, a pressing need exists for a post-KEDO framework for North Korean energy, which is the analytical focus of this paper.

North Korea's Dire Current Energy Realities

Like South Korea, North Korea has historically had a high-energy-use economy (Noland 2000, 143; Calder 2000, 2–9). Primary commercial energy use in the DPRK was approximately three times the level of China in 1990 and about half the level of Japan, which had a gross domestic product (GDP) per capita 20 times as high as North Korea at that time (Noland 2000, 144). North Korean energy use has been relatively high for three reasons:

- Industrial structure, with a high concentration of energy-intensive sectors like steel and fertilizer production;
- Inefficient use of fuels owing to obsolete equipment as well as lack of market pricing; and

- Reliance on relatively less efficient fuels, such as coal, as a source of energy.

This high energy intensity of the economy, together with a critical lack of oil and the importance of oil to North Korea's military, make energy in general, and oil in particular, priority concerns for the DPRK's political-military leadership.

North Korea's domestic energy situation needs to be considered in terms of four basic dimensions, and the DPRK's circumstances are dire in all four. The energy problems that the DPRK confronts in all these areas are interrelated, yet the nature of the difficulties involved is somewhat different in each area.

Supply of basic energy.   In terms of basic energy supply—that is, the availability of coal, hydroelectric power, oil, natural gas, and nuclear power—North Korea's energy insecurities are broadly similar to those of South Korea, Taiwan, and Japan. North Korea has, for example, no operating oil fields, although mostly since mid-2002 Sweden's Taurus Petroleum and Singapore's Sovereign Ventures have conducted some modest positive seismic surveys. A Norwegian firm, Global Geo Services, reportedly contemplates initial off-shore seismic work in the first half of 2004 (DOE 2002b).

Most of North Korea's neighbors experience underlying energy-resource scarcity similar to the scarcities confronting the DPRK. Indeed, not a single major producing oil field exists in the vast, economically powerful swath of Northeast Asian territories stretching from Hokkaido and the rest of the Japanese archipelago, across the Korean peninsula, to the southern tip of Taiwan (Calder 1996, chap. 1). And there are no major natural gas fields either. With respect to oil and gas, the economies of Northeast Asia are all heavily dependent on the politically volatile Middle East. For North Korea, Iran is an important traditional energy supplier as well as a political-military ally, even though it is 7,000 miles distant from Pyongyang.

With virtually no indigenous oil or natural gas production, North Korea's only substantial domestic fossil-fuel source is coal. The DPRK has substantial reserves of anthracite and lignite coal, mostly produced from underground mines (Von Hippel et al. 2002, 12). This domestic coal is North Korea's main fuel for electricity generation, but coal mining itself usually requires electricity for lighting, jackhammers, and transporting coal out of the mines. In addition, many important coal seams are actually beneath the seabed, especially off the western coast near Anju, which requires sea water to be continuously pumped out for the mines to operate. Several of these mines were flooded in the mid-1990s. The coal that can be produced is uneven in quality, creating significant operational problems, especially for new coal-fired power plants.

In 2001 coal provided about 86 percent of North Korea's primary energy consumption, a share that has been rising as the country's isolation from the broader world has intensified since 1990 (DOE 2002a). Yet estimated coal output in the DPRK declined more than 50 percent between 1990 and 1996, and it has probably declined considerably more since then (DOE 2002a, 10). Coal shortages thus contribute substantially to North Korea's overall energy problem, even though the country has, ironically, relatively plentiful domestic coal supplies. In addition, most coal supplies for coal-fired power plants are transported by rail, as is 90 percent of North Korean freight cargo generally, so chronic problems with rolling stock and railroad safety further constrain electricity production. As a consequence, most coal-fired plants in the DPRK operate well below capacity owing to difficulties in securing suitable inputs.

Electric-power generation. Electric-power generation is a second serious domestic energy problem that North Korea confronts. In 2001, hydroelectric power plants generated about 69 percent of North Korea's electricity, and thermal plants 31 percent (DOE 2002a, 2). All except one thermal plant, which relies on the heavy fuel oil that the United States has been supplying to the North since 1995 under the KEDO agreement, is coal fired and thus subject to the difficulties described above. As much as 85 percent of the DPRK's hydroelectric capacity has also been damaged by flooding (Ivanov 2002, 13). Overall, as little as 20–30 percent of installed capacity for electric-power generation may actually be operable (Von Hippel et al. 2002, 13).

Electric-power transmission. Electric-power transmission is, as noted, a third major domestic energy-supply difficulty. North Korea's original power grid was created in Japanese colonial days, well over 60 years ago, and was decimated during the Korean War. Refurbished by the Soviet Union in the 1960s and 1970s, the grid has had inadequate servicing since the collapse of the USSR more than a decade ago. The lack of spare parts, scavenging of metal (as barter for food) from remote lines in the countryside, and general physical deterioration have severely degraded the system. Power outages are thus common throughout the country—even in Pyongyang—and energy loss through inefficient transmission is enormous.

The poor state of North Korea's power-transmission grid has major implications for the functional role of the Agreed Framework and KEDO in North Korea's relations with the world. The grid is in such a deplorable state of disrepair that the LWRs to be provided through the KEDO framework could not be connected to the grid without raising major safety problems. Without an extensive modification of the grid and a connection to another system, such as that of South Korea, Russia, or China, the promised nuclear reactors could not be used. In addition, as Von Hippel and Hayes (2003) point out, LWRs need a stable source of backup power for coolant pumps and other equipment and must be operated such that the sudden loss of load is kept to an absolute minimum (DOE 2002a, 12). Neither of these requirements could be met with the DPRK grid as it is currently configured.

Secondary energy use apart from electric power.   North Korea's energy problems are even more acute outside the electric-power sector than within it. Since 1990, when China and the former Soviet Union began demanding payment at commercial rates in hard currency for oil, crude oil imports into North Korea have dropped by roughly 85 percent (Harrison 2002–03, 31). China has also recently been using oil supplies as a strategic lever, reportedly suspending pipeline deliveries for three days in early 2003 to protest North Korea's HEU nuclear program.

Oil shortages have immobilized important petroleum-dependent industries, including fertilizer factories. These bottlenecks have in turn precipitated low agricultural production, intensifying the impact of the 1995–96 famines. Oil shortages also shut down tractor operations and many of the power generators in rural areas that were needed to run irrigation pumps.

The energy sector of the North Korean economy, in short, is in a highly precarious state. Underlying resources are scarce outside the coal sector, and production and distribution of coal itself are antiquated and inefficient. Moreover, the energy generation and distribution systems themselves are close to nonfunctional.

Implications for the North Korean Political Economy and Beyond

Energy is clearly North Korea's Achilles' heel. Neither its military nor its organized civilian economy can function effectively for any prolonged period without adequate energy supplies. Therein lie both the danger and the opportunity for the broader world as it addresses North Korea's energy problems. Ignoring the security dimensions of energy could make North Korea prospectively more dangerous as an adversary and enhance its ability to aid subversive, even terroristic, efforts by others. Yet, failing to see the positive contribution that, under the right security circumstances, energy cooperation with North Korea could make to Northeast Asian and, indeed, global economic growth—not to mention its positive impact on the miserable living circumstances of the North Korean people—would be equally short-sighted. It is thus crucial to stand back and assess the linkages between North Korean energy and broader national, regional, and global concerns.

Energy shortages have clearly inhibited DPRK economic performance in recent years. They have, for example, constrained rail and motor transport as well as industrial production. The lack of energy also contributed to the chronic food shortages of the mid-1990s and to the massive famines of 1995–98 through their impact on fertilizer production. More recently, energy shortages and the constraints that the lack of functional electric pumps places on rural water supply have also been linked, by UNESCO and others, to deterioration in public sanitation (Choi 2004, 3).

Beyond North Korea itself, the DPRK's energy situation has broader implications for nations throughout the North Pacific. For the United States, of course, the central concern is security related: the potential of North Korean nuclear programs for generating fissile materials that might be used as warheads and other explosive devices, either by the North Korean military or by terrorists. For Russia, China, and South Korea, an additional, and often more immediately expressed, concern is more cooperative: the prospect of addressing North Korea's energy problems through regional solutions such as natural gas pipelines and electric-power grids, potentially transiting North Korea and thus transforming South Korea from a geostrategic island, as it has been for over a half century, into an interactive part of the Asian continent.[1]

The resolution of North Korea's energy problems could potentially be linked to the broader resolution of the entire Northeast Asian region's fundamental energy need: to diversify its supply of energy away from oil and away from heavy dependence on the Middle East. Northeast Asia is, after all, the only major region of the industrialized world without a well-developed natural gas grid, and the region has a correspondingly low reliance on that highly attractive fuel source: natural gas.

As is suggested later in greater detail, there are strong complementarities between South Korea and China's rapidly rising energy demand, on the one hand, and the massive natural gas reserves and hydroelectric power potential of Siberia, on the other. This equation could be resolved through pipelines and power grids someday transiting North Korea once the nuclear crisis is resolved. Virtually all parties to the ongoing six-party talks[2] on North Korean nuclear issues—which, after all, represent the major participants in the prospectively integrated Northeast Asian energy economy of the future—also have economic interests in a cooperative resolution of the nuclear crisis. Such a resolution could rationally involve large, new infrastructural projects in the area of energy if security concerns are resolved, and any such resolution should certainly also involve technical assistance to cope with the extraordinary energy inefficiency now prevailing in the North.

KEDO as a Vehicle for Addressing Northeast Asian Energy Issues

It is increasingly clear that KEDO, in its present form, does not and cannot address North Korea's central energy problems, pressing as they are. KEDO emerged originally to defuse a security crisis, not to address an economic agenda. KEDO's deficiencies as a vehicle for resolving energy problems—together with its subtle value as a forum for midlevel technical communica-

---

1 On the geopolitical transformations implicit in a changing relationship of North Korea to Northeast Asia, see Calder (2001, 106–22) and Kim and Lee (2002).

2 Participants in the six-party talks are China, Japan, North Korea, Russia, South Korea, and the United States.

tion with North Korea—are clear from a brief review of that fragile, controversial organization's origins and original mandate.

KEDO emerged after a long history of confrontation and North Korean belligerency on the Korean peninsula. In the spring of 1993, North Korea test-fired a potentially nuclear-capable missile, the No-dong 1, into the Sea of Japan, and threatened to withdraw from the Nuclear Non-Proliferation Treaty. In May 1994, the DPRK defied the antiproliferation regime by removing spent fuel from its experimental reactor at Yongbyon, thus making verification of its nuclear stockpile impossible and precipitating a major crisis with the United States. After a confrontation that came, in the view of many participants and observers, perilously close to war, Jimmy Carter and Kim Il-sung achieved a breakthrough in informal discussions leading ultimately to the formal Agreed Framework of October 1994. Even the negotiators of the agreement admitted it to be imperfect, viewing it only as the best among many unsatisfying options. At its heart were calculated ambiguities that made this agreement controversial and difficult to operationalize from the start.

KEDO itself was created in March 1995 to implement the Agreed Framework between the United States and the DPRK, under which North Korea agreed to freeze and ultimately dismantle its existing nuclear program. In return KEDO was to provide the DPRK with alternative sources of energy in the form of two 1,000 MW light-water reactors by a target date of 2003, and 500,000 metric tons of heavy fuel oil annually until the reactors were operational, to replace the potential energy supply from the suspect nuclear projects on which North Korea was to suspend construction under the Agreed Framework. Upon completion of the reactors, North Korea was to begin repaying the cost of these new reactors over 17 years, after a 3-year grace period.

Effectively, the Agreed Framework, upon which KEDO was and is based, traded ambiguity about past North Korean nuclear activities for a cessation of future activities. It thus postponed the moment of reckoning about the North Korean nuclear program and gave the North for nearly a decade the advantage of a certain strategic ambiguity that the militant, yet vulnerable, economically depressed, and isolated, nation found valuable in balancing the growing relative power of the outside world (Noland 2000, 152). The moment of truth under the agreement was to come around 2003, when KEDO was obligated to deliver the reactors and the North Koreans would be obligated to submit to unrestricted International Atomic Energy Agency inspections to which they had previously been highly resistant.

Once formally established, KEDO experienced a long series of political frustrations,[3] rooted partially in the ambiguous character of the Agreed Framework and partially in the broader relationships between the United States and the DPRK. Snyder (2000, 21–2) has pointed out that early tactical mis-

---

3 For details, see Pollack (2003) and Noland (2000, 151–70).

takes by the Clinton administration—chiefly in consultations, or lack thereof, with Congress—may well have compounded KEDO's problems. Congress was never enthusiastic about either the Agreed Framework or KEDO, voting to provide only half the money needed to purchase the heavy fuel oil in 1996 and coming close to appropriating no funds at all in 1998.

On its side, the North clearly poisoned the atmosphere for cooperation with its Taepo-dong missile launch of August 1998 and by minor, yet politically damaging, steps such as demanding exorbitant salaries for the North Korean workers detailed to the Kumho reactor-building project. And the final blow to the Agreed Framework was North Korea's admission in October 2002 of its continuing covert HEU nuclear program, a step that led to the freezing of heavy-oil deliveries in December 2002 and the one-year freeze on the Kumho reactor project in November 2003.

The KEDO project, to be sure, has achieved a few modest successes. It has slowly and quietly built unprecedented interpersonal networks, mainly of technical specialists, between North and South Korea. It has likewise established previously unknown forms of direct communication, including an air link initiated on 15 October 2002 between Yangyang airport in South Korea and the reactor project site at Kumho in the North as well as a training program for North Korean workers. KEDO has stationed eight KEDO employees on-site in North Korea for the past several years and has installed flow meters, provided by the United States under the agreement, at seven North Korean power plants to monitor the flow of heavy fuel oil (KEDO 2002).

The KEDO framework also has the important geopolitical merit, from a U.S. perspective, of providing a framework for trilateral interaction among the United States, Japan, and South Korea on Northeast Asian issues. In contrast with the four-party framework inherited from Korean War armistice negotiations (the United States, the People's Republic of China, the ROK, and the DPRK) that it succeeded, KEDO's trilateralism has provided an unprecedented opportunity to consolidate the comprehensive security relationship among U.S. allies in Northeast Asia. It gave birth to the Trilateral Coordination and Oversight Group (TCOG) consultation talks among ranking U.S., Korean, and Japanese officials that since the North Korean missile test of 1998 have become a significant part of diplomacy in the North Pacific. This process, however, is now well institutionalized and is in no sense dependent on KEDO for future momentum.

Despite the modest technical successes and the opportunity for U.S.-ROK-Japan trilateral dialogue that it provided, KEDO has failed; its failure was perhaps unavoidable given its small staff, precarious mandate, and lack of enforcement and monitoring capacity. It failed, in particular, to prevent North Korean subversion of the Agreed Framework in 1998 as it conducted its missile test and, more seriously, as it proceeded with its covert HEU program. Since December 2002, heavy-fuel-oil deliveries to the North have been suspended and, since November 2003, construction on the Kumho reactor project itself has been in abeyance. Given KEDO's original imperfections, as a result in significant part of the crisis circumstances in which it originated, the irrelevance of its original time framework, and its loss of legitimacy because of persistent violations of its provisions, the KEDO framework should be seriously rethought and revised to make it relevant to the new circumstances of Northeast Asian energy now emerging.

New Options for the Future

As suggested above, there are serious problems with KEDO, and the Agreed Framework on which it is based, as a comprehensive blueprint for North Korea's energy future. With fuel-oil deliveries and reactor construction at Kumho now suspended and with six-party talks on the nuclear question in progress, the time is right to think analytically and dispassionately about what sort of mechanism should supplant KEDO—a mechanism that can capitalize on KEDO's achievements in network building and on sunk investments already made, while it addresses North Korea's acute energy problems more directly, fundamentally, and efficiently than KEDO has.

A basic problem in the original Agreed Framework was that the accord made no provisions regarding connection of the two 1,000 MW reactors to be built under the agreement with North Korea's electric-power grid. Indeed, differences in technical standards and recent degradation of the network would make it both technically difficult and quite dangerous to attach the Kumho reactor currently under construction, or its prospective counterpart, to the North Korean grid. The power to be produced through the KEDO venture could presumably be exported to South Korea or elsewhere in the world, but it would be very difficult to use within the DPRK itself.

The two large reactors contemplated under KEDO would not only be virtually impossible to connect to the North Korean power grid; at a projected cost of $5 billion, they would also be extraordinarily expensive compared with alternative energy projects.[4] Roughly $1.5 billion has been expended since 1996 on the construction of the first reactor. These sunk costs, and the possibility of exporting the power produced to South Korea or elsewhere in the region once a modernized regional grid is established, would plausibly justify to South Korea and Japan the completion of at least one reactor. Yet cancellation of the second reactor and substituting a more rational, cost-effective energy infrastructure should definitely be a central element of any post-KEDO arrangement.

The indispensable condition for any alternatives to KEDO—indeed, for any form of continued energy cooperation with North Korea at all—must be a verifiable nonproliferation agreement. Provided that such an agreement is

---

4 These reactors, at around $5 billion, would reportedly cost more than the prospective cost ($3 billion to $3.5 billion) of the proposed Seoul-to-Sakhalin natural gas pipeline (Harrison 2002–03, 33).

forthcoming, the nuclear dimension of the energy-support program should be scaled down or eliminated. In place of this, the overriding imperatives are threefold:

- To modernize the North Korean electric-power grid, with an emphasis on increased efficiency;
- To proceed, in a related fashion, with pipeline proposals that would allow both North and South Korean access to Russian gas, thus generating much needed electric power; and
- To pursue greater energy efficiency within the North Korean industrial and transport sectors through expanded technical assistance.

The feasibility of connecting a refurbished North Korean grid directly to the South Korean power system, which could inhibit destabilizing political-economic actions on the part of the North, might also be considered.

Northeast Asia at present is the one major region of the industrialized world that still lacks a regional natural gas grid, and the region has remarkably little reliance on natural gas despite that fuel's many attractive properties. Natural gas is one of the most energy efficient and environmentally attractive energy sources in the world, in the view of ever-growing numbers of energy experts worldwide. With one-quarter of the world's population, the region has little more than 5 percent of its natural gas usage (Calder 2000, 12; BP Amoco 2000, 26–27). Korea, like its Northeast Asian neighbors, uses relatively little gas despite that fuel's intrinsically attractive properties. Only 12 percent of South Korea's primary energy is derived from gas, compared with about 21 percent in Germany and 26 percent in the United States (BP Amoco 2003, 38). Indeed, South Korea's total gas use, as a share of overall energy consumption, remains significantly less than levels in Japan despite a vigorous recent support policy in Seoul for natural gas.[5] In North Korea, gas use is negligible.

Considerable potential exists for expansion in gas consumption on the Korean peninsula as a whole, particularly in the North. And Russia is the logical source of supply. Russia has nearly one-third of the proven natural gas reserves in the world, many of them located within commercial distance of the Korean peninsula. South Korea, to be sure, can easily access liquefied natural gas (LNG) from the Persian Gulf and is, in fact, the world's second-largest LNG importer following Japan. Yet Middle Eastern LNG is a much less attractive proposition for North Korea, for both geographical and infrastructural reasons.

The costs of large-scale pipeline development could be massive, however. There are three basic pipeline options between Russia and Korea. The simplest would run roughly 3,200 km from Sakhalin through the Russian Far

---

5 In 2002, natural gas provided 11.5 percent of South Korea's primary energy consumption compared with 13.7 percent in Japan (BP Amoco 2003).

East and North Korea, down the Korean east coast, toward Seoul. The Japanese—and, more recently, U.S. and Anglo-Dutch interests—have been discussing these reserves with the Russians since the mid-1960s (Burrows and Windrem 1994, 435). The Sakhalin route, a central piece of the Soviet Union's Vostok Plan of the early 1990s (Valencia and Dorian 1998, 5–7), has substantial attraction for the Russians because it could provide important gas infrastructure to urban centers of the Russian Far East such as Khabarovsk and Vladivostok en route. It also has a substantial informal constituency in South Korea as well, and it could prospectively involve Exxon-Mobil, the largest of the multinational U.S. energy firms, which is a major participant in the Sakhalin gas and oil fields that this pipeline option would access.

The second pipeline option—a longer and more complex route—would run from the massive Kovykta gas field, northwest of Lake Baikal, through Manchuria and either under the Yellow Sea or along the western coast of North Korea, toward Seoul. Two variants have been proposed: one via Mongolia and a second solely within Russian and Chinese territory. The Chinese have strongly preferred the latter route and have promoted it above other Russian pipeline alternatives, as it would provide fuel directly to Northeast Chinese urban centers before it would pass on to Korea. In November 2003, KOGAS, CNPC, and RUSIA Petroleum completed a detailed feasibility study regarding this route.

The third pipeline option between Russia and Korea, and the most attractive alternative to Sakhalin from a Korean perspective, is the Sakha Republic (Yakutia) option. Yakutia is a sprawling area more than 3,000 km north of Korea, covering one-fifth of the vast Russian Federation (3.1 million km^2) but hosting a population of only 1.3 million people. Much of Yakutia's desolate Arctic and sub-Arctic terrain remains unprospected.

Initial recoverable gas reserves in Sakha/Yakutia are estimated at more than 8 trillion m^3, at depths from 1 to 4 km. Together with the massive South Pars field of Iran/Qatar, the Sakha fields are thus the largest gas fields ever discovered on Earth. They could supply Korea, and potentially much of the rest of continental Asia as well, with natural gas for at least another half century, at an estimated present-value development cost of around $20 billion.

The Sakha/Yakutia route has the considerable merit, from a Korean perspective, of being prospectively a Korea-centric, rather than a Japan-centric, concept, in contrast with Sakhalin. The Japanese, to be sure, held 10 years of discussions during the Soviet era over Yakutsk gas, involving Bechtel and El Paso Natural Gas of the United States at one point. Yet disagreement over pipeline routes, liquefaction sites, and security (the Soviet invasion of Afghanistan) stalled the project. Since a dramatic January 1989 initiative by Chung Ju-yung, founder of the Hyundai Group, South Korea has been a central player with respect to Yakutsk.[6]

---

6 On the complex, frustrating history of Siberian and Sakhalin projects, see Paik (1995, 207–21).

Chung's bold notion, on which discussions have since proceeded, was to construct a 3,200 km gas pipeline across Russian territory near the Chinese border along the Amur and Ussuri Rivers, across North Korea, toward Seoul. Korean President Kim Young-sam and Russian President Boris Yeltsin jointly agreed to support a detailed feasibility study at their 1994 summit. Nevertheless, the project remains in abeyance. Uncertainties in energy demand and financing since the Asian financial crisis exploded in late 1997, including the collapse of the major *chaebol* Daewoo in November 1999, compounded the short-run difficulties of proceeding further. Despite its long-term attractiveness from a Korean point of view, the Yakutia option thus appears to have less short-term feasibility than the other two pipeline alternatives.

All of the three basic Russia-to-Korea gas pipeline options, it is important to note, at least consider the prospect of transiting North Korea. The ultimate locus of consumption, after all, is South Korea, and the source of supply is one of the three Siberian locations mentioned above—all located to the north of the Korean peninsula. In the absence of a verifiable nuclear nonproliferation agreement with the DPRK, it is obviously premature to move toward agreement on a trans–North Korea pipeline from any of the three major prospective sources of Russian gas, even though it would be cheaper than alternatives and more attractive to most Korean parties concerned.

The recent international feasibility study on the Kovykta field, recommending a 4,887 km, $12 billion pipeline under the Yellow Sea to South Korea—bypassing the North—was thus the correct decision.[7] Yet if North Korea is forthcoming on the nuclear issue—within the six-party talks framework or elsewhere—the issue of transit pipelines across North Korea from either Kovykta or Sakhalin or, ultimately, from Yakutia should be revisited. Indeed, all these options have prospectively strong political-economic merits that could make them the heart of a realistic "grand bargain" between North Korea and the nations of the North Pacific, provided that the nuclear issue is satisfactorily resolved. Such a grand bargain, with natural gas pipeline projects at its heart and also involving a related modernization of the North Korean electric-power grid and power generation systems, could be a highly constructive element of a broad, long-range Northeast Asian economic development plan. Indeed, a grand bargain could be a crucial political-economic catalyst for moving regional gas and electric-power-grid projects forward, given the immense scale, financial cost, and geopolitical coordination issues that are involved.

From the perspective of North Korean economic development as well as political preference, the Sakhalin route is definitely more attractive than Kovykta. The DPRK apparently fears that China, with its rapidly growing domestic demand for gas and geopolitical leverage, would not be willing for

---

7 For details, see *Gas Matters Today*, 3 February 2004.

very long to let Kovykta gas go to Korea. Kim Jong-il has repeatedly conveyed his preferences to Russian president Vladimir Putin for a Sakhalin pipeline (Harrison 2002–03, 30).

One possible alternative to a gas pipeline—or a long-run supplement, should Korea's explosive growth in energy demand continue—would be a long-distance electric-power transmission line approximately 235 miles long from Vladivostok into North Korea. Russian hydroelectric potential is massive and could help ameliorate Korea's prospective energy shortages. The electric-power transmission line option would also be substantially cheaper than the long-distance gas pipeline.

Connecting selected economic centers in North Korea to the South Korean electric-power grid has also been suggested. This seems most technically and politically feasible in the case of special economic zones (SEZs) isolated from the dilapidated North Korean power system as a whole, such as the Kaesong SEZ along the Demilitarized Zone. There a connection to the South Korean grid would provide a symmetrical combination of economic advantage and geopolitical benefits to the major parties involved, sufficient to make it a realistic short-term proposition.

The Northeast Asian pipeline options could be highly synergistic with North Korean energy development, addressing many of the problems discussed above. Such options could harness long-term regional energy imperatives to the solution of serious local North Korean infrastructural problems. Concretely, gas-fired power stations could be built along the pipeline route, with two 500 MW combined cycle stations that combine optimal energy efficiency and positive environmental traits and compensate for the electric power prospectively forgone in the cancellation of one of the 1,000 MW reactors contemplated under the KEDO agreement. Three such gas-fired stations were contemplated in the 2001 understanding between a consortium of three Dutch trading companies (one since acquired by Bechtel although it has indicated a desire to scuttle the deal) and North Korea, and the underlying conception would seem to have economic logic (Harrison 2002–03, 32).

Another possibility would be building a network of smaller 250 MW gas-fired power stations along the pipeline route, connected to a series of small local transmission grids. This could be an alternative to constructing a large-scale national transmission grid, which would likely be much more expensive. Korean energy specialist Paik Keun-wook has calculated that it would cost roughly $1.4 billion to construct such a network of eight regional gas-fired power stations linked to a trans–North Korea pipeline and connect them with a decentralized transmission grid such as that discussed above (Paik 1995, 33). At that cost, this proposal would be one-third as expensive as the estimated total cost of the two oversized reactors promised under the Agreed Framework, and much better adapted to North Korea's basic energy needs.

Although Japan does not appear likely to establish a national gas grid anytime soon because such a grid could cost as much as $25–$40 billion to build, calculations appear to be somewhat different in South Korea. Since 1999 South Korea has built a network of domestic pipelines that already surpasses Japan's and is pursuing much more varied and ambitious uses for national gas than is Japan. Seoul, for example, has been promoting demand for natural gas through tax incentives, aid for introduction of natural gas vehicles such as gas-powered buses, and expansion of the domestic natural gas grid. This growing gas network would appear to be establishing a solid economic basis for key Korean involvement in regionwide pipeline ventures in the foreseeable future—potentially including trans–North Korea pipelines.

The attractiveness for Korea of piped gas, as opposed to LNG or other fuel choices such as nuclear power, depends to an important degree on the interrelationship between global energy prices and the progress of major North-South political-economic détente on the Korean peninsula itself. If global energy prices are predictably high and the prospect of North-South détente with Korea is also strong, there would be a strong political-economic rationale in Korea for rising dependence on Russian piped gas and for the construction of the extensive Northeast Asian pipeline system that is often discussed. Conversely, if the political prospects are for North-South confrontation, the case for nuclear power may be strengthened.[8]

Apart from the economics of a natural gas–based alternative to KEDO's nuclear bias, there is also a geopolitical rationale—one especially relevant under the assumption of a nuclear nonproliferation agreement and intrusive inspections as a precondition for the energy initiatives toward North Korea that are outlined here. The trans–North Korean pipelines contemplated here—like the railroads and regional electric-power grids also frequently discussed—would transform North Korea (or a united Korea that could well succeed it) from an outsider in the regional political economy into a central player. North Korea's crucial transit role for a panoply of infrastructural projects, including pipelines and railways as well as transnational electric-power grids, would yield it ongoing revenue to offset the otherwise depressed state of its domestic economy. Yet this transit role would also provide—through the advantages it would bestow on neighboring nations—positive international economic leverage for a transformed North Korea as well. This leverage would compensate, at least in part, for the increased vulnerability that the DPRK or a successor state would experience through abandonment of its nuclear program. It would clearly provide a much healthier basis for political equilibrium in the region than would otherwise exist if the North continued to rely, as it has done for so long, purely on military might and brinkmanship to gain recognition from the broader world.

---

8   For the political-economic assumptions involved, see Calder (2000, 17).

In the absence of both a conclusive elimination of North Korean nuclear-weapons-related capabilities and a clear transformation of North Korea's regional role in more peaceful directions, more limited incremental options can also be considered. Clear political-military progress should obviously accompany such incremental steps, but they need not involve the comprehensive grand bargain that large-scale pipeline or electric-grid overtures would necessarily entail. Apart from the selective connection of North Korean SEZs to South Korean, Russian, or Chinese power grids, technical assistance in improving the efficiency and reliability of electric-power transmission in the North, including the training of North Korean engineers and other specialists, could be a constructive incremental step. Regardless of the details, it is clear that the legitimate policy interdependence of the economic and security aspects of North Korea's energy problems must not be forgotten.

Conclusion

North Korea has faced a severe energy crisis over the past decade along several dimensions: primary energy supply (apart from coal); electric-power generation and distribution; and fuel for transportation. Indeed, energy has been the Achilles' heel of the economy as a whole, with energy shortages also crippling industry and agriculture. These shortages have inhibited North Korean military adventurism, to be sure, but they have also crippled economic growth, in both the DPRK and surrounding areas.

KEDO helped defuse the dangerous military confrontation of 1994–95 and helped reinforce the important triangular relationship among the United States, Japan, and South Korea. It also helped forge delicate but often useful interpersonal ties, mainly technical, between North Korea and the outside world. Yet the organization could not forestall the covert North Korean HEU nuclear program, and it has been continually weakened by political cross fire. Given the inappropriate energy choices with which it started, the body needs to be fundamentally transformed, with due consideration for the sunk costs and the residual benefits involved.

A post-KEDO energy development body for North Korea should of course include all the nations involved at present as central members of that organization, with a central role for the United States. To elicit needed political support in the United States, any successor will also need to provide significant commercial opportunities for U.S. firms, and at least some jobs for U.S. workers. Yet a successor body to KEDO should also broaden to include Russia and China in more systematic ways. With a more substantial mandate centering on developmental issues such as transnational natural gas and electric-power grids that naturally involve neighboring nations as well as North Korea, such a post-KEDO body could reasonably expect to avoid the nuclear-power-specific resentments and sourcing difficulties that have rendered relationships between KEDO and its massive neighbors so complex. By including all the nations now involved in the six-party talks on the North Korean nuclear crisis, a "KEDO II" could also appropriately institutionalize that six-party forum to promote the long-term energy development of the Northeast Asian region as a whole.

A new Northeast Asian energy-development body, based on the emerging six-party-talks framework, should keep its energy-specific character, but broaden its mandate and focus particularly on the development of natural gas resources in the region. Because of sunk costs, one of the 1,000 MW nuclear reactors proposed under the Agreed Framework should be continued, but the other should be cancelled and succeeded by a systematic network of medium-scale gas-fired power plants connected to a trans-Korean pipeline grid. All such planning, of course, needs to be contingent on a resolution of the nuclear crisis consistent with the imperatives of global security.

References

BP Amoco. 2000. *Statistical Review of World Energy 2003*. London: British Petroleum Company.

BP Amoco. 2003. *Statistical Review of World Energy 2003*. London: British Petroleum Company.

Brooke, James. 2004. Two Energy Plans for North Korea. *New York Times*, 3 February, sec. W1.

Burrows, William E., and Robert Windrem. 1994. *Critical Mass*. New York: Simon and Schuster.

Calder, Kent E. 1996. *Pacific Defense*. New York: William Morrow and Company.

Calder, Kent E. 2000. Korea's Energy Insecurities. Policy Forum Series, report no. 13. Washington, D.C.: Johns Hopkins University, School for Advanced International Studies (SAIS). December.

Calder, Kent E. 2001. The New Face of Northeast Asia. *Foreign Affairs* (January–February).

Choi, Soung-ah. 2004. North Korea Desperately Needs Clean Water. *Korea Herald*, 18 March.

Department of Energy (DOE). 2002a. *Country Analysis Brief: North Korea*. Washington, D.C.: DOE.

Department of Energy (DOE). 2002b. *International Energy Outlook*. Washington, D.C.: GPO.

Harrison, Selig S. 2002–03. Gas and Geopolitics in Northeast Asia. *World Policy Journal* (Winter).

Ivanov, Vladimir I. 2002. North Korea, The Korean Peninsula Energy Development Organization, and Russia. Paper presented at the International Workshop on Energy Security and Sustainable Development in Northeast Asia, Seoul, 29–31 March.

Kim, Samuel S., and Lee Tai Hwan. 2002. *North Korea and Northeast Asia.* Lanham, Md.: Rowman and Littlefield.

Korean Peninsula Energy Development Organization (KEDO). 2001. Annual Report. New York: KEDO.

———. 2002. Annual Report. New York: KEDO.

Noland, Marcus. 2000. *Avoiding the Apocalypse: The Future of the Two Koreas.* Washington, D.C.: Institute for International Economics.

Paik, Keun-wook. 1995. *Gas and Oil in Northeast Asia: Politics, Projects, and Prospects.* London: Royal Institute of International Affairs.

Pollack, Jonathan D. 2003. The United States, North Korea, and the End of the Agreed Framework. *Naval War College Review.* Summer: 11–49.

Sigal, Leon V. 1998. *Disarming Strangers: Nuclear Diplomacy with North Korea.* Princeton: Princeton University Press.

Snyder, Scott. 2000. The Korean Peninsula Energy Development Organization: Implications for Northeast Asian Regional Security Cooperation, North Pacific Policy Papers Series, no. 3. Vancouver: University of British Columbia. www.iar.ubc.ca/pcaps/pubs/snyder.pdf.

Valencia, Mark A., and James Dorian. 1998. Multilateral Cooperation in Northeast Asia's Energy Sector: Possibilities and Problems. Working paper, East-West Center, Honolulu. www.ciaonet.org/wps/shsol/igcc36ac.html/.

Von Hippel, David F., and Peter Hayes. 1996. Engaging North Korea on Energy Efficiency. *Korean Journal of Defense Analysis* 8:177–221.

Von Hippel, David, Peter Hayes, Masami Nakata, Timothy Savage, and Chris Greachen. 2002. *Modernizing the U.S.-DPRK Agreed Framework: The Energy Imperative.* Berkeley: Nautilus Institute for Security and Sustainable Development.

Von Hippel, David, and Peter Hayes. 2003. Regional Energy Infrastructure Proposals and the DPRK Energy Sector: Opportunities and Constraints. Paper presented at the KEI/KIEP Policy Forum on Northeast Asian Energy Cooperation, Washington, D.C., 7 January.

Kent E. Calder is the Director of the Reischauer Center for East Asian Studies, SAIS/Johns Hopkins University.

12

Mobilizing Private Capital for North Korea: Requirements for Attracting Private Investment

Malcolm Binks and Carl Adams

The topic posed might seem to be a mission impossible: North Korea (the Democratic People's Republic of Korea) is a country that has been largely cut off from the global economy for more than 50 years, and even before that time it was hardly a center of foreign investment. However, the same held true for many countries until relatively recent times; China and Russia come to mind. In an environment where investors now feel free to roam pretty much anywhere, it is important to recognize that things can change very quickly and often in a surprisingly positive fashion.

Although a theoretical approach to how North Korea would go about attracting foreign investment would be feasible, a more practical approach would be preferable. It entails facing up to the realities of the situation in the country, in the region, and in the global context. This paper takes the practical approach because the hoped-for result will be achieved only if several basic issues are confronted. This approach is mandated by the nature of what confronts North Korea and the risks that any foreign investor of private capital will have to undertake.

This paper therefore seeks to address what will be required to attract foreign investment and how North Korea might go about making itself a desirable location for such investment. The focus here is on private investment; others at this conference will address the potential for investment from public sources such as the World Bank. It may also be important to look at this in a Northeast Asian context because of North Korea's location and its potential ability to attract capital in preference to other locations in the region.

The Nature of the Problem

All private-sector investors in developing countries are familiar with the risks they undertake. Apart from all the normal investment risks, there is always the question of the underlying creditworthiness of the country in question, which can be affected by the availability of resources, geographic location, stability and cohesiveness of the workforce, a harsh climate, and, above all, the issue of political stability in the global context. All developing countries go through a process of maturation and many, especially Asian, countries make it to the other side, become politically stable, and evolve into developed economies.

South Korea is a case in point although, ironically, its A3 (negative outlook) rating suffers because of the perceived North Korean risk, either because of the military threat or because a total collapse of the North Korean regime would result in a huge liability for South Korea to repair the collapsed economy. China is rated A2 and is closer to winning recognition as a developed investment-target country. Vietnam has some distance to go, but with a B1 (positive outlook) rating the country is on an improving track. Myanmar is far off; but, of all the economies in Asia, North Korea is the farthest away. If it were to be rated, it would most likely be in the C category, reserved for countries such as Cuba. North Korea's foreign debt, estimated to be in excess of $12.5 billion and contracted in the 1970s, has long been in default. North Korea presents an immense challenge and will make substantive progress only if it can persuade the global community and, in particular, its immediate neighbors that it is prepared to make the necessary changes to create an attractive investment climate.

Private Foreign Investment Alternatives

Traditional channels of private capital mobilization offer suggestions for investment funding alternatives in North Korea. The primary sources of private investment for an emerging nation include:

- Project financing, in which the investor looks directly at the viability of the project (for example, a power station);
- Corporate direct investment in a defined activity such as a manufacturing operation, often a joint venture with a local entity;
- Portfolio investment in a listed company, undoubtedly less likely in North Korea for the foreseeable future;
- Venture capital, generally in an unlisted company; and
- Trade-related and finance arrangements secured by assets with an established value or by secured cash flows from ongoing, proven operations and activities.

The bulk of foreign investment in emerging economies almost always comes from public sources or with public-sector guarantees and from project financing and corporate investment. North Korea will need to focus for the time being on these primary, secured-financing sources until such time as the economy establishes itself as fundamentally viable.

Political Context

For all private-sector investment interests, there is no way of avoiding the North Korean political reality as a critical and basic issue. Private-sector investors have multiple alternatives as to where they may put their money. They will invest only if it makes sense to them in the context of gaining a market, gaining an attractive source of production, and, above all, getting a measurable and maximum return on their investment. Security of the investment is therefore fundamental. Although no investment location offers absolute certainty, especially in developing markets, the perception of risk and a clear understanding of political risk and its proper pricing are overriding criteria.

The question of receptivity is related to this: Does North Korea really want foreign investment? Is North Korea prepared to make the necessary adjustments to its economy to gain those investments? Are the political costs—both domestic as well as external—of more open investment in North Korea acceptable to the ruling regime and to the self-interest of its elites? The importance of this cannot be overstated or underrated.

In the Asian context, China's ability to attract direct investment and portfolio investment may have been one of the most surprising turns of events of the past 25 years. China is a country that has not undergone any fundamental change in its underlying political philosophy, but in the space of a generation it has become the largest single destination for capital in the developing world. Maybe Deng Xiaoping never sat down and thought "we must become user friendly" to foreign investors, but Deng made China a destination of choice by his direct and indirect support for greater political security, and his successors have continued his policy. The Organization for Economic Cooperation and Development (OECD) reports that foreign direct investment (FDI) in China grew from almost nothing in 1978 to $360 billion by 2000.

Notwithstanding the Tiananmen Square event, the Asian financial crisis of 1997, on-and-off problems with Taiwan, and some significant differences with the United States, foreign investment into China has continued unabated. China's adoption of and entry into the World Trade Organization (WTO) arrangements will further boost FDI inflows, as ample evidence during 2003 confirms. It would be simplistic to attribute such FDI expansion to foreigners' interest in a billion-plus population market overcoming concerns about Chinese politics. It can be argued that India should always have been a more attractive venue, but it is only in recent years that India has started to match China's ability to attract foreign investment and achieve the kind of growth rate that has become the norm in China. Political security and the country's own openness and receptivity to inward investment by the private sector are the key distinctions.

North Korea is a much smaller nation, it has much less going for it in terms of opportunity, it is high on President Bush's black list, and it is widely viewed in the media as reclusive and reactionary. To make meaningful progress, North Korea will need to find some way of diffusing the "big" political issue of nuclear materials deployment and making a conscious effort at becoming a reasonable and opportunistic destination of choice for private foreign capital. At the most basic level, the North Korean leadership will need to demonstrate that it is willing to renounce confrontational politics with the United States and with its neighbors. North Korean leaders need to demonstrate they can launch and sustain a coherent plan of reform suitable for private-sector perceptions of risk and their own country's prospects.

China to some extent progressed by stealth to a market-driven economy. However, the severity of North Korea's problems really requires a full commitment at the outset, simply because so much needs to be done. It has become unremarkable for even the most backward of emerging nations to have a stock market, to allow participation in that market by domestic and foreign investors, and to attempt to make the market open and transparent. North Korea is so far from the starting line of a market economy that it should not waste a moment of time even thinking about the possibility of a stock market.

Why North Korea Presents Special Problems for Private Capital

It is tempting to think that North Korea could follow the route of China or Vietnam toward reform and become an economy that could attract substantial foreign private capital. Both these countries offer experiences in development that suggest some potentially useful guidelines, and Vietnam may be a better model because China is a unique case. At the point when China started to open its doors to foreign investment, it had a number of advantages:

- **A well established, if grossly inefficient, industrial base.** Notwithstanding many mistaken industrial policies, China had a steel industry, a substantial electric power industry, a somewhat broken telephone system, and all the components of an industrial economy. Although the private sector possesses little intelligence about North Korea that is known to be valid and reliable, it has concluded that North Korea has only a very minimal industrial base.

- **An established banking system.** Throughout China, several very large banks as well as a widespread branch-banking system were in operation. The Bank of China, which had international experience and a well-established system for dealing with remittances both into and out of China, had always maintained a presence in major financial centers. North Korea has none of that capability and no evidence of available technical and human resources capacity that shows an adaptability to such banking-system structures.

- **A very large group of overseas Chinese that had maintained family contacts in China.** Many members of the Chinese diaspora were running successful businesses in their new locations but, importantly, were ready, eager, and willing to re-enroll in the Chinese economy. They saw China, as it opened to FDI, as a land of opportunity. North Korea's long isolation from the global economy, with no significant numbers of overseas Koreans returning, has left it with few connections for potential private capital mobilization.

- **Willingness to experiment with open market policies while adhering to political philosophy and party organization.** Although many of China's initiatives to attract foreign capital were touted at the outset as experiments (for example, the special economic zones), the Chinese government did pursue a long and successful strategy of opening up the economy, which culminated in its membership in the WTO. Many of its financial and regulatory systems were (and still are) imperfect, but the determination to move through reforms has been unmistakable. This could still happen in North Korea, but evidence and indications thus far suggest that those with vested interests in the current system in North Korea will be much less open to experiments in which their own good fortune and advantaged status are challenged.

Vietnam is somewhat different than China. It started later but to some degree presents a more useful model for North Korea. Vietnam had been somewhat isolated from the global financial world, but it is more comparable in size with North Korea. A potential tourist destination with a well-educated population, a large group of interested overseas Vietnamese, and remnants of a functioning economy, Vietnam offered a base to get started. Above all, Vietnam committed to learn from the outside, welcomed assistance from the World Bank, and initiated a crash course to educate key personnel in international finance. Similar prospects in North Korea seem extremely dim at this time.

Proposed Strategy to Mobilize Private Capital for North Korea

North Korea needs to instill confidence in its political intentions before outsiders perceive the North as a destination for capital investment.

Foundation of Basics for Real and Political Capital

The first and absolute requirement for a good investment climate for North Korea is that the political situation that hangs over the country must be defused. Others are better qualified to suggest how that might be done, but the result must be persuasive and convincing to independent, private-sector investors. Also, efforts to find a resolution on the defaulted debt must begin, and an economy that is not viewed as being in crisis needs to be created. This will require North Korea's willingness to work with international financial institutions (IFIs) such as the International Monetary Fund (IMF) and the World Bank.

Defusing North Korea's political situation will require a proactive program to attract foreign aid, not only foreign aid as money but also in oversight, training, and technical assistance as to how and where the money gets spent. Merely announcing that North Korean doors are open to foreign investment will not do very much so far as the private investment sector is concerned. This is a case in which actions will speak for themselves and words will do very little. Northeast Asian regional powers must be persuaded that there has been a real change in attitude before they will willingly participate in a program of recovery; and they must believe that their participation will be welcomed—or at least not be held hostage and manipulated—by North Korean government officials, prominent persons, and political elites. Central to this basic foundation of governance and political ambition are the essential requirements of commitment to openness, transparent disclosure, and avoidance of graft, corruption, and connivance among commercial and political players.

Creation of Capital Infrastructure
for Observable Best-Practices Behavior

North Korea will need to bend over backward to welcome foreign investment and avoid needlessly irritating potential private-sector investors and partners. Projects will need to be approved on a timely basis, and commitments to make payments when due will need to be fully honored. Investors will need to be persuaded that the climate for business and foreign investment is open and transparent. Public declarations of support and interest in best practices for capital mobilization will be needed often and in earnest. It may take years to complete the process, but the North Korean government will need to get started on establishing institutions that can manage a market economy and be seen to be doing it in a manner that, over time, will create private-sector confidence.

A minimum guideline for such infrastructure requirements is the list of 12 key codes and standards for sound financial systems provided by leading global public authorities for the Financial Stability Forum (FSF) of the Bank for International Settlements. There is no better checklist of infrastructure requirements for private-sector capital mobilization. The 12 key standards, shown in *Table 1*, are grouped in the three broad areas of macroeconomic policy and data transparency, institutional and market infrastructure, and financial regulation and supervision.

Table 1: Key Codes and Standards for a Sound Financial System

Area	Key standards	Issuing body
Macroeconomic policy and data transparency		
1. Monetary and financial policy transparency	Code of good practices on transparency in monetary and financial policies	IMF
2. Fiscal policy transparency	Code of good practices in fiscal transparency	IMF
3. Data dissemination	Special data dissemination standard (SDDS)/general data dissemination system (GDDS)[1]	IMF
Institutional and market infrastructure		
4. Insolvency	Note 2 below.	World Bank
5. Corporate governance	Principles of corporate governance	OECD
6. Accounting	International accounting standards (IAS)[3]	IASB[4]
7. Auditing	International standards on auditing (ISA)	IFAC[4]
8. Payment and settlement	Core principles for systematically important payment systems/recommendations for securities settlement systems	Committee on Payment and Settlement Systems (CPSS)/IOSCO
9. Market integrity	The 40 FATF recommendations of the FATF/8 special recommendations against terrorist financing	Financial Action Task Force (FATF)
Financial regulation and supervision		
10. Banking supervision	Core principles for effective banking supervision	Basel Committee on Banking Supervision (BCBS)
11. Securities regulation	Objectives and principles of securities regulation	IOSCO
12. Insurance supervision	Insurance core principles	IAIS

Source: FSF 2004.
1 Economies with access to international capital markets are encouraged to subscribe to the more stringent SDDS and all other economies are encouraged to adopt the GDDS.
2 The World Bank is coordinating a broad-based effort to develop a set of principles and guidelines on insolvency regimes. The United Nations Commission on International Trade Law (UNCITRAL), which adopted the Model Law on Cross-Border Insolvency in 1997, will help facilitate implementation.
3 Relevant IAS are currently being reviewed by the International Association of Insurance Supervisors (IAIS) and the International Organization of Securities Commissions (IOSCO).
4 The International Accounting Standards Board (IASB) and the International Federation of Accountants (IFAC) are distinct from other standard-setting bodies in that they are private sector bodies.

Although not often itemized by the private sector when it assesses investment opportunities and prices the risk and return necessary to endorse capital commitments, each of these key areas is an essential (but not sufficient) factor to assure funds commitment and investment success. Capital movement infrastructure may take many local and cultural forms, but, in essence, compliance with each of these 12 areas facilitates funds inflow and provides the private sector with sufficient information to improve risk predictability.

Some of the areas on Table 1, such as insurance supervision and securities regulation, may seem far-fetched for consideration by North Korea at this stage of its development. Some areas, such as data dissemination, corporate governance, or, to be sure, market integrity—and the entire spectrum of best practices to avoid money laundering—seem to be especially outrageous recommendations for a regime known to use illegal funding practices and to be fully suspect regarding corruption at many levels. However, the rule of best practices, even among thieves, is a compelling truth for capital mobility; and, at this early stage of interest in mobilizing capital from the private sector for North Korea, full accommodation of these codes and standards deserves due diligence and enactment of compliance oversight mechanisms.

Many of these infrastructure issues will be fully addressed during consideration of North Korea's membership in the various United Nations organizations and IFIs, should the regime in control choose to join. All will be defining measures for private capital, and they will determine the form and time they are implemented by whatever local custom prevails. Human society is quite capable of providing accommodation to all of these 12 codes and standards in unique and untried ways, but the spirit of compliance along with transparency, disclosure, and language that may be commonly understood and trusted are surely basic ingredients for eventual mobilization of capital into North Korea.

The building blocks for private capital infrastructure mobilization rest on the first group shown on Table 1—macroeconomic policy and data transparency. Because precise foreknowledge of future North Korean monetary and fiscal policies is lacking, one fact will make a difference for private capital inflow: are these monetary and fiscal arrangements transparent? In other words, do responsibilities and accountabilities have proper and identifiable disclosure, and do the key players in the economy have reasonable prospects for fair valuation and pricing information? North Korea's recent casino-type so-called bond issues show that North Korea needs to go a good distance before fiscal and monetary policies are adequately open, even for the local population—not to mention foreign private sources of capital. Likewise, the assessments of data dissemination will need to achieve a minimum level of international competence, with verifiable accuracy to validly and reliably assess that the data measure what is actually happening.

The second group of financial-market standards and codes for best practices is next in importance to the private sector for adequate, investment-enabling infrastructure. Institutional and market infrastructure need not have Western capitalist detail, but they must hold hallmarks of fairness, balanced rules of conduct, and some checks and balance on competing influences so that no one party in the North Korean system holds unlimited power to determine all investment and valuation results. The fact that many tyrannies in the history of human society also addressed these institutional and market requirements suggests that private capital mobilization into North Korea has some possibility. If the rules and language of the commercial and investment order are consistent and openly understood, there is no reason that private capital would not pursue reasonable returns for the identifiable risks of the markets and institutions in the economy. Again, the keys are open disclosure, consistency of the rules, transparency among all actors, and relevant issues for price discrimination and market clearance.

The details of the third group of standards for codes of best financial-market practices are the technical rules of financial-market functional activities—banking, securities dealing, and insurance. These more technical rules for money and capital arrangements are in essence the local scheme for risk allocation and risk price discovery among functional roles in the commercial order. Gathering deposits for intermediation and redistribution in loans, bonds, and common equity may occur in many workable variations. It is hoped that even the unique and isolated society in North Korea will further develop its own order for banking and mobilization of capital—in such a way that private external investors, too, might participate. Insurance functions are also likely to find a useful role in the longer-dated liabilities for North Korean society and in the employment of longer-dated local assets. All 12 areas of financial-market best practices serve to define the infrastructure necessary for successful private capital mobility—from both external and domestic sources. They are the markers, too, for proper pricing of risk in North Korean investment activity by the private sector and should not be neglected or misunderstood if they take on unique, local characteristics.

eStandards Forum. The eStandards Forum Web site is a useful and informative body of information that describes independent assessments of country compliance with the FSF's codes and standards for sound financial infrastructure. This information portal provides an organized public record of assessments by public- and private-sector authorities as to country compliance with the 12 standards. The Web site covers 83 countries, both developed and developing, and is monitored and updated weekly to capture ongoing initiatives by countries to progress toward fullest compliance with the global best-practices codes. North Korea is not covered by the eStandards Forum initiative, but clues to eventual private-sector interest in investment in North Korea are offered by examination of other similar or regional nation-states (see *Table 2*).

The eStandards Forum effort also provides a numerical index of country compliance with the standards and codes so that the best-conforming country, the United States, ranks number one among all 83 countries; yet the numeric score of the United States out of a possible 100 is only 77.69. Readers should note for contrast that South Korea, recently intent on upgrading

Table 2:   Assessment of Country Compliance with Key Codes and Standards for Sound Financial Systems

Area	Key standards	Full compliance	Compliance in progress	Enacted	Declaration of intent	No compliance	No assessment available
Macroeconomic policy and data transparency							
1. Monetary and financial policy transparency	Code of good practices on transparency in monetary and financial policies	United States	—	Japan, South Korea	China, Russia	—	Vietnam
2. Fiscal policy	Code of good practices in fiscal transparency	United States	Japan	South Korea	Russia	China	Vietnam
3. Data dissemination	Special data dissemination standard (SDDS)/general data dissemination system (GDDS)	—	United States, Japan, South Korea	—	Russia	China, Vietnam	—
Institutional and market infrastructure							
4. Insolvency	Principles and guidelines for effective insolvency regimes and creditor rights systems	—	United States	Japan	South Korea, Russia	—	China, Vietnam
5. Corporate governance	Principles of corporate governance	United States	—	Japan, South Korea, Russia	—	China	Vietnam
6. Accounting	International accounting standards	—	—	China	Vietnam	Japan	United States, China
7. Auditing	International standards on auditing (ISA)	—	South Korea	Russia	Vietnam	Japan	United States, China
8. Payment and settlement	Core principles for systematically important payment systems/ recommendations for securities settlement systems	United States	South Korea	—	—	Russia	Japan, China, Vietnam

Area	Key standards	Full compliance	Compliance in progress	Enacted	Declaration of intent	No compliance	No assessment available
9. Market integrity	The 40 FATF recommendations of the FATF/8 special recommendations against terrorist financing	—	United States, Japan	China, South Korea, Russia	—	Vietnam	—
Financial regulation and supervision							
10. Banking supervision	Core principles for effective banking supervision	United States	—	South Korea, Russia	Japan	—	China, Vietnam
11. Securities regulation	Objectives and principles of securities regulation	United States	South Korea	—	Russia	—	Japan, China, Vietnam
12. Insurance supervision	Insurance core principles	—	United States, South Korea	Russia	—	—	Japan, China, Vietnam

Source: eStandards Forum 2004.

openness, transparency, and financial oversight following the 1997 crisis, currently ranks number eight out of 83 countries; the numeric index for its compliance as indicated by the assessments shown in Table 2 is 63.08 out of a possible 100. Japan, despite the reality of being the second wealthiest economy in the world, ranks only 33rd out of 83; the numerical index for Japan is 41.54 from a potential total score of 100. Russia, ranked 36 and just slightly less compliant with FSF standards and codes than Japan, is by numeric index recorded at 40.00. China is assessed by authoritative observers such as the IMF, the World Bank, the rating agencies, and private-sector authorities to be ranked as 68th among the 83 countries reported by eStandards Forum. China's numerical score is 13.85. Finally, for reference to contrast with North Korea, Vietnam scores only 6.92 and ranks a lowly 76th out of 83 among the nations reported.[1]

Sovereign ratings. Sovereign ratings by the international rating agencies offer another useful insight for investment contrast among countries. Bond ratings for several states in Africa, emerging areas in Central Asia, the Middle East, remote sections of South and Central America, and other developing countries in Asia provide private investors with a type of infrastructure "gap analysis" that points out weaknesses and risk. Bond ratings also serve to highlight advantages or unrecognized benefits possibly available in places like North Korea—at least by contrast with more established or traditional location targets. To be sure, no ratings of North Korean creditworthiness are currently known or planned by any of the major agencies. But often the examination of developing countries that are rated may be informative.

Recent rating agency assessments of some sub-Saharan African countries, for example, resulted in sovereign credit ratings at or better than similar ratings for established emerging-market investments. Ghana was rated B+ (stable) by Standard & Poor's, and Mozambique was rated B (stable) by Fitch Ratings—remarkably strong assessments relative to similar ratings for Indonesia, Brazil, or Turkey, where private-sector investors are well traveled and have been exposed for many years. North Korea may not soon earn assessments as high as B by the international agencies, but the international agencies' well-detailed output on similar high-risk, low-rated countries offers private investors informed perspectives on resources and government behavior.

Development and Maintenance of Key Institutions for Private Capital Investment

The following are summary suggestions of key institutions that will most likely be needed to help make the mobilization of private capital in North Korea happen.

---

1 For a fuller discussion of these assessments, see the eStandards Forum Web site (www.estandards forum.com/servlet/home) or contact Matt Zimmer (212/692-0828; matt.zimmer@eStandards Forum.com).

Economic czar.   A person of prominence and influence will have to lead the pursuit of business and financial-market best practices. North Korea already demonstrates the characteristic of single personality leadership; for economic development in such a highly political country, economic leadership will be no exception. Although there might be potential for a stealthy evolution to a market system, such a prospect from the perspective of private-market players is very remote indeed at this time. Further, as long as the North Korean economy remains in a state of crisis, decisive leadership and action are imperative for getting things on a positive track. Other countries have adopted various mechanisms to achieve visible progress. In North Korea's case, a minister who has the full and unquestioned support of the President and the national elites could be appointed to execute economic policy. Such a czar could be a minister of finance or a minister of economic reconstruction and development, but this person must have the power to get things done.

Ministry of Finance.   Such a ministry would be the organ of the government to institutionalize the political empowerment necessary for economic policy implementation. The Ministry of Finance would be a key ministry and would need to have the ability to find the best available minds in North Korea, or elsewhere, to start to build economic policy. The ministry would need to have broad authority to hire experts as needed from outside North Korea and to mobilize public resources as needed to enable and encourage private capital mobility. This kind of capability can be found in multinational institutions, such as the World Bank and Asian Development Bank, as well as in private institutions in neighboring countries. Multinational institutions should be encouraged to establish their presence in Pyongyang as a priority.

Ministry for Economic Reconstruction and Development.   Such a ministry would be a formal state organ for the creation, promotion, development, and monitoring of development projects; this ministry is an essential institution for best mobilization of private capital. Especially when there is evidence of collusion, collaboration, fraud, and graft in a central authority system, like North Korea's, some institutional effort is needed to guide the local population as well as outsiders to progressive and improved rules of engagement for reconstruction of existing economic infrastructures as well as development of new and greenfield investment projects. This can be especially helpful with the reeducation of the economic players toward less conflicted, self-serving grasps for corrupt rewards and more open, transparent, legal, and fair activities. Such an institution for reconstruction and development will also play better to the external community for private capital investment and also offer an efficient channel into North Korea for training and technical assistance.

Central bank and functioning commercial banking system.   Any system that seeks to appeal to private capital investment must have an orderly arrangement for payments, settlements, deposits collection, and remobilization through lending or capital markets for useful applications of the funds. The role for the state is to authorize a central monetary authority that the private sector may believe will act in the interests of all market players and will evidence the enlightened self-interest of a sovereign seeking to increase the welfare and progress of the population. Thus, the character and efficient implementation of a central monetary authority is a key ingredient for successful private capital enrollment.

Likewise, a banking network and a branch-banking system connecting the central monetary authority to the real-world microeconomic commercial services in the country are critical for private capital mobility and its success. As a practical matter, we know of no country's economic development—with or without private capital inflow support—that has succeeded without a proper and dynamically expanding banking system. Capital intermediation is in fact intermediation of systemic risk among users and providers of resources. Whether it is a centrally planned system as in North Korea today and in the former Soviet Union in the past, or it is an open and liberal democratic capitalist market order that has been the trend since 1989, a functioning banking order and system of collection and distribution of financial risk are essential institutional requirements. Private capital in particular will not respond efficiently in any country without the support and benefit of a well-defined (or at least promising) banking system.

Other Steps for Attracting Private Investment to North Korea

In conjunction with these big-picture steps, North Korea's leadership and government will need to initiate a number of direct and focused programs to cultivate and stimulate foreign investment. A comprehensive investor relations plan and public relations plan will need to be designed to educate and overcome what is likely to be substantial investor resistance. Because of this resistance, North Korea will need to make private capital opportunities in the country as attractive as possible and take extra steps to overcome what will be a very dubious investor audience. Some of the more important initiatives are listed below.

Investor education and a professional country presentation.   A very complete presentation of North Korea as an investment target must be prepared in conjunction with an outside expert experienced in producing rating-agency presentations for sovereign nations. It would not be appropriate to seek any kind of credit or political risk rating of North Korea until it is apparent that the measures referred to above are taking effect. Such a presentation should be a live and dynamic document that, once prepared, can be updated as the situation requires. The work on preparing the North Korean country presentation will need to be done with the authority and support of very senior ministers, such as the minister of finance, and will carry proper regard by the private sector if it is fully backed by the head of state. It will become apparent during the preparation of a country investor-relations report that there are many serious problems in the North Korean story. Thus it will be necessary to have an authoritative spokesperson in the government to establish remedial steps to correct those problems or at least offer an official response and explanation of the issues.

Identification of key industries and projects to revitalize the economy. The country's leaders and strategic planners with development oversight responsibilities must promote a master plan for North Korea. Such plans featuring serious designation of key industries and projects prioritized to rebuild and revitalize the economy are essential as signals to private investors. The plan will need to be developed to identify infrastructure projects and potential industries that will be critical to the economy's revival with respect to political process and actual capacity possibilities. Some of these will need the support from multinational institutions. Others, such as natural-resources projects, may attract private industry. But no project can be known and sanctioned by investors unless it is articulated in an official strategic plan for the future of North Korea's economy.

Data and information on the economy.   Data and information need to be provided regularly by respectable sources and in conformity with international standards and terminology. North Korea will need to start publishing accurate and timely data regarding key elements of its economy. The private sector is quite unforgiving of special circumstances and irregular reporting of standard data on economic growth, fiscal and monetary reference information, and timely, unadulterated metrics of what is happening in a country. Creative reporting and propaganda will not be tolerated for long in the twenty-first century. Globalization confirms that technology and information developments assure all leaders that few material facts can be kept secret for long; thus truth and transparency are best for technocrats and tyrants alike. The good news for North Korea is that the globalization of capital and economic resources continues to lower the costs of data assembly, packaging, and speedy distribution. The unfortunate counterpoint to this good news is that, without adequate data and information about a country, its resources, and its commercial practices, there is no participation in the world order for money and business. Recent examples of Cuba, Syria, Albania, and extremely poor countries in Africa underscore for the North Korean situation that without data and information—available and transparent—there is no ticket to the market for economic growth and sustainable development.

Willingness to allow foreign control of North Korean businesses.   Such control should be encouraged and not resisted. As a country with virtually no internal sources of capital, North Korea has few options and should welcome foreign ownership. This will bring expertise and discipline as the country seeks to move forward. Recent economic and political success in India is now evident and is caused by its recent willingness to liberalize and open up for foreign ownership and direct participation in the economy. Such measurable observations fully underscore this suggestion.

Creation of special mechanisms for foreign currency transfer and settlement of disputes.   In the early stages it is unlikely that there will be institutions in place to deal with these kinds of problems, and some interim mechanisms will need to be put in place. As demonstrated in China and perhaps less elegantly in Russia since the currency disaster in 1998, there are progressive regimes for currency trading, transfer, and settlement that can actually boost the North Korean economic expansion goals in a technology-safe arrangement. Both public-sector IFIs and private-market initiatives are available to help regimes such as North Korea's implement favorable currency systems and mitigate commercial code and business dispute issues.

Tax holidays.   Tax holidays or exemptions for foreign entities establishing businesses and entering into joint ventures are a good idea. This may indeed be a useful management tool for bringing local vested interests into alignment with broader, more robust economic expansions, as has been demonstrated in several former Soviet states and in parts of Central Asia today.

Conclusion and Focus

Given the magnitude of the task, North Korean policymakers will need to be focused on the most important topics for economic revival and sustained expansion. The outreach to market initiatives, although only a low-key one, and the recent military-first programs of the current regime are not necessarily hostile to long-term economic expansion objectives. Initially, programs to promote economic growth should be coordinated with the IFIs and other multinational agencies that can bring expertise and know-how. Developing a road map for mobilizing private-sector capital will require substantial input from these institutions. The 12 areas of codes and standards for financial-market soundness offer unquestionable markers for the infrastructure that are essential for the entry of private investors. In seeking foreign investment, the most likely opportunities will be in project financing and contractual, secured deals with foreign corporations and financial institutions or with official sector (external) guarantees. These techniques can be used even in an economy lacking the capability to support debt payments and more traditional market arrangements for collecting resources and redistributing financial allocations.

Reconciliation with its key neighbors will bring North Korea resources to finance such projects and activities as well as valuable expertise in the form of technical assistance and training. South Korea, Japan, and, to an increasing extent, China should be helpful in supplying suitable expertise, personnel, and financial resources to mobilize the private capital inflows.

But, above all else, political will and attention to the resolution of current political tensions inside the state and among its global counterparts will be imperative for attracting reasonable interest from any part of the private-investor universe. All these efforts—an effective communications program and display of interest by the North Korean state combined with strong investor relations, persistent education initiatives, and positive, creative marketing outreach—will be necessary to win investment regard and to usher in private capital resources. General and well-documented experience suggests that private capital mobility does not require incentives that are inappropriate or costly to a country like North Korea. But private capital will not mobilize on lies, half truths, and obfuscations by shortsighted business or political elites—not in the United States, not in Europe, not in developed Asia, not anywhere. When the North Korean state is honest and transparent with its elites, its population, and the outside world, private capital inflow will be steady, and the economy will expand in a sustainable fashion. Truth, transparency, and earnest disclosure are the simple requirements for private capital mobility—in any country, in any location, and without regard to political legacy and ideological flavor.

References

eStandards Forum. 2004. Assessment of Country Compliance with Key Codes and Standards for Sound Financial Systems. www.estandardsforum.com/servlet/home.

Financial Stability Forum (FSF). 2004. 12 Key Standards for Sound Financial Systems. Basel: FSF, Bank for International Settlements. www.fsforum.org/compendium/key_standards_for_sound_financial_system.html.

Malcolm Binks, currently an independent consultant, was previously Senior Vice President for Merrill Lynch International with responsibility for business development in the Asia-Pacific region. Carl F. Adams is founder and manager of Capital Framework Advisors LLC, a consultancy for support of private sector initiatives and public policy applications; he was previously Global Director of Country Risk for Merrill Lynch World Headquarters.

Possible Role of South Korea and Other Major Stakeholders

13

A Proactive Approach
to Engaging North Korea:
Boldness, Flexibility, and Inclusiveness

Choo Yong-shik and Wang Yun-jong

In October 2002, Pyongyang officials implicitly agreed to Assistant Secretary of State James Kelly's charge that the Democratic People's Republic of Korea (DPRK, or North Korea) had been pursuing a new course of nuclear development through nourishing highly enriched uranium (HEU). The issue of North Korea's nuclear development returned to the front page of the world's major newspapers, and this renewed international attention augured a second nuclear debacle on the Korean peninsula. Before that point, North Korean nuclear developments had theoretically been frozen since the 1994 Agreed Framework, in which Pyongyang pledged to cease and gradually dismantle any nuclear development program in exchange for economic, political, and security benefits from the outside (particularly the United States).

The Agreed Framework has been praised as one of the Clinton administration's greatest foreign policy achievements. The South Korean (ROK) administration of Kim Dae-jung followed a more accommodating version of engagement and accomplished the epochal South-North summit meeting while it broadened extensively the social, economic, and political exchanges between the two sides. Kim's approach, which has come to be known as the Sunshine Policy, has effected significant ideological change in South Korean society. South Koreans began to perceive the South-North relationship more from a perspective of reconciliation and cooperation with the "northern national partner" than from an attitude of containment of and confrontation with "the Communists." Thus, liberals and progressives who had long opposed conservatives' hard-line policies have raised their voices, and their ideas have become the core of Seoul's policies.

However, when the Kim Dae-jung government's illegal under-the-table payment to Pyongyang was revealed, the crafty and duplicitous management style of the Sunshine Policy brought a political backlash against engagement and raised public doubts of its effectiveness. Moreover, the recent discovery of a new North Korean nuclear program requires a fundamental review of engagement with Pyongyang. This paper explores the current status of North Korean issues and proposes a more effective approach to engagement from a proactive perspective.

Background

North Korea's clandestine HEU program is clearly in violation of the 1968 Nuclear Non-Proliferation Treaty (NPT) and the South-North accord on denuclearization of the Korean peninsula (that Pyongyang signed in 1985 and 1991, respectively) and, more important, the 1994 Agreed Framework—its spirit if not its letter. Subsequent to the discovery of the HEU program, North Korea's brinkmanship tactics of overtly stating its intent to reprocess spent nuclear fissile material provoked a diplomatic crisis that called for urgent action. Policymakers in the international community were compelled to present a panacea for North Korea's delinquency. And, as was the case during the 1993 version of Pyongyang's nuclear adventure, diverse diagnoses and prescriptions emerged; most of them supported engagement or containment, but some proposed coercive diplomacy—and even preemptive strikes.

International discourse on the nuclear endgame varied from "liv[ing] with the unthinkable," to launching "a bold initiative," and to "containment with the long-term goal of regime change" (Carpenter 2003–04; Wright 2003; Schmitt 2002). Neoisolationists in the United States and, one imagines, extreme progressives in South Korea preferred to tacitly tolerate Pyongyang's nuclear weapons program. Supporters of engagement instead touted the resumption of diplomacy. Hard-liners, in contrast, decried the futility of the Agreed Framework and called for replacing it with an "inevitable" containment of the North or even with preemptive strikes on North Korea's nuclear facilities. Alongside it, the myth (or, if one prefers, the necessity) of North Korea's imminent collapse resurfaced. Such a pattern of responses closely matched the shape of public reactions during the 1993 nuclear episode. And history seems to repeat itself.

The Need to Modify Current Practices of Engagement

Is engagement the sole effective means of dealing with the North Korean nuclear issue? Certainly not. The Agreed Framework made considerable achievements. North Korea shut down a nuclear reactor in operation and suspended construction of two reactors of bigger production capacity that, had they been completed, could have brought a nuclear nightmare. But the agreement did not solve the nuclear issue, as it did not succeed in eliminating North Korea's nuclear facility. The crisis was temporarily frozen and defused. As shown by the fact of Pyongyang's secret HEU program, however, nuclear threats from North Korea continue to haunt the international community, particularly South Korea and the United States.

Nevertheless, engagement is preferred, first of all, to avoid human casualties. It is highly plausible that aggressive containment and preemptive strikes would incite North Korea's military retaliation. U.S. forces in Korea as well as South Koreans are perpetually threatened by the specter of a North Korean artillery barrage. About 500 of the North's 12,000 artillery tubes are deployed within range of Seoul. With their capacity for firing several rounds per minute, a North Korean bombardment could incur many tens of thousands of South Korean deaths and many tens of billions of dollars in damage, even if the ROK military swiftly responded to destroy them, using counter-artillery radar (O'Hanlon and Mochizuki 2003, 73–74). Such scenarios are hardly acceptable to South Korea.

Engagement is also favored as a reasonable or second-best—though not optimal—solution because alternatives are less effective or much too risky. Technically, the United States cannot preemptively strike the nuclear facilities. The HEU programs have not been located; thus, they are not even a visible target for preemptive strikes. Other facilities are not easy targets, either. If North Korea had reprocessed spent fuel rods into plutonium and removed it outside Yongbyon, it would be almost undetectable (O'Hanlon and Mochizuki 2003, 93). The other option of allowing a nuclear North Korea to exist would provoke Japan, South Korea, and possibly Taiwan to proliferate, which would outrage China and could escalate nuclear competition in East Asia.

Even though engagement is preferred, at this time engagement must be reexamined from an overall perspective. In the main, engagement has been a defensively motivated strategy to preclude devastating effects (such as a war on the Korean peninsula) by providing economic and security incentives. Some criticize it on the grounds that such a reactive or defensive engagement only succeeds in feeding an enfeebled regime in Pyongyang while allowing it to snatch cash by bluffing. They say that such practices actually encourage North Korea's old habit of extortion, in other words (O'Hanlon and Mochizuki 2003, 84), "developing destabilizing weapons and then bargaining to give them up for huge amounts of aid." Furthermore, they argue that engagement simply bought time for Kim Jong-il to consolidate his totalitarian, dynastic-style reign (Armitage 1999).

There are persistent suspicions that foreign economic and humanitarian assistance funds have been diverted and used in North Korea for strengthening and encouraging the military, Kim's powerful last resort. From 1995 to 2002, the United States provided humanitarian aid worth $1,021.7 million, which also includes U.S. contributions to the Korean Peninsula Energy Development Organization's pledges of heavy oil supplies as outlined in the Agreed Framework (Manyin and Jun 2003, 1). South Korean government aid including agricultural fertilizers, grains, and medical services amounted to $172.8 million during the four years of 1998–2001 (Lee et al. 2003, 523). Also providing food aid were the United Nations Food and Agricultural Organization, the World Food Program (WFP), and UNICEF. However, the Pyongyang regime, unlike other countries, has never allowed the standard practice of monitoring aid distribution. Moreover, one recent study on regime fragility in North Korea assesses that the hazard of regime change in Pyongyang has passed its peak and, despite resurgences in the likelihood of change between mid-1996 and mid-1998, has since declined (Noland 2004, 38–40).

In spite of such massive humanitarian assistance, North Korea still remains a leading violator, invariably ranked as one of the most repressive regimes because of its control of the populace in nearly all aspects of people's social, political, and economic lives. Those sentenced to jail or work camps are reportedly often tortured or even killed. Varying estimates state that between 10,000 and 300,000 North Koreans have fled the country and are living—and hiding—in China.[1] The justification for public criticism of engagement with North Korea is that engagement will actually delay resolution of North Korean problems, particularly issues of weapons of mass destruction (WMD) (Wolfowitz 1995). If an engagement framework does nothing but help to prolong Kim Jong-il's totalitarian reign, even as an unintended consequence, without eliminating North Korea's potential for WMD development and improving human rights conditions there, it cannot be regarded as a reasonable policy option.

Therefore, history shows engagement must be part of a larger approach toward North Korea, even as history teaches that engagement must be tempered with four other considerations:

First, with its formidable capability for developing WMD, North Korea would neither easily surrender to diplomatic pressure nor compromise in order to receive only a small reward. A bold diplomatic initiative would be needed.

Second, North Korea should not be allowed to use brinkmanship as a means of extracting cash from the international community. A disciplined means of engagement backed up with coercive measures is required in order to call Pyongyang's bluff.

Third, engagement should be comprehensive and inclusive, addressing pending economic, political, and military issues. Because North Korea's attempts at nuclear development were driven by a sense of regime crisis and essentially related to its survival, a specifics-based approach would only bog down diplomatic efforts.

Fourth, the conduct of engagement should be based on long-term perspectives on the Korean peninsula, particularly prospects for the northern

---

1 For human rights conditions in North Korea, see Freedom House (1972–2002, 2003) and Human Rights Watch (2002).

regime's sustainability and the question of Korean reunification. Seoul's North Korea policy must be guided toward a regime change through engagement and, at the same time, prepare for the contingency of a regime collapse in the North.

Taken together, these considerations call for a proactive strategy to minimize risk as they address North Korean issues in incremental yet flexible and comprehensive ways.

North Korea's WMD Capabilities

North Korea's formidable capabilities for developing WMD are a major problem that calls for a bold diplomatic breakthrough. Without detailed and verifiable information on North Korea's nuclear activities, it is not yet clear whether Pyongyang has produced nuclear bombs and/or weapons-grade fissile material. However, it seems reasonable to say that Pyongyang's potential nuclear capabilities seem to have expanded.

In January 2003, North Korea announced its withdrawal from the NPT and restarted the 5 MWe nuclear reactor at Yongbyon, which can reprocess spent fuel rods into weapons-grade plutonium.[2] Three months later, North Korea announced that it possessed nuclear weapons, and it showed its intention to reprocess spent fuel rods it extracted from the reactor in 1994.[3] In June, Pyongyang went further, overtly threatening to develop a nuclear deterrence force; later, at the first six-party meeting in August 2003, North Korean delegates privately warned U.S. officials that they could export nuclear weapons. Finally, in October 2003, North Korea declared the completion of its nuclear deterrence capability by turning its stock of 8,017 uranium fuel rods into enough weapons-grade plutonium to produce six bombs (Wehrfritz and Wolffe 2003). Through both direct and oblique public statements, North Korea has hinted that it possesses nuclear weapons, although it often terms them a "nuclear deterrence capability," while it wholly denies evidence of its HEU programs.

Many intelligence sources believe that the DPRK may possess enough plutonium to produce one or two bombs. On *Meet the Press* on 29 December 2002, Secretary of State Colin Powell said that North Korea was believed to have "a couple of nuclear weapons." The Central Intelligence Agency also estimates that North Korea may have two or three nuclear weapons.[4] The

---

2 See CIA (2003). Since 1994, North Korea has frozen the operation of its 5 MWe nuclear reactor at Yongbyon in accordance with the 1994 Agreed Framework. However, it hastily discharged the fuel from the reactor without permitting meaningful verification from the International Atomic Energy Agency (IAEA). In fact, North Korea is believed to have removed some of the fuel rods in 1989.

3 North Korean officials even announced that they were successfully reprocessing the spent fuels, although later they rephrased their statement as "successfully going forward with reprocessing."

4 This was a comment by a senior U.S. official at a conference on U.S.-Japan Track II Cooperation for Arms Control, Nonproliferation, and Verification; the official also commented that North Korea may have two or possibly three nuclear bombs. See Furugawa (2003).

Table 1: North Korea's Nuclear Potential

Nuclear facility	Annual plutonium production	Annual weapons production
5 MWe reactor	6 kg	1
50 MWe reactor	56 kg	11
200 MWe reactor	220 kg	44

Source: Cirincione (2002).

logic behind this belief is that in the early 1990s Pyongyang extracted enough material from the 5 MWe reactor's spent fuel rods to make one to two bombs.[5] On 17 October 2003, Kyodo News reported that South Korea's minister of unification stated that North Korea might have approximately 12 kg of nuclear materials; and, in general, international intelligence has no doubt that North Korea has reprocessed spent fuel rods—estimated at 2,000 by the IAEA and at 2,500 by U.S. and ROK intelligence. Observations of a recent U.S. unofficial delegation to North Korea appear to confirm that Pyongyang "has processed all 8,000 spent fuel rods" although no conclusive evidence for the existence of weapons-grade plutonium was found (Kessler 2004). If this is true, as a recent report (Chipman 2004, 2–3) by the International Institute for Strategic Studies (IISS) estimates, then 25–30 kg of plutonium could have been produced, enough to build two to five nuclear bombs.

The IISS report warns that North Korea could be equipped with four to eight nuclear bombs over the next year and thereafter add thirteen more per year. Currently, North Korea's nuclear capability is limited to its 5 MWe reactor, which it restarted in February 2003. However, the report cautions that, after the completion of the 50 MWe reactor now under construction and after the production of any material from HEU programs, the North's nuclear capability could grow enormously, allowing it to reprocess 130 kg of plutonium, enough for another eight to thirteen bombs per year.[6] Another study (Cirincione 2002) draws a similar conclusion (*Table 1*): if left unchecked, Pyongyang's nuclear drive will reach potentially catastrophic levels—a production capability for 36 bombs from three reactors, exclusive of the nonconfirmed HEU facility.

Factoring in the level of documented weapon device developments would seem to discount North Korea's nuclear weapons capability. The CIA reportedly states that no information exists to confirm a successful North Korean nuclear test, but it assesses that "North Korea has produced one or two simple

---

5 North Korea has insisted that the 5Mwe reactor was shut down in April 1994. However, most analysts think that some (or possibly all) spent fuels were extracted in 1989. See Squassoni (2003).
6 Frankel (2004) reports that the HEU program is estimated to produce 75 kg of plutonium per year.

fission-type nuclear weapons and has validated the designs without con-ducting yield-producing nuclear tests (FAS 2003)."[7] However, as important as the nuclear programs and as essential to their weaponization are North Korea's missile developments that enable delivery of nuclear bombs. North Korea has developed ballistic missiles of various ranges. It produces Scud-B and Scud-C short-range ballistic missiles with launching distances of 300 and 600 km, respectively, as well as its No-dong medium-range ballistic mis-siles (in the 1,300 km range). These missiles can reach anywhere in the ROK and nearly anywhere in Japan. North Korea also launched a three-stage Taepo-dong 1 missile (in the 2,000 km range) over the Japanese island of Honshu. It is also developing the Taepo-dong 2 that could reach the west coast of the United States.[8]

In addition to developing WMD, Pyongyang has exported such weapons. In 2001 alone, the regime is believed to have earned $560 million by selling missiles to some of the world's most anti-U.S. regimes, including Iran, Libya, and Syria (Lintner and Stecklow 2003, 12–15). The formidability of WMD developments and possibilities for proliferation precisely into the hands of terrorist organizations and rogue states intensify the urgency of resolving this issue, one that greatly enhances North Korea's negotiation leverage. The regime will only bargain for a major deal. Certainly, North Korea's WMD developments have proved to be the primary shield against the fall of the regime there; at the same time, WMD developments are a chief impediment to Pyongyang's engagement with the international community.

Regime Dynamics

Whether the Pyongyang regime will sustain itself or collapse has been one of the most argued and fundamental questions to approaching the riddle of North Korea. Even the fact of the enfeebled state's considerable sustainability during the preceding decade has not dispelled the myth of its imminent collapse. Some realist advocates of engagement now suggest that engage-ment is more effective in inducing a regime change.

Scholars' and analysts' views on the future of North Korea can be divided broadly into three groups:

- **Engagement is necessary.**   Engagement adherents argue that the Pyongyang regime will not easily fall without incurring immense secu-rity risks and exacting a tremendous humanitarian toll on the North Korean people.

---

7 The South Korean government doubts such assessments; it believes that North Korea's nuclear potential has not been weaponized. In some aspects, the South Korean Kim Dae-jung and Roh Moo-hyun administrations have been reluctant to officially accept intelligence reports on the nuclear status of North Korea that would undermine the logical grounds of their engagement policies of buying security with economic assistance.

8   On North Korea's missile developments, see Bermudez (1999) and Feikert (2003).

- **Regime will collapse suddenly without engagement.** Those who see the sudden collapse of the regime cite as signals economic deprivation, the absence of mass rallies, and defections of the elite (such as former member of the Central Committee of the Korea Workers' Party and chairman of the Supreme People's Assembly, Hwang Jang-yop). These observers also consider the rise of the military and the withering of normal political institutions (such as Kim Jong-il's power base) indicative of the regime's increasing fragility.

- **Regime's resilience calls for a middle ground.** Others argue that the North Korean regime's survival through a decade of hardship has demonstrated its resilience and that it will at least muddle through the foreseeable future. Surely, the regime's prospects for survival depend heavily on external environments (Noland 2004, 40); the regime needs outside aid to muddle through and secure at least a minimum of economic life for North Korean citizens. Although adoption of this muddle-through hypothesis involves the risk of reinforcing North Korea's cash snatching, its advocates hold that, from a long-term perspective, making the regime stagger toward a soft collapse and ultimate absorption into South Korea would be desirable because it would prevent the shock of its sudden demise and reduce the burden of unification for South Koreans.

Another factor that would have enormous impact on regime dynamics is a centrifugal pull from South Korea because of its shared national identity; one good example is the German reunification. Therefore, in judging the regime's sustainability, the analysis of three factors is critical: North Korea's economic reform, its political stability, and the dynamics of the inter-Korean relationship.

Economic Reform

North Korea has undergone a devastating economic experience. According to the Bank of Korea, North Korea's per capita gross domestic product (GDP) declined by approximately 25 percent during the 12-year period of 1990–2002 (an average of 2 percent annually) (Noland 2004, 22). It experienced sharper declines in per capita GDP in 1992 and 1997 (approximately −5 percent in both years). The 1992 decline was mainly due to the collapse of Communist regimes in Eastern Europe that drastically reduced North Korea's external trade. The 1997 depression occurred because natural disasters in the mid-1990s severely curtailed agricultural production and caused famine on a massive scale, resulting in the deaths of an estimated one to two million North Koreans.

The economic depression also affected grain production. The ROK Ministry of Unification estimates that, since the early 1990s, grain production has been between 3.5 and 4 million tons, and the annual food shortage during

Table 2: Resilience of Various Regimes

Regime	Duration of regime (years)	Longest economic downturn during the existence of the regime		
		Duration of downturn (years)	Cumulative decline in per capita income during downturn (percent)	Annualized rate of decline in per capita income during downturn (percent)
DPRK	55	8	−33	−5
Cuba	44	4	−28	−8
Kenya	39	4	−7	−2
Togo	36	4	−26	−7
Syria	33	3	−11	−4
Haiti	29	2	−8	−4
Romania	24	4	−3	−1
Zambia	19	6	−17	−3

Source: Noland (2004, 26).
Note: Noland used (ROK) Bank of Korea statistics on North Korea.

the same period has been between 1.5 and 2 million tons. In 1990, rice production dropped by 32 percent and the total crop by 26 percent. During the 1992–2001 period, the annual average domestic food deficit was 1.66 million tons. Even with foreign imports (including North Korea's imports and foreign aid), the North lacked approximately 770,000 tons of food from 1992 to 1999. During the same period, the North's annual average food imports and foreign aid were estimated at 1 million tons.

The North Korean economic record is not unique. World Bank data (cited in Noland [2004, 22–24]) show that, since 1960, 42 countries have suffered declines of more than 25 percent in their per capita incomes over a 12-year period. Nations experiencing more than a 33 percent fall in per capita income over eight years numbered 67. In light of the DPRK's economic underperformance, the regime's political stability—its survival, in fact—is remarkable. One study ([Noland 2004, 22–24] see *Table 2*) of regime resilience shows that, among eight regimes with severe economic depressions that have existed more than 18 years, North Korea has experienced the most prolonged economic depression (eight years) and the greatest cumulative decline in per capita income (more than 33 percent); yet this regime is of the longest duration: "its combination of longevity and underperformance is unparalleled."

One critical question related to regime change is economic reform. A principal premise of engagement is that North Korea will become open to the world and will inevitably undergo system reforms, beginning in its economic sector. Many refer to the July 2002 economic reforms—taken broadly in four fields: microeconomic policy, macroeconomic policy, special economic zones, and quest for foreign aid—as an indication of Pyongyang's willingness to engage the outside world. The reform package was comprehensive in terms of its effects on national economic and social systems. The core elements of the reform measures were increasing state prices and income, partially revising the distribution system, making the foreign exchange rate more realistic, decentralizing state planning and expanding corporate sector autonomy, and strengthening the merit system. Does this reform package indicate a shift to a market economy? Are North Korean leaders willing to implement genuine economic reform, probably following the Chinese lead? Analysts' answers have diverged.

The introduction of capitalist elements even in limited scope—the state preserved its basic frame of a public distribution system and an administered price structure—notably departs from the North's previous reform moves. Skeptics say that it was aimed at shifting from a material-based control mechanism to a money-based mechanism (Newcomb 2003; Oh 2003). One cautious view (Noland 2004, 51) emphasizes the drastic—and particularly inflationary—effects the reform may bring onto North Korean society that could cause social differentiation: "North Korea has moved from the realm of the elite to the realm of mass politics." Such skeptics argue that, unlike in the Chinese reform case, North Korean leaders did not take those economic reform measures as imperatives but rather as a policy option to meet political needs.

Political Stability

In North Korea as in other totalitarian states, politics has permeated almost every aspect of the economic and social systems. In such a society, extensive reform tends to lead to revolutionary, not soft, regime change. Blitzkrieg economic reforms may spark political revolutionary movements that could break down the existing totalitarian regime. Thus, economic rationality in terms of enhancing performance is bounded by imperatives for preserving political stability.

Another consideration with regard to North Korean economic reforms is South Korea. The two states share an ethnic identity and are geographically proximate and economically complementary (the South has well-developed industries and the North has cheap labor). Market-oriented reform in the North could enforce its opening to the outside world, and the South would be the most plausible economic partner. In such a case, it is not hard to imagine the North's initial integration into the South via the economic sphere, a process that could spill into the political sphere under ROK domination. The Pyongyang leadership regards such a scenario as a nightmare to be avoided at all costs.

Gravitational Pull from South Korea

During the past 50 years of a divided Korean nation, the essence of conflict between the two Koreas has been about which side can claim exclusive legitimacy to represent the nation and, with it, the right to claim and control unification. Within such a framework, the two Korean states have struggled to achieve hegemonic unification in which one system prevails over the other. At bottom lies a contest over the identity of a unified Korea. Both Korean states have claimed exclusive legitimacy and so have projected their modern identities into the process of unification. This hegemonic vision of unification necessarily involves demolition of the other's "illegitimate" and "treacherous" system, followed by imposition of sovereignty over the other half of the peninsula. Clearly, such ambitions pose a fatal threat to the legitimacy and even survival of the leadership on each side and serve to reinforce the hostility separating the two Koreas.[9]

The upshot here is that there remains at the heart of the inter-Korean relationship a dilemma between reconciliation and hegemonic unification. Within the larger framework of Cold War ideological and military confrontations around the globe, the additional factor of the pursuit of hegemonic unification by each Korean state has only raised greater barriers to their reconciliation. The Korean War epitomized the struggle for hegemonic unification through extreme violence. After the war, this life-or-death contest has continued in the form of consolidating one's own legitimacy and working to erode the legitimacy of the other side (Choo 2003, 40–50).

One aspect of this contest for exclusive legitimacy has been to show off one's system as superior to that of the other, thus undercutting the opponent's performance legitimacy. Each Korean state has struggled to demonstrate that its system better serves the political, economic, and security needs of the people. The method of demonstration does not necessarily require exposing the other's active pursuit of hegemonic unification. One side's economic prosperity itself would serve to undermine the other's legitimacy when the latter suffers severe economic hardship, as was the case in Germany. In terms of per capita income, the South surpassed the North by more than 12 times as of 2001 (see *Table 3*). If there were political turmoil in North Korea, an economically thriving South would act as a "gravitational pull" for the North Korean people.

Realist supporters of engagement argue that engagement would enhance Seoul's leverage over Pyongyang by broadening North Korea's exposure to

---

9   For the contest of the two Koreas over exclusive legitimacy, see Shin (1998).

Table 3: Comparison of Per Capita Incomes between South Korea and North Korea, 1990–2001

Year	North ($)	South ($)	South/North
1990	1,142	5,886	5.2
1991	1,115	6,810	6.1
1992	1,013	7,183	7.1
1993	969	7,811	8.1
1994	992	8,998	9.1
1995	1,034	10,823	10.5
1996	989	11,380	11.5
1997	811	10,370	12.7
1998	573	6,742	11.9
1999	714	8,581	12.0
2000	757	9,628	12.7
2001	706	8,900	12.6

Source: Ahn (2003, 36).

South Korea, thus increasing the effects of the gravitational pull. However, engagement's effectiveness will depend on the ways and means of its implementation. The Sunshine Policy's accommodating engagement has tended to provide North Korea with room to maneuver; in other words, North Korea can continue to play its nuclear card as it holds the Korean peninsula hostage.

The Need for a Proactive Version of Engagement

The foregoing analysis and the diplomatic history of North Korea lead to several implications.

First, the threshold for engaging North Korea will be high. Put another way, North Korea would move toward engagement only in return for a great many benefits. With more formidable nuclear weapons development potential now than in 1994, Pyongyang has good reason to ask a higher price to eliminate the basis for the brinkmanship diplomacy it has exploited as a principal source of cash. We need to strike what O'Hanlon and Mochizuki (2003, 43) call "a grand bargaining" to break ground for engagement. Such a grand bargaining encompassing a broad range of pertinent issues can provide vision and a road map to parties involved in engagement and help prevent negotiations from becoming bogged down in marginal issues.

Second, such a grand bargaining does not necessarily mean an all-at-once approach. There is no feasible—let alone effective—silver-bullet therapy.

Engagement will inevitably lead to the gradual opening of North Korea to the outside world and again compel reform of its system. The Pyongyang regime is acutely sensitive to the snowball effect of social and economic reforms on politics, and the regime will not make a hasty and extensive reform through engagement. Moreover, in world historical terms, the regime has shown unsurpassed sustainability under economic and social duress. This indicates that engagement should be implemented phase by phase over time.

Third, the grand bargaining cannot be successful without some coercive measures. Once North Korea enters the engagement sphere, each forward step toward deeper engagement must be conditioned on the North's compliance with binding obligations. Any violation of or noncompliance with obligations should be met with withdrawal of positive rewards or with sanctions. Countries engaged with North Korea should be ready to use a mix of containment and engagement in a flexible manner.

Fourth, during engagement, there will be the risk of breakdown and North Korea's degeneration into blackmail diplomacy. Such a contingency can lead to extreme instability and even military conflict. Deterrence capability should therefore be preserved. A grand bargaining should certainly include reduction of conventional weapons. However, such arms reduction should not hamper the deterrence capability of the United States and South Korea.

Fifth, if the external environment does not turn adversarial, it is probable that North Korea will muddle through for a foreseeable period by implementing reform measures to the minimum extent necessary to defuse the peoples' dissatisfaction. But the regime's inelastic and rigid nature may cause total system breakdown. All countries involved with North Korea need to be ready to meet the contingency of such a regime collapse.

Sixth and most important, and once again from O'Hanlon and Mochizuki (2003, 50), engagement should be aimed at "a soft, velvet form of regime change." North Korea's problems have fundamentally arisen from the underperformance of its regime, caused by the regime's totalitarian rigidity and overall ineffectiveness.

Therefore, engagement should be proactive (to provide a long-term vision and road map), bold (to break through the current stalemate), comprehensive (to address the full range of pending issues), flexible (to use both punishments and rewards appropriately), and, finally, contingent (to be ready to manage uncertainties).

So complex! However, complexity is intrinsic in the problem. Although it may be daunting, complexity can be disentangled by prioritizing a plan for action. First, proactive engagement should be aimed at regime change in North Korea. Imminent threats must be addressed first: eliminate the nuclear and missile threats, then bring about the economic recovery of North Korea, and finally improve human rights conditions. Yet all the way through it, the world needs to be prepared to cope with contingencies. North Korea has proved its unpredictability more than once.

Role of South Korea

Where lies South Korea's role? South Korea is a key player but is in a delicate position. At one extreme, it can be a catalyst of a regime collapse; on the other, it can act as a stabilizer. In a proactive engagement model, South Korea should promote extensive reforms in North Korea. Until Pyongyang moves forward to a great degree of engagement with the outside world, North Korea remains more of a target for the South to transform than a partner with which the South may cooperate. As a promoter of reform, South Korea could do the following:

First, persuade nations concerned with North Korea that the final goal is a regime change through reforms. The interests of powers in the area of the Korean peninsula have converged to the point that peninsular disturbances that disrupt geopolitics will not be welcome. Thus, neighboring nations may not support a plan for abrupt regime collapse in North Korea. All have agreed, however, on the need to eliminate North Korea's WMD and its continual threatening actions and to help it to develop into a normal state.

Second, maintain a solid relationship with the United States and transform the role of the alliance into a peninsular and regional stabilizer. The establishment of a peace system between the United States and the two Koreas by concluding either peace treaties or nonaggression agreements is a primary goal of proactive engagement. In preparation for a peace settlement, the U.S.-ROK alliance should begin to take up tasks of monitoring the peace process and stabilizing disturbances and should also prepare for possible contingencies arising from a post-regime-change North Korea.

Third, take a leading role in engineering international cooperation. Such cooperation is a key to successful proactive engagement. South Korea has to skillfully mobilize the support of other nations.

Fourth, continue humanitarian aid to and exchanges with North Korea—but with discipline. Particularly, inter-Korean exchanges do not need to be based on strict reciprocity that would be unfavorable to North Korea in terms of the balance of power. However, use of humanitarian aid has to be closely monitored to prevent diversion for other purposes. Economic exchanges should be enacted so as to promote market principles in North Korea.

Fifth, muster domestic public consensus. Seoul's North Korea policy is very sensitive to the South Korean public because it directly affects their lives and intimately relates to nationalism. Without solidified public support in the South, proactive engagement cannot bear fruit.

These prescriptions are not basically different from the current policy of South Korea's government. They share the fundamental premise that regime change is the ultimate solution to North Korean problems. They diverge, however, on the details of disentangling the riddle and implementing the process.

Since the end of the global Cold War, the main focus of South Korea's North Korea policy has gradually shifted from containment to engagement. Kim Dae-jung's Sunshine Policy marked a watershed in this transition. Kim's policy assumed that North Korea's erratic and hostile behavior stemmed from its sense of insecurity and vulnerability and that North Korea, in order to survive, would ultimately choose to align itself more with the outside world through economic and political reforms. With such logic, Kim's administration tried to promote inter-Korean reconciliation on the basis of two principles: one was to place priority on a model of reconciliation that foresees two Koreas coexisting for a considerable period into the future (Sunshine Policy architect Lim Dong-won often-mentioned de facto unification); the other was a spirit of accommodating North Korea that meant not imposing principles of strict reciprocity upon inter-Korean relations.

The current Roh Moo-hyun administration's North Korea policy is designed to build on the Sunshine Policy, but it departs from it by broadening the scope of its vision of security. President Roh sees security as encompassing the areas of unification, national security, and foreign relations. This new security concept has been publicly presented in the policy for peace and prosperity, the idea of Korea as a Northeast Asian economic hub, and discussions of national self-defense.

Roh Moo-hyun bases his policy for peace and prosperity on the premise that peace on the Korean peninsula and peace in Northeast Asia reinforce each other. In other words, a peace settlement on the peninsula will both require and strengthen cooperation among powers—Japan, China, Russia, and the United States—that have security interests in North Korea. Furthermore, North Korea's economic development will also require international assistance. Reciprocally, the establishment of an enduring peace on the peninsula would promote regional peace in Northeast Asia, and economic prosperity on the peninsula would contribute to economic cooperation and development in the region. The upshot of the Roh Moo-hyun policy for peace and prosperity is therefore that both *minjok gongjo* (inter-Korean cooperation) and international cooperation must proceed in parallel.

On the basis of such a strategic vision, the Roh administration has presented an action plan (MOU 2003):

- **Peaceful resolution of the North Korean nuclear issue.** The North Korea nuclear issue must be resolved peacefully through dialogue on the basis of national consensus and in close coordination and cooperation with the international community.
- **Comprehensive approach to North Korea.** The Roh administration believes that, to eliminate North Korea's sense of insecurity, a comprehensive approach encompassing economic and humanitarian aid as well as security measures is needed. Thus, it would pursue a security policy that takes into account the positive impact of inter-Korean economic

cooperation on the promotion of peace. However, the Roh administration differs from the accommodations of the previous administration in that it seeks a balance between security and economy.

- **Establishment of a durable peace regime on the Korean peninsula.** The Roh administration seeks to establish a lasting peace between the two Koreas by replacing the current armistice with a peace treaty. Improvement of North Korea's relations with the United States and Japan and the development of regional institutional arrangements safeguarding the security of the Korean peninsula should also be pursued.

- **Rise of Korea as a hub in the Northeast Asian economy.** The Roh administration foresees that the policy for peace and prosperity will lay the foundation for the rise of Korea as a Northeast Asian economic hub. Once the North Korean nuclear issue is resolved, South Korea would expand economic cooperation with North Korea toward the creation of an economic community on the Korean peninsula. It would also endeavor to construct a positive environment for cooperation in trade, industry, energy, and finance in Northeast Asia. By doing so, the Korean peninsula could emerge as a gateway connecting the Eurasian continent with the Pacific Ocean.

Roh's policy, however, includes some elements that contradict the lessons from previous experiences with North Korea:

- Economic cooperation with or a comprehensive approach toward North Korea has been tried and did not lead to a peaceful resolution of WMD issues, as functionalists predict will happen. Bold and even coercive measures should accompany economic engagement to gain leverage over the Pyongyang regime. Otherwise the engagement could remain oriented on defense.

- Despite Seoul's stated emphasis on the importance of *minjok gongjo* as well as the necessary cooperation of the international community, since the time of the Kim Dae-jung administration, South Korean positions have been leaning toward South-North cooperation, most probably so as not to lose its premier position in resolving North Korean issues and, perhaps more, to promote domestic political interests by appealing to popular South Korean nationalist sentiments. No longer national in scope, however, North Korean issues have become regional and international issues. North Korea intends to resolve WMD issues directly with the United States, not with South Korea; therefore the nationalist logic of *minjok gongjo* is confronting a practical contradiction.

- A multilateral security arrangement should not be considered a substitute for the U.S.-ROK alliance. Without the construction of a common identity among countries in Northeast Asia, a durable security regime in the region will be difficult to create. It is not clear, however, that South

Korea's national interests could be enhanced under such a multilateral security arrangement. In some sense, the six-party talks have given China leverage to deal with North Korea and have decreased the significance of South Korea's strategic positions. In the past, the United States, Japan, and South Korea together tackled the issue. But now, with China's ever-rising prominence, the Sino-U.S. axis is altering the political landscape with regard to North Korea.

In consideration of the above, South Korea should adopt a more adamant attitude toward North Korea and maintain more intimate relations with the United States. By doing so, South Korea can play a role as a promoter of reform and a leading principal in this North Korean game. One model for South Korea—a possible grand strategy for managing the Korean peninsula—in a proactive engagement framework follows.

1. Master Plan

- Develop a long-term plan in cooperation with other nations (in particular the United States and China) and submit it to North Korea at a six-party meeting. Such a plan must be bold and inclusive, addressing elimination of WMD and conventional weapons and the improvement of human rights conditions in North Korea. The plan must also include rewards, such as guarantees of security and economic aid, for North Korea's commitment to resolving those issues as well as coercive measures in case of its noncompliance with the action plan.

- To break the ground for engagement, South Korea should persuade the United States to propose a resumption of the oil supply and a pledge of nonaggression on the condition that Pyongyang act to freeze current nuclear development toward the ultimate dismantlement of nuclear facilities in complete, verifiable, and irreversible ways.

2. Keep *Minjok Gongjo* in Pace with International Cooperation

- Except for humanitarian aid, temporarily suspend economic exchanges —including the Kaesong industrial complex project—with North Korea.

- Renew economic assistance and resume political exchanges with North Korea upon North Korea's actions toward resolving nuclear issues. North Korea should permit on-site inspection of key nuclear facilities, particularly HEU programs, and remove plutonium and spent fuel rods from the country.

3. Massive Economic Engagement toward Political Liberalization

- With all the WMD issues cleared, increase the scale of economic collaboration and cooperation with North Korea in mutually beneficial ways for both South and North.
- As human rights conditions improve, begin industrial development in North Korea. South Korea should take a mediating role in inducing international investment and other economic involvement.

4. Establish a ROK-U.S. Security Council for Stabilization of the Korean Peninsula

- The U.S.-ROK alliance should be transformed into a kind of security council in which both nations take a leading and cooperative role in preventing and stabilizing disturbances that occur during the process of achieving peace and unification and in the aftermath of a unified Korea.
- Move toward conventional arms reduction and establish a peace system under the umbrella of the ROK-U.S. Security Council.

5. South-North Economic Commonwealth and Move toward Unification

- Begin to build institutions for constructing a South-North economic commonwealth.
- As economic interdependence makes significant progress, move toward political integration.

Implementing the above plan depends on North Korea's compliance with binding obligations proposed at each phase. The key to the plan is the premise that engagement should be directed to make North Korea into a "normal country." South Korea should also be prepared for contingencies—such as a drastic change in its political system—that could erupt in the process of normalizing North Korea.

The twenty-first century is the era of globalization. South Koreans must prepare to solve current North Korean issues from a broad perspective of building a new nation that will arise as a leading member of the international community. Great nations have always had great visions for their future. It is beyond doubt that the great vision for the Korean nation begins with plans for normalizing North Korea.

References

Ahn Choong-yong, ed. 2003. *North Korea Development Report 2002/2003*. Seoul: Korea Institute for International Economic Policy. August.

Armitage, Richard. 1999. A Comprehensive Approach to North Korea. Presentation at the Strategic Forum, National Defense University, Washington, D.C., March.

Bermudez, Joseph S., Jr. 1999. A History of Ballistic Missile Development in the DPRK. Monterey, Calif.: Monterey Institute of International Center for Non-proliferation Studies. Occasional paper no. 2. http://cns.miis.edu/pubs/opapers/op2/.

Carpenter, Ted Galen. 2003–04. Living with the Unthinkable. *The National Interest* (Winter): 19–98.

Central Intelligence Agency (CIA). 2003. Appendix A: Unclassified Report to Congress on the Acquisition of Technology Relating to Weapons of Mass Destruction and Advanced Conventional Munitions, 1 January through 30 June 2003. Washington, D.C.: Central Intelligence Agency. www.cia.gov/cia/reports/721_reports/jan_jun2003.htm.

Chipman, John. 2004. North Korea's Weapons Programmes. London: International Institute for Strategic Studies. January. www.iiss.org/news-more.php?itemID=590.

Cirincione, Joseph, with Jon B. Wolfsthal and Miriam Rajkumar. 2002. *Deadly Arsenals: Tracking Weapons of Mass Destruction*. Washington, D.C.: Carnegie Endowment for International Peace.

Choo, Yong-shik. 2003. "Rethinking Ethnic Homogeneity: A Dilemma between Reconciliation and Unification in Korea." PhD. diss. Johns Hopkins University, 2003.

Federation of American Scientists (FAS). 2003. Intel Agencies Answer Questions for the Record. *Secrecy News* 2003 no. 95. 31 October. www.fas.org/sgp/news/secrecy/2003/10/103103.html.

Feikert, Andrew. 2003. North Korean Ballistic Missile Threat to the United States. Washington, D.C.: Congressional Research Service. 25 March. www.nautilus.org/DPRKBriefingBook/missiles/CRS-RS21473_DPRKMissileThreatUS.pdf.

Frankel, Glenn. 2004. Report Cites Potential of N. Korean Arsenal. *Washington Post*, 22 January.

Freedom House. 1972–2002. Freedom in the World Country Ratings. New York: Freedom House. www.freedomhouse.org/research/freeworld/FHSCORES.xls.

———. 2003. *The World's Most Repressive Regimes*. New York: Freedom House. www.freedomhouse.org/research/mrr2003.pdf.

Furukawa, Katsuhisa. 2003. North Korean Nuclear Reality: Intention and Capability. Paper presented at conference, "North Korea, Multilateralism, and the Future of the Peninsula," organized by the Institute of Foreign Affairs and National Security, Center for Strategic and International Studies, Ilmin International Relations Institute, Institute 21 for Peace Studies, Friedrich Naumann Foundation, Shizuoka Research Institute, and the Asia Foundation, 20–21 November, Seoul. www.csis.org/isp/pastprojects/031120_papers.pdf.

Human Rights Watch. 2002. *The Invisible Exodus: North Koreans in the People's Republic of China*. New York: Human Rights Watch. November. www.hrw.org/reports/2002/northkorea/index.htm#TopOfPage.

Kessler, Glenn. 2004. N. Korean Evidence Called Uncertain. *Washington Post*, 2 January.

Lee, Jong-seok, Cho Myoung-chul, and Dong Yong-seung. 2003. Inter-Korean Economic Relations. In *North Korea Development Report 2003*, ed. Ahn Choong-yong. Seoul: Korea Institute for International Economic Policy.

Lintner, Bertil, and Steve Stecklow. 2003. Paper Trail Exposes Missile Merchants. *Far Eastern Economic Review*. 13 February.

Manyin, Mark, and Ryun Jun. 2003. U.S. Assistance to North Korea. Washington D. C.: Congressional Research Service. 17 March.

Ministry of Unification (MOU). 2003. The Policy for Peace and Prosperity. Seoul: MOU. www.unikorea.go.kr/data/eng0403/000113/attach/eng0403_113A.pdf.

Newcombe, William. 2003. Reflections on North Korea's Economic Reform. *Korea's Economy 2003* 19:72.

Noland, Marcus. 2004. *Korea after Kim Jong-il*. Washington, D.C.: Institute for International Economics.

O'Hanlon, Michael, and Mike Mochizuki. 2003. *Crisis on the Korean Peninsula: How to Deal with a Nuclear North Korea*. New York: McGraw-Hill.

Oh, Seung-yul. 2003. Changes in the North Korean Economy: New Policies and Limitations. *Korea's Economy 2003* 19:72.

Schmitt, Gary. 2002. U. S.-North Korea Policy. Project for the New American Century (PNAC) Memorandum. 4 November. www.newamericancentury.org/northkorea-20021104.htm.

Shin, Gi-wook. 1998. Division and Politics of Representation in Korea. Paper presented at conference, "The Republic of Korea after 50 Years: Continuity and Convergence," Georgetown University, Washington, D.C., 2–3 October.

Squassoni, Sharon. 2003. North Korea's Nuclear Weapons: How Soon an Arsenal? Washington, D.C.: Congressional Research Service. 29 July. http://fpc.state.gov/documents/organization/29649.pdf.

Wehrfritz, George, and Richard Wolffe. 2003. How North Korea Got the Bomb. *Newsweek*. 27 October.

Wolfowitz, Paul. 1995. The North Korean Nuclear Deal and East Asian Security. Testimony before the Senate Foreign Relations Committee, Washington, D.C., 25 January. www.fas.org/irp/threat/fp/b19ch10.htm.

Wright, Jonathan. 2003. S. Korea suggests US take bold initiative. Reuters, 28 March.

Choo Yong-shik is with the Johns Hopkins School of Advanced International Studies. Wang Yun-jong was with the Korea Institute for International Economic Policy at the time this paper was written.

14

Payback Time:
Japan–North Korea Economic Relations

Richard J. Samuels

For historical and ideological reasons, relations between Japan and North Korea (the Democratic People's Republic of Korea, or DPRK) are among the most contentious and mutually distrustful of any in the world today.[1] From Pyongyang's perspective, Japan's military alliance with the United States and its history of harsh colonial rule are impediments to normal diplomatic and economic relations. From Tokyo's perspective, North Korea's brazen abduction of Japanese nationals during the late 1970s and early 1980s and its flagrant militarism make the DPRK a particularly repellent neighbor. In December 2001, the Japanese coast guard actually fired upon and sank a North Korean spy ship in what was the first incident of Japanese hostile fire since World War II. The two countries do not have formal diplomatic relations, a situation that significantly impedes normal intercourse.

Still, after a protracted negotiation conducted in secret by officials in the Ministry of Foreign Affairs (MoFA), Prime Minister Koizumi Junichiro visited Pyongyang in September 2002.[2] Whether this was designed to establish independence from the United States or to distract public opinion from stalled economic reforms, the visit followed a warming of Republic of Korea (ROK)-DPRK relations and was an important effort to get Japan-DPRK relations on track. Koizumi's initiative was nearly derailed by U.S. government revelations that Pyongyang had begun a secret program to generate highly enriched uranium, violating the 1994 Agreed Framework. The North Koreans

---

1 For concise histories of the North Korea-Japan relationship, see Green (2001) and Manyin (2003).

2 The details of the diplomacy that led to the meeting are hazy, and the degree of interaction between Japan and other regional partners prior to the meeting remains open to conjecture. Newspaper reports suggest that Tanaka Hitoshi, the director general of the Asia and Oceania Bureau of the MoFA, who played a pivotal role in setting up the visit, was approached by North Korean officials. Tanaka was criticized for keeping the information hidden from the foreign minister and for directly advising the prime minister and the chief cabinet secretary.

subsequently withdrew from the International Atomic Energy Agency and reactivated their Yongbyon nuclear reactor, adding to Japan's security concerns. Now Pyongyang had programs to build a stockpile of enriched uranium and plutonium. As a result, the Pyongyang Declaration, signed by Prime Minister Koizumi and Chairman Kim Jong-il, was clouded by greater diplomatic uncertainty than ever.[3]

A large portion of this uncertainty was also tied up in the abduction issue. After a decade of lobbying by aggrieved Japanese families, the Japanese government prevailed upon Pyongyang in January 1998 to search for abductees—then formally referred to as "missing persons." But these early talks soon broke down, and Pyongyang abandoned the effort, insisting there had been no abductions. Before the September 2002 summit, the Japanese government suspected that North Korea had abducted 11 Japanese citizens from coastal towns across the archipelago and in Europe.[4] During the meeting, however, Prime Minister Koizumi was surprised by Chairman Kim's admission that North Korea had abducted thirteen Japanese citizens, of whom only five were still alive. During the meeting, Kim also stated that North Korean spy ships entering Japanese waters were somehow beyond his control. He promised to investigate further and to ensure that no more ships were sent.

Following the meeting, a North Korean spokesperson stated that North Korea would allow the families and relatives, as well as Japanese government officials, to meet with the five abductees still living and to let them and their families return to Japan if they so wished. The Japanese government responded by sending a delegation to meet with the abductees, visit the graves of those who had died, and obtain information about the cases. Following negotiations, in mid-October, the five living abductees returned to Japan, where they currently reside. Their families remained in North Korea and did not obtain permission to leave until after Koizumi returned to Pyongyang in late May 2004.

Confirmation of these abductions, the subsequent hostage taking of their families, and the blatant flexing of Pyongyang's military capabilities hardened the attitude of the Japanese public toward North Korea. After some initial euphoria, Prime Minister Koizumi was harshly criticized for the "secret diplomacy" of his Foreign Ministry. After information about North Korea's nuclear program became known and the public focused on the scale of the abduction issue, bilateral talks became deadlocked.

The breakdown of these talks and the clouding of the prospects for the Pyongyang Declaration had a particular impact on Korean residents in Japan. The group that represents them is Chongryun (the General Association

---

3 See MoFA (2002a) for the English text of this declaration.
4 For the MoFA account of the abduction issue prior to the Koizumi visit, see MoFA (2002b), Manyin (2003), and Hiramatsu (2003).

of Korean Residents in Japan; also known as Chosen Soren in Japanese). Its eight executives are members of North Korea's parliament, the Supreme People's Assembly. Established in 1955, it is estimated to have approximately 200,000 members out of the 660,000 ethnic Koreans living in Japan and has been instrumental in the limited economic interactions between the DPRK and Japan. In 1972, Chongryun was recognized by Tokyo's leftist governor, Minobe Ryokichi, as North Korea's de facto representative in Japan, and it was granted· tax-free status.

There have been occasional acts of violence against Chongryun officials, as in the case of the murder of a branch vice chairman in Chiba whose office was torched soon after Pyongyang tested a missile over Japanese airspace in 1998. In July 2003 a bullet was fired into a Chongryun office in Niigata, and a bomb was found in a credit union used by North Korean residents. The following month, a phalanx of 42 right-wing sound trucks accosted buses carrying Korean residents of Japan to a Niigata port to greet a North Korean ship. According to a press account in the *Guardian* on 3 October 2003, in just two weeks in the autumn of 2003, Chongryun received nearly 300 threatening phone calls and experienced nearly 30 cases of violence or attempted violence.

In July 2003, Tokyo's governor, Ishihara Shintaro, who previously had publicly condoned a right-wing bomb scare at the home of the MoFA official who had negotiated the Pyongyang meeting for Prime Minister Koizumi, took official action against Chongryun. Ishihara ordered the Tokyo metropolitan government to rescind Chongryun's tax-exempt status and to levy a 60 million *yen* tax on their Tokyo properties. When Chongryun did not comply, Ishihara ordered attachment of three Chongryun properties and planned to auction them off. The auction has been frozen while Chongryun has appealed the decision. Other local governments have begun to follow suit, demanding taxes from Chongryun. The accelerating pace of "out-marriage" (nearly 90 percent of Korean residents now marry Japanese citizens) and the increasing numbers of Korean residents who choose South Korean over North Korean citizenship have reduced Chongryun's membership dramatically.[5]

The Japan-DPRK Economic Relationship

Postwar economic ties between Tokyo and Pyongyang first were stimulated after Hatoyama Ichiro became the Japanese prime minister in 1955. Hatoyama had pledged improved economic relations with North Korea as well as the restoration of diplomatic relations with the Soviet Union and the People's

---

5   For a remarkably frank analysis of its deepening problems, see Chongryun (2004). Two demographic nuggets from this report: Last year there were 7,000 births to parents in "international marriages" (i.e., North Korean residents and Japanese) and only 3,000 to parents who were "compatriots"; the number of students attending Korean schools in Japan has dropped by 6,000, and 30 of these schools have been closed. (No time period was specified.)

Republic of China (PRC). But as soon as three small firms (Toko Bussan, Toho Shokai, Wako Koeki) signed direct contracts with North Korean trading houses in October, the Japanese government banned all exchange with the DPRK. Instead, Japanese firms turned to the Chinese as formal intermediaries to triangulate Japan-DPRK trade. Japanese manufactured goods, including tires and chemicals, were shipped first to China and then on to North Korea in exchange for corn. After the Mitsui and Sumitomo Banks established correspondent relations with the Foreign Trade Bank of North Korea in the early 1960s, smaller Japanese financial institutions followed suit (Hughes 1999, 135). Large Japanese trading companies used dummy corporations (Murakami 1996).[6]

In November 1962, Japan and North Korea began direct cargo shipments on a very small scale. Two years later, in July 1964, trade agreements were signed. The first direct Japanese sales/trade show was held in Pyongyang in May 1965, with the participation of some 20 Japanese trading firms displaying nearly 400 products, including machine tools. While their North Korean hosts purchased all the products on display and ordered more, payments were not forthcoming. This continued through the first North Korean trade exhibition in Japan in 1970. But it was only after North Korea defaulted in 1972 on payments to the Kyowa Bussan Trading Company—comprising 20 large Japanese firms (including Nippon Steel and Toshiba)—that Japan's Ministry of International Trade and Industry (MITI) finally suspended all export credits in 1974. At that time it was reported that half the debt owed to Japanese firms was held by Shinwa Bussan, a Mitsui Trading Company subsidiary (Hughes 1999, 135, 141). By 1975, Japanese creditors claimed nearly 80 billion *yen* in unpaid notes, and in October 1986 MITI provided 300 billion *yen* in compensation for losses incurred by Japanese firms that had traded with North Korea (Hughes 1999, 136).

Still, limited trade continued between Japan and North Korea. After North Korea announced its Law on Joint Ventures in 1984, a Mitsui Trading Company subsidiary backed a gold-mine venture with North Korean residents of Japan, and an Osaka-based firm established a cement factory in North Korea in 1990 (Hughes 1999, 132). Although Japan became North Korea's second largest trading partner after China in 1993 and soon thereafter became its largest partner (at least temporarily), overall trade volume soon began to decline. By the end of the first half of 2003, bilateral trade was at its lowest level in a decade.[7] Japanese firms that had been commissioning manufacture—textiles and electrical machinery—from North Korean plants found the DPRK too risky and Chinese alternatives too attractive. The DPRK has

---

6 Mitsui Bussan created Daiichi Tsusho for this purpose.

7 Note, however, a report in Jiji Press on 11 September 2003 that bus and truck exports from Japan to North Korea "soared" 46 percent in that period. For Japan-DPRK trade statistics, see www.customs.go.jp/toukei/info/index.htm.

exported pine nuts, mushrooms, fishery products (for example, shellfish), and other primary products. Japanese importers have also had limited experience with subcontracting apparel (suits, sweaters, underwear) from North Korean needleworks, a business that has now been largely diverted to China. Japanese firms can provide every variety of manufactured product, from motor vehicles to key infrastructure such as railways, ports, and communications.

There have been periodic, largely feeble attempts to enhance DPRK economic relations with the outside world, including Japan. In the mid-1990s Pyongyang scrapped its special currency for foreigners, allowing them use of the North Korean *won,* and in April 2001 the DPRK promulgated a law to encourage manufacturing for exports. In 1997 Pyongyang hosted a series of visits by International Monetary Fund (IMF) and World Bank officials (Hughes 1999, 138). In 2001 Pyongyang applied for membership in the Asian Development Bank (ADB), a potential new source of loan capital for economic reconstruction. Its application has been supported by the ROK but opposed by both the United States and Japan, the two largest shareholders in the ADB (Takeuchi 2001). Meanwhile, bilateral Japan-DPRK trade declined, and Japanese firms have made no direct investment in North Korea since 1997.

The largest part of Japan-DPRK trade by far has involved either businesses established by North Korean citizens living in Japan or illegal narcotics traffic (or both). More than 100 Chongryun joint ventures were created in the wake of the 1984 North Korean Joint Ventures Law, but failures of Chongryun "patriotic plants" in North Korea and Japanese government investigation of their finances have dampened this *cho-cho* economic relationship. Meanwhile, a Japanese government crackdown on drug smuggling has caused much of the North Korean narcotics traffic to be rerouted through China, which has more than doubled its arrests of Japan-bound shipping from North Korea, reported the *Tokyo Shimbun* on 25 November 2003. Periodically there also have been highly visible crackdowns on illegal exports from Japan; on 6 November 2003, just before the election, the *Nihon Keizai Shimbun* reported that a Korean resident of Japan was arrested in Tokyo for falsifying the end user of electrical equipment currently banned for sale to the DPRK.

Japanese trading company officials occasionally speak about the attractiveness of investing in DPRK infrastructure development (railroads, ports, electric power), but neither the Keidanren nor the Keizai Doyukai has committees that deal with North Korean issues, and neither business association has issued a North Korean trade and investment white paper.[8] The same Japanese firms that would be the most active in such investments—such as Hitachi and Toshiba, which had won a turbine contract under the now-suspended KEDO program—also are the ones that stand to gain the most from increased procurement of weapons systems by the government of Japan

---

8 One official states, "Keidanren intentionally avoids the issue" of trade and investment with North Korea.

in response to the DPRK threat.[9] Mitsubishi Heavy makes the H-II rocket and Aegis destroyers and is seeking a license to produce the PAC-3 missile; Mitsubishi Electric is the prime contractor for the spy satellite that was authorized immediately after the DPRK tested its Taepo-dong missile over Japanese airspace in August 1998.[10]

While the *South China Morning Post* on 18 September 2002 optimistically predicted that "a surge of Japanese investment in North Korea" would result from Prime Minister Koizumi's September 2002 visit and a subsequent normalization, the Japanese press reported widespread skepticism in the Japanese business community.[11] Meanwhile, although Japan remains one of North Korea's more important economic partners—about one-quarter of DPRK exports went to Japan in 2002—there was a dramatic drop-off in bilateral trade after Japan tightened port controls in 2003 (Manyin 2003).

Party Positions

In the absence of pressure from the business and financial communities, the Liberal Democratic Party (LDP) has been free to define the DPRK issue in purely political terms. The LDP has insisted that settlement of the abduction issue and denuclearization of the peninsula are the sine qua non for normalization of relations. In May 2003, a group of younger LDP Diet members formed a caucus to revise the Foreign Exchange and Foreign Trade Control Law to make it possible for Japan to stop remittances (*sokin*) to North Korea from Japan that have been estimated at upwards of 60 billion *yen* per year (Green 2001, 117).

But the LDP hardly needed to be goaded into action. The party played the North Korea card to great effect in the November 2003 election campaign. By promising sanctions, the LDP isolated the Socialists and made the Democratic Party of Japan (DPJ) look passive on an issue of clear concern to the Japanese electorate. Indeed, the establishment of an Abductee Policy Center in October and the appointment of its chairman, Abe Shinzo, as chief cabinet secretary underscored the political salience of the abduction issue. Abe has called for a halt to all remittances from Japan to North Korea until the abductee issue is resolved. The LDP policy statement on North Korea in its autumn 2003 election manifesto calls for the return of abductee families to Japan, the resolution of unsolved cases, and the provision of financial support to abductees and their families.[12] Within two weeks after the election,

---

9 KEDO—the Korean Peninsula Energy Development Organization—was created in 1995 under the 1994 Agreed Framework. The DPRK agreed to freeze and ultimately dismantle its existing nuclear program. In return, KEDO would supply heavy fuel oil and a light-water reactor that would reduce the risk of weaponization. See Hughes (1999, 152–4) for analysis of Japan's participation in KEDO.
10 See Green (2001, 124–8) for more on Japanese and U.S. reactions to the missile test.
11 See reports in Jiji Press on 13 September 2002 and Kyodo News on 30 August 2002 and 17 September 2002.
12 The LDP manifesto also advocates a normalization of relations that includes the comprehensive

the LDP introduced Diet legislation to allow Japan to impose unilateral economic sanctions on North Korea, and within three months it had become law. The Koizumi government again played a Pyongyang card to position the LDP in the July 2004 upper house elections. The prime minister revisited Chairman Kim in late May and secured the realease of the family members of the abductees still in Japan. He also arranged for the reunion of one abductee with her U.S.-born husband, Charles Jenkins, and their daughters in Indonesia two days before the election.

The LDP's coalition partner, the Komeito, took no independent position on North Korea, and the LDP's tough stand trumped all of the opposition parties in the earlier vote. The largest Japanese opposition party, the DPJ, also identified the abduction and nuclear issues as the most important problems to be resolved as part of any normalization talks. But its calls for a written apology, reparations, the return of all abductees and their families, and a commitment to cease abductions in the future seemed derivative of the LDP position to many voters. Likewise, its criticism of the government for signing the Pyongyang Declaration despite knowledge of the DPRK's recommenced nuclear program struck many as grasping at straws. In short, although the DPJ called the abduction issue "important," it found itself following in a strong LDP wake throughout the campaign. It has continued in this pattern by echoing the LDP; on 26 November 2003 the *Yomiuri Shimbun* reported that the DPJ had also established a party committee to manage policy on the abduction issue. It promised to tighten controls on remittances, but only after the LDP had already revealed a stronger line toward the North Koreans and only after Chairman Kan Naoto was criticized effectively by Secretary General Abe of the LDP for having once advocated release by the South Korean government of a North Korean agent jailed for abducting Hara Tadaaki in 1980. Of those in the DPJ who were elected, three-quarters favored tougher sanctions against the DPRK.

The Japan Communist Party (JCP) has released a number of statements outlining its policies on North Korea.[13] The party calls for removing the nuclear threat, solving the abductee problem, and accepting North Korea into international society without resorting to war. It also argues for the return of the abductee families, a formal apology, and payment of compensation to the abductees. The JCP reminds the public it had harshly criticized the DPRK for many years, insisting that the greater danger is a confrontation between the United States and North Korea.[14] In part because the JCP platform called for

---

resolution of the abductee, nuclear, and missile problems. It supports the six-party negotiations framework. It is found (in Japanese) at: http://www.jimin.jp/jimin/jimin/sen_syu43/sengen/07.html.

13 For a list in Japanese, see www.jcp.or.jp/seisaku/index-02-05gaiko.html.

14 The relationship between the JCP and the North Korean Workers' Party worsened in the 1970s, and the JCP severed formal relations following the October 1983 terrorist attack in Rangoon orchestrated by North Korean agents who killed 21 people (including 4 cabinet members) and injured 46. The rupture of JCP-DPRK relations has not prevented the Komeito from publishing a book pillory-

the resumption of talks without conditions attached, the party was decimated in the November election. It is now left with only nine seats in the Lower House.

The Social Democratic Party (SDP), once closely tied to the Korean Workers' Party, has tried to refocus on the nuclear issue, arguing for its resolution through multilateral dialogue. But during the November campaign the Socialists were embarrassed by LDP and media reminders that it once had insisted that the abduction issue was a fake. The SDP, which had long held a conciliatory stance toward the DPRK, had arranged and participated in the 1990 visit to Pyongyang by Kanemaru Shin. Voters remembered, and punished the SDP severely in November 2003 for having turned a blind eye to Japanese abductees and then denying it had done so. Party Chair Doi Takako was defeated in her home district and held onto her seat only in the proportional representation list. She resigned soon after the results were posted. The Socialist Party that once accounted for more than one-third of lower-house seats now has only six representatives in Diet and is in danger of disappearing altogether.

Thus, the most recent lower house elections seem to have closely reflected a strongly anti–North Korean public sentiment, one that was read most clearly and massaged most effectively by the ruling LDP. Stimulated by support groups for the families of Japanese abductees, some two-thirds of those elected to the lower house in November 2003 supported tougher measures against the DPRK, including tightened foreign-exchange controls and restrictions on entry by North Korean ships to Japanese ports.[15] The LDP used the North Korea issue to generate positive media attention once again in the upper house elections, which followed seven months later.

Japanese Interests and Policies toward the DPRK

There is no question that reduction of Pyongyang's military threat is atop the list of Japanese priorities alongside resolution of the abductee issue. But it is not only Pyongyang's military threat that troubles Japanese security planners. They are also concerned that a marked deterioration of political stability in North Korea or a military miscalculation by Pyongyang would invite great-power intervention, markedly affecting Japanese interests on the peninsula (Akaha 2002). Thus, Japan also has an interest in restraining the United States, especially in a post-9/11 world in which the Bush administration has outlined a national security strategy based on preventive war. This is why the

---

ing the JCP for its relationship with the North Korean leadership and for encouraging North Korean citizens in Japan to return to North Korea from the 1960s to the early 1980s. From 1959 to 1984, the Japanese and North Korean Red Cross associations assisted people of Korean descent to move from Japan to North Korea, with 93,000 returning by 1984, of whom 6,800 were Japanese citizens (many families of North Korean citizens in Japan).

15 See Kyodo News on 10 November 2003 and *Sankei Shimbun* on 11 November 2003.

Koizumi administration warmly welcomed the Bush administration's October 2003 offer of a security guarantee to Pyongyang.

Prime Minister Koizumi's visits to Pyongyang in 2002 and 2004 may have been the last efforts to place unilateral initiatives alongside multilateral ones in Japan's policy quiver. Japan depends more than ever on U.S. and ROK leadership. Moreover, even acknowledging the improvement of bilateral relations between Seoul and Tokyo, it is not at all clear that the prospect of a nuclear-armed North is significantly more threatening to Japan than a nuclear-armed and unified Korean peninsula (Akaha 2002, 81). As a result, the Japanese government has made a sustained effort to coordinate policy not only with the United States but also with Russia and China. In January 2003, Prime Minister Koizumi visited Moscow, where the two countries signed an action plan (MoFA 2003c) that outlined cooperation on a range of issues, including North Korea; and both Koizumi and Foreign Minister Kawaguchi have stayed in regular contact with their counterparts in China as well (MoFA 2003c; MoFA 2004b). This summitry is symbolized by the meetings held by Koizumi in St. Petersburg with President Putin and President Hu Jintao of China on subsequent days in May 2003.[16] Further, Koizumi has used the various regional multilateral bodies as opportunities to meet with his Chinese, Russian, and South Korean counterparts and coordinate on North Korean and other issues; he has met with Hu Jintao and Vladimir Putin at the sidelines of the APEC Economic Leaders' meeting in Bangkok in October 2003 and with Wen Jiabao at the ASEAN+3 meeting in October 2003 in Bali, Indonesia (MoFA 2003b).

Nor is all the activity merely diplomatic. The DPRK is responsible for Japan's coming out of its postwar security shell as well. The initial decision to cooperate with the United States on missile defense research and development was prompted by North Korea's test of a Taepo-dong 1 ballistic missile over Japan in August 1998. Since the eruption of the latest crisis, Japan has moved closer to implementing a missile defense system as well as launching its own intelligence satellites. Tokyo also has reminded Pyongyang of its long-standing claim of a right to use preemptive military force. In the MoFA's *Blue Book 2003*, North Korea is listed ahead of the war on terror and weapons of mass destruction as Japan's greatest diplomatic concern. The MoFA states Japan's basic policy toward North Korea as aimed at achieving normalization through a tripartite cooperation among the United States, the ROK, and Japan that contributes to peace and stability (MoFA 2003a). Meanwhile, the 2003 defense white paper issued by the Japan Defense Agency (JDA) (Boeicho 2003, 44–45) is blunt about the North Korean threat:

---

16 For information on the Japan-Russia summit meeting, see www.kantei.go.jp/foreign/koizumiphoto/2003/05/30russia_e.html.

North Korea has sought as a basic national policy to transform itself into a "strong and rising great power" and adopted a "military-first policy" to realize this aim. . . . Despite the serious economic difficulties it faces, North Korea continues to give the military preferential allocation of resources, and is dedicating considerable effort into maintaining and improving its military capabilities and readiness. North Korea possesses weapons of mass destruction, ballistic missiles, and large-scale special operations forces, and the country appears to be maintaining and strengthening its asymmetrical military capabilities. North Korea's suspected development of nuclear weapons impinges on the security of Japan and is also a matter of concern for the entire international community. . . .

Normalization talks have been the main mechanism through which Japan and North Korea have engaged at a government level. These talks have been conducted intermittently since the agreement to begin them was reached during the visit of Kanemaru Shin to Pyongyang in September 1990. Talks were broken off in 1992 after eight meetings, and efforts by LDP leaders Watanabe Michio in 1995 and Mori Yoshiro in 1997 to get them restarted failed. Efforts stalled again after the 1998 missile test, when Japan responded by freezing charter flights, suspending humanitarian aid, and stopping payments to KEDO (Akaha 2002, 83). Normalization talks finally recommenced in April 2000, when MoFA bureaucrats took the lead for the Japanese side. The most recent talks were held in October 2003 in Kuala Lumpur, where Japanese negotiators requested the return of the abductee families to Japan, maintenance of the Pyongyang Declaration, submission to responsibilities under the Nuclear Non-Proliferation Treaty, and the nontargeting of Japan by North Korean No-dong missiles.[17]

From the beginning of the Cold War, Japan's North Korean diplomacy— and much related domestic policy—has been hitched to the U.S. wagon. In 1950, with the outbreak of the Korean War, Japan assembled its first postwar military force, the 75,000-man National Police Reserve, the direct antecedent of the Ground Self-Defense Force. The trade restraints imposed by the Eisenhower administration in the mid-1950s loomed large throughout the rest of the Cold War. In 1994, the Clinton administration devised the Agreed Framework, which required Japanese contributions to KEDO that were resented by some officials in Kasumigaseki who were not entirely convinced that Pyongyang's threat was serious.[18] More recently—this was expressed in Diet testimony of Hori Toshikazu—it seems that Japanese support for Operation Enduring Freedom in Iraq is tied to the belief that, if Japan does not support the United States in the Middle East, it risks either that the United States would provide insufficient support in the event of a Korean contin-

---

17 For a Japanese government summary of the results of these talks, see MoFA (2002c).
18 For an insider's account of the development of the Agreed Framework and Japan's reaction, see Kanter (1998) and Green (2001, 125) on the "heavy pressure" exerted on Japan to sign onto KEDO.

gency or that the United States would act unilaterally on the peninsula in ways that would be contrary to Japan's national interests. Thus, Japanese diplomacy has focused directly and enthusiastically on promotion of six-party talks.[19] It has engaged partners multilaterally, as exemplified by its sponsorship of a conference to establish Asia's first export control regime, as well as bilaterally—both within the region and abroad—to impress other states with the importance of the abduction and nuclear/missile issues. Japan has received assurances from the ROK that a nuclear North Korea will not be tolerated.[20]

Apart from the abduction issue and the military threat—the two most important issues impinging on normalization—there are at least three subsidiary matters defining Japanese government policy vis-à-vis North Korea. The first concerns refugees. Currently Japan takes very few refugees and concentrates on providing support through the United Nations (UN). Refugees seeking asylum can apply only from inside Japan, ruling out the use of foreign embassies for this purpose. In January 2003, the MoFA Asia and Oceanic Affairs bureau chief, Mitoji Yabunaka, confirmed that the Japanese government has put "dozens" of Japanese citizens—Japanese spouses of North Korean nationals who fled North Korea to China and want to return to Japan—under its protection. Japan has stayed quiet about this out of consideration for China, which has allowed the refugees to return to Japan even though the PRC has had a repatriation order with North Korea since 1986. Still, the Japanese government does not accept political asylum seekers and does not issue travel documents to allow travel to Japan in order to apply for refugee status.

The second area concerns the regulation of remittances to North Korea. Press reports, such as that by Yonhap on 1 November 2003, estimate that cash remittances from pro-Pyongyang residents in Japan amount to more than $1 billion a year, a sizable portion of North Korea's annual expenditures, although these may be exaggerated.[21] Even if much less, however, these remittances constitute a large share of the total North Korean economy. While most of the funds transfers are voluntary, some have been extorted (Hughes 1999, 137). It has been reported that the Japanese government has begun pressuring the Tokyo-based Ashikaga Bank, used by Korean residents of Japan to send money to North Korea, to halt the flow of remittances. In 1994 the Ministry of Finance temporarily suspended all dollar-based remittances from the Ashikaga Bank, and in late 2003 it nationalized the bank (FEER 2003). In early 2004, the Japanese Diet amended the Foreign Exchange Con-

---

19 Participants in the six-party talks are China, Japan, North Korea, Russia, South Korea, and the United States.

20 For the Japanese government's official statement and a list of bilateral overtures, see MoFA (2004a).

21 A Japanese foreign ministry official (whom I interviewed on 6 March 2004) insists this figure is exaggerated, and Manyin (2003, 5) places it in the tens of millions of dollars annually.

trol Law to allow for unilateral economic sanctions, including the suspension of remittances to North Korea via Japanese banks.

The third policy concerns the regulation of trade and investment. In 1983, after the DPRK defaulted on its debts to Japanese creditors, the Japanese government ceased underwriting trade insurance for Japanese firms doing business there. As noted, this has effectively frozen any large-scale economic interaction between Japanese firms and North Korea. Although resolution of the debt problem is not the major obstacle to normalization, there can be no trade incentives unless and until these debts are satisfied. In May 2003, the Japanese government announced that it could legally invoke a complete trade ban with the DPRK. The government cited not only Japanese law, but a bilateral treaty with the United States: Because Japanese law allows the government to restrict trade if it affects the healthy development of Japan's economy, the government concluded that a Japanese failure to comply with U.S. sanctions would seriously undermine the U.S.-Japan relationship and, hence, Japan's economy.

The Japanese government has taken small, but significant, steps to regulate trade with the DPRK, starting with tighter safety inspections. In much the same way that the Chinese government cut off oil shipments to North Korea in 2003 to show Pyongyang that it meant business, the Japanese Ministry of Land, Infrastructure, and Transport began spot inspections in August that hampered the ability of North Korean vessels to travel to Japan. Kyodo News reported on 25 August 2003 that the inspections, nominally designed to ensure seaworthiness, had found safety problems on 70 percent of the North Korean ships, including such minutiae as defective exhaust ducts in the galleys, misplaced emergency exit signs, and missing fire extinguishers. The *Man Gyong Bong-92*, a passenger and freight vessel connecting North Korea and Niigata that has ferried between Japan and Korea up to 20 times annually since 1971, became a special focus of attention on the suspicion that it was transporting narcotics, illegal remittances of cash, and missile parts.[22]

Conclusion

Given the history of this difficult relationship, Japanese participation in a "grand bargain" among six parties presumes normalization—and, given the array of political interests at home, normalization presumes satisfactory outcome to the issues of greatest concern to Tokyo: the abductees and Pyongyang's military threat.

But there are demands for payback on both sides: The first item on Pyongyang's agenda is reparations for three decades of Japanese colonial

---

22 In November 2002, Tokyo metropolitan police seized documents that included instructions from Pyongyang for spying in South Korea; the documents were reportedly passed to an operative by the captain of the vessel.

rule and the forced migration of thousands of Koreans—including for sex slavery and corvée. The DPRK is demanding up to $10 billion, although some estimate that normalization can be achieved for half that amount (Green 2001, 307; Manyin 2003, 9). Therefore, given the mobilization of Japanese antipathy toward the North Korean position on history and on Japan's war responsibility and given the centrality of the reparations issue to the North Korean regime, it is very difficult to imagine a grand bargain in which the demands of both sides are ignored.

Still, for the purposes of this analysis we can suspend disbelief and ask what Japan might contribute to a multilateral grand bargain with the DPRK. After all, Japan is working very hard to have its bilateral concerns addressed multilaterally. Moreover, the Pyongyang Declaration does stipulate bilateral agreement on what normalization would require and entail. Prime Minister Koizumi and Chairman Kim agreed that history could be accounted for in actions by both sides (MoFA 2002a):

> Both sides, pursuant to the basic principle that when the bilateral relationship is normalized both Japan and the DPRK would mutually waive all their property and claims and those of their nationals that had arisen from causes which occurred before August 15, 1945.[23]

> With respect to the outstanding issues of concern related to the lives and security of Japanese nationals, the DPRK side confirmed that it would take appropriate measures so that these regrettable incidents, that took place under the abnormal bilateral relationship, would never happen in the future.

And the way to economic cooperation also could be cleared:

> Both sides shared the recognition that, providing economic cooperation after the normalization by the Japanese side to the DPRK side, including grant aids, long-term loans with low interest rates and such assistances as humanitarian assistance through international organizations, over a period of time deemed appropriate by both sides, and providing other loans and credits by such financial institutions as the Japan Bank for International Cooperation with a view to supporting private economic activities, would be consistent with the spirit of this Declaration, and decided that they would sincerely discuss the specific scales and contents of the economic cooperation in the normalization talks.

---

23 This is characterized as a "Provisional Translation." A better translation might be: Both sides, pursuant to the basic principle that the respective governments and their nationals mutually relinquish pre-August 15, 1945, holdings of, and claims on, real and financial assets to achieve normalization of the bilateral relationship, agreed to discuss this issue of settlement of claims in concrete terms in the normalization talks.

These pledges—and the suspension of disbelief—notwithstanding, it remains difficult to 'imagine getting there from here. First of all, despite its labor shortage, Japan is unlikely to allow the resettlement of a massive number of economic refugees as its part of such a six-party grand bargain. Chinese and Southeast Asian migrants have already become a domestic political problem in some areas of Japan. North Korean migrants would make matters even more difficult. Nor will political asylum likely be acceptable grounds for resettlement in Japan.[24]

But what of the promise of increased financial flows? The most likely initial source of such flows would come from DPRK-friendly residents. Although the Chongryun is the most active group doing business with North Korea, its resources are extremely limited, and its political clout has shrunk to near zero. In the event of normalization, Korean residents of Japan will play a much diminished role, largely as go-betweens or facilitators for large firms. Local governments and local business groups in the coastal areas near North Korea, such as Niigata, are expected to increase their trade and investments. But here, too, resources are very limited—and declining. Japanese investors have displayed only limited interest in multilateral regional development programs, such as the Tumen River Area Development Program sponsored by the UN, to develop the border area of China, Russia, and North Korea (Hughes 1999, 133).

Substantive increases in the form of direct investment would have to come from large Japanese firms and financial institutions. But this would depend on two things. First, it would depend upon resolution of the DPRK debt. As noted, North Korea owes Japan more than 100 billion *yen* in unpaid export bills after its default in 1975. If forgiven by the government of Japan and/or picked up by an international financial institution, the path would be cleared for significantly more direct foreign investment. Still, Japanese firms are wary of doing business in North Korea, and they have very attractive alternatives in China and elsewhere.

Given these alternatives, the second barrier—the abduction issue—looms even larger. Although the Japanese government has expended enormous diplomatic effort to place this issue on the six-party table, *Nikkei Shimbun* on 3 October 2003 reported that the Chinese premier, Wen Jiabao, had told Prime Minister Koizumi that China prefers this issue be handled bilaterally between Japan and the DPRK. And, in the absence of economic pressure in the other direction, the political costs of backing away from this issue are growing. On 12 September 2003, *Nikkei Shimbun* reported that Secretary General Abe of the LDP had declared that, if the eight families of the abductees are not allowed to return to Japan, bilateral relations will not be normalized.

---

24 On 11 November 2003, Kyodo News reported that the Ministry of Justice had rejected a recommendation by Tokyo Regional Immigration Bureau to grant asylum to a Korean resident who had been a DPRK spy.

And, in what was the first time a government official had attached a figure to potential levels of Japanese aid to North Korea, Abe added: "If relations are not normalized, then economic assistance of hundreds of billions of *yen* will not flow to North Korea."

Short of normalization—the current sine qua non for any Japanese initiative within a grand bargain—even Japan's tried-and-true tied aid seems a nonstarter. This option—official development assistance to North Korea in an amount equal to the outstanding debt Pyongyang owes to Japanese firms (possibly extended through Japan Bank for International Cooperation/Japan International Cooperation Agency)—could be used to repay long-standing debts and free larger Japanese firms to begin to explore business opportunities in the North, particularly for infrastructure projects. Of course, the Japanese government would also have to reinitiate its trade insurance for Japanese commercial activities in the DPRK, and there is no evidence this program is under active review. Finally, without normalization, there can be no most-favored-nation status, without which DPRK exports would continue to be severely disadvantaged.

Thus, Japan's willingness to participate in a grand bargain is restricted by a number of thorny bilateral issues that remain to be resolved. Japanese-DPRK economic relations remain hostage to political solutions that seem beyond either country's grasp. In the interim, one possible alternative is for Japanese firms to act as a secondary engine, that is, by nesting their investments inside projects negotiated and led by South Korean firms, hardly the first choice for Japanese or Korean interests.[25]

Although there is no question that Japan has an important part to play in any engagement process with North Korea, progress is stymied by difficult bilateral issues, crowned by the thorny problem of the abductees. The now latent Pyongyang Declaration remains an important breakthrough and an important road map for managing historical and debt issues, both of which are prerequisites for normalizing relations. But, as Secretary General Abe of the LDP stated in February 2004 (reported in the *Mainichi Shimbun* on 2 February) after his plan for unilateral economic sanctions against the DPRK became law: "A lack of pressure has resulted in delaying resolution of the abduction issue."

This underscores above all that the problem is not about economics. The question of abductions hangs heavily as a deal breaker over Japanese engagement in any grand bargain. Management of the issue is made more difficult by the emotional involvement of many of Japan's citizens in the fate of the abductees, driven by a genuine sense of horror at the actions of the North Korean government, but also nurtured for political gain by the LDP. While Prime Minister Koizumi's willingness to take risks has had benefits, his use

---

25 Hughes (1999, 134) uses the term secondary engine.

of populist politics is a double-edged sword: it connects to the Japanese people while it simultaneously constrains the ability of Japan's bureaucrats to reach a hard-headed bargain in the national interest.[26]

References

Akaha, Tsuneo. 2002. Japan's Policy toward North Korea: Interests and Options. In *The Future of North Korea*, ed. Akaha Tsuneo, chap. 5. London: Routledge.

Boeicho, ed. 2003. *Heisei 15 Nenban Nippon no Boei: Boei Hakusho* [The defense of Japan 2003: Defense white paper]. Tokyo: Gyosei.

Chongryun. 2004. 21 Seiki: Chosen Soren no Saisei no tame no Teigen [Proposal for the regeneration of Chongryun in the 21st century] (in Japanese). http://www13.plala.or.jp/forum/.

Far Eastern Economic Review (FEER). 2003. 27 March.

Green, Michael J. 2001. *Japan's Reluctant Realism.* New York: Palgrave.

Hiramatsu, Kenji. 2003. Leadup to the Signing of the Pyongyang Declaration. *Gaiko Forum* 2:20–30.

Hughes, Christopher W. 1999. *Japan's Economic Power and Security: Japan and North Korea.* London: Routledge.

Kanter, Arnold. 1998. The Coming North Korean Crisis: Back to the Future? Berkeley: Nautilus Institute for Security and Sustainable Development. www.nautilus.org/fora/security/23A_Kanter.html.

Manyin, Mark E. 2003. Japan-North Korean Relations: Selected Issues. Washington, D.C.: Congressional Research Service. 26 November. http://fpc.state.gov/documents/organization/27531.pdf.

Ministry of Foreign Affairs (MoFA). 2002a. Japan-DPRK Pyongyang Declaration. Tokyo: MoFA. www.mofa.go.jp/region/asia-paci/n_korea/pmv0209/pyongyang.html.

———. 2002b. Outline and Background of Abduction Cases of Japanese Nationals by North Korea. Tokyo: MoFA. www.mofa.go.jp/region/asia-paci/n_korea/abduct.html.

———. 2002c. Twelfth Round of Japan-North Korea Normalization Talks (Evaluation and Outline). Tokyo: MoFA. www.mofa.go.jp/region/asia-paci/n_korea/nt/round12.html

———. 2003a. *Blue Book 2003* (in Japanese), chap. 1, sec. 1. Tokyo: MoFA. www.mofa.go.jp/mofaj/gaiko/bluebook/2003/gaikou/html/honpen/index.html.

---

26 For more on Japanese leadership, see Samuels (2003).

———. 2003b. Japan-China Summit Meeting at the ASEAN+3 Summit Meeting (Summary). Tokyo: MoFA. www.mofa.go.jp/region/asia-paci/asean/pmv0310/china.html.

———. 2003c. Japan-Russia Action Plan. Tokyo: MoFA. www.mofa.go.jp/region/europe/russia/pmv0301/plan.html.

———. 2004a. Japan-North Korea Relations. Tokyo: MoFA. www.mofa.go.jp/region/asia-paci/n_korea/index.html.

———. 2004b. Japan-Russia Relations. Tokyo: MoFA. www.mofa.go.jp/region/europe/russia/index.html.

Murakami, Sadao. 1996. Nitcho Boeki Kandei no 40 Nen. *Chuo Koron* (May).

Samuels, Richard J. 2003. *Machiavelli's Children: Leaders and Their Legacies in Italy and Japan.* Ithaca: Cornell University Press.

Takeuchi, Yukifumi. 2001. International Groups Could Help Pyongyang Reform. Tokyo: Asahi Network. www.asahi.com/english/asianet/report/eng_2001_13.html.

Richard J. Samuels is the Ford International Professor of Political Science at the Massachusetts Institute of Technology (MIT) and Director of the MIT-Japan Program. He is grateful to Llewelyn Hughes for research assistance.

15

China's Role in the Course of North Korea's Transition

Liu Ming

The North Korea (Democratic People's Republic of Korea [DPRK]) nuclear drama offers a good chance for fundamentally curing the North's structural problems and routine crises. All the countries on North Korea's periphery plus the United States have formed a consensus that it is urgent to find a way out of the current North Korean nuclear stalemate, which also touches upon other sectors in North Korea and that country's long-standing concern toward the outside. In other words, any solution to the problem of North Korea needs a kind of comprehensive approach and arrangement or, as called by many Korea experts, a great bargain; economic leverage or incentives will play a significant role.

China has a long history of a client relationship with North Korea; during the current nuclear crisis, it draws the world spotlight through its proactive shuttle diplomacy. If all the participants in the six-party talks—North Korea, South Korea, China, Japan, Russia, and the United States—can finally work out a package of solutions, China must be an indispensable guarantor and a contributor in the implementation process.

Asymmetrical Ties between Beijing and Pyongyang

The status of China-North Korea ties has always been inconclusive and an issue for debate among Korea experts. In fact, their relationship reflects inherent contradictions. Given that China played a significant role in salvaging the DPRK from its total failure in the early period of the Korean War through a million-strong fighting force, its special status in maintaining a quasi alliance (described as being "as close as lips and teeth") with the North since the end of the war on the basis of their same ideology, its continuing exchange and symbolic policy consultation—albeit not too close—with North Korea leaders, and its endless economic assistance to North Korea, many people hold that Beijing's relations with Pyongyang are much closer than any relations North Korea has with any other country in the world. Thus, China has a special influence on the DPRK. As for the tension and bitter feelings toward each other during the mid-1990s: they could be compared with a married couple with many grievances or distrust who still live together under the same roof but in different rooms. They know clearly that a divorce would bring more harm than good to both of them.

Generally speaking, China is North Korea's political and security protector and a long-tested ally; the two countries have indeed managed to maintain their fragile relations without being openly at odds in the face of periodic global and local-environment transformations. Because of its disadvantage and uncertain position in its sense of security on the Korean peninsula, North Korea has to rely on China's and Russia's support; and because of its insufficient energy and food supply and poorly performing economy, North Korea constantly depends for survival on China's and other countries' assistance, although this dependence has been reduced in both absolute and relative terms (Mansourov 2003). As long as Pyongyang's diplomatic, economic, and security maneuvering room is limited or its strategic and political environment has not been greatly turned in its favor, it must regard Beijing as its indispensable patron. In theory, therefore, China could keep a certain degree of its influence over North Korea through the use of specific leverage.

However, the scale of Chinese assistance and China's perceived big-brother position vis-à-vis North Korea do not match its practical role and influence in shaping North Korea policy and behavior. One reason is that Pyongyang is wary of Beijing's international influence, its ability to collaborate with the United States and South Korea, its willingness to foster traditional friendship, and its credibility in fulfilling its commitments to the DPRK in case of crisis. Therefore, both openly and privately, the DPRK will try to limit or downplay China's role and influence during the resolution of the current crisis and as it affects North Korea's future, even though a certain level of involvement for the PRC in tandem with multilateral efforts is reluctantly acknowledged by the DPRK. Pyongyang generally seeks to avoid any linkage between its requests to China for economic aid and China's views on Korean peninsula issues, and to diversify its other potential sources of aid, such as Russia and international organizations. It would also attempt to raise the stakes by balancing its two neighboring giants—China and Russia—against each other (Zong 2003). Because China is aware of North Korean suspicions and perceives the difficulty of influencing the DPRK, China has seldom used its leverage for a political purpose; this in turn restrains China's influence.

The dependence of North Korea on China is not totally one way. Before 1992, China regarded North Korea mainly in political and strategic contexts. After normalization of relations with Seoul, this kind of strategic mentality in China's North Korea policy decreased greatly. To China, North Korea is no longer a necessary buffer between itself and the United States and South

Korea. This does not mean that Beijing considers the DPRK a redundant and unvalued neighboring country even though the DPRK is an economic burden and causes political trouble for China in a certain sense. In the minds of Chinese leaders, a socialist North Korea is instrumental in keeping a balance of power in Northeast Asia and could hinder the trend away from socialism that is spreading across East Asia and that is producing a backlash against Chinese ideological legitimacy (Scobell 2002, 278–9). More important, China is not sure the United States would feel it necessary to develop constructive relations with Beijing if Washington successfully demolishes all the "rogue countries" in the world, including North Korea (Zong 2003). Last but not least, the survival and stability of North Korea amounts to security, peace, and order for the Chinese border area.

Traditional Political Relations in Flux

The astonishingly fast warming of relations between Beijing and Seoul and the death of Kim Il-sung played key roles in cooling down the close China-North Korea relations in the years before 2000. After Kim Jong-il visited Beijing at the end of May 2000, the two sides' relationship gradually warmed up. However, the nuclear crisis and the arrest in China of Yang Bin (immediately after North Korea had announced his appointment as governor of the Sinuiju special administrative region) demonstrated once again the fact that China-DPRK relations are now fragile and can no longer return to their high point of the 1950s and 1960s, when the older generation of leaders was in power. Their traditional close ties are clearly facing unprecedented challenges in both their internal systems and their foreign policies.

Beginning in November of 2002, Chinese fourth-generation leaders came to power, but the new top Chinese leader, Hu Jintao, did not meet Kim Jong-il until April of 2004. Ostensibly, it was not the leaders' intention to disrupt the momentum of the fence-mending process; instead it has been the nuclear issue that keeps them apart, at least at the top leadership level.[1] Hu Jintao must have thought that if he met Kim Jong-il in 2003 at the climax of nuclear deadlock, before all parties concerned could sit down seriously to explore possible outcomes, the meeting would likely have aroused criticism from the United States and other members of the international community for appeasing North Korea, and it would also have made it awkward for the two leaders to touch upon the situation.

---

1 According to some reports, Kim Jong-il planned to visit China at the end of December in 2002 but, because of the nuclear crisis, China declined his visit. Beijing didn't officially admit to such a request, let alone the cancellation; at a regular press conference at China's Ministry of Foreign Affairs on 13 December 2002, spokesperson Liu Jianchao denied a report that Kim Jong-il would visit China. Observers believed, however, that Kim Jong-il would ask for such a visit because he had praised highly the Chinese economic reform and wanted to learn more about it; the nuclear crisis also would push him to seek support of Chinese leaders.

Of course, the exchanges of visits at other levels seem to have continued as usual from 2002 until today. But those formal visits also reflected a kind of dynamic change in the relationship between Beijing and Pyongyang. They were not conducted only to foster traditional friendship. Instead, they were more centered on adjusting relations and on advising North Korea on overall policy transformation and on the nuclear issue.

During the late October 2003 trip to Pyongyang of China's second in command, Wu Bangguo, Wu reiterated the "four points" principles on the development of China-North Korea relations; simplified, the principles are inheriting tradition, facing the future, good-neighborliness and friendship, and strengthening cooperation. These principles are not new in format, but the reinterpretation implies some new directions:

- **Inheriting Tradition** encouraged cherishing and safeguarding their traditions, permitting further expansion.
- **Facing the Future** was designed to let their ties keep abreast of the times, including a focus on peace and development so as to assure vitality and vigor in their relations.
- **Good-Neighborliness and Friendship** demanded understanding and mutual support for each other, attaching importance to issues of concern to both countries as well as addressing these issues.
- **Strengthening Cooperation** highlighted the need to explore how to deepen and expand the cooperation, rendering cooperation more diversified.

From the four points above, we can infer:

- The two countries have not gotten along well in the area of preservation of tradition, such as consultation and coordination between them on important issues. In other words, Beijing wants Pyongyang to pre-notify China more about North Korea's important activities and decisions that relate to international concerns and Chinese interests.

- In the Chinese view, the framework of PRC-DPRK relations, or rather North Korea policy, has not been adapted to the current international situation, and both countries should pursue a common policy that integrates them into the international community on the basis of peaceful diplomacy and cooperation. Their new relations framework should suit the trends of the post–Cold War and post–September 11 worlds.[2]

- North Korea should not always adopt a unilateral policy that endangers China's and other countries' security and interests, and the DPRK

---

2   In 2003, some reports claimed that China was preparing to negotiate with North Korea about the revision of the quasi-military treaty. Chinese officials denied the reports, but some Chinese scholars have encouraged revision of the treaty, which is a by-product of the Cold War (Shen 2003, 57–58).

should understand Chinese concern about dismantling its nuclear program.

- PRC-DPRK economic cooperation should not limit the manner of Chinese official economic assistance. Both sides need to develop new ways to rejuvenate North Korea's economy and reform its system. These include China offering technical and agricultural guidance, introducing reform and market economy transition experiences, diverting official assistance to the commercial cooperation between enterprises in the light of market practice, and collaborating to use international funding and technology for industrial restructuring and infrastructure.

In addition to the adjustment of relations, the nuclear issue almost took up the agendas during the visits by Chinese senior officials and three visits by the DPRK between 2003 and May of 2004. Chinese visits included:

- Vice Premier Qian Qichen flew to Samjiyon on 8–9 March 2003 for discussions with Kim Jong-il to propose three-party talks.
- Vice Foreign Minister Dai Bingguo met Kim Jong-il on 14 July 2003 during arrangements for six-party talks and presented a letter from Hu Jintao.
- Xu Caihou, director of the political department of the Chinese army, on 19–20 August 2003 conversed with Jo Myong-rok, vice chairman of the National Defense Commission of North Korea, and Kim Jong-il about the six-party talks.
- Liu Hongcai, deputy minister of the International Liaison Department of the Chinese Communist Party (CCP) Central Committee, on 19 August 2003 led a party delegation to visit Pyongyang and met with the Korean Workers' Party secretary, Choi Tai-bok, on the nuclear issue.
- Wu Bangguo met with Kim Jong-il on 31 October 2003.
- Wang Yi, vice foreign minister, went to Pyongyang on 25–26 December to discuss with his counterparts details of the next round of six-party talks.
- Hu Jintao secretly sent a Chinese high-level official to Pyongyang in a bid to coordinate with Kim Jong-il over the first six-party talks (this is an unconfirmed report; the visit is said to have taken place soon after Xu Caihou's mid-August 2003 visit).
- Minister of the International Liaison Department of the CCP Central Committee Wang Jiarui on 19 January 2004 met with Kim Jong-il, but the official news agency did not disclose the theme of the talks (they reportedly discussed issues of interest).
- Foreign Minister Li Zhao-xing of China on 23–25 March 2004 visited Pyongyang for talks with Kim Jong-il and other North Korean leaders that covered issues of nuclear plans and Sino-North Korean relations.

On the North Korea side, all of the visits were related to the six-party talks:

- Kim Yong-il, vice foreign minister, visited Beijing on 22–24 November 2003;

- Jo Myong-rok, vice chairman of the DPRK's defense committee, came to China on 2 December 2003; and

- North Korea's deputy foreign minister, Kim Kye-kwan, visited China on 7–9 February 2004 for consultation on the next round of six-party talks.

Intensified problem-solving visits do not mean the two countries have real policy consultations and fundamentally resume closer ties; such visits can possibly indicate just that the nuclear issue has an urgent importance for both of them and other issues of mistrust and resentment have to be covered or shelved. Beijing wants to keep continuous pressure on Pyongyang and keep the ball rolling for multilateral talks. It is perceived that China-North Korea ties have become more complicated since the PRC has given priority to denuclearization on the Korean peninsula in light of questions of strategic balance and consequences; the PRC ostensibly sides with the U.S. position. China also worries that North Korea could move into a more perilous status of resisting the U.S. coercive stance and maneuvering. It is not in the Chinese interest to see the United States toppling the North Korea regime. Thus China-North Korea political relations are restrained by China's concern and anxiety over the nuclear issue. Beijing has begun to use its long-neglected or unwillingly used leverage to influence and shape North Korea's thinking and behavior and to cautiously intervene in North Korea's adventurous policy in the face of escalated tension and a likely showdown during the development of North Korea's next phase.

The nuclear issue does not simply create trouble for relations between the two countries, however; it also produces some positive effects:

- Pyongyang clearly perceives Beijing's uncommon pressure on its recalcitrant position.

- North Korea is showing some flexibility and is listening to Chinese advice to a certain degree, given that the United States has mounted pressure on North Korea without making concessions on the form and content of the talks (so far, Russia and South Korea have been unable to achieve a level of influence comparable with that of China).

- China has begun to reevaluate its policy of negligence toward North Korea, and it has attempted to bolster its substantive influence on the DPRK through increased goodwill, communication through reason and understanding, and certain incentives.[3]

---

3 The press (China Will Offer Free Aid to North Korea—300 million Korea *Won* [30 November 2003], http://chinese.chosun.com) and China's Ministry of Foreign Affairs (www.fmprc.gov.cn) report that to induce North Korea to participate in the next round of six-party talks, China pledged to

As a result, Chinese influence, though not reaching its earlier heights, has rebounded a bit, which can be seen mainly within the limited bounds of the nuclear issue. This was noticed (and reported by Xinhua on 31 October 2003) when North Korean leader Kim Jong-il made an unusual comment in discussing with Wu Bangguo that the two countries' ties had a strategic significance in maintaining peace and stability in Asia. On other occasions of meetings of other senior officials, North Korea also tended to tout its relationship with China, now at a new high since ties worsened in 1992. This shows explicitly the DPRK efforts to ensure Chinese support during the resolution of the nuclear crisis and in case of other conflicts. Beijing also understands, however, that North Korea has its own interests and its own bottom line; North Korea will not give in to U.S. pressure and Chinese persuasion if it does not find a way to reach its basic goals.

Unbalanced and Backward Economic Cooperation

For a long time during the Cold War, China was North Korea's biggest economic supporter; since 1992, however, China's economic assistance to the DPRK has dropped sharply because of China's internal reform, the market orientation of its international relationships, and the soured ties between Beijing and Pyongyang. The scope of PRC-DPRK economic relations is very narrow in comparison with Chinese trade with South Korea, the United States, Japan, Taiwan, and other East Asian regions.

PRC-DPRK economic relations exhibit several characteristics. Following 1992, when China switched from a bilateral barter system to a cash payment system for trade between the two countries, the amount of PRC-DPRK trade declined steadily until recently. With the peak year of 1993 as a frame of reference, the amount of trade dropped from $899 million to $370 million in 1999.[4] In 2000, the situation began to improve a bit: PRC-DPRK trade totaled $488 million, with a growth rate of 31.8 percent in comparison with 1999. In 2001, trade increased again, reaching $739 million, with a growth rate of 51.6 percent. In 2002, trade was maintained at almost the same level, at $738 million, a figure close to the 1993 level. According to a 28 March 2004 announcement by China's Ministry of Commerce (www.mofcom.gov. cn), this growth maintained its momentum in 2003, when the total amount of PRC-DPRK trade reached an astonishing $1.023 billion, up 38.51 percent, which broke down to $628 million in Chinese exports and $395 million in Chinese imports.

---

offer $50 million of additional assistance to the DPRK; Wu Bangguo, chairman of the Chinese People's Congress offered this when he visited Pyongyang in October of 2003. On 13 January 2004, China denied the linkage between the assistance and the talks but confirmed the grant and the ongoing discussion of how to use this amount of money.

4 These 2000 data were from the Web site of China's Ministry of Foreign and Economic Cooperation (www.moftec.gov.cn); the ministry has since been merged into the new Ministry of Commerce.

The reasons for the growth are diverse:

- North Korea's economy has improved a bit, especially after it adopted a reform policy toward wages and prices, loosening control on markets and on border trade with China and Russia. Because its minerals production has recovered considerably, other enterprises that had suspended operations in recent years because of energy shortages resumed production. Therefore North Korea has a few more goods to export and more money to import industry-related or processing materials, which has ended its export decline of the preceding years.[5] The goods North Korea exports to China are mainly minerals, base metals, and wood. According to Chinese businesspeople who trade with their North Korean counterparts in the PRC-DPRK border area, DPRK companies now are able to pay with foreign cash when they purchase goods.

- There are growing numbers of new trading companies and various kinds of enterprises across the DPRK border, which expands the chances and the channels of trade.

- In the years preceding 2002, North Korea imported more food, agricultural goods, and daily necessities, which were sold to North Korea at a relatively low price. But now the DPRK imports more machinery and chemical goods, which are more costly and which could be increasing the total value of trade.

- In 2002, North Korea started to increase its capacity to process on commission, encouraging enterprises to import as many materials as possible to be processed and then reexported, in order to expand the country's processing trade (An 2003, 3). The composition of trade also tells us that China still accounts for a large share of North Korea's exports ($451 million in 2000 and $573 million in 2001); in other words, the improvement in trade is limited, and the prospects are not seen optimistically because the DPRK's consumption capacity is very low, its large trade imbalance is irreversible in the near future, and the market still lacks vitality (An 2003, 3).

Chinese investment in North Korea is also disappointing. At the end of 1999, there were 13 Chinese enterprises in the North, with investments of $2.73 million, but in 2001 China had only two investments in North Korea, totaling $3.95 million (contractual amount). Chinese investments are mainly in equipment, materials, and technical knowledge for restaurants, shops, mineral water production, aquatic breeding, and other light industry. Except for restaurants and shops, China's Ministry of Foreign Trade and Economic Cooperation reports that most of these investments have not been profit-

---

5   In the border city of Dandong, North Korea's exports to China rose to $150 million in 2002, 2.8 times earlier levels, but its imports decreased by 10 percent (An 2003, 2–3).

able. Besides such investments, the economic cooperation centers mainly on labor contracts. At the end of 1999, the cumulative Chinese labor contract value in North Korea was $98.71 million; in 2001, the newly signed labor contract value in North Korea was $32.84 million, turnover was $18.28 million, and the number of laborers in North Korea was 1,485 (MOFCOM 2000).

The causes of the difficulties in China-North Korea economic cooperation are complicated, but the main reason lies in the differing economic systems and North Korea's poor investment environment. The Chinese economy is now market based; no matter whether the enterprise is a state enterprise or a private company, its prime focus is profits, and it requires a partner with good commercial credibility and an economic environment that corresponds to international rules. So far the North Korean economy is still operated under the highly centralized command system, which does not meet minimal commercial requirements for Chinese companies. In addition, there is no evidence indicating that North Korea wants Chinese businesspeople to play an active role in reviving the DPRK's decaying economy through their typical practice of marketing. Given that background, aside from the limited government assistance projects, most Chinese companies would only reluctantly invest their money in North Korea as long as the current status remains. As long as China-North Korea economic cooperation cannot be fully expanded in a profitable way, Chinese businesspeople will remain uninterested in developing economic relations with the North, and it is unlikely that China will play a big role in buoying up North Korea's economy in a commercial way.

In addition to normal economic cooperation, China continues to support massive economic assistance to North Korea, but the amount of this aid is not stable; it fluctuates according to variations in North Korea's shortage of fuel and food, the closeness of their ties, the frequency of the leaders' reciprocal visits, the Chinese premier's personal attitude in pursuing commercial practice in developing external economic relations, China's interest and imperatives in playing a role or exerting specific influence in some cases, and Chinese strategic thinking. In a normal year, China offers 500,000 tons of fuel and provides 500,000 to 600,000 tons of grain (worth approximately $500 million) to North Korea (Liu 2003).[6] China is aware that such free assistance supplies North Korea only minimum sustenance, but it is not helpful for its reform. Should China not provide such assistance, however, the DPRK would likely collapse, which would seriously affect Chinese security and strategic interests. Thus, as long as North Korea is not determined to

---

6 Nemets and Scherer (2003) report that Beijing increased its economic support of Pyongyang following the May 2000 meeting. Exports from China to North Korea—primarily crude oil, oil products, grain and food items—jumped from around $330 million in 1999 to a little more than $450 million in 2000. Chinese imports from North Korea decreased from nearly $42 million to $37 million. Exports minus imports amount to subsidies from Beijing to Pyongyang, and these grew from $288 million to $413 million.

completely change its system and it has not built normal security relations with other countries, China will have to continue this kind of assistance.

Joint Role for China and Surrounding Countries in the "Grand Bargain"

There may be diverse reasons that contribute to the developing nuclear program by North Korea. However from an outside observer's view, the main causes for the DPRK's pursuit of nuclear weapons, which runs counter to the world trend, are the lack of accurate knowledge of world developments and its abnormal relations with the developed countries. These factors lead to an isolated ideology, a shortage of confidence in security, suspicion of the Western world, a policy of brinkmanship, and poor economic performance. Thus, to prod North Korea to fundamentally dismantle its nuclear program and other weapons of mass destruction as well as other conventional threats, we need to not only set up a rigid inspection regime and maintain a strong military deterrence but also arrange a reasonable and attractive multilateral approach to induce North Korea to build its confidence and open its doors to the outside. We should also assist it to revitalize its economy and be engaged with the international community.

A possible "grand bargain" between the multilateral parties and the DPRK for a solution to the North Korea threat would involve two parts. One part concerns terminating all North Korea nuclear and conventional threats in a verifiable and complete approach. The other concerns economic rewards and incentives for North Korea consistent with the progress in addressing part one (O'Hanlon 2003, 5–6). In that grand plan, all five of the other parties should form a unanimous voice and demand what North Korea should implement just as they should have a clear division of labor to carry out inspections, technical work toward dismantlement, and the obligation for sharing the costs of denuclearization and economic assistance to the DPRK.

China's role and its obligation should become an important part of the integral plan:

- China needs to play a role in two aspects of the denuclearized arrangement: one aspect is to serve as an inspector to check the progress of North Korea's implementation of the accord in tandem with the other parties; the other is to take on a role of guarantor for North Korea's security and the U.S. commitment to the North. At this point, Beijing might dilute its role as a mediator and shift to the multilateral common position. Because the deal would likely be a phased process, China's role should stand out at each stage and press North Korea to faithfully follow the designed procedures as well as urge the United States to take prescribed actions as an incentive. In the midst of the implementation, if there appears some friction, frustration, or misunderstanding between the DPRK and the United States, China will need to find a way to iron out the difference by persuasion, explanation, and sometimes by strong joint action or unilateral compensation and symbolic placation.

- To reduce the buildup of North Korea's conventional forces and to build confidence, China can also play a positive role, but this may be a bit different from that of the allied countries. Beijing would support in principle the same proportional cuts in North Korean, South Korean, and U.S. weaponry and forces (O'Hanlon 2003, 6–8). However, given the facts that the DPRK's weapons are quite outdated and of low quality and that the United States has reinforcement forces in the other parts of the western Pacific, the proposed reduction in quantity would not be acceptable to North Korea. North Korea would surely demand that the United States withdraw certain types of advanced weapons from the Korean peninsula or that South Korea dismantle some of its modern equipment, or it could propose an asymmetrical reduction that takes the unbalanced military capabilities on both sides of the DMZ into account, which would allow the DPRK to reserve more forces and some offensive weapons. The PRC would not side completely with the North's positions but would show understanding toward the DPRK's security vulnerabilities, hoping the United States and South Korea give North Korea a bit of advantage in the numbers of forces and weapons.

- On the political level, China has several missions. One is to do its utmost to push forward inter-Korean reconciliation and cooperation during meetings with Kim Jong-il and other DPRK leaders; this means particularly urging Chairman Kim to make a reciprocal visit to Seoul after a nuclear deal is reached if the atmosphere in South Korea is amicable. Another is to encourage Washington and Tokyo to adopt conciliatory stances to engage North Korea and solve the major pending issues by bold and flexible action in order to achieve normalization. China should also offer practical advice to North Korea on how China has been able to maintain political stability while fully opening its doors to the world and integrating itself with the global economy and international standards. In view of North Korea's concern about its security, political stability, independence, and dignity in undertaking reform and developing cooperative relations with the Western countries, China would likely continue to provide political support for North Korea in a symbolic and substantive way.

- China needs to gradually or partly transform its traditional bilateralism to deal with North Korea in a multilateral setting for economic cooperation; that is, China should move a portion of its routine assistance to North Korea to a multilateral package deal. This could serve four purposes: adding the strength of developing a common position among surrounding countries; linking China's contribution with a multilateral arrangement, thereby gaining the lion's share of economic reconstruction projects in DPRK; rendering North Korea's behavior and survival subject to international economic cooperation; and mitigating China's dilemma in dealing with North Korea's endless demands for economic assistance during crisis or other economic difficulties.[7]

- China, together with South Korea and other countries, should help North Korea join several key international financial organizations. China also could share with the DPRK its experiences with the procedures and qualifications to join the World Bank, the International Monetary Fund (IMF) and the Asian Development Bank. As a full member of these three international financial institutions (IFIs) and as a transitional country that not long ago moved from a planned economy to a market economy, China is quite aware of North Korea's problems and how North Korea could make efforts to solve them. Beijing could provide some useful advice to Pyongyang, urging it to take concrete measures to adapt to the requirements of these international bodies and make full preparations for the time when the United States is ready to strike the DPRK from its terrorist list. In the meantime, China can join with South Korea to press the United States and Japan to accelerate the process of handling North Korea's applications for the international banks and IMF. Only when Pyongyang fully enters international financial organizations and develops economic relations with the rest of the world on the basis of international commercial norms will North Korea be able to consider forgoing its isolated ideology and military-first strategy. China already has an ambitious plan to first draw the DPRK into the organization on Asia-Pacific Economic Cooperation (APEC), in which North Korea could work together with members of the various working groups on topics such as agricultural technical cooperation and industrial science and technology. Furthermore, the Shanghai APEC Finance and Development Program and the APEC School in China also could train North Korean financial officials and organize study groups to address urgent economic issues suggested by North Korea.[8]

- China wants to continue all levels of contact with North Korea's officials, officers, artists, scholars, correspondents, and ordinary people in order to make clear the achievements of its reforms and help North Koreans know more about the outside world. It would be worthwhile for China to set up more fellowship programs for North Korean young people and middle-level officials. Some prominent Chinese institutions

---

7   Some expect that rebuilding the DPRK will fall largely to the ROK because it has the deepest pockets and the PRC and Russia have less interest in paying for extensive redevelopment. This is not true for China because Beijing already contributes a great deal of money to North Korea. If the prospects are clear that North Korea will reform and open its doors on the basis of international standards, Chinese entrepreneurs would actively invest in the DPRK (Brooke 2003, W1).

8   The Finance and Development Program was founded in the State Accounting School in Pudong, Shanghai; it is now part of the Chinese central government.

and universities have already begun such educational courses for North Koreans; for example, the Shanghai Academy of Social Sciences admitted two batches of North Korea study groups—three scholars in each team—in 2002 and 2003. And the PRC would also like to keep providing free sanatoriums to delegations of North Korean officers.

With regard to North Korea's economic system and situation, the Chinese contribution may focus on the following:

- Both China and South Korea could advise North Korea to continue its financial reforms and price reforms, but it should make use of more sophisticated calculations, moderate steps, and a long-term blueprint based on a market orientation while it maintains party leadership on macroeconomic management and policy guidance. China and South Korea should encourage North Koreans to explore all possibilities for better living and increased wealth by best using their distinct wisdom, specialties, and materials available throughout the country, which would certainly revitalize the DPRK's overall economic atmosphere and expand the size of its markets. They should also urge the DPRK to loosen its grip on contacts between the North Korean people and foreigners and on restrictions on foreigners traveling to the DPRK.

- Recognizing the scarcity of capital for infrastructure construction in North Korea, China could introduce to North Korea three concepts, or financing modalities, that were used successfully in Chinese infrastructure development—lease on batches; differential ground rent, and building operation transfer. If North Korea can agree to lease some pieces of land in the coastal areas to foreign companies for dozens of years, it could not only receive back a great deal of developed land after a certain time but also could obtain sufficient capital for infrastructure in the other areas. All the land should be leased on the basis of differential ground rent, in other words, the amount of rent should be decided according to the distance from the urban area and the potential for commercial development of the land. The need for infrastructure for South Korean companies that invest in North Korea could be handled by Chinese, South Korean, and European joint ventures if they are allowed by the DPRK to operate the finished projects for a period of years to retrieve the yields.

- China and South Korea could collaborate in other ways to help salvage North Korea's economy. Because Pyongyang is unable to join the IFIs and receive concessional loans in a short time, China and South Korea can consider organizing several consortia to finance companies investing in North Korea and develop some badly needed joint projects there.[9] For

---

9 Two South Korean scholars (Chae and Zang 2001) propose an Interim North Korea Development Assistance Group (INKDAG).

example, they can jointly explore oil in the East Sea and natural gas in Russian Siberia, extending to North Korea the joint China-South Korea-Russia-Japan natural gas pipeline. The funding could come from government donations as well as a specific bond issued by the DPRK government and the consortium.

- China and South Korea also could set up training schools in various parts of China to teach North Korean officials and scholars as well as managers and technicians about international law, business management, finance, agriculture technology, and the methods and rules of negotiation with foreign companies and IFIs for business agreements. Furthermore, China and South Korea could jointly or separately dispatch farming experts to North Korea to alleviate its agricultural problem; they could help to improve seeds, ameliorate soil problems, select the best plants to grow, and breed aquatic products (certain plants and aquatic products are suitable for export in the international market and could be exchanged for needed food). China and South Korea also could help North Korea remold old industrial facilities and relink the Kyongui rail line, which could finally connect Europe to China by rail.[10]

- China is concerned about gambling, money laundering, and the impact on Chinese border management of the Sinuiju Special Autonomous Region (SAR). If the countries involved in the six-party talks can reach a package deal—agreement on the nuclear issue, DPRK agreement to a reform policy, and with all parties to the talks willing to assist the DPRK with its reforms—and if the DPRK changes the focus of its economic development efforts in the Sinuiju SAR, China would be willing to consult with North Korea about the design and development of the Sinuiju SAR and would like to actively participate in its development. It might even evolve into a large free economic zone that includes Dandong, a Chinese border city.

All Chinese contributions and efforts should be carried out through consultations with North Korea and on the basis of the DPRK's policy alternatives. Before the DPRK makes decisions on reform, the PRC should avoid advising it to take any specific road or make any radical suggestions.

---

10 The South Korean National Institute of Territory reports that the connection of the Kyongui rail line with the Chinese border city of Dandong and then with Russia's railways will divert passengers and cargo (which usually arrive and depart Shenyang and Beijing through the ports of Dalian and Tianjin) from ships to railroads. The Busan-Shenyang line could become an optimal tool to facilitate Northeast Asian economic cooperation. This rail line would divert 32 percent of the passengers from the Seoul-Beijing air route and 27.1 percent of the passengers from the Beijing-Seoul air route (An 2002).

Conclusion

The nuclear crisis offers a chance for China to increase its influence on North Korea and adjust its traditional relations with and approach to the North. But China's role in North Korea's nuclear issue is limited because North Korea has its own interests and China does not want to let North Korea collapse. More important, current China-North Korea ties are not particularly good and the level of trust is not great, and North Korea especially wants to obtain U.S. rewards. If the United States and North Korea reach an agreement on a comprehensive plan, it could broaden China's role and allow China to fully explore its potential to help North Korea feel secure, confident, and outward looking enough to finally reform its system and revitalize its malfunctioning economy. North Korea must be determined to carry out its reforms, and the United States must be flexible enough to adjust its policies.

References

An, Zhenli. 2002. Lianjichaxianbandaozhiyaoutilu: yiyijiduicexianze (Connection of Korean peninsula and Euro-Asia railway: Implications and options). Paper presented at the conference, "Promoting the Korean Peninsula and Northeast Asian Cooperation," jointly sponsored in Beijing by the Institute of Asia-Pacific Studies, the Chinese Academy of Social Sciences, and the Korea Economic Institute of America, 7–8 June.

An, Zhenli. 2003. Recovery amid Adjustment: Observing North Korea Economy Trend from China-North Korea Economic Exchange. Paper presented at a seminar at Fudan University, summer.

Brooke, James. 2003. Quietly, North Korea Opens Markets. *New York Times,* 19 November.

Chae, Su-chan and Zang Hyoung-soo. 2001. Creating an Interim North Korea Development Assistance Group. Paper presented at the conference, "North Korea in the World Economy," Korea-America Economic Association and the William Davidson Institute at the University of Michigan Business School, Washington, D.C., 26–28 August.

Liu, Ming. 2003. China and the North Korean Crisis: Facing Test and Transition. *Pacific Affairs* 76:3.

Mansourov, Alexandre. 2003. Giving Lip Service with an Attitude: North Korea's China Debate. San Francisco: Nautilus Institute. December. www.nautilus.org/DPRKBriefingBook//china/Mansourov_DPRKChinaDebate.html.

Ministry of Commerce (MOFCOM). 2000. Beijing: MOFCOM (formerly Ministry of Foreign Trade and Economic Cooperation). www.moftec.gov.cn (accessed in 2000).

Nemets, Aleksandr, and John L. Scherer. 2003. Fair Comment: U.S. Must Stand Its Ground on the Korean Peninsula. *Insight on the News.* 7 July. www.insightmag.com/news/446179.html.

O'Hanlon, Michael E. 2003. A "Master Plan" to Deal with North Korea. Policy Brief no. 114. Washington, D.C.: Brookings Institution. January. www.brook.edu/comm/policybriefs/pb114.htm.

Scobell, Andrew. 2002. China and North Korea: The Close but Uncomfortable Relationship. *Current History.* September.

Shen, Ji-ru. 2003. Weihu Dongbeiyaanquandedangwuzhiji (The urgency for safeguarding Northeast Asia Security—Curbing the dangerous game on the North Korea nuclear issue). *Journal of World Economy and Politics* (in Chinese) 9.

Zong, Hairen. 2003. Hu Jintao Writes to Kim Jong-il to Open Door to Six-Party Talks. *Hong Kong Economic Journal* (Hong Kong hsin pao) (in Chinese), 28 August. Cited in Special Report, Northeast Asia Peace and Security Network. San Francisco: Nautilus Institute. 5 September 2003. www.nautilus.org.

Liu Ming is with the Shanghai Academy of Social Sciences.

16

Russian–North Korean Relations and the Prospects for Multilateral Conflict Resolution on the Korean Peninsula

Alexandre Y. Mansourov

Russia fought two limited wars against Pacific powers on the Korean peninsula: first against Japan in 1904–05 and then against the United States and its overseas allies 50 years later, in 1950–53. Both times Russia suffered considerable setbacks and failed to achieve its primary goal: keeping the peninsula free of the expanding maritime influences hostile to Russia's continental power.

Now, at the dawn of the new millennium, Korea is faced with the possibility of another major geopolitical shock, namely the upcoming unification of the peninsula. Obviously, such a radical transformation of the existing political and socioeconomic frameworks cannot leave Russia uninterested and passive (even despite its lingering internal woes) and is sure to focus Russian attention on peninsular affairs once again. How does a reborn Russia—itself in transition to democracy and open markets—react to the simmering North Korean nuclear crisis and the intensifying inter-Korean reconciliation? Will Russia try to influence these developments in the direction of favoring Russian national interests? Will Moscow sit on the sidelines as it did in the 1990s, or will it actively participate in shaping the future of the Korean nation as it used to do during Soviet times? Will the Kremlin prefer the application of force, as in the past, or creative peaceful diplomacy?

Some Generalizations about Russian Policy Approaches to Korea

First, the Korean peninsula tends to occupy a secondary place in the Russian Far Eastern policy that places its primary emphasis on relations with the regional heavyweights—the People's Republic of China (PRC), Japan, and the United States. Russian-Korean relations are often subordinate to broader goals and depend on the dynamics of Russian relations with other regional powers. Historically, Russian national interests in Korea tend to be strategic in nature, rather than economic. At present, the meteoric rise of China, economic decline and remilitarization of Japan, and U.S. global hegemony inevitably shape the Northeast Asian geopolitical context within which Russian policy toward the Korean peninsula has to be formulated.

Second, as a rule, Korean affairs tend to be handled primarily by the department-level bureaucrats within the Ministry of Foreign Affairs and the Ministry of Defense and by trade officials. Rarely is an issue of Korean policy brought to the attention of national leadership or made a subject of domestic political debate. Hence, policy breakthroughs are rare, and policy innovations tend to be incremental and slow. Three glaring exceptions to this rule were Stalin's personal role in decision making regarding the Korean War in 1950–53, Gorbachev's personal involvement in the normalization of Soviet-Republic of Korea (ROK) relations in 1989–90, and President Putin's personal diplomacy with Kim Jong-il in 2000–02.

Third, by and large, Russian policy toward Korea has always been passive, reactive, and rather cautious; the exception was Stalin's underwriting of Kim Il-sung's Korean War initiative. Since the collapse of the Soviet Union, a dramatic decline in Russian conventional military capabilities in the Far East and Russia's military preoccupation with the extremist Islamic terrorist threat in the South (emanating from the Caucasus and Central Asia) have contributed to further moderation of Russian foreign policy goals on the Korean peninsula. Russia's foreign policy goals vis-à-vis Korea are fundamentally and essentially conservative, status quo oriented, and consensus seeking.

Fourth, the geopolitical concerns, ruling ideologies, and political affinities of governing regimes tend to play a relatively larger role in Russian policy toward the Koreas than the consideration of Russian economic interests or humanitarian concerns. Moreover, currently unresolved mutual debt issues and the increasing fragility of the Russian Far East and its economy, stemming from progressive depopulation and deindustrialization, perennial economic crises, rampant local corruption and crime, and the looming threat of political disintegration in the past decade, tend to undermine the languid central government efforts aimed at encouraging cross-border and regional economic cooperation between the Russian Far Eastern provinces and the two Korean states.

One of the leading indications of renewed Russian positive interest in Korean affairs was the first-ever official state visit paid by the Russian president, Vladimir V. Putin, to the Democratic People's Republic of Korea (DPRK) on 19–20 July 2000. In the centuries-old history of bilateral Russian-Korean relations, the Russian czars refused to notice this proud, tiny hermit kingdom on the remote border of the Russian Far East. The Soviet Communist leaders loved to pamper the North, whereas the first post-Communist Russian rulers despised and isolated it. Hence, Putin's Pyongyang trip was an accomplishment of historical significance, unimaginable even during the glorious years of the tight USSR-DPRK military alliance during the 1940s–80s, not to mention the decade of mutual Russian–North Korean abandonment and estrangement in the 1990s.

Summit Diplomacy in the 2000s

At the onset of the third millennium, a new political leadership in the Kremlin, headed by a young, dynamic, and pragmatic premier-elected-president, Vladimir V. Putin, decided to capitalize on all the positive changes that had been accumulated in Russian-DPRK relations since 1996 and opened a new era in state-to-state relations between the two countries. After several delays and exhaustive diplomatic consultations, the Russian foreign minister, Igor S. Ivanov, visited Pyongyang on 9–10 February 2000 and signed a new bilateral Treaty on Friendship, Good-Neighborliness, and Cooperation to replace the defunct USSR-DPRK alliance treaty of 1961.[1] The conclusion of the new treaty ensures the continuity of traditional friendship; takes into account the national interests of both countries; and provides a contemporary legal framework for further development of Russian-DPRK relations on the basis of new principles of equality, state sovereignty, territorial integrity, non-interference in domestic affairs, good-neighborliness, and mutually beneficial cooperation.

The Pyongyang Summit

To cement a new phase in Russian-DPRK relations and open new constructive possibilities for Russia to participate in the international peaceful resolution of the Korean problem and other issues of multilateral concern in Northeast Asia, President Putin led an official state delegation[2] to visit the DPRK on 19–20 July 2000.[3] The visit came a month after the historic inter-Korean summit in Pyongyang on 13–15 June. This was the first official visit by any Soviet or Russian head of state to North Korea. President Putin was also the first foreign leader to visit Pyongyang at the invitation of General Secretary Kim Jong-il since 1994.

---

1   The Russian State Duma ratified the new treaty by the overwhelming majority of 363 votes on 19 July 2000. The Russian Federation Council approved of this ratification on 26 July 2000. President Putin signed the law on the ratification of this treaty on 5 August 2000 (MOFA 2000).

2   The official delegation included Deputy Prime Minister I. I. Klebanov, Foreign Minister I. S. Ivanov, Defense Minister I. D. Sergeyev, First Deputy Director of the Presidential Office D. A. Medvedev, Deputy Director of the Presidential Office S. E. Prukhodko, Minister of Education V. M. Filippov, General Director of the Federal Governmental Agency of Communications and Information (directly under the president) V. G. Matyukhin, chief delegate of the president of the Russian Federation to the Far East District K. B. Pulikovsky, Governor of the Maritime Territory E. I. Nazdratenko, member of the State Duma of the Russian Federation Yu. M. Jong, and the Russian ambassador to the DPRK, V. I. Denisov.

3   Contrary to some news reports, the initiative for the visit originated in Russia. In late April 2000, the Kremlin used diplomatic channels to indicate to Pyongyang that if Kim Jong-il invited President Putin, he would accept the invitation and travel to the DPRK in the summer of 2000. Kim sent a hand-written invitation to Putin, and the Russian president said yes.

At Pyongyang Sunan Airport, General Secretary Kim Jong-il, together with high-ranking officials of the Korean Workers' Party (KWP), the DPRK government, and the Korean People's Army (KPA), warmly greeted the Russian leader.[4] Tens of thousands of Pyongyang residents turned out at the airport with the flags of the two countries and bouquets in their hands to greet the guests from Russia.

Putin and Kim Jong-il had two rounds of summit talks at the Paekhwawon State Guesthouse in Pyongyang. At the talks, "both sides informed each other of the situation in their countries, had an exhaustive and in-depth exchange of opinions on further expanding and developing bilateral friendly and cooperative relations and a series of issues of mutual concern, and reached a consensus of views on all the matters discussed (KCNA 2000a)." Ministerial-level talks were also held between the two sides. Both sides discussed matters of mutual concern in such fields as foreign trade, economic cooperation, education, forestry, and military affairs. President Putin invited General Secretary Kim Jong-il to visit Russia at an appropriate time, and the invitation was accepted with gratitude.

After successfully completing the summit talks, the DPRK and Russia issued an 11-point joint declaration (KCNA 2000b), in which Pyongyang and Moscow vowed to strengthen the traditional relations of friendship, good-neighborliness, mutual trust, and multilateral cooperation.[5] Describing the meeting and talks in Pyongyang as a "landmark event" in the history of friendly relations between the two countries, the KWP official newspaper, *Rodong Sinmun,* on 20 July 2000 said that "the declaration demonstrated each other's desire to strengthen the traditional relations of friendship, good-neighborliness, mutual trust, and multilateral cooperation and to make positive efforts for disarmament and global stability and security against all the policies of aggression and war." But, more important, President Putin was able to develop a good personal rapport with Kim Jong-il and referred to his counterpart as a very intelligent, pragmatic, and rational leader, "the man with whom one can deal."

---

4 The official DPRK delegation at the summit talks comprised Kim Yong-nam, president of the Presidium of the DPRK Supreme People's Assembly; Jo Myong-rok, director of the General Political Department of the KPA, who is also first vice-chairman of the DPRK National Defense Commission; Kim Yong-chun, chief of the General Staff of the KPA, who is also a member of the DPRK National Defense Commission; Kim Il-chol, minister of the People's Armed Forces, who is also vice-chairman of the DPRK National Defense Commission; Jon Pyong-ho, member of the DPRK National Defense Commission and secretary of the KWP Central Committee; Choe Thae-bok, chairman of the DPRK Supreme People's Assembly; Choe Yong-rim, prosecutor-general of the Central Public Prosecutor's Office; Kim Kuk-thae and Kim Yong-sun, secretaries of the KWP Central Committee; Paek Nam-sun, minister of foreign affairs; Pak Ui-chun, DPRK ambassador to Russia; and additional leading officials of party, armed forces, and power institutions, commissions and ministries of the cabinet, and national institutions.

5 In a symbolic gesture of reaffirmation of traditional Russian-North Korean friendship, on 20 July 2000, President Putin and General Secretary Kim Jong-il laid a wreath before the Liberation Tower and observed a moment of silence in memory of the soldiers of the Soviet army who had fallen in sacred battles for the liberation of Korea in August 1945.

Russia expressed its support for the North Korean position, stressing the need to resolve the question of Korean reunification independently by Koreans themselves in a peaceful and democratic manner. Moscow and Pyongyang reiterated the shared belief that the outside powers concerned should support but refrain from intervention in this process of Korean reconciliation. President Putin confirmed his support for the 15 June North-South Joint Declaration and promised to work toward ensuring a peaceful reunification of the divided peninsula. In their joint statement, the two leaders expressed their opposition to Washington's national missile defense plans and theater missile defense plans, saying that U.S. concerns about a possible threat from Pyongyang were "groundless." The joint declaration stated that the DPRK's missile program "does not pose any threat to anybody but is purely peaceful in its nature." Moreover, Kim Jong-il indicated to President Putin that the DPRK was willing to forfeit further development of its intercontinental ballistic missiles if the United States and other countries concerned were to agree to assist Pyongyang in its space exploration efforts and in its plans to launch two or three North Korean satellites per year at their expense. In a sense, in his conversations with Putin, the DPRK leader outlined a framework for a possible new deal between Pyongyang and Washington, which could settle the so-called North Korean missile question.

The Moscow Summit

Kim Jong-il made a return visit to Russia from 26 July to 18 August 2001, traveling more than 20,000 km in his personal armored train from the Russian-DPRK border at Khasan to St. Petersburg on the Baltic Sea and back. An official state visit in Moscow took place on 4–5 August 2001. This landmark journey[6] dramatically improved Kim Jong-il's and the North Korean elite's perceptions of Russia, its new generation of reformist leaders, and its struggling peoples, as well as increased their understanding of Russian institutional reforms and socioeconomic and political changes unfolding in the country. The coverage of the visit in the world media lifted somewhat the dark veil over the personality of Kim Jong-il and considerably improved his image in the world.[7] The fact that Kim (the "Dear Leader") felt confident enough to leave his country for a whole month and even celebrate its official

6   Kim Jong-il said that the purpose of the journey was "not to discuss the railway question, which is a technical problem for specialists to resolve," but to observe how the Russian Far East, Siberia, Moscow, and St. Petersburg have changed since his previous trip to what was then the Soviet Union, more than 40 years ago (Pulikovsky 2002, 47). Some experts also stress the symbolic significance of the train trip and its similarity with Kim Il-sung's six-week travel to the Soviet bloc in the summer of 1984. Kim Il-sung's 1984 rail trip is credited with launching a period of warmer relations and increased aid from Moscow in the mid-1980s. In the same vein, Kim Jong-il's rail trip in 2001 is credited with improving Russian-DPRK relations in the 2000s.

7   The best account of Kim Jong-il's visit to Russia in summer 2001 is Pulikovsky (2002). Konstantin Pulikovsky, plenipotentiary representative of the president of the Russian Federation to the Far Eastern District of Russia, was President Putin's personal envoy escorting Kim Jong-il on his train during his month-long journey across Russia.

Liberation Day of 15 August in a foreign land was further proof that he was firmly in control of his government, enjoyed total popular support, and did not fear opposition challenges while he was away.

Summit talks at the Kremlin on 4 August 2001 covered global politics and various bilateral relations in the Asia-Pacific, prospects for bilateral trade and military-technical cooperation, the question of linking the Trans-Korean railways (TKR) with the Trans-Siberian Railway (TSR), Russian commercial use of the port of Rajin, and many other important issues. In the end, President Putin and Chairman Kim Jong-il signed an eight-point joint declaration.

The Moscow Declaration stated the two countries' belief in the rule of international law, the principle of equality of states, and the leading role of the United Nations in world affairs. Against the background of escalating tensions in U.S.-DPRK relations caused by President George W. Bush's inclusion of North Korea in the so-called axis of evil in January 2001, the Moscow Declaration stressed the need to resolve international disputes by political means, through negotiations on the basis of nonconfrontation; and it underlined the right of every state to an "equal degree of security," regardless of its size or political system. Both sides agreed to join efforts to combat international terrorism and militant separatism. Pyongyang reiterated its support for Russia's position on the Anti-Ballistic Missile Treaty "as a cornerstone of strategic stability" in exchange for Russian welcome of the DPRK's position on its missile program, which "has peaceful character and does not pose a threat to any country that respects the sovereignty of the DPRK."

Moscow welcomed the North-South 15 June declaration and all related inter-Korean agreements, and promised to continue to play a "constructive and responsible role in positive processes on the Korean peninsula." Both sides warned against any external obstructions to the process of inter-Korean reconciliation. A real breakthrough for Pyongyang was Moscow's unexpected expression of understanding for the clarification of the DPRK's official position on the U.S. military presence in Korea, namely that "the withdrawal of the U.S. troops from South Korea is an urgent problem that must be resolved without delay in the interests of maintaining peace and security on the Korean peninsula and Northeast Asia" (paragraph eight). Russia stressed the need to provide for peace and security on the peninsula by "nonmilitary means." The declaration did not mention the nuclear question, which was supposed to have been resolved by the U.S.-DPRK implementation of the 1994 Geneva Agreed Framework. Russia welcomed the process of normalization of relations between the DPRK and the United States and Japan.

As for the future of bilateral relations, the Moscow Declaration emphasized the "deep historical roots of traditional Korean-Russian relations of friendship and cooperation" (paragraph three) and highlighted significant progress made in resolving a number of pressing bilateral economic problems, including Pyongyang's official recognition of its past debts to the former Soviet Union, the desirability of third-party (in other words, ROK) financing of certain joint projects involving the reconstruction and modernization of the old Soviet-built electric power stations in the North, and, finally, the principle of mutual profitability during the construction of the TKR-TSR railway transport corridor connecting South Korea, North Korea, Russia, and Europe.

In sum, when Kim Jong-il was commenting in private on the significance of the Moscow Declaration, he reportedly said, "These days, people like to talk about 'partnerships,' 'strategic partnerships,' and so on. Foreign news media noticed that there was no reference to 'strategic partnership' between us. But I told President Putin that we did not need to come up with any term of that kind, because all that was about diplomacy, whereas what we needed was sincerity. And he agreed with me. I do not want to be a 'partner,' because between friends we do not call each other 'partners' (Pulikovsky 2002, 41–2)."

Moreover, when Kim Jong-il was passing through Moscow on his way back from St. Petersburg to the North, President Putin unexpectedly invited him for a last-minute lunch at his private residence at the Kremlin, on 8 August 2001. That private lunch with Putin's family reportedly made quite a difference in further improving Kim Jong-il's perceptions of Russia and its young, innovative leader. What both leaders had in common was the desire to build a powerful and prosperous nation for their respective peoples in a rather hostile international environment. They developed a great deal of personal chemistry, mutual respect, and understanding. Some even say that they became "true friends." Kim Jong-il summed it up as follows: "When people treat me in a diplomatic fashion, I become a diplomat myself. In contrast, Putin was very straightforward with me, and I opened my soul to him (Pulikovsky 2002, 46)." In general, the Dear Leader was very satisfied with the journey, which definitely cleared up many misunderstandings and misperceptions about Russia and its policies in his mind.

Some Russian analysts believe that the wealth of information gathered and lessons learned by Kim Jong-il and his entourage during his first journey across Russia provided the foundation for the July 2002 policy decisions announced in Pyongyang, such as partial liberalization of prices and wages, marketization of services and utilities, introduction of partial convertibility of the *won* currency, and relaxation of labor-market controls. They interpreted those "economic improvement measures" emanating from Pyongyang not as the initiation of Chinese-style market-oriented reforms but as the North Korean government's attempt to make a quantum leap from the Brezhnev-style redistributional socialism of the 1970s to the Gorbachev-style perestroika of the late 1980s–early 1990s in the former Soviet Union (Alexeyev 2002). Although North Koreans continued to view the Gorbachev period in Soviet history with a great deal of negativity, Russians began to regard Kim Jong-il as the North Korean statesman-reformer, much like Mikhail Gorbachev.

The Vladivostok Summit

On 20–24 August 2002, Kim Jong-il again traveled by train around the Russian Far East,[8] specifically to the cities of Khabarovsk and Komsomolsk-upon-Amur. On 23 August 2003, he held a third summit meeting and had a private dinner with President Putin in Vladivostok.[9]

During his second visit to Russia, Kim Jong-il met many Russian provincial and local government officials, private businesspeople, and defense industry managers; he was very interested in further studying the positive and negative sides of ongoing Russian economic and political reforms. He paid special attention to the so-called Russian model of transition toward market economy, defense industry conversion, and market adjustments in the Russian military-industrial complex. Russian analysts believe that in 2004 the DPRK government will continue the country's economic reforms, especially in its military-industrial complex, following some of the lessons learned during Kim's 2002 trip to the Russian Far East.

From a geopolitical standpoint, the Dear Leader may have played a Russian card again. By postponing his scheduled PRC trip and inserting instead an unplanned visit to the Russian Far East in his "busy calendar" at the last minute, the Dear Leader may have tried to demonstrate to the PRC, considered by many the main sponsor of the DPRK in the international arena, that Pyongyang does have a Russian alternative. The intent may have been to put in doubt any exclusive status for Beijing in Korean affairs and, perhaps, to push Beijing to increase its economic assistance to North Korea and to intensify its political support for Pyongyang to counter worsening DPRK-U.S. relations. Bearing in mind President Putin's words at a news conference after the summit that "Russia must build the TKR for the simple reason that if it does not, then our dear friend China would do it," one may speculate that Kim Jong-il may have attempted to stimulate traditional Russian-Chinese contradictions on the Korean peninsula by playing Russia off against China on the railway issue.

At the summit, President Putin is said to have assured Kim Jong-il that Moscow would not support any U.S. efforts to impose a so-called Iraqi scenario on its North Korean neighbor, and that Russia would not join any anti-DPRK international coalition. Moreover, Russia would try to help the DPRK distance itself from the so-called axis of evil and extricate itself from its U.S.-

---

8   During his 2002 journey to Russia, Kim Jong-il was accompanied by Kim Yong-chun, a member of the National Defense Commission (NDC) and chief of the general staff of the KPA; Yon Hyong-muk, member of the NDC; Kim Yong-sun, secretary of the KWP Central Committee; Kang Sok-ju, first vice minister of foreign affairs; Pak Nam-gi, chairman of the State Planning Commission; Kim Yong-sam, minister of railways; and Jang Song-thaek and Ju Kyu-chang, first vice department directors of the KWP Central Committee.

9   The summit idea was discussed and agreed upon during the visit of the Russian foreign minister, Igor Ivanov, to Pyongyang on 29 July 2002. Kim Jong-il held talks with Ivanov for several hours, during which he described in great detail the economic reforms unfolding in the DPRK. They also exchanged views on outstanding issues of regional security and of bilateral concern (Alexeyev 2002).

sponsored international isolation. Further, the Vladivostok summit allowed Kim Jong-il to regain the initiative in inter-Korean relations—an initiative that was frozen as a result of the June 2002 naval clashes in the Yellow Sea—and to revive the discussions about the railway reconnection project. Moreover, President Putin is rumored to have encouraged Kim Jong-il to invite Prime Minister Koizumi of Japan to Pyongyang and make necessary concessions in order to normalize the DPRK-Japanese relations for the sake of future prosperity of the North Korean people and peace and stability in Northeast Asia.

Kim Jong-il's second Russia trip cemented propitious conditions for an unprecedented upswing in DPRK-Russian interstate and political relations. Even during the decades of fraternal friendship that was based on socialist internationalism, North Korean and Soviet leaders did not enjoy the high degree of interpersonal trust and credibility that President Putin and Chairman Kim appear to share these days.

The North Korean leader currently demonstrates a marked warmth and a special attentiveness to Russia. Since the beginning of 2003, he has frequently met with the Russian ambassador, Andrei A. Karlov, in a very cordial atmosphere[10] and has held more than a dozen prolonged conversations with high-ranking officials from Russia's Ministry of Foreign Affairs, including Deputy Foreign Minister Losyukov and senior diplomats at the Russian embassy in Pyongyang. The North Korean leaders appreciate the fact that President Putin alone continues to communicate personally and deal with them directly on the basis of equality, sincerity, and mutual respect, despite the increasing anti-DPRK international campaign sponsored by the United States to fight "rogue states" and other members of the axis of evil.

At long last, the North Korean leaders seem to have grasped new Russian realities and realize that their country and people actually have more in common with Russia and Russians than is usually believed. North Korean–style socialism was an offspring of the Soviet Stalinist model. The North Korean and Russian elites share a common genesis. The mentality of the two peoples was formed within the same Soviet socialist paradigm and evolved along similar lines during the period of mutually reliant socialist construction. As part and parcel of the Soviet-centric world, they used to share the values, benefits, problems, and deficiencies of the same Soviet socialist civilization. All these developmental similarities make it easier for the North Korean elites to understand where Russia is coming from, why things evolve the way they do there, and what the future might hold for them. At the same time, they offer useful insights to Pyongyang as to how it can approach various new developmental challenges on its own road to economic restructuring and political liberalization. For North Korea, Russia serves as a role model of

---

10 These repeated visits by Kim Jong-il to the Russian embassy are noted because it is highly unusual for the head of state to frequent a foreign embassy so often.

sorts and a window into modern civilization. It offers an example of what may actually happen in the North should that country seriously embark on a road of internal reformation.

Now Pyongyang seems to be willing to maintain stable and intimate dialogue at the highest possible level with Moscow. In turn, Moscow, too, values a close bilateral relationship with its North Korean neighbor and is reluctant to jeopardize it for the sake of unproved multilateral formulas. A high degree of interpersonal trust and intense political dialogue allow Russia to not only obtain credible information about the latest developments on the Korean peninsula from the North Korean leaders themselves, but also open the possibility for Moscow to influence these events as they unfold and nudge Pyongyang in the direction of further socioeconomic and political reforms at home and more constructive behavior abroad.

Russian Views on the North Korean Question

The Russian government seems to assume that, following the historic inter-Korean summit on 15 June 2000, the slow-moving process of Korean reintegration has already begun. It is rather unstable and erratic because of frequent fluctuations in North Korea's security position, financial difficulties, political squabbling inside the ROK, and a U.S. policy seemingly designed to slow Korean reunification (President of Russia 2003, 5, 8). The two Koreas are on their way to formal political unification, however, and the process is likely only to accelerate in the years to come.

To position itself in a way that would enable it to benefit from its friendly and close relationship with the first leader of a unified Korea, Russia strives to keep up the reunification momentum by creating a proper balance in its individual relations with Seoul and Pyongyang; by mediating inter-Korean differences; and by hampering the further development of the Korean processes in accordance with the perceived U.S. scenario, thereby reducing the possibility of the expansion of the U.S. military presence on the peninsula and its redeployment closer to the Russian Far Eastern borders (President of Russia 2003, 8).

Many Korea experts in Russia tend to dismiss U.S. moralizing regarding Kim Jong-il's regime.[11] They praise the acceleration of the North Korean reforms and encourage more assistance and support from South Korea. Most Russians understand that the Dear Leader's regime is totalitarian in nature, and they do not particularly like it because they had their own terrible historical experience with Stalinist totalitarianism. Russia, however, is against any regime change through foreign intervention or export of democratic revolution to North Korea. The ongoing economic liberalization and political

---

11 Experts include Vadim Tkachenko, director of the Center for Korean Research at the Institute of the Far East of the Russian Academy of Sciences, and Alexander Vorontsov, head of the Korea section at the Institute of Oriental Studies at the Russian Academy of Sciences.

decompression in Pyongyang are likely to gradually soften up the regime beyond recognition, and, with time, the Kim clan is sure to pass away from the historical scene, thereby opening the gates for Korean unification. That process must unfold naturally, without foreign military intervention (Arbatov 2003).

On the other hand, many believe that the U.S. hard-line policy and adamant insistence on North Korea's unconditional unilateral nuclear disarmament fortifies the siege mentality in Pyongyang and only strengthens Kim Jong-il's regime. Intensified international hostility around the DPRK simply allows the DPRK government to impose harsher security measures on the society, puts the KPA on the center stage of domestic politics at the expense of other social and political forces, drains productive resources from economic reform and development, and increases popular support for and the domestic legitimacy of Kim Jong-il (Titarenko 2003).

In what is reminiscent of the Cold War mentality, quite a few analysts contend that the United States purposefully exaggerates the North Korean nuclear threat because of the "U.S. permanent interest in aggravating tensions on the Korean peninsula" in order to justify its long-term military presence in Korea and East Asia as a whole (Titarenko 2003). They believe that the North Korean nuclear crisis is not about nuclear nonproliferation; neither is it really a security crisis between Pyongyang and Washington. Instead, it is a great diplomatic game between Washington and Beijing, with huge stakes, and played for long-term strategic control and dominance over the entire Korean peninsula as well as the future shape of the East Asian security order. In other words, the question is not whether the United States will fight a war against North Korea over a couple of dubious nuclear warheads but, instead, whether the United States will choose to engage in a major conflict with a 1.3-billion-strong China that is rapidly emerging as the second superpower and potential primary challenger to U.S. global supremacy over strategic preeminence in Korea. It is also a question about what the historical consequences of such a mega-confrontation between the two Asia-Pacific giants could be for the security situation in the whole of East Asia (Bubnov 2003).

Some Russian military experts believe that, in contrast with Iraq or Yugoslavia, the United States lacks fundamental economic or political interest in initiating a major war in Korea. There is no oil in the DPRK—it is poor, hungry, and underdeveloped (in the military experts' words, "there is nothing to plunder in the North"), and, despite its official label of a "terror-sponsoring nation," Pyongyang is not known for extremist Muslim connections. Besides, Washington may not want to have any serious trouble with Beijing at present (Gareyev 2003). In addition, Russian experts consider Pyongyang's suspected nuclear arsenal and artillery forces located near the Demilitarized Zone (DMZ) as sufficient military deterrents, able to prevent a U.S. military attack against North Korea (Safranchuk 2003; Konovalov 2003).

Precision strikes from offshore bases alone are unlikely to resolve the Korean crisis, and Washington is clearly not interested in any protracted, large-scale military conflict on the peninsula (Titarenko 2003). Moreover, seeming U.S. failure in rebuilding postwar Iraq puts a damper on more aggressive U.S. plans in Korea (Rogov 2003).

However, other military analysts argue that, if the Bush administration were to decide to attack the North preemptively, it would be mostly for domestic reasons and causes unrelated to the Korean peninsula. In that case, Washington is not going to ask anyone's permission, including the United Nations, the ROK, Russia, or even China, and is likely to strike first when U.S. Forces Korea (USFK), U.S. Forces Japan (USFJ), and augmentation forces are militarily and logistically ready for a major sustainable offensive operation. In their opinion, U.S. war planners are not afraid of Kim Jong-il's imaginary nuclear deterrent or of his rusting long-range artillery tubes. They are likely to carpet bomb everything from nuclear facilities to Kim Jong-il's palaces, as they did in Iraq, and then parachute the ROK's special forces into all major North Korean cities and key installations in order to reunite the country from within (Vladimirov 2003). Given all these expert opinions that by and large allow for the possibility of war in Korea, it is no wonder that, in mid-August 2003, the Russian General Staff and Pacific Command conducted large-scale joint civilian and military exercises designed to, among many other things, test the Russian operational response to the possibility of the outbreak of hostilities on the Korean peninsula in light of the escalating DPRK-U.S. confrontation (Kravchenko 2003; Pulikovsky 2003).

Whatever happens on the Korean peninsula in the immediate future and in the years to come, it is clear that Russia's national security interests and its economic and political interests will be directly affected. Therefore, the Russian government is sure to continue its active, balanced engagement policy with both Korean states through separate bilateral channels; within various multilateral frameworks, including the six-party talks; and in cooperation with third parties, especially China.

Prospects for Multilateral Conflict Resolution on the Korean Peninsula

Russia half-heartedly endorsed the Geneva talks, the four-party peace talks, and the Korean Peninsula Energy Development Organization (KEDO) mission in the DPRK throughout the 1990s; expressed conditional diplomatic support for the three-party peace talks in Beijing in April 2003 (Losyukov 2003); and is actively participating in the six-party North Korean crisis-resolution process.[12] Russia's goal in the Beijing process is to be an honest broker

---

12 Participants in the four-party talks were China, North Korea, South Korea, and the United States. Participants in the three-party talks were China, North Korea, and the United States. Participants in the six-party talks are China, Japan, North Korea, Russia, South Korea, and the United States.

that strives to achieve denuclearization of the Korean peninsula, obtain credible assurances of mutual nonaggression and confidence-building measures across the DMZ, and advance better governance based on democratic values and free markets in North Korea.

Most experts in Russia are relatively pessimistic, however, about the prospects for the six-party talks. They tend to predict a troublesome continuation of the existing status quo, which will be shaken up sporadically by emotional walkouts and abrupt terminations. The status quo may be occasionally adjusted at the margins during the on-again, off-again rounds of six-party plenary sessions devoted to endless debates about the virtues, flaws, costs, benefits, and credibility of something like an Agreed Framework Lite or Very Lite, an Agreed Framework Two (stipulating North Korean nuclear disarmament in exchange for multilateral security guarantees and international economic assistance), an Agreement to Disagree, or even an Agreement on Working Groups. These experts expect such talks to head slowly toward an unannounced death—like the notorious four-party peace talks of 1997–99.

At worst, Russians who specialize in Korean affairs predict a dramatic failure for the Beijing six-party talks. In particular, these talks are believed to be a venue for both Washington and Pyongyang to buy time for further advancement of their respective sinister aggressive plans against each other as well as an opportunity to delegitimize each other in the eyes of the international community of nations: "See, we told you so. . . . We made concessions time and again, but they just refused to listen and compromise. . . ." At the end of the day, these experts expect that the United States may succeed in fully delegitimizing the North Korean regime in front of other participants in the six-party talks, especially its Chinese Communist ally.

Consequently, they believe that Washington may try to use the talks to form an ad hoc, multilateral, anti-DPRK coercive coalition of the intimidated (the ROK and the PRC), the weak (Russia), and the greedy (Japan) and may attempt to bring down the North Korean regime by intensifying blockades, increasing international pressure, and using force if necessary to resolve the North Korean security crisis once and for all. They urge the Russian government to stay ahead of the game in order to prevent such an eventuality.

In general, Russian government officials are frustrated with the dramatic shift toward belligerence in U.S. policy toward the DPRK. They argue that Pyongyang largely abided by its obligations under the Agreed Framework and is receiving the short end of the stick, which, ironically, confirms their long-held belief that Washington was never serious about providing Pyongyang with alternative sources of nuclear power for peaceful use. Washington's arbitrary decision to not certify Pyongyang's compliance with the Agreed Framework is interpreted as a manifestation of a growing U.S. tendency in international affairs toward unilateral rejectionism and increasing reliance on the use of force instead of the rule of law. Moscow does not really share the U.S. concerns over the North Korean missile and nuclear weapons programs. Furthermore, Russian officials believe that the U.S. designation of the DPRK as part of an axis of evil, despite clear evidence of positive domestic evolution in the North in recent years, may seriously undermine the efficacy of President Roh Moo-hyun's peace and prosperity policy and prospects for peace, stability, and inter-Korean reconciliation on the peninsula. Thus, without naming names, Moscow unambiguously holds Washington responsible for the current absence of dialogue and escalation of tension between Washington and Pyongyang.

It is clear that the Russian government will not support any attempt by the North Korean leaders to blackmail Seoul through threatened military aggression; that would be counterproductive and hinder Russia's expanding national interests in the South. Neither will Moscow encourage any kind of head-to-head challenge by Pyongyang against Washington because Moscow understands the devastating consequences that would result for the North and the highly destabilizing impact such a challenge would be for all of Northeast Asia.

It is also evident, however, that Russia will be receptive to Kim Jong-il's personal overtures and pleas for political, diplomatic, and military-technical support and, possibly, even expanded economic assistance. Moscow is committed to providing enough spare parts for defensive weapons to Pyongyang to ensure the North Korean regime's self-defense sufficiency and the restoration of the North's credible military deterrent capability on the peninsula. It goes without saying that Russia will not support any kind of international coalition that has as its goal the military crushing of North Korea.

If the international community succeeds in reaching a new "grand bargain" with the DPRK at the negotiation table in the ongoing six-party talks in Beijing—and this is a big "if"—there will be practical limits to Russian participation in any such scheme. Moscow may be willing to participate in offering some vague multilateral security assurances to Pyongyang and in implementing the international inspection and verification regimes to be created to verify and monitor the North Korean compliance with its future nuclear disarmament obligations. The Russian role in the DPRK's economic rehabilitation as part of a new package deal is likely to be very limited, however. Substantive and mutually beneficial railroad cooperation, energy cooperation, enterprise rehabilitation cooperation, and debt relief cooperation are all myths for now. At present, many obstacles (domestic and international, economic, financial, and political) to these cooperative bilateral or multilateral projects are too high, stakes are too low, and payoffs are delayed too far into the future, making Russian interests just too marginal. Despite all the talk, Russians are not willing to walk the walk toward implementation any time soon. In sum, as far as Russia is concerned, there will be no Trans-Siberian Railway–Trans Korean railways connection, no Russian-

Korean gas/oil pipeline, no debt relief, and no more money thrown into the North Korean "money pit" until Korean reunification.

Moscow, however, is likely to continue its efforts to convince the North Korean leaders that domestic change is good; that change should not necessarily threaten the DPRK's survival; and that the more open and market oriented the DPRK becomes, the more benefits the DPRK is likely to receive in terms of the advancement of its economy, social welfare, and national security. In this vein, Moscow will continue its policy of encouraging the North-South economic, cultural, and political exchanges by placing a greater emphasis on the need for the North to show more reciprocity and transparency in its relations with its dialogue partners from the South.

References

Alexeyev, Yuri. 2002. North Korean Leader Is Interested in Russian Experience with Economic Reforms (in Russian). 15 August. http://www.strana.ru/.

Arbatov, Alexei. 2003. Reasonable Defense Is Required for Firm Peace (interview). 28 July. www.smi.ru/.

Bubnov, Vasily. 2003. China Getting Ready for Severe Blitzkrieg. *Pravda*. 1 August. http://english.pravda.ru/world/20/91/366/10637_korea.html.

Gareyev, Makhmoot. 2003. Interview; Gareyev, an army general, is president of the Russian Academy of Military Sciences. Vladivostok: Vostok-Media News Agency. 29 July.

Konovalov, Alexander. 2003. Interview; Konovalov is president of the Institute of Strategic Assessments. Vladivostok: Vostok-Media News Agency. 29 July.

Korean Central News Agency (KCNA). 2000a. Talks Held between Kim Jong Il and V. V. Putin. 19 July.

———. 2000b. DPRK-Russia Joint Declaration Released. 20 July.

Kravchenko, Victor. 2003. Interview; Kravchenko is chief of main staff of the Russian Pacific Fleet. Vladivostok: ITAR-TASS. 18 August.

Losyukov, Alexander. 2003. Interview; Losyukov is deputy foreign minister of the Russian Federation in charge of the Asia-Pacific region. Moscow: Kyodo News Agency. 17 April. www.mid.ru/; no. 947-19-04-2003.

Ministry of Foreign Affairs (MOFA). 2000. Press release no. 755. Moscow: Ministry of Foreign Affairs. 11 August.

President of Russia. 2003. Recommendations of the Far Eastern Federal District aimed at improving cross-border cooperation, trade and economic exchanges, and cultural ties with the CIS partners and neighboring countries, presented for the consideration of the ninth session of the Presidential State Council, devoted to the analysis of current international activities of the Russian Federation. Moscow: President of Russia, Kremlin. 22 January. www.kremlin.ru/.

Pulikovsky, Konstantin B. 2002. *Oriental Express: Across Russia with Kim Jong Il*. Moscow: Gorodets Publishers.

————. 2003. Interview; Pulikovsky is permanent representative of President Putin to the Far Eastern Federal District. Khabarovsk: ITAR-TASS. 19 August.

Rogov, Sergey. 2003. Interview; Rogov is director of the Institute of the United States and Canada. Moscow. September.

Safranchuk, Ivan. 2003. Interview; Safranchuk is director of the Defense Information Center, Moscow. Vladivostok: Vostok-Media News Agency. 29 July.

Titarenko, Mikhail. 2003. Americans themselves strengthen the North Korean regime. 2 September. www.smi.ru/.

Vladimirov, Alexander. 2003. Interview; Vladimirov, a major general, is vice president of the Council of Military Experts within the Russian Ministry of Defense. Vladivostok: Vostok-Media News Agency. 29 July.

Alexandre Y. Mansourov is an Associate Professor who is with the Asia-Pacific Center for Security Studies, Honolulu, Hawaii. The views expressed in this chapter are personal opinions of the author and do not reflect the official positions of the APCSS or the U.S. government.

17

Expected Role of South Korea and Major Stakeholders: NGO Contributions to and Roles in North Korea's Rehabilitation

Scott Snyder

In response to the food crisis of the 1990s, the Democratic People's Republic of Korea (DPRK) for the first time began to accept humanitarian assistance from the outside world. This opening was one of the first cracks in the hermetic seal of self-imposed isolation that the DPRK leadership had sought to impose on its people for decades. It came about as a result of desperately needed food, a situation caused by the failure of the People's Republic of China (PRC) and the Soviet Union to provide the resource flows that had sustained the DPRK and allowed it to enjoy its relative isolation throughout the Cold War. The scarcity of food in the DPRK gave proof in the starkest possible terms to the lie of North Korea's claimed capacity to stand as an autonomous, self-reliant actor (according to the *juche* ideology).

The famine became an opportunity for the establishment of new relationships between the DPRK and United Nations (UN) organizations such as the UN World Food Programme (UNWFP), as well as a variety of nongovernmental efforts to promote exchange between the two Koreas and between the DPRK and the rest of the world. The famine also provided an initial entry point and opportunity for nongovernmental humanitarian-aid workers to be catalysts for change and representatives of the good intentions of the outside world toward North Korea's people, who had been closed off to the outside world for many decades.

With the advent of a sustained economic boom in Asia and a shift in development assistance philosophy away from direct aid to often corrupt local governments to support through organizations with local implementation capacity on the ground, the 1980s saw the rapid development of nongovernmental organizations (NGOs) in a variety of roles—humanitarian, disaster relief, service provision, and technical assistance—in response to various crises around the world. The NGO community had developed over the years initially as an outgrowth of religious-based humanitarian efforts and subsequently as broader vehicles for efficient service provision through subcontracting of government-funded humanitarian and technical development efforts. Over time, organizations emerged with specialized expertise that resulted in the professionalization of service delivery, especially in the areas of humanitarian response and technical development.

These organizations developed as more effective counterparts than governments because they were able to support local efforts inside the target country by developing relationships with a variety of governmental and nongovernmental organizational counterparts at the local level. The development of international NGOs as major players in humanitarian crisis response and delivery of technical services has been given a boost in recent years by the end of the Cold War and the accompanying increase in space for depoliticized nongovernmental roles and functions. The growth of NGOs has been aided as well by the trend on the part of governmental development agencies of supporting NGO service providers as effective vehicles for rapid deliveries of humanitarian and technical resources on the ground (Salamon 1994, 109–22).

The development of international NGO efforts also may be seen as part of the development of grassroots or people-to-people exchanges at the global level because much of the interaction is not necessarily constrained by government policy, although governments as major funders of NGO efforts may indirectly influence the effectiveness of such efforts. The trend of greater space for nongovernmental activities in a sphere outside of the direct control or influence of governments is another development that has gathered speed with the end of the Cold War. These technological developments have facilitated the creation and strengthening of issue-based virtual communities that share an interest in specific issues or developments and can organize more effectively to advocate for attention to the issues about which they are concerned. NGO advocacy with less regard for national borders has thus become one mechanism for influencing government policy, as issue-based interest groups organize to advocate for particular policies in line with their own organizational interests.

In South Korea (Republic of Korea, or ROK), the development of the NGO sector was a natural by-product of Korean democratization and development of civil society. The growth and influence of the nongovernmental sector in South Korea has been a significant part of Korea's deepening democratization, as nongovernmental organizations have played significant advocacy and service provision roles in South Korean society as part of the deepening of democracy. The rise of South Korean NGO involvement as part of inter-Korean relations reflects democratic changes in South Korea and has become an influential and relatively new aspect of the development of the inter-Korean relationship in recent years. The rise of South Korean NGOs has influenced the development of inter-Korean relations, and, as vehicles for expanded grassroots exchange, NGOs are likely to play an even more important and complex role in the future development of inter-Korean relations in the fields of advocacy, service delivery, and grassroots exchange. This paper will attempt to draw out and highlight some of the likely roles that both international and South Korean NGOs will play in the rehabilitation of North Korea.

Constraints and Conditions on NGO Roles in the Absence of Diplomatic Relations

To properly define at the outset the constraints and opportunities NGOs may face in working with North Korea, it is necessary to clarify the range of roles that NGOs have been able to play in situations analogous to that which exists with North Korea. The scope and nature of NGO involvement in situations analogous to that with North Korea have been limited substantially by politics on both sides. Only with political support from governments is it possible for NGOs to play an effective role in opening the way for diplomatic normalization efforts (for example, the "ping-pong diplomacy" between the United States and the PRC in the early 1970s).

The story of NGO interaction with North Korea thus far has illustrated most starkly the limits of apolitical humanitarianism (represented by the Reagan-era aphorism, "a hungry child knows no politics") as NGOs seeking humanitarian space to perform their work apart from political constraints have come up against North Korean perceptions that everything about NGO activity in North Korea is fundamentally political. At the same time, in certain cases, NGO advocacy efforts have been successful in heightening political pressure to open roles and opportunities for NGOs to become involved on the leading edge of interaction with the target country. In the case of North Korea, one of the most interesting results of the accumulation of NGO experience in the country is the extent to which the NGO community has become divided and has pursued political advocacy efforts on both sides of the political question of how to manage the future of humanitarian aid work with North Korea.

Although NGOs have been on the leading edge of engagement to provide and support the development of an infrastructure in failed states where political control and order are lacking, NGOs—if both political and financial support are forthcoming—may play important roles in place of governments and in the absence of diplomatic relations as precursors to the establishment of new relationships between governments. NGOs have been on the front lines of engagement with actors or counterparts that have not yet gained formal diplomatic recognition of governments or in situations where political factors have constrained formal governmental roles or relationships with other counterparts. In such highly politicized circumstances, however, the deepening of NGO involvement is usually dependent on the financial support and political encouragement of state actors, financial or otherwise, to carry out that role. NGOs have very tough going and in many cases may not succeed in the absence of governmental support or in an environment in which financial or political support is otherwise unavailable.

In circumstances where the political support is unavailable for NGOs to reach out and become active at the grass roots, NGOs may pursue advocacy as a vehicle by which to build political support for the government to allow experimental efforts to go forward, to provide financial support for particular activities, or to test the possibility for establishing new relationships. If such advocacy efforts are successful, it may be possible for NGOs to expand the political support for establishing new relationships or developing new programs in areas where prior relationships have not existed. However, in the absence of political support or in the context of a weak advocacy effort with insufficient constituent support, it may become virtually impossible, as a result of existing political constraints, for NGOs to carry out their specialized work.

Thus, in the context of complex humanitarian emergencies or in the case of postconflict situations when a lack of trust has prevented the restoration of formal diplomatic relations (Vietnam, Cambodia, Iran, Myanmar, and North Korea), humanitarian NGOs may step in to play dual roles of provision of humanitarian aid or technical skills as well as advocacy to shape the political space, expand the terms of interaction, and develop the grassroots support that will be necessary to allow them to carry out their work. In the arena of advocacy, however, various NGOs may be primary actors in conflict with each other. For example, issue-based advocacy groups that focus on issues of human rights or democratization may seek to mobilize support to contest interactions supported by relief and development NGOs that could lead to increased political opening or the establishment of new government-to-government relationships. NGOs often are the chief vehicles for mobilizing grassroots participation on such issues, both pro and con, depending on the issue orientation and focus of the specific NGO involved.

The South Korean NGO Experience with North Korea: History, Advocacy, Action

The South Korean NGO experience with North Korea has included as part of its agenda both advocacy efforts and pioneering work to open new relationships with North Korean counterparts. South Korean NGOs, in a little more than a decade of involvement with North Korea, have faced extraordinary political constraints at various times in their relationships with both the governments of the ROK and DPRK. South Korean NGO roles and responsibilities vis-à-vis North Korea have focused on both advocacy and action in response to North Korea's humanitarian needs. However, actions have been constrained beyond expectations in working with the North while NGOs have also responded to the needs of North Korean refugees in China and in South Korea. Also, the experience with North Korea has produced advocacy on both sides of the policy debate about the future of North Korea.[1]

Origins of South Korean NGO Advocacy for Projects with North Korea

South Korean NGO efforts to respond to North Korean food shortages in fact began as public advocacy campaigns to "share rice in love" (*sarang ssal nanugi*) in the early 1990s. This campaign was initiated by South Korean religious organizations that wanted to respond to reports of starvation in North Korea. At that time, the South Korean government opposed citizen efforts to contact the DPRK or to provide nongovernmental assistance. Some groups attempted to provide aid through China, however, and these efforts represented a source of growing opposition to South Korean government policy through the mid-1990s. President Kim Young-sam of South Korea recognized public sentiment and launched a costly governmental humanitarian effort to provide 150,000 tons of South Korean rice to North Korea just prior to local elections in 1995, but this effort did not fundamentally change the extraordinary political tensions in the inter-Korean relationship. It is interesting that these offers, as well as a Japanese government agreement to provide 500,000 tons of rice to North Korea, were negotiated with the DPRK before the massive floods in the summer of 1996 that led to the opening of the DPRK to international humanitarian assistance. (See *Table 1* on page 370 and *Table 2* on pages 372 and 373).

In 1996 and 1997, a range of grassroots activities led by the Korean Sharing Movement developed in opposition to the Kim Young-sam administration policy that restricted humanitarian aid to the DPRK to the single channel of the South Korean National Red Cross. Despite political obstacles, a grassroots public campaign promoted by members of the Korean Sharing Movement, the YMCA, and other South Korean NGOs attracted support from 4 million Koreans and raised approximately $4.5 million in cash, a remarkable feat given government opposition to the movement.

Sunshine Policy and Expansion of South Korean NGO Activity in North Korea

South Korean NGO efforts to help North Korea faced opposition from the South Korean government until the beginning of the Kim Dae-jung administration's Sunshine Policy in 1998, which marked a dramatic change in South Korea's orientation toward the North and toward South Korean NGO involvement in inter-Korean activities. From that time forward, South

---

1 For a more detailed description of South Korean NGO experiences with North Korea, see Chung (2004, 81–110).

Table 1: Aid by the Government of South Korea to the DPRK, 1995–2003

Year	Amount of aid (U.S. dollars)	Details of aid
1995	232,000,000	Rice: 150,000 tons
1996	3,050,000	UNWFP: $2,000,000 (mixed grain)
		UNICEF: $1,000,000 (powdered milk 203 tons)
		WHO: $50,000
1997	26,670,000	UNWFP: $6 million (mixed grains 9,852 tons)
		UNICEF: $340,000 (ORS factory cost)
		UNWFP: $10,530,000 (corn 50,000 tons; powdered milk 300 tons)
		UN: $9.8 million, comprising: UNWFP: $4 million (CSB 8,389 tons) UNICEF: $3.6 million (powdered milk 781 tons) WHO: $700,000 UNDP: $1.2 million FAO: $300,000
1998	11,000,000	UNWFP: $11,000,000 (corn 30,000 tons; flour 10,000 tons)
1999	28,250,000	Fertilizer: 1.15 million tons (total: 33.9 billion *won*)
2000	78,630,000	Fertilizer: 500,000 tons; additional fertilizer aid: 100,000 tons
2001	70,450,000	Underwear: 1.5 million articles
		Fertilizer: 200,000 tons
		UNWFP: corn 100,000 tons
		WHO: medicine for malaria
2002	83,750,000	Includes food, medical/health, fertilizer, etc.
2003	87,010,000[a]	
Total (1995–2003)	620,810,000	

Source: MOU, various years.
a   Does not include the 400,000 tons of rice sent as in-kind credit.
Note: FAO, Food and Agriculture Organization of the United Nations; UNDP, United Nations Development Program; UNICEF, United Nations Children's Fund; UNWFP, United Nations World Food Programme; WHO, World Health Organization. Some ROK aid arrives in the DPRK through UN agencies; on this table ROK aid through the UN is itemized.

Korean NGO involvement in humanitarian activities toward the North began to expand as private donations flowed and as the Kim Dae-jung government began to provide financial support to some South Korean NGOs for provision of various types of assistance to North Korea. Chairman Chung Ju-young of Hyundai paved the way for expanded South Korean humanitarian efforts: first by the provision of more than 1,000 head of cattle to North Korea in two different donations and, subsequently, through an agreement to develop and allow South Korean tourism to the Mount Kumgang area in a project that was developed in close cooperation with the South Korean government. Aside from Chung's private-sector efforts, which included provision of humanitarian aid, approximately 20 South Korean NGOs were registered with the Ministry of Unification (MOU) to conduct exchange activities with North Korea in a variety of areas, from promotion of contact among North and South Korean children, to health projects, to technical assistance in the agricultural sector.

Although there was growing interest among the South Korean NGO community in providing various types of assistance to North Korea, a variety of obstacles remained, including harsh restrictions by the DPRK government that came in a variety of forms. South Korean NGOs were very closely observed through either the DPRK's Asian Pacific Peace Committee, which was led by the high-ranking party official, Kim Young-sun, or the Committee for Overseas Compatriots, a branch of the DPRK government that had been most active in promoting United Front activities and pro–North Korean support abroad. Despite significant donations of assistance in a range of areas, travel by South Koreans was restricted, and South Korean NGO representatives were required to be accompanied by North Korean minders at all times. In addition, the level of South Korean NGO monitoring of donations to the North that was permitted by the DPRK was considerably less than even the unsatisfactory monitoring arrangements the DPRK had approved for food and other assistance received through the UN agencies and international NGOs.

As the severity of the humanitarian crisis in the DPRK abated at the end of the 1990s, South Korean NGOs moved away from emergency relief and, as a means of trying to expand access and as a more effective way of contributing meaningfully to the quality of life in North Korea, toward the direction of capacity building and technical assistance projects designed to support North Korea's development. For example, since 1999, World Vision Korea has provided greenhouse equipment designed to support the development and transplantation of high-quality potato strains, and the International Corn Foundation has worked for several years on improving strains of corn that can grow effectively under conditions found in North Korea. Although the implementation of such projects has required more significant inter-Korean interaction, requiring education and training in certain technical areas, the North Korean side has remained wary of expanding South Korean interaction beyond the specialist level or beyond institution-based interaction to allow contact with end users of the services provided.

The price of entry for South Korean NGOs has remained significantly higher than for international organizations or for Europe- and U.S.-based NGOs because of North Korean suspicions about the intent of the South Korean NGOs and concerns that South Korea's presence would negatively influence the North Korean population. Ironically, a further constraint on NGO activ-

Table 2: South Korea's NGO Aid to the DPRK, 1995–2003

Period	Comment	Amount of aid (U.S. dollars)	Breakdown
Sept. 1995– May 1997	Through the IFRC	4,960,000	Flour (3,664 tons), powdered milk (94 tons), blankets (10,000), vegetable oil (1.86 million tons), ramen (100,000 packages), socks (305,000 pairs), potatoes (1,900 tons), radish seeds (4.8 tons), cabbage seeds (6.4 tons), corn (4,980 tons)
June 1997– July 1997	Korean Red Cross, first shipment	8,500,000	Corn (41,511 tons), flour (2,000 tons), ramen (150,000 boxes), fertilizer (2,000 tons), corn standard (53,841 tons)
Aug. 1997– Oct. 1997	Korean Red Cross, second shipment	8,900,000	Corn (17,100 tons), sorghum (14,576 tons), flour (5,501 tons), vegetable oil (270,000 tons), potatoes (1,300 tons), baby food (96.74 tons), powdered milk (100 tons), children's vitamins (30,000 bottles)
March 1998		170,000	Fertilizer (800 tons)
April 1998– June 1998	Korean Red Cross, third shipment	9,350,000	Corn (16,585 tons), flour (13,500 tons), vegetable oil, powdered milk, fertilizer, salt, rice, potatoes, socks, Korean cows, and others
Sept. 1998– Dec. 1998	Additional aid	11,330,000	Chung Ju-young: corn, cows[a] NGOs: corn, flour, white rice, powdered milk, sugar, vegetable oil, etc.
Jan. 1999– Dec. 1999		18,630,000	Korean Red Cross: fertilizer (3/30-6/5), (40,000 tons) Through Korean Red Cross: 3.4 trillion *won* from 24 organizations: flour (3,139 tons), corn (4,015 tons), powdered milk (42 tons), sugar (165 tons), seed potatoes (180 tons), vegetable oil (15,845 liters), ramen (9,930 boxes), clothing (215,448 articles), medical, etc.
			Independent channel (bilateral): 6.6 trillion *won* from 10 organizations; EBCF: medical equipment, worth 1.2 trillion *won*
			South-North Sharing Campaign: clothing, flour, fertilizer, sprayer, shovel, etc., worth 1.1 trillion *won*
			Good Neighbors: pasteurizing tank, cream separator, veterinary medicine, etc., worth 33 million *won*
			JTS: fertilizer (384 tons), dental equipment, sugar (52 tons), powdered milk (30 tons), notebooks, pencils, etc., worth 356 million *won*

ity came as a result of the inter-Korean summit, which resulted in a dramatically improved government-to-government relationship but also had the effect of marginalizing both South Korean governmental financial support for

Table 2: South Korea's NGO Aid to the DPRK, 1995–2003 (continued)

Period	Comment	Amount of aid (U.S. dollars)	Breakdown
Jan. 1999– Dec. 1999 (continued)			WVK: medicine, greenhouse material, seed potatoes (1.5 tons), clothing (24,871 articles), etc., worth 390 million *won*
			KSM: clothing (46,500 articles), fabric, medicine, corn (1,000 tons), flour (51 tons), ramen (300 boxes), eggs (5 million), tangerines (585 tons), goats (450), etc., worth 2.6 trillion *won*
			Korean Rotary Foundation: ambulance, medicine, etc., worth 40 million *won*
			ICF: 10 types of seed potatoes, worth 1 million *won*
			National Episcopal Committee for the Reconciliation of Korean People: fertilizer (1,000 tons), corn (3,000 tons), clothing (5,500 articles), shoes (1,000 pairs), etc., worth 791 million *won*
			National Reconciliation Buddhist Committee: shoes (5,000 pairs), clothing (6,828 articles), etc., worth 207 million *won*
Jan. 2000– Dec. 2000		35,130,000	Korean Red Cross: approx. $94,416 (16 organizations) Independent channel: approx. $256,166 (13 organizations)
Jan. 2001– Dec. 2001		64,940,000	Korean Red Cross: approx. $238,333 Independent channel: approx. $465,000 (19 organizations)
2002		51,170,000	General aid, medical aid, agricultural reconstruction
2003		70,610,000	Same as above categories
Total (1995–2003)		283,690,000	

Source: MOU, various years.
a   Chung Ju-young was founder and chairman of the Hyundai Group; this reflects aid supplied by him during visits to the DPRK in 1998.
Note: EBCF: Eugene Bell Centennial Foundation; ICF, International Corn Foundation; IFRC, International Federation of Red Cross and Red Crescent Societies; JTS, Join Together Society; KSM, Korean Sharing Movement; WVK, World Vision Korea.

NGO activities and North Korean attention to South Korean NGOs. Immediately following the summit, the DPRK focused on government-to-government projects with the ROK government at the expense of projects with South Korean NGOs partly because government-led projects involved less risk of contamination through promotion of unfiltered people-to-people contact. In some cases, the same DPRK counterparts who had been working with

Figure 1: Aid to North Korea from South Korea's Government and South Korea's NGOs, 1995–2003

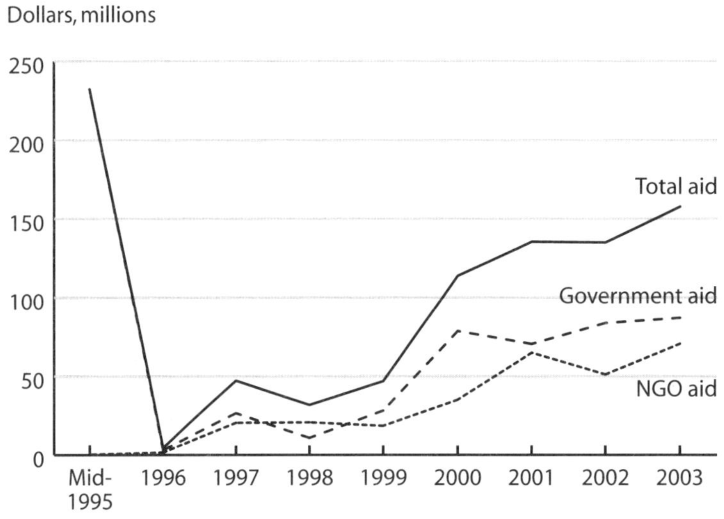

Source: MOU, various years.

South Korean NGOs were simply too busy managing government-led exchanges to be bothered with South Korean NGO activities, a situation that led to delays and inattention to grassroots-led technical exchanges or other efforts. Nonetheless, the overall level of aid from both governmental and nongovernmental sources increased (*Figure 1*), partly as a result of the fact that, following the summit, the ROK government also increased governmental support from the Inter-Korean Cooperation Fund for South Korean NGO activities.

All of these factors have led to a certain degree of disillusionment on the South Korean side, but the perceived need among South Korean mainstream NGOs to continue grassroots exchange efforts goes beyond technical assistance to the matter of erecting a political framework for inter-Korean reconciliation. Despite the setbacks and considerable frustrations imposed by the North Korean context, many South Korean NGOs have quietly persisted in their efforts, working together with North Korean counterparts to provide technical assistance despite difficulties, with the hope that hard-won opportunities for expanded grassroots relationships might also lead to a change in North Korea's attitude toward exchange possibilities.

Some of these South Korean groups can claim to have witnessed gradual changes in North Korea and a more practical and cooperative response at an individual level to South Korean NGO efforts, but access has come slowly and at a high financial price, often with little to show in the way of concrete progress. Some of these projects have led to significant infrastructure and technical process improvements in the North that may, in turn, enhance efficiency and productivity within the North Korean system. But is such progress catalyzing or inhibiting the systemic reforms that are ultimately necessary for a transformed North Korea to survive and thrive? Although there are no definitive answers to such questions, the answer to exactly how soon South Korean NGOs will find expanded opportunities in their work with their North Korean counterparts in effectively promoting humanitarian assistance and grassroots technical exchanges ultimately hinges on this question.

Refugee Relief and South Korean NGO Advocacy for North Korean Human Rights

Alongside the continuing activities of NGOs that are engaged directly in activity with North Korea is a set of advocacy activities that not only infuses the specialized focus of South Korean NGOs which have taken up work with North Korea but also serves as part of the broader agenda and ideological orientation of the progressive mainstream within the civic society movement in South Korea. This progressive mainstream set of NGOs is primarily focused on domestic political reform, anticorruption, and social renewal efforts in South Korea, but included as part of this progressive worldview is a broadly supportive attitude toward inter-Korean reconciliation and a strong critique of the George W. Bush administration's containment policy toward North Korea.

Activities and exchanges with North Korea have been led by more specialized NGO efforts that are included but are not necessarily at the forefront of the mainstream of South Korean NGO concerns, although those activities are strongly endorsed as part of the progressive political agenda of inter-Korean reconciliation promoted by mainstream South Korean citizens' organizations. These organizations, including the Civil Network for a Peaceful Korea, the People's Solidarity for Participatory Democracy, Women Making Peace, and other groups, are actively engaged in advocacy to support inter-Korean reconciliation and are strongly opposed to President Bush's more confrontational approach toward North Korea. This view appears to have public support from a range of public opinion polls that during recent years have consistently shown widespread support among Koreans for reconciliation and engagement efforts with North Korea.

Meanwhile, another set of seemingly contradictory South Korean NGO activities has developed that focus on resettlement and advocacy on behalf of North Korean refugees who have left North Korea for China and South Korea. This work has roots in the broad South Korean response to North Korea's humanitarian crisis of the mid-1990s. However, because of opposition by North Korean government authorities who oppose efforts by NGOs to respond simultaneously to DPRK government requests for assistance and work with refugees in northeastern China—authorities in Pyongyang resist working with organizations found to be active in assisting North Korean refugees—the South Korean NGO response has become a two-pronged effort. Some NGOs take the lead in delivery of humanitarian and technical assistance inside North Korea while other South Korean NGOs such as the Join Together Society focus on helping North Korean refugees in China. These service-delivery NGOs have been joined by a range of South Korean activist NGOs with conservative roots or foreign funding (for example, from the National Endowment for Democracy), many of which are opposed to the North Korean regime and are conducting human rights advocacy against North Korea. A range of NGOs, often religiously based and led by individual activists working in China as missionaries in the ethnic Korean-Chinese communities in the vicinity of Yanbian, has focused on saving North Korean refugees and bringing them to South Korea via an "underground railroad" or, because of the PRC's opposition to recognition of North Korean refugees in China, through South Korean embassies in Mongolia and Southeast Asia.

Differences in approach and perspective among various South Korean NGOs have caused conflict in advocacy approaches between groups such as the Civil Network for a Peaceful Korea and NGOs focused on human rights and refugee assistance such as Citizens' Alliance for North Korean Human Rights (CANKHR), which has been quite active in human rights–based advocacy on behalf of North Korean refugees and, increasingly, in direct work with North Korean refugees in South Korea. The Civil Network for a Peaceful Korea and like-minded groups have criticized the approach of conservative, human rights–focused South Korean NGOs; they stress that it must be recognized that North Korea's international circumstances have contributed to its isolation, that the use of humanitarian assistance as leverage for political purposes is itself contrary to basic concepts of human rights, and that the political objectives of containment and regime change, rather than real concern for human rights, appear to be the primary motivators of the human rights criticisms of conservatives.[2]

Since 2001, South Korean religious-based refugee assistance efforts have been joined by a more visible and activist set of actors that have tapped into the international human rights community and linked with conservative and activist democracy-promoting counterparts in the United States. These groups highlight the plight of North Korean refugees in order to mobilize political support to increase pressure on the DPRK government in hopes of a political collapse and regime transition. These advocacy efforts by a coalition of conservative South Korean NGOs that wants to promote regime change in North Korea have a distinct base among a strong conservative minority in South

---

2 See an unpublished thesis by Song (2002), in which she cites Jung Wook-shik of the Civil Network for a Peaceful Korea (www.peacekorea.org/nkright/wooksik.html). Opposing views may be found on the Web site of CANKHR (http://nkhumanrights.or.kr/NKHR_new/index_eng_new.htm).

Korea, but the greatest effects of their advocacy thus far have been to draw attention to these issues in the United States among a developing coalition of religious conservatives and human rights advocates, especially on Capitol Hill. Perhaps the high point thus far and the best example of the influence and relative success of these efforts is the North Korean Freedom Act—which would legislate in many areas consistent with the approach of this human rights–focused coalition—currently under consideration in the U.S. Congress.

In addition, South Korean NGOs concerned with human rights have become more active in supporting refugee resettlement programs in South Korea beyond the initial assistance given for refugee resettlement by the ROK government through the MOU. In support of the basic education program offered by the Hanawon, an MOU-run educational facility for newly arrived North Korean refugees, South Korean NGOs such as the YWCA, Full Gospel Central Church, CANKHR, North Korean Refugee Legal Support Association, and various North Korean defector/refugee support associations have provided supplementary programs particularly focused on helping children adjust to life in South Korea. Programs include job training and job search networks, children's camps, legal support, women's health education, and similar programs designed to ease the adjustment of North Korean refugees to South Korea. According to a variety of MOU sources, development of these programs has been encouraged by the South Korean government, which has reduced the length of the course for new arrivals from three months to two and has spread initial government support for new arrivals over a longer period of time so as to facilitate adjustment to life in South Korea.

Historical Context of U.S. and European NGO Experiences with North Korea

Compared with the role of South Korean NGOs working with North Korea, U.S. and European NGO experiences, respectively, have been much more limited in their scope and influence toward the DPRK. In both cases, NGO involvement with the DPRK has been more a function of government policy than has been the case with South Korean NGOs; and, with the notable exception of the U.S. NGO response to the North Korean famine at its height in 1996 and 1997, U.S. and European NGOs have played marginal roles in policy advocacy toward the DPRK. Structural differences in the requirements that accompany governmental funding of European NGO work in North Korea and the relatively depoliticized European response to DPRK needs—in contrast with the highly political lens through which the U.S. response has been considered—have thus far made European NGOs much more successful than their U.S. counterparts in establishing sustained programs in the DPRK.

U.S. NGO Involvement in North Korea[3]

Following disastrous flooding in the summer of 1996, the DPRK government for the first time expressed a willingness to open itself to receiving assistance from outside organizations. In the initial stages, the UNWFP was the primary vehicle through which U.S. government assistance was delivered because of the lack of on-the-ground experience of any U.S. NGO in the DPRK and the political sensitivities associated with the establishment of direct bilateral assistance to the DPRK. Even the initial U.S. government contribution of 25,000 tons of food assistance in late 1996 drew strong criticism from the ROK government because it was made under PL 480, the same mechanism through which food assistance had been offered to South Korea following the Korean War in the 1950s.

Despite the lack of a U.S. NGO presence on the ground, the U.S. government played a major role behind the scenes in pushing the UNWFP to get up and running in the DPRK, even requesting that the UNWFP issue emergency appeals so that the United States could respond in accordance with the Clinton administration's own political objectives as part of the effort to establish a multilateral negotiating mechanism with the DPRK in early 1997. In addition, the UNWFP received unprecedented contributions to alleviate the North Korean famine from U.S.-based NGOs, largely because there was no other mechanism established whereby U.S. NGOs could respond quickly to North Korea's need.

Three types of U.S.-based NGOs responded to the North Korean food crisis: the traditional public-campaign NGOs that sought to raise money through campaigns, conveyance NGOs, and religious NGOs. The public-campaign NGOs ran into difficulties because of DPRK sensitivity to external criticism and its unwillingness to cooperate in showing the worst of the famine to outsiders. Conveyance NGOs foundered on the rocks of political distrust and skepticism about the political appropriateness of U.S. bilateral assistance to the DPRK. Religious NGOs, however, flew below the radar screen and have been able to maintain small operations based on nongovernmental funding streams that have allowed for the establishment of small sustainable programs in niche areas such as humanitarian relief, establishment of bread and noodle factories, and limited educational exchange and technical assistance.

Conveyance NGOs such as Mercy Corps, World Vision, and CARE are the traditional mainstream early responders to humanitarian disasters, and the North Korean food crisis was no exception. Top representatives visited North Korea in early 1997 and began to form a North Korea working group under the auspices of InterAction, an umbrella advocacy group of humanitarian development organizations that worked closely in coordination with USAID and the U.S. Department of State to highlight and advocate for U.S. govern-

---

3 This section draws substantially from and summarizes Flake (2004, 15–46).

ment responses to global humanitarian crises. These NGO advocates in 1996 also convened a conference, the Musgrove Conference, to discuss the political obstacles to an effective humanitarian response to North Korea. This conference of humanitarian-service-providing NGOs continued on an annual basis through the latest conference in 2001 in South Korea. Some humanitarian advocates pushed for an active U.S.-based publicity campaign and pressed the U.S. government to allow USAID-supported bilateral assistance to the DPRK as a way of gaining a foothold there. This advocacy resulted in the establishment of the Private Voluntary Organization Consortium (PVOC) comprising CARE, Catholic Relief Services, Mercy Corps, World Vision, and Amigos Internacionales. In 1997 this NGO consortium was assigned to deliver USAID-funded humanitarian assistance on a bilateral basis but, for political reasons, was not allowed to move beyond humanitarian assistance and consider development assistance projects.

The U.S.-based NGO coalition—the PVOC—that was eventually formed to operate in the DPRK faced a host of problems derived from the unique difficulties of cooperating with DPRK government authorities in-country and from deep-seated and continuing political mistrust on the part of both NGOs and the DPRK authorities. The greatest obstacle was that all U.S. food assistance was already negotiated between the United States and the DPRK in what came to be characterized as "food for talks," in which the United States sought DPRK participation in multiparty dialogue, participation that the DPRK conditioned on U.S. performance in meeting the DPRK's food assistance demands. The net result was that NGOs had no leverage on the ground to insist on proper monitoring requirements once their groups' representatives finally arrived in Pyongyang. Moreover, DPRK counterparts established an interagency organization, the Food Damage Rehabilitation Committee (FDRC) to manage foreign NGOs and limit as much as possible the ability of NGOs to penetrate DPRK society.

The lack of diplomatic relations and the innate suspicion of DPRK authorities led to the DPRK assumption that requests for information were spying; NGO reports, particularly to the international media and to the U.S. Congress, were indeed regarded by the North Koreans as spying. As a result, the DPRK authorities demanded non-Korean-speaking food monitors and one week's advance notification to prepare for monitoring visits, and they limited U.S. NGO representatives to short-term stays and nonresident status. The PVOC lasted for only three years and dissolved in failure following the politically directed provision of potato seeds in a project that was indirectly connected with the inspection of suspected nuclear facilities at Keumchangri.

Subsequent efforts by U.S. NGOs to work in North Korea have been sporadic. USAID attempts to delink humanitarian assistance for North Korea from the overall political environment have succumbed to the views of hardliners in the Bush administration who believe that North Korea can be squeezed to death through the DPRK government's own intransigence, unwillingness to respond, and refusal to allow a proper monitoring system for food aid. A proper system would include on-the-spot inspections and assurances that food is truly reaching end users.[4] Under current circumstances, it is unlikely that USAID assistance to the DPRK will continue in any form that would allow space for U.S. conveyance NGOs to reengage. Even the U.S. response to UNWFP appeals has been curtailed by frustrations with North Korean noncooperation and the press of competing humanitarian emergencies in many other parts of the world.

European NGO Experience and Historical Context in North Korea[5]

The European NGO experience in North Korea has been less influenced by political considerations than either U.S. or ROK NGO efforts, yet European NGOs have encountered many of the same restrictions on the ground as other NGOs. The initial decision among European NGOs to work in North Korea was primarily a response to North Korea's humanitarian appeal in the mid-1990s. However, one condition of assistance from the European Commission's Humanitarian Aid Office (ECHO) is that European NGOs must establish local offices on the ground in the concerned country. This requirement meant that the DPRK had to accept a resident presence for European NGOs in order to receive assistance from European NGOs. As of October 2002, eight European NGOs had residency status in the DPRK, and five other European NGOs that had once worked inside the DPRK decided to pull out on the basis of judgments that further humanitarian relief efforts could no longer be justified as effective in meeting the greatest humanitarian needs.

As with other NGOs, the initial focus of the work of European NGOs was on humanitarian relief, but gradually projects have shifted in the direction of technical assistance in the medical and agricultural areas. The European NGOs that remain resident in the DPRK include Campus für Christus (Switzerland), Concern Worldwide (Ireland), Cooperazione e Sviluppo (CESVI, Italy), German Agro Action, Adventist Development and Relief Agency International (Switzerland), PMU Interlife (Sweden), Triangle Génération Humanitaire (France), and Handicap International (Belgium). Despite the practical limits imposed on their work, representatives of those organizations that remain resident in the DPRK are gaining practical experience and building an understanding of the types of technical and development assistance most needed in the DPRK.

Among the European NGOs that left the DPRK were several that pulled out because of their frustrations with the monitoring restrictions imposed by the DPRK. These NGOs—Action contre la Faim, Médicins Sans Frontières,

---

4   The current system of advance-notice inspections can guarantee only that food has reached institutions; it does not eliminate suspicion of diversion or misuse.

5   This section draws from Schloms (2004, 47–80).

Médicins du Monde, and Oxfam, for example—departed out of frustration with their inability to establish direct contact with individual end users. The feeling among some of these NGOs was that the environment was so restricted that it was often impossible to carry out effectively the intended work that was necessary to meet the greatest humanitarian needs. These organizations assessed that there was little freedom to even determine and respond to the greatest humanitarian needs. Other European organizations, less focused on delivery of services to individuals in greatest need or more focused on technical assistance in specific sectors that did not require close contact with the end user, determined that, despite the restrictions of the DPRK government, it was important to remain and continue the work. They gradually appealed to DPRK counterparts to show flexibility in the implementation of the work. The fact remains, however, that flexibility has been hard-won in an environment where the restrictions imposed on resident NGO representatives remain designed to restrict grassroots contact with the average North Korean.

On the ground, the experience of European NGOs, which initially came to the DPRK with the least politicized motives compared with counterparts in the United States and South Korea, led to starkly contrasting advocacy positions that were based on their respective experiences. European NGOs that found the North Korean environment too restrictive departed believing that humanitarian aid was not reaching the population in greatest need and that the effect of continued assistance was to stabilize the regime by "feeding the dictator" (Schloms 2004, 73–75). These criticisms led in the late 1990s to an intense discussion and review of principles for humanitarian aid in North Korea. European NGOs that have remained in the DPRK argue that "change through rapprochement"—the philosophy behind West German *Ostpolitik*—is the principle that should be applied in North Korea. These NGOs argue that, beyond simply providing assistance, their efforts contribute to better relations between North Korea and the international community, a factor that can open the minds of North Korean counterparts who gain practical experience by working daily with Europeans in project implementation.

Role of NGOs in North Korea's Future Rehabilitation

What are the likely future roles that NGOs may play as part of North Korea's rehabilitation and integration with the outside world? On the basis of NGO experiences with North Korea accumulated thus far, South Korean NGOs are playing decisive—but contested—advocacy roles to influence South Korean policy toward the North, and they have played significant roles in resource delivery and technical assistance projects that are important to North Korea's rehabilitation. As long as the DPRK continues to gradually expand inter-Korean cooperation and allow greater in-country space in which South Korean NGOs can work, it is likely that South Korean NGOs will continue to make a substantial contribution, alongside ROK government efforts, to expand inter-Korean relations. However, if the DPRK acts to sour inter-Korean relations or continues to limit South Korean NGOs to only service delivery without opportunities for grassroots interaction (for example, the slowdown in 2002 of ROK NGO assistance to North Korea following the second West Sea confrontation), donor fatigue and frustration will set in even among South Korean NGOs, and the level of support for the DPRK will decrease. To the extent that South Korean NGOs continue to play active roles in promoting inter-Korean reconciliation in ways that draw a positive North Korean response, advocacy and action in favor of broadening inter-Korean relations will continue to receive broad support from the South Korean public.

More specifically, South Korean NGOs can bring to bear considerable resources to promote effective technical training for North Koreans as one means of exposing more North Koreans to information shared by counterpart specialists in many areas. This would be one natural means for South Korean NGOs to powerfully assist the North Korean people through short-term specialized training activities, longer-term stays at South Korean universities, and provision of educational and other resources that might be helpful. South Korean NGOs will be likely to bear the bulk of the responsibility to promote inter-Korean reconciliation through such exchanges. Because there is no language barrier, aid provision via South Korean NGOs is immensely more efficient than provision of assistance via international NGOs and, in the long term, should be the preferred vehicle for provision of technical assistance and training for North Korean beneficiaries of assistance.

The role of European NGOs has been notable because of the absence of other NGOs with a permanent presence in North Korea. Through on-the-ground experience, European NGO representatives have a practical understanding of some of the technical infrastructure and development needs that exist in the DPRK, although North Korean limits on interpersonal interaction still remain obstacles to gaining a full understanding of how to best meet many DPRK needs. However, the political atmosphere resulting from the second North Korean nuclear crisis has constrained even European NGOs to a relatively low level of activity and support for the DPRK compared with what would be possible if the DPRK government were to show a sincere commitment to opening and, in particular, to allowing European and other international NGOs the opportunity to conduct more in-depth training programs and host and support North Korean students for study abroad. It is likely that, in the aftermath of a transformation of the priorities of the North Korean regime, there will be a substantial increase in international assistance and exchange with international NGOs from Europe as well as from the United States and Japan and with other interested organizations.

With the exception of a few religious NGOs whose activities remain relatively quiet, there is no significant U.S. NGO activity with the DPRK. Under current circumstances, U.S. NGO advocacy comprises only several human rights–focused NGOs that are advocating against the current regime in the DPRK. Nor is there likely to be significant interest in the DPRK among mainstream U.S. conveyance NGOs, absent either a major humanitarian crisis or a regime transformation that would justify the promotion of a much broader range of U.S. NGO activities in the DPRK than would otherwise be possible. Currently the likelihood of U.S. government funding for U.S. NGO involvement in North Korea is highly unlikely, with the possible exception of a resumption of humanitarian assistance in some form. Although many restrictions on humanitarian exchange with the DPRK have been exempted from the U.S. trade ban, the overall political atmosphere still has a dampening effect on such activities and increases the likelihood that there will be no U.S.-government-funded bilateral assistance in either humanitarian assistance or technical assistance. After a resolution of current tensions over North Korea's nuclear weapons development efforts and a fundamental change in the direction and composition of North Korea's leadership, it will be possible to imagine an increase in U.S. NGO activity in the rehabilitation of North Korea, although U.S. NGO roles would likely be relatively smaller and supplementary to South Korean NGO efforts.

References

Chung, Ok-nim. 2004. The Role of South Korea's NGOs: The Political Context. In *Paved with Good Intentions: The NGO Experience in North Korea*, ed. L. Gordon Flake and Scott A. Snyder. Westport, Conn.: Praeger.

Flake, L. Gordon. 2004. The Experience of U.S. NGOs in North Korea. In *Paved with Good Intentions: The NGO Experience in North Korea*, ed. L. Gordon Flake and Scott A. Snyder. Westport, Conn.: Praeger.

Ministry of Unification (MOU). Various years. *Statistical Report on Intra-Korean Exchanges and Cooperation and Humanitarian Aid Projects.* Seoul: Ministry of Unification.

Salamon, Lester M. 1994. The Rise of the Nonprofit Sector. *Foreign Affairs* 73, no. 4 (July/August).

Schloms, Michael. 2004. The European NGO Experience in North Korea. In *Paved with Good Intentions: The NGO Experience in North Korea*, ed. L. Gordon Flake and Scott A. Snyder. Westport, Conn.: Praeger.

Song, Ji-young. 2002. Rights Approach to North Korea: Combining Criticism and Constructive Engagement. Thesis submitted to LLM Human Rights Programme, University of Hong Kong.

Scott Snyder is Senior Associate at The Asia Foundation/Pacific Forum CSIS. The author would like to thank Asia Foundation program officer, Ban Seon-young, for her research assistance.